The Soldiers' General

STUDIES IN CANADIAN MILITARY HISTORY

The Canadian War Museum, Canada's national museum of military history, has a three-fold mandate: to remember, to preserve, and to educate. It does so through an interlocking and mutually supporting combination of exhibitions, public programs, and electronic outreach. Military history, military historical scholarship, and the ways in which Canadians see and understand themselves have always been closely intertwined. Studies in Canadian Military History builds on a record of success in forging those links by regular and innovative contributions based on the best modern scholarship. Published by UBC Press in association with the Museum, the series especially encourages the work of new generations of scholars and the investigation of important gaps in the existing historiography, pursuits not always well served by traditional sources of academic support. The results produced feed immediately into future exhibitions, programs, and outreach efforts by the Canadian War Museum. It is a modest goal that they feed into a deeper understanding of our nation's common past as well.

The Soldiers' General: Bert Hoffmeister at War

Douglas E. Delaney

UBCPress · Vancouver · Toronto

15 14 13 12 11 10 09 08 07   5 4 3 2

Printed in Canada on acid-free paper.

Library and Archives Canada Cataloguing in Publication

Delaney, Douglas E. (Douglas Edward), 1964-
   The soldiers' general : Bert Hoffmeister at war / Douglas E. Delaney.

(Studies in Canadian military history 1499-6251)
Includes bibliographical references and index.
ISBN 0-7748-1148-X (bound): ISBN 0-7748-1149-8 (pbk)

   1. Hoffmeister, Bert, 1907-1999 – Military leadership. 2. World War, 1939-1945 – Campaigns – Western Front. 3. Canada. Canadian Army – Officers – Biography. 4. Generals – Canada – Biography. 5. World War, 1939-1945 – Canada – Biography. I. Title.

U55.H63D45 2005   940.54'1271'092   C2005-901100-9

Canadä

UBC Press gratefully acknowledges the financial support for our publishing program of the Government of Canada through the Book Publishing Industry Development Program (BPIDP), and of the Canada Council for the Arts, and the British Columbia Arts Council.

This book has been published with the help of a grant from the Canadian Federation for the Humanities and Social Sciences, through the Aid to Scholarly Publications Programme, using funds provided by the Social Sciences and Humanities Research Council of Canada.

Publication of this book has been financially supported by the Canadian War Museum.

UBC Press
The University of British Columbia
2029 West Mall
Vancouver, BC V6T 1Z2
604-822-5959 / Fax: 604-822-6083
www.ubcpress.ca

In memory of my grandfather, R55453 Corporal Gerard Aery Power, RCAF

Contents

Maps, Figures, Photographs

Foreword

Bert Hoffmeister was Canada's best fighting commander of the Second World War. A militiaman in the Seaforth Highlanders in Vancouver before the war, Hoffmeister went overseas in 1939 as a company commander. By the time of the invasion of Sicily in July 1943, he was the commanding officer of his regiment and, within months, he was first an infantry brigade commander and then the General Officer Commanding the 5th Canadian Armoured Division. He led his division through the Hitler Line and Gothic Line battles in Italy and then through the last months of the war in Northwest Europe. Well before the end of the conflict, the 5th was "Hoffy's Mighty Maroon Machine," the only Canadian formation with a clear sense of its own identity. Deservedly so, too, for Hoffmeister's division, like his battalion and his brigade before it, had fought with notable success against formidable opponents.

Hoffmeister stood out among his peers. He was intelligent, for one thing, a man with a very good intellect. He had a powerful charisma, that unlearnable and god-given capacity to inspire others. No other Canadian general in the 1939-45 war had that trait. Harry Crerar was sly and cool, for example, while Guy Simonds was cerebral and cold, and Charles Foulkes had the personality of a cod fish. Hoffmeister was hot by comparison, a commander who understood that if soldiers were to go willingly into danger, their leaders had to lead and be seen to do so. He was as brave as a lion, literally the officer who would not ask his men to do anything that he himself would not do. Because they understood this, Hoffmeister's men accomplished miracles time after time. Leadership mattered in the Second World War just as it has in wars before and since. The story, almost certainly apocryphal, that Hoffmeister had led a counterattack to stop a Nazi breakout in the Netherlands in the last weeks of the war may not have been true. But it could have been; it was credible that the General would have done so. That the story was embellished by having Hoffmeister wearing his pyjamas during the action added an affectionate verisimilitude to the tale. No one would have expected Foulkes or Crerar to lead a counterattack, but Hoffmeister ... of course, he would do so whether in uniform or in pyjamas. Courage still counted. Image and reputation still mattered. Leaders won battles and wars.

What Doug Delaney has written here is the first full story of Bert Hoffmeister as a commander. Few Canadians today know of Hoffmeister, and with reason: very little has hitherto been written about him. Now, sixty years after the end of the Second World War, there is no excuse for this ignorance of a great soldier and leader.

Delaney's splendid book has told his story – and the story of the units and formations he led – with clarity and grace. Because he is an infantry officer, Delaney
understands what leadership is and how hard it is to command soldiers. He knows
the importance of ground in battle, and he can read a map. (Neither are traits
common to most military historians in Canada or elsewhere!) He understands
what weapons are supposed to do and what they can do. These soldierly characteristics inform his biography of Hoffmeister and make it all but unique in our
literature.

His is, I suppose, a "top-down" study, an examination of the commander rather
than the commanded. "Bottom-up" military history is in fashion in Canada now,
thanks to Terry Copp's fine revisionist examination of the Canadians in Normandy
in 1944. There is, however, still a place for the top-down studies, and there will be
so long as there are no satisfactory biographies of Hoffmeister's fellow division
commanders, or the Canadian corps' commanders, or even a published biography
of Harry Crerar, First Canadian Army's commander from early 1944 through to
the end of the war. Why Canadian military historians have been so loathe to look
at the generals who led the army in the Second World War is inexplicable. On the
other hand, almost a century after the Great War no Canadian general of that war
other than Sir Arthur Currie has been studied in a book-length scholarly manuscript yet. In Canada, in truth, there is no conflict of interpretation between top-
down and bottom-up studies so much as a gaping historical vacuum that needs to
be filled by good scholarship however it is written. Of course, we need more than
biographies of the most senior officers. Studies of battalion and brigade commanders scarcely exist and the histories of the divisions of the First and Second
World Wars still remain to be written. There are dozens of other Canadian military topics from the wars of the twentieth century that remain completely un-
touched. We know surprisingly little about our soldiers and how they fought in
1915 and 1943; we know almost nothing about the officers who led them into battle
at Vimy, Ortona, or the Scheldt.

Major Delaney's biography of General Hoffmeister therefore stands all but un-
challenged. And so it should, for he has produced a first-rate book, well researched
and well written, a study that at last assigns Bert Hoffmeister his proper place in
the Canadian pantheon.

J.L. GRANATSTEIN
Author of *The Generals: The Canadian Army's Senior Commanders in
the Second World War* and of *Canada's Army: Waging War and Keeping
the Peace* and director and CEO of the Canadian War Museum from
1998 to 2000

Acknowledgments

I have many people to thank.

To start, this book would have been a much poorer product were it not for the generous help of many soldiers and scholars. Bill McAndrew and Jane Errington steered this work through its first life as a doctoral dissertation and have continued to be exceptional sources of advice and encouragement. Jack Granatstein literally shared boxes of his own research material and provided the occasional prod to keep me on track. I have also benefited from the guidance of Terry Copp, Patricia Roy, and Ken MacLeod and their knowledge of sources. Mary McRoberts helped me understand Hoffmeister's civilian work experience and place it in its proper perspective. Major-General (retired) Lewis Mackenzie, Desmond Morton, David French, and Lieutenant-Colonel (retired) Jack English reviewed earlier drafts, offered comments, and in a few cases, saved me from some gaffes. So did Emily Andrew and Camilla Gurdon of UBC Press; both have been a pleasure to work with. In spite of all this help, some mistakes may have made their way into the narrative. Those are my fault, no one else's.

One of the most rewarding aspects of this undertaking has been meeting so many Canadian veterans of the Second World War. Colonel David Fairweather, Colonel Syd Thomson, Denis Meade, Jock Gibson, Ron Hurley, and Al Worrington all kindly consented to be interviewed. Battery Sergeant-Major Gordie Bannerman shared his very enjoyable memoir drafts. Sergeant Meade, Colonel Fairweather, and Colonel Thomson even reviewed earlier chapter drafts to offer a soldier's perspective and make sure that I was not off the mark in my interpretations. To all these veterans, I wish to extend my deepest thanks not only for the assistance they have given me but for the service they have rendered their country. Canadians have never thanked them enough.

Rod Hoffmeister kindly allowed me access to his father's collection and scrapbooks, all beautifully kept by his wife, Pat. He also introduced me to his mother, Donalda, who agreed to be interviewed, and he put me in touch with some of his father's childhood friends and business associates, Dot Moore and Ralph Shaw among them. Margot Ketcham (née Hoffmeister) was also very helpful.

To the staffs of the Massey Library of the Royal Military College, the British Columbia Archives, the University of British Columbia Special Collections, the City of Vancouver Archives, Library and Archives Canada, the Seaforth Highlanders of Canada, the Imperial War Museum, and the Liddell Hart Centre for Military Archives, I want to express my appreciation for all their efficient help and service.

I am also grateful to the Directorate of History and Heritage at National Defence Headquarters, and to Reg Roy for allowing me to draw from their maps. I am indebted as well to the Canadian War Museum and the John Dobson Foundation, Montreal, for a grant that kept the research going.

I wish also to thank my family, starting with my wife, Christine, and my two "troops," Allison and Connor. Over the past few years, Christine has proofed more chapters than she cares to remember, and all three have had to endure my preoccupations, my absentmindedness, and my occasional inattentiveness. I am a lucky man. They make me happy. My morale would not have weathered this book's completion without them. Mum and Dad have kept up the chorus of cheerleading that they started forty years ago. That helped too.

Finally, this book is dedicated to the memory of my grandfather, who passed on his own stories of the Second World War and first got me interested in history. Probably more than anyone, he guided me toward the happiest accident of my life – my becoming a soldier.

Abbreviations

AA & QMG	Assistant Adjutant and Quartermaster General
ADC	aide-de-camp
armd	armoured
att	attached/attachment
bde	brigade
br	bridge
BCD	British Columbia Dragoons
CAB	Canadian Armoured Brigade
CAD	Canadian Armoured Division
CBH	Cape Breton Highlanders
Cdn	Canadian
CIB	Canadian Infantry Brigade (also Cdn Inf Bde)
C-in-C	Commander-in-Chief
CID	Canadian Infantry Division (also Cdn Inf Div)
CJWSC	Canadian Junior War Staff Course
CMHQ	Canadian Military Headquarters (London)
CO	Commanding Officer
Comd	commander
comms	communications
conc	concentration
coy	company
CPX	Command Post Exercise
CRA	Commander Royal Artillery
CRE	Commander Royal Engineers
CR Sigs	Commander Royal Signals
CTR	Canadian Tank Regiment
CSM	Company Sergeant-Major
def	defence
Div	Division
engr	engineer
FOO	Forward Observation Officer (artillery)
Gen	General
GGHG	Governor General's Horse Guards
GHQ	General Headquarters
GOC	General Officer Commanding

GS	General Staff
GSO	General Staff Officer
H&PER	Hastings and Prince Edward Regiment
inf	infantry
instr	instruction
int	intelligence
LdSH	Lord Strathcona's Horse (Royal Canadians)
LO	liaison officer
NBH	New Brunswick Hussars
NCO	non-commissioned officer
NDHQ	National Defence Headquarters
OC	Officer Commanding
OO	Operation Order
OP	Observation Post
ops	operations
PF	Permanent Force
PLDG	Princess Louise Dragoon Guards
PPCLI	Princess Patricia's Canadian Light Infantry
PW	prisoner of war
RCD	Royal Canadian Dragoons
RCR	Royal Canadian Regiment
recce	reconnaissance
regt	regiment
reorg	reorganization
res	reserve
RMC	Royal Military College (of Canada)
RSM	Regimental Sergeant-Major
tac	tactical headquarters
TCP	traffic control point
tk	tank
tp(s)	troop(s)
trg	training
SC	Staff Captain
sit	situation
sp	support
SP	self-propelled
sqn	squadron
SHC	Seaforth Highlanders of Canada
TEWT	Tactical exercise without troops
veh	vehicle
WD	War Diary
W.O. 1	Warrant Officer First Class

The Soldiers' General

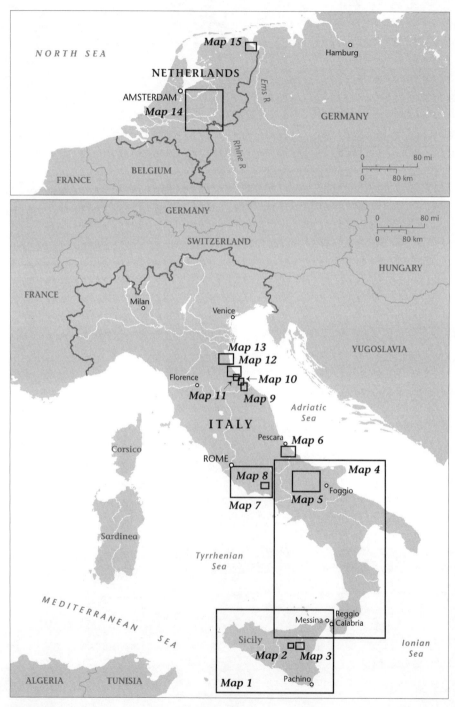

Key to maps

1
Looking at Command

Military Command has always required technical skill and spiritual power and quality; both are essential. The great commanders in history have been those who had a profound knowledge of the mechanics of war and the stage-management of battles, and who were able to focus and call forth the spirit and qualities of their soldiers.

FIELD-MARSHAL THE VISCOUNT MONTGOMERY OF ALAMEIN[1]

By almost any measure, Major-General Bertram Meryl Hoffmeister was the most successful Canadian battlefield commander of the Second World War. No Canadian officer spent more time in combat.[2] With few respites, Hoffmeister confronted the enemy from the Allied landings on Sicily in July 1943 to the victory in Northwest Europe in May 1945. During that time, he fought six battles as a battalion commander, four as a brigadier, and eight in command of an armoured division.[3] With one, possibly two, exceptions, all his actions succeeded. He earned three Distinguished Service Orders – one at each of battalion, brigade, and division levels of command. He was made a Commander of the Most Excellent Order of the British Empire for piercing the Gothic Line. And, after his division's sweep out of the Arnhem bridgehead in April 1945, Hoffmeister was admitted as a Companion of the Most Honourable Order of Bath. So impressed were Canadian military authorities, they saw fit to appoint the Vancouver native commander of the Canadian contingent in the war against Japan.

This would have been an extraordinary record of success for a soldier who had spent a lifetime in uniform. That it belongs to a man who started the war as a poorly trained militia captain whose most formative experiences had been in the world of business is truly remarkable. Only three officers from Canada's Non-Permanent Active Militia – Hoffmeister, A.B. Matthews, and R.H. (Holly) Keefler – commanded divisions in action. Of those, only Hoffmeister and Matthews could be regarded as truly successful. Two others, Victor Odlum and C.B. Price, although appointed to divisional command overseas, were relieved before taking their formations into action. Arthur Potts, Hardy Ganong, and P.E. Leclerc went on to command divisions in Canada after being removed from brigade command in England. Hoffmeister was an exception.[4]

Surprisingly, Canadian military historians have had little to say about Hoffmeister. What little they have written has tended to be tangential to operational histories, focusing on tactics and doctrine at the formation level.[5] Several studies, for example, have looked at the 2nd Canadian Infantry Brigade's (2 CIB) struggle for the Italian town of Ortona,[6] and a few others have probed the actions of the 5th Canadian Armoured Division (5 CAD) in the battles of the Liri Valley and the Gothic Line.[7] But none have been specifically devoted to the study of Hoffmeister as a military commander. This work is the first.

Despite his exceptional war record and his rapid advancement in rank, Hoffmeister did not become an able military commander overnight. His story is anything but a confirmation of the old militia myth, which purported that Canadians, inherently rugged and conditioned by their harsh environment, only needed a healthy dose of once-weekly military training to prepare them for war whenever it came.[8] He did not glide from business to the battlefield, nor did he move up the command ladder without stumbling. He worked at it – and worked at it hard – every step of the way. When, as a militia captain, he joined the Canadian Active Service Force in the autumn of 1939, he joined an army that was ill prepared to give him what he needed most: effective training. For a young self-starter, that was disappointing. Indeed, personal and professional frustration characterized the better part of his first two years in England. But, eventually, as the Canadian Army and its training practices improved, so did Hoffmeister, but the process was gradual. In fact, Hoffmeister's military acumen was the culmination of a lifetime of character development and learning. Family, sports, business experience, military training, and, most of all, combat: all of these contributed to some degree or other. Only by examining *how* he exercised command at the various levels of command does the extent of each of these influences become clear.

Of course, any analysis of command is fraught with difficulties. To begin with, the term "command" has several different connotations. As a noun, it can refer to the exercise or tenure of authority vested in an individual ("the officer addressed the soldiers in his command") or it can mean the actual order given by the controlling authority ("the officer gave the command to advance"). As a verb, it can denote something that authoritatively requires attention ("this problem commands your attention") or it can mean the direction or leadership of subordinates ("he commanded his men to advance"). This book is concerned with the last of these definitions. In other words, the primary focus of this study is *how* Hoffmeister, as a military commander, did his business – how he organized and employed the men and resources under his authority.

But even with that focus, analyzing command is no simple matter. As the quotation from Field-Marshal Montgomery at the beginning of this chapter states, the exercise of command requires the ability to direct and to inspire, to lead and to manage, to coordinate and to motivate, to think and to feel. Few works capture these subtle dichotomies; many confuse them. Martin Van Crevald, for example, consciously excluded "moral forces" as a function of command in order to give rigour to his analysis of the organizations, systems, and technologies that commanders have used throughout the ages.[9] In a more theoretical vein, Ross Pigeau and Carol McCann have offered an over-intellectualized perspective based on the relationship between the components of *competence, responsibility,* and *authority,* while Lieutenant-Colonel Peter Bradley has boiled the matter down to the twin activities of *leadership* and *management.*[10] Some, such as Martin Blumenson and James L. Stokesbury, have rejected such abstract approaches: "Since man is the only creature who defies wholly quantifiable terms, since each historical event, no matter how similar to one of the past, is still unique, there is no formula, and therefore no science."[11] If the existing literature makes anything clear, it is that the exercise of command is neither wholly art, nor wholly science; hence the underlying dichotomies. What Field-Marshal Montgomery termed "technical skills" – tactical analysis, decision making, planning, direction, monitoring, supervision – can be gauged or measured in some degree, and are therefore more "scientific." On the other hand, the ability to call forth the spirit and qualities of soldiers, to make them do willingly, and in the face of danger, what is necessary to achieve a military goal, defies quantification and is therefore more of an art.

What can be loosely termed the human and technical dimensions of command are not only interrelated, they are interdependent. All the charm and influence in the world, for example, cannot guarantee the success of a poorly conceived and inadequately managed plan. Conversely, even the most brilliant of plans flounders if not executed by enthusiastic, willing, and well-trained subordinates. Montgomery understood this. In his 1961 book, *The Path to Leadership,* he explained that a leader needed both:

> A thorough knowledge of his job, of his profession is an absolute pre-requisite; and then a never-ending study to keep himself up-to-date ...
>
> A leader must also have a genuine interest in, and a real knowledge of humanity – which will always be the raw material of his trade. He must understand that bottled-up in men are great emotional forces and these must have an outlet in a way which is positive and constructive and which will warm their hearts and excite their imagination. If this can be done and the forces can be harnessed and directed towards a common purpose, the greatest achievements become possible. But if the approach to this human problem is cold and impersonal, little can be achieved.[12]

Such complexities should remain foremost in any analysis of command.

The historian trying to appreciate how a general exercised command must consider a variety of sources. The technical dimension of command is predominantly rational, and the human dimension is predominantly non-rational; information about each of these dimensions is found in different types of evidence. The more rational aspects of military command – intelligence gathering, tactical analysis, decision making, direction, and coordination among them – can be analyzed by considering battle plans, doctrine, weapons' capabilities, command structures, force ratios, or schemes of manoeuvre. Such things are best discovered in the documentary evidence of written battle estimates, orders, and correspondence and, therefore, offer at least some quantifiable criteria by which to study the commander. However, the less rational aspect of calling forth the spirit and qualities of soldiers, because it implies willing, even emotional, compliance on the part of the follower, cannot be quantified with any certainty.

This is the essential difficulty: while the commander may undertake certain actions to harness those "great emotional forces" better, only the performance of the followers will testify to the commander's success. The reason for this is plain – leaders do not exist without the led. Oftentimes the decision of the soldier to follow is rational. Just as often, however, it is non-rational. For example, on a rational level, the follower may do what a leader orders because the consequences of inaction, whether disciplinary or the result of enemy action, are so grave. On a non-rational level, the follower may take a certain action because of an attachment to the leader, or to avoid letting leader, peers, and country down. This is what Field-Marshal Sir William Slim referred to as "that intangible force which will move a whole group of men to give their last ounce to achieve something, without counting the cost to themselves; that makes them feel they are part of something greater than themselves."[13] This is a key element of success in command, something the best commanders cultivate. In analyzing how a commander commanded, consideration must therefore be given to *how* and *why* subordinates did what they did.

The perspective of subordinates is important. Too frequently, historians have dismissed the reminiscences of soldiers as anecdotal, unscientific, and, therefore, unimportant. They have derided interviews conducted more than a few days after a combat action as unreliable because, for a variety of reasons, such evidence tends to be inaccurate in terms of details or the sequencing of events.[14] That is true; but, at the same time, that is not what makes interviews and memoirs useful. An example or two demonstrate their worth.

One soldier, who won a Military Medal for his action in the Battle of Agira in July 1943, recently confessed that, despite the assistance of maps and a visit to the same Sicilian hills where he had distinguished himself some fifty-seven years earlier, he could not recall the sequence of events that earned him the award. Given the passage of time, this is understandable. He was, however, able to recount the occasion of his being awarded the decoration by Montgomery. What remains clear in the old soldier's mind is the memory of Montgomery pinning the medal on his chest and then fastening an errant button afterward.[15] This is a small point, some would say insignificant, but it illustrates just how profoundly a commander can affect a subordinate. No soldier forgets an encounter with a commanding general.

Will R. Bird's First World War memoir, *Ghosts Have Warm Hands,* related the positive impression that Major-General Louis J. Lipsett's frequent visits to the front-line trenches left on Bird and his fellow soldiers: "He was nearer to us than any brass hat, being often in the trenches. I had never heard a man speak against him, and I had my own memory of running into him in the trench that night during

1917."[16] The eminent military historian Sir Michael Howard similarly believed that just hearing the news that the commander of the Allied Armies in Italy, General Sir Harold Alexander, had landed on the precarious Salerno beachhead in September 1943 steadied him and his hard-pressed comrades in the Coldstream Guards.[17]

Conversely, the absence of a commanding general can have the opposite affect. W.H.A. Groom's vituperative memoir of the Great War conveyed something of why the British Army's morale sagged so much in 1917: "In twenty months [at the front] I saw our brigadier once only ... They knew nothing about the conditions and were completely out of contact with the men."[18]

All of this says that impressions count, by lasting longer in memory than facts, by filling in the human dimension, and by giving us a more complete, more balanced understanding of command. As Montgomery expounded: "Military command is, fundamentally a great human problem and no good results will follow unless there is mutual confidence and sympathy between the known commander and the regimental officers and men – the former being seen frequently in the forward area by the soldier."[19] Even if the accuracy of interviews or memoirs does not match contemporary sources, such as personal journals, war diaries, and operations logs, the impressions they do reflect, particularly as they pertain to commanders, are important.

It stands to reason that all evidence must be weighed, cross-referenced, and compared in order to cobble together the most accurate representation of the events and their causes. In piecing together the events, contemporary documents are unquestionably more valuable than the more filtered, and sometimes sanitized, sources of war diaries, memoirs, and interviews conducted long after the events. Still, in dealing with command, it would be a mistake to focus solely on what a soldier did, to the exclusion of any examination of why he did it. That would be as unbalanced as relying solely on interviews. A comprehensive analysis of command – which involves a relationship between the commander and the commanded – must give equitable consideration to both the technical and human dimensions of command, and to the different types of evidence that support each.

That no historian has undertaken a major study of Hoffmeister as a military commander should come as no surprise. Studies of Canadian commanders are rare. Unlike their American or British counterparts, few of Canada's Second World War generals have captured the attention of historians. Only A.G.L. McNaughton, H.D.G. Crerar, and G.G. Simonds have been the subject of major works,[20] while others such as E.L.M. Burns, A.B. Matthews, M.A. Pope, K. Stuart, and Hoffmeister have received only minor treatment.[21]

The only examination specifically devoted to Hoffmeister as a military commander appeared in J.L. Granatstein's *The Generals,* a collective biography that looks at Canada's Second World War generals as a group.[22] It is a short narrative, thirteen pages in a chapter shared with Matthews, but here we get a quick look at a true exception in a group of "pallid, colourless figures."[23] Here we see a battlefield commander with good technical skills *and* remarkable ability to motivate soldiers – all in an officer who had not spent a lifetime in the profession of arms.[24] Granatstein sought to make the exception understandable by giving us a brief glimpse of Hoffmeister's background – his upbringing in interwar Vancouver, his cadet experience, his life as a militia officer, his wartime training, and his personal crises. More important, he raised a number of questions that too often have been unasked. How did this commander motivate his soldiers and staff officers? How did they respond to him? And still more questions need asking. How exactly did Hoffmeister acquire the skills to command an armoured division in battle when others proved incapable of doing the same? How did he make his decisions? The roots of Hoffmeister's technical acumen require further investigation as well.

That is the central purpose of this book: to look at *how* Hoffmeister did his business as military commander. It is not to judge him, merely to look at what he did, how he did it, and how he learned to do it. As such, it examines command in a manner that has not hitherto been done. Arguing that the exercise of command has both human and technical dimensions, this book attempts to achieve greater balance than exists in the current literature. It builds on the existing scholarship that has established the state of pre-war training, the influence of doctrine, and the combat experience of the Canadian Army between 1943 and 1945. It uses a wide array of evidence and sources, including contemporary documents, war diaries, personal journals, memoirs, and interviews. And it analyzes what is impossible to quantify: the human element. The testimonies of subordinates is accorded greater weight than has previously been the case, not so much for their recollection of events but for soldiers' impressions of their commander and of how their relationship with him affected their performance. Factors that influenced Hoffmeister's abilities to stage-manage battles and tap into the talent and energy of subordinates – his family, his childhood, his education, his civilian work experience, his military training, and his years of combat experience – are presented and probed in a biographical narrative, restricted to the general's military career and the antecedents that affected it.

There is a second purpose of this book, and that is simply to chronicle the military career of a remarkable soldier about whom most Canadians – soldier, scholar, citizen – know very little. In a way, that may be the real value of this work. It addresses that most important, yet most forgotten, purpose of history: to tell a story.

2
A Young Man before the War

He always seemed to be doing something for someone.

Dot Moore, recalling Hoffmeister as a young man[1]

A combination of benevolence and ambition – that is the subtext of the remark by Dot Moore, a friend from adolescence. Hoffmeister liked helping people, but, at the same time, he worked hard to get ahead. Both traits played an important part in his business and military careers, and, as Dot Moore's comment suggests, both were present at a very early age.

In fact, many of the personal qualities that contributed to Hoffmeister's command success are traceable to his experiences in his first 32 years. His ambition, his work ethic, his physical toughness, his strong interpersonal skills, his organizational ability, and his understanding of the human condition: all of these were shaped, to some degree or other, by family, participation in sports, work experience, and military training. This pre-war period was the foundation of his development as a military commander.

On 15 May 1907, Bert Hoffmeister was born in Vancouver, a city on the rise. During his early childhood and adolescence, Vancouver's size, population, and economy exploded. It had benefited from the Klondike gold rush of the 1890s and the turn-of-the-century Prairie wheat boom, both of which had spiked demand for lumber, manufactured goods, and produce, a demand that continued well into the first quarter of the twentieth century.[2] Lumber and manufacturing were not the only economic sectors to benefit. Other industries expanded in proportion. The railways were extended and the port of Vancouver was expanded to accommodate the new economy. These were good times.

With work to be had and money to be made, the city attracted plenty of newcomers. Between 1891 and 1911, Vancouver grew from a municipality of 13,709 residents to a metropolis of 100,401. In 1921, the city incorporated the neighbouring municipalities of South Vancouver and Point Grey, boosting the population to 163,220, and that number nearly doubled to 246,593 by 1931.[3] In 1911, well over half of Vancouver's population was foreign born, the majority coming from the British Isles.[4] Of Canadian-born Vancouverites, those born in Ontario were, by far, the largest group,[5] and Bert Hoffmeister's father, Louis, was one of them.

Louis Hoffmeister, a second-generation German immigrant, was one of seven brothers who moved west from Wellington County, Ontario, in the 1880s and 1890s.[6] A hard-working and ambitious lot, they fit well into the hustle and bustle of the burgeoning West Coast metropolis. Louis's brother, Reinhardt, built Vancouver's first electrical power generator in 1888 and established his own successful electrical business, despite his lack of formal training in the field. Bold and ambitious, Reinhardt rode the economic wave, making a very profitable living selling electrical generators to mining and lumber companies throughout British Columbia. Brothers Harry, George, and Fred had the same spirit for enterprise. They formed Hoffmeister Brothers Incorporated, a motor-car dealership that had the distinction (good or bad) of being the first to sell an electric car in the province.[7] Even a tertiary review of the family history reveals that the Hoffmeisters were a gutsy and driven group, willing to assume risks to capitalize on opportunities. Growing up in that kind of milieu affected young Bert.

Although Louis Hoffmeister was a little less adventuresome than his brothers, he did work hard. For most of his adult life, he toiled as a low-level manager at the Rat Portage Lumber Company, invested his savings where he saw opportunity, and provided a comfortable existence for his family. But in 1923, Louis's fortunes took a turn for the worse. First, a work-related accident forced him to leave his place of employment. Then, in the mid-1920s, most of his investments failed.[8] These developments forced Louis's son into the workforce early. Bert was not especially close with his father, but he was a dutiful son, and immediately after his matriculation, the younger Hoffmeister assumed the role of sole family provider, taking a job as a labourer in the same lumber company that had employed his father.[9] The burden of responsibility came early.

Bert's income allowed the family to keep the sturdy, though not extravagant, two-storey house that Louis had built on West First Avenue, in the Vancouver neighbourhood of Kitsilano.[10] Though by no means the poorest residential neighbourhood in the city, the Kitsilano of 1925 was a "lower middle income" area, the residents being mostly "skilled workmen, salesmen and clerks" of the lumber industry and the Canadian Pacific Railway.[11] Unlike Vancouver's East End, which had sizeable Italian and Chinese enclaves, Kitsilano was a largely homogeneous area. Most of its residents were Canadian and foreign-born of British lineage. Compared to other south-side neighbourhoods, however, Kitsilano lagged in mean income. The well-to-do managers and executives of the Vancouver business community preferred the "upper middle income" municipality of Point Grey or the very exclusive and affluent Shaughnessy. Young Bert Hoffmeister, who inherited the ambition and entrepreneurial drive of his uncles, noticed the difference.

Strong as the influence of the Hoffmeisters may have been, the family member who affected Bert most was his mother.[12] Born of British stock, Flora Hoffmeister (née Rodway) was not fond of her husband's family or its German ancestry. Part of that familial discord may have been purely personal, but a large part of it undoubtedly had to do with the First World War backlash against German immigrants and Canadians of German ancestry. Bert Hoffmeister never discussed any such animosities, but they were there. In her book *Vancouver: An Illustrated History,* Patricia E. Roy related the illustrative story of a German-born real estate and mining mogul whose position in Vancouver society changed dramatically from community leader to *persona non grata* with the advent of the First World War.[13] Eventually, he left Vancouver to live out the remainder of his days in Seattle, Washington. He was not the only German resident to leave Vancouver as a result of anti-German sentiment. According to census statistics, the number of German-born residents in the city dropped from 733 in 1911 to 264 in 1921.[14] What is more, unlike Italian and Chinese immigrants who settled in their own neighbourhoods, the German immigrants of Vancouver were much fewer and were scattered throughout the city. Flora Hoffmeister anglicized the pronunciation of her surname to "Hoffmaster" to blend in with the largely Anglo-Canadian community of Kitsilano.[15]

Flora wanted the best for Bert and his older sister, Aldyne, and she took the lead in their upbringing. She was not only the primary caregiver of the Hoffmeister household but also its disciplinarian. From the time they were young, she encouraged her children to work hard, treat people with respect, and assume the responsibilities that life foisted upon them. But Flora was also an affectionate parent. She adored her children and took particular pride in her son's achievements.[16] She collected newspaper clippings and photographs that chronicled Bert's accomplishments in sports, business, and the military, preserving these keepsakes in family scrapbooks.[17] One surviving piece of documentation that indicates the depth of her affection is a letter she sent to her son during his wartime service overseas. Like all mothers with sons at war, Flora Hoffmeister worried for Bert's well-being and she wanted him to know it, so she hand-copied "A Mother's Prayer" into her letter: "God, Father of Freedom, look after that boy of mine, wherever he may be ... Nourish him with the love that I gave to him at birth, and satisfy the hunger of his soul with the knowledge of my daily prayer. He is my choicest treasure. Take care of him, God ... Keep him in health and sustain him under every possible circumstance. I once warmed him under my heart. You warm him anew in his shelter under the stars. Touch him with my smile of cheer and comfort, and my full confidence in his very brave pursuit."[18] Flora Hoffmeister also left her son with a prominent sentimental streak. Hoffmeister carried the letter with him throughout the war, and it was still among his possessions when he died in 1999.

The comment by Dot Moore that opens this chapter suggests that Hoffmeister's good-heartedness showed itself from a very early age. The young man who enjoyed doing favours for friends and associates was the same man who, as a retired general, worked assiduously to find work for returning soldiers and committed himself to numerous charities.[19] He liked people, plain and simple. In fact, had he been given his first choice of vocation, Hoffmeister would have been a physician.[20]

One wartime subordinate summed up Hoffmeister's disposition with typical soldier's simplicity: "You could just tell he cared."[21] That helped Hoffmeister tap into
those "great emotional forces" when he needed them later on.

However, young Bert Hoffmeister was a complex individual; an exceedingly
strong competitiveness curiously accompanied his benevolence. He enjoyed success, and despite a lifelong reluctance to discuss his achievements, he collected
mementos of his accomplishments, taking pride where pride was due. Sports nur-
tured his will to win from an early age.[22] As a student at Henry Hudson Grade
School, and later at Kitsilano High School, Hoffmeister played basketball in a league
organized by St. Mark's Anglican Church. In his teen years, rugby captured his
interest, forging his physical robustness and ameliorating his appreciation for teamwork as a prerequisite for winning. But it was in the sport of rowing that the solid
six-footer attained his greatest success as an athlete.[23] He represented the prestig-
ious Vancouver Rowing Club on several crews and even captained the club during
the 1935 season.[24] Rowing for an exclusive club also allowed Hoffmeister to rub
shoulders with some of Vancouver's most prominent lawyers and businessmen,
many of whom were work associates residing in the more exclusive Vancouver
neighbourhoods. Building credibility with influential people certainly did not hurt
his career aspirations.

Perhaps the most enduring aspect of Hoffmeister's sporting experience – aside
from a lifelong interest in physical fitness – was the mark it left on his leadership.
It was a subtle one. In stewarding his teams and inspiring his teammates,
Hoffmeister learned a leadership style that was not rooted solely in authority, but
also in competence, personal example, and charisma.

He carried the same drive to succeed into his work experience. In accepting his
new responsibilities as a labourer at the Rat Portage Lumber Company, he applied
himself with a vigour that offers some insight into his character. In 1980, he remembered,

> Very early on, I realized that it was important to move around as much as I could, so
> I was willing to take on any job that I could in order to get experience ... Not long
> after there was a vacancy for an office boy and I jumped at the chance ... I was moved
> into the office and I pursued the same principle there, trying to learn as much as I
> could in a very short order. I was assisting in the sales and other departments and
> gained quite a good experience there ... I realized, however, that my practical experi-
> ence was not sufficient and went back out to the mill, in the shipping department,
> where I was able to learn a lot more about lumber and grading, and everything else
> about the practical side. Then I was able to go back into the office again.[25]

He was ambitious, a self-starter, and also inquisitive. That much seems clear from
Hoffmeister's reflection on his seven years with Rat Portage. More important, however, his actions revealed an acute understanding that adequate technical knowl-

edge and training had to be acquired before moving to the next level. That was why he asked to be put back – to make up the deficiency. Then, with the necessary technical expertise in hand, he moved on to greater managerial responsibilities.

Not long after Hoffmeister joined the Canadian White Pine Company as a junior salesman in 1930, he caught the eye of H.R. MacMillan, the owner and president of H.R. MacMillan Export Company.[26] At the time, MacMillan's company, the largest private exporter of lumber in the world, owned Canadian White Pine. Drive and determination propelled Hoffmeister from salesman to sales manager in less than three years. As a manager, he exhibited the same verve and inquisitiveness that had marked his performance as an office boy. "Again," Hoffmeister recounted, "I made it my business to get to learn everything that was going on in that office."[27] He also achieved exceptional results in whatever he did. Hoffmeister oversaw the acquisition of a dilapidated nearby mill and its integration into the Canadian White Pine operation. Under his influence, production at Canadian White Pine rose sharply, and the entire enterprise became more flexible and responsive to an expanding list of orders.[28] MacMillan noticed.

Based on Hoffmeister's performance at Canadian White Pine, MacMillan summoned the young sales manager to the company's Vancouver head office to deal with one of the most precipitous crises in the company's history. In 1935, most of MacMillan's lumber suppliers formed a cartel – Seaboard Lumber Sales – to market and ship their lumber directly to clients, thereby eliminating the clients' need to deal with MacMillan's export enterprise.[29] MacMillan met the challenge with an aggressive and risky two-pronged strategy: first, he garnered all the orders he could, in order to deny them to Seaboard; and, second, he sought alternative suppliers to fill those orders. The job of finding and training the alternative suppliers fell to Hoffmeister. As Hoffmeister recalled, he required all of his technical and human skills for the task – it was his first big test within the MacMillan organization. "We were in a desperate situation ... I immediately set to work to organize a number of small to medium-sized mills in the lower mainland and Vancouver Island areas and, in many instances, talked them into getting into the export business, which they weren't – in some cases – at all anxious to do. And, I shudder now to think of the miserable little mills we had producing lumber for export on export grade rules; however, they performed reasonably well ... It was a very difficult, trying period but the fact remains that we shipped those orders."[30]

This was no small accomplishment. It involved a "long period of educating the mills" on standards for export production and on the importance of contractual commitments.[31] One co-worker at MacMillan Export offered the following explanation for Hoffmeister's success: "he was clear thinking, logical ... and had the courage to make decisions and stick by them. Employees and mill owners responded well to him."[32] For Hoffmeister, the significance of the Seaboard crisis was this: his first major success in the H.R. MacMillan Export Company depended on how well those working for him – in this case, the "miserable little mill" owners –

performed. Had they been unwilling or unable to produce to export standards, and in sufficient quantities to fill the orders that MacMillan had so vigorously pursued, Hoffmeister would have failed. It was a lesson he never forgot.

MacMillan was pleased, and for good reason. His company had weathered the Seaboard crisis and was well positioned to expand into the production end of the lumber business. With his sights set squarely on future opportunities, MacMillan skilfully set about building the team to do it, and Hoffmeister, who figured prominently in the future scheme of things, learned much from his mentor. During those years, MacMillan fingered Hoffmeister as a future company president.[33]

Selecting and developing capable subordinates were things that MacMillan did well. Said one of MacMillan's chosen few: "H.R. MacMillan was an extremely effective teacher, communicating ideas and knowledge – he spent a lot of time at that – with the result that it was very stimulating to the young men working with him."[34] With the other half-dozen or so men that MacMillan had selected for higher office, Hoffmeister learned much about foreign affairs and the most current business practices. In short, MacMillan made a mark on Hoffmeister, not only for what he taught the young manager, but also for the way he put his stamp on an organization. Hoffmeister watched and learned.

The tutelage he received under MacMillan later proved valuable in his military career as well: "H.R. MacMillan was a great teacher ... My training experience with MacMillan Co. stood me in good stead in the war."[35] For instance, the decision-making method taught by MacMillan was, in Hoffmeister's estimation, essentially the same as that practised in the military – "a matter of assembling the facts and then making a decision based on the facts."[36] The sequence was both logical and simple: first one had to determine the *object* or *aim* – what was to be done; the second step was to analyze the *factors* that would influence the outcome; third, one weighed the *courses open*, both to oneself and to the opposition; and then, finally, came the selection of a course of action and the plan.[37] A 1939 official Army publication noted the similarities between business and military planning:

> The ordinary citizen who is planning a business transaction, goes through much the same steps as the commander in the field who is planning an operation. Both begin by informing themselves as fully as possible; both, if they are wise, limit their enterprise to suit their means; both can best arrive at a decision by summing up to themselves in the form of a balanced statement of pros and cons of the various choices before them; both have to take into their calculations the possible schemes of rivals without allowing their judgment to be upset by fear of their action; both, if they be men of character, will abide by a decision once made and carry out what they have planned.[38]

As a young sales manager in MacMillan's organization, Hoffmeister had many practical opportunities to practise the art of decision making.

Making a decision was only part of the process. Studying under MacMillan, Hoffmeister learned the machinations of a system in which situations were assessed, decisions made, solutions implemented, and actions supervised. MacMillan described the cycle in this way: "Analyze, organize, deputize, supervise, energize, and if necessary excise."[39] It was a logical and sensible manner of doing things, but it was too onerous a set of activities for one man, and MacMillan knew it. For that reason, he created an organization capable of handling the many and complex undertakings of this continuous process, as it pertained to the lumber export business (see Figure 2.1).[40] To assist with planning and direction, MacMillan assembled a nucleus of advisors. Chief among them was W.J. VanDusen. Analytical, meticulous, and more introverted than MacMillan, VanDusen's role was one of "receiving, evaluating, and commenting on the ideas that HR MacMillan might have."[41] In effect, VanDusen acted as a trusted chief of staff for the company president. As the vice president in charge of production and shipping, VanDusen also oversaw the operations of MacMillan Export's most important holdings: the Canadian Transport Company, the Australia-British Columbia Shipping Company, Canadian White Pine, and Japan Warf. In addition to VanDusen, there were two other vice presidents whose responsibilities MacMillan divided based on function: one he assigned to sales, the other to finance and administration. With responsibilities for planning and execution so delegated, MacMillan could give his full "attention to correlating and supervising operations, to general policy, to new commitments."[42] Later, when studying the Canadian Army staff system, Hoffmeister would see many similarities.

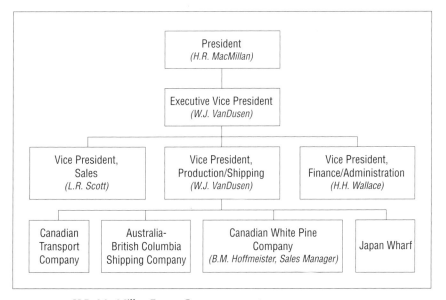

FIGURE 2.1 *H.R. MacMillan Export Company, c. 1936*

Hoffmeister learned a lot during his time at the H.R. MacMillan Export Company, and not just about sound management practices. Throughout the latter 1930s, he studied the personality of the company's charismatic leader. MacMillan energized every member of his team with his vision for the company, and they responded by working exceedingly hard. They succeeded as a team and they took pride in their accomplishments as a group. Hoffmeister also admired MacMillan's decisiveness: "There was never any waffling ... I was very impressed by HR's [MacMillan's] ability ... to grasp the essentials of any situation and to deal with them."[43] He respected MacMillan's moral courage and his willingness "to face up to problems and deal with them; they were there; they were real and they had to be dealt with."[44] In all, the environment at MacMillan Export during the 1930s was conducive to learning the fundamentals of good leadership and competent management. As had been his practice from a very early age, Hoffmeister set out to learn everything he could, and he made the most of the experience.

During his busiest years at MacMillan Export, Hoffmeister married and started a family with Amber Donalda Strauss, a university-educated schoolteacher from a fairly affluent family.[45] They met in 1932, dated for some four years, and married in September 1936. In 1938, shortly after Donalda gave birth to the first of their two children (Margot), Bert Hoffmeister set to building a new house for his family. When he did, he chose not the neighbourhood of his youth, but the upscale environs of his business associates, West Point Grey. A fast-rising star in the lumber industry, Hoffmeister wanted a home comparable to those of his new colleagues, even if it stretched his finances, which it did. The young couple could barely afford the property on Belmont Avenue, let alone the house. In fact, construction of the building still was not complete when Hoffmeister left for England in December 1939.[46] But Hoffmeister was a resourceful and dutiful provider, and they managed, despite the demands of his very heavy workload. Hoffmeister worked almost incessantly in the eighteen months between the birth of his daughter and his departure on wartime service, and unfettered family time was at a premium. Still, despite the often-conflicting demands of family, work, and military service, Hoffmeister's affection for his family ran deep. Later, during his six years at war, he wrote to them weekly and without fail.[47]

Another formative experience for Hoffmeister came through his association with the Seaforth Highlanders of Canada. It started when he entered the regiment's cadet corps at the age of twelve. Hoffmeister went so far as to state that his cadet experience was, to some extent, "a substitute for university. It furthered my education and built up my self-confidence."[48] He started at the bottom, but he advanced steadily in cadet rank, gradually acquiring greater responsibilities as an instructor and cadet officer. He accepted each additional duty – and the rank that came with it – willingly. The same work ethic and self-discipline that characterized his civilian work experience also surfaced during this time. During one of his earliest attempts at drill instruction, Hoffmeister's lack of preparedness led to a lesson that was, by his own admission, "not good." But after considerable self-study and re-hearsal, subsequent drill sessions went "much better indeed."[49] It was a simple lesson, and he learned it early: knowledge and preparation were directly linked to self-confidence, which in turn affected his ability to command.

As a cadet, he spent the bulk of his cadet time drilling and performing ceremonial duties. Even this narrow range of activities taught him two lessons applicable to the human element of command: discipline and the importance of pride in group achievements. Hoffmeister took pride in his uniform, the regiment, and the cadet corps, as did his fellow cadets. To look smart for their monthly parade down Granville Street, they practised regularly and diligently. This diligence born of pride showed itself in the hours of preparation the cadet corps put into a ceremonial guard for the 1926 visit of the deputy chief of the General Staff, Brigadier A.G.L. McNaughton. Hoffmeister, then only eighteen, commanded the Guard of Honour. His attention to detail, and the hours of effort put forth by his cadets, paid off. After reviewing the guard, McNaughton reportedly told Hoffmeister, "I've never seen a better guard anywhere."[50] Hoffmeister and his subordinates were delighted: "I relayed this [McNaughton's compliment] onto the troops of course and they were just super-smart. They were ... young people who had a goal in mind and ... [became] very efficient ... We took pride in it and, while our training was limited, we moved a lot of people, put a lot of boys through the ranks, and developed quite high morale."[51] Even at a very young age, Hoffmeister had an appreciation, conscious or unconscious, of a potent motivator: the link between individual pride and group success or failure.

The same regimental pride characterized the Seaforth Highlanders of Canada, the militia regiment into which Hoffmeister was commissioned as a provisional lieutenant in October 1927.[52] As Hoffmeister recalled: "The officers and other ranks became familiar with the history of the regiment, they developed pride in the regiment, they were proud to be in uniform, to be seen in uniform, and it was a damn smart regiment on parade."[53] They celebrated the accomplishments of their members – such as when Lieutenant-Colonel R.M. Blair won both the King's prize and the Grand Aggregate for rifle shooting at Bisley, England – and they paraded often in the community. The regiment also competed in a number of sports throughout the city of Vancouver and won many competitions in its military district.[54] Winning was not a bad habit for any military organization.

That the Seaforths were so well connected politically, socially, and financially made membership all the more attractive, particularly for officers. For instance, John Arthur Clark, the man who was the honorary lieutenant-colonel of the Seaforth Highlanders from 1924 until 1957, and whom many believed was the "regimental godfather," had a prominent Vancouver law practice and served as a Conservative Member of Parliament from 1921 to 1930. He looked after the regiment, and he carried the clout to make things happen. When a new armoury was needed in 1934, he used his political connections to secure funding for a new one.[55] When import duties on regimental kilts seemed exorbitant in 1938, letters to the Leader of the Opposition and the Prime Minister resulted in the tariffs being waived.[56] Clark also chaired the committee that selected officers for the regiment. The list of officers he picked was a "who's who" of Vancouver society. Cecil Merritt was a descendant of Prime Minister Sir Charles Tupper, Henry "Budge" Bell-Irving came from an extremely wealthy family that made its fortune in the canning industry, and Douglas Forin was a lawyer, like so many Seaforth officers, and the son of a judge.[57] Many of these officers received no pay for weekly parades, more often than not assigning what little remuneration there was to the regimental fund.[58] The regiment drew consciously from the professional classes of the city, and Hoffmeister, whose upbringing was humbler than most, had much to gain in belonging to such an exclusive group.

It is a wonder that the regiment was able to maintain any *esprit de corps* at all, given the miserly budgets and the concomitant training deficiencies of the interwar years. During the 1920s and 1930s, militia units were ill equipped and undertrained. What little equipment they had was largely of Great War vintage.[59] Units of the Non-Permanent Active Militia had none of the grenades, submachine guns, mortars, or even gas masks of modern fighting armies, and training was, therefore, limited to rudimentary individual skills such as drill, marksmanship, first aid, and map reading. Sports and other physical training activities filled gaps in the training calendar when resources or funds were scarcest. Only occasionally did soldiers exercise at the section, platoon, or company level.

One such rare occasion was an amphibious exercise off the coast of Vancouver Island in June 1929. As part of the amphibious landing force, the Seaforths enjoyed the novel experience, but the training was of dubious value.[60] Few of them, officers or non-commissioned officers (NCOs), knew much about small-unit tactics, let alone amphibious operations. The fact that the exercise, like all other exercises, took place under the supervision of equally neglected and cash-starved Permanent Force (PF) soldiers did not help matters.[61] Many of the PF exercise staff knew little more than their militia counterparts, and Hoffmeister's impression of them was not good. In the main, he regarded them as "sad", "lethargic," and "overweight" – soldiers who "drank too much" and who were, for the most part, "useless."[62] The net effect of inadequate tactical training during the interwar years was summed up best in Hoffmeister's succinct reflection on the state of his own training on mobilization: "I knew damn all about tactics."[63] Thus, by the time war was declared, the 32-year-old Hoffmeister may have had well-developed human skills, but he still lacked the technical tools for effective battlefield management.

That said, inadequate training did nothing to prevent young men from filling the regiment's ranks in the fall of 1939. On 1 September, the strength of the regiment was 30 officers and 260 other ranks.[64] Many serving Seaforths, like Captain Hoffmeister, chose the occasion of the Canadian declaration of war on 10 September to leave their civilian jobs and join the Canadian Active Service Force.[65] New recruits caused the regiment's numbers to swell to 416 all ranks by 11 September, and then to 787 by the end of the month.

Integrating and training that many newcomers presented huge challenges, particularly in light of the fact that there was precious little time.[66] Orders that assigned the Seaforths to the first Canadian contingent heading overseas arrived on 21 September, and a frenetic period of training and reorganization ensued as the battalion prepared for its upcoming mission.[67] Enlistments, medical examinations, inoculations, and reorganization consumed most of September. Only after the addition of a cadre of PF soldiers did mobilization training begin in earnest, though even that was limited.[68] Most of the training focused on fairly low-level individual skills: basic fieldcraft, chemical defence drills, and field defences (how to build a trench).[69] Seaforth soldiers marched, stripped and assembled small arms, fired their rifles and one or two light machine guns on a nearby range, but that was it. Neither Hoffmeister nor his fellow officers added to their understanding of tactics or battlefield decision making. Even had there been enough time to learn it – and there most certainly was not – there was no one available to teach it.

Training deficiencies notwithstanding, on the morning of 15 December, the Seaforth Highlanders of Canada, to the tune of "Scotland the Brave," marched out of their armoury, crossed the Burrard Street Bridge, and made their way to the train station for the first leg of a long deployment to England. The streets were lined with people – a mixture of family members, friends, and curious onlookers. Donalda Hoffmeister and her eighteen-month-old daughter, Margot, were among them. A *Vancouver Sun* reporter captured the mood of the intensely emotional event:

> There was kissing and shouting and tears and brave smiling and long, long waving of hands and hearty back slaps and shouts of "Good Luck!" and half strangled "God Bless yous" and more kisses and girls weeping and tucking pathetic little notes into uniform pockets to be found later, and an exchanging of souvenir badges and brooches and all the immemorial, sad, tear-dimmed ritual.
>
> And in the midst of it a few civic dignitaries and important personages looked on bewilderedly as their dignity and importance dwindled to nothing in the swelling of common emotion.
>
> And when it was all over, the place was empty and the streets around were filled with a thinning crowd of sad-faced men and women, some of whom had not cried before but were crying now.[70]

The scene amplified the gravity of the regiment's undertaking, particularly for those charged with leading the sons and husbands of those well-wishers in the days, months, and years ahead. It was a scene that would resonate in Bert Hoffmeister's memory for years to come.

3

The Years of Company Command and Personal Turmoil

My mind reverted to the farewell party at the armoury, when the wives and sweethearts and other relatives were all there ... and these people came up to me and said: "Now my boy is in your company, look after him, we have every confidence in your officers to bring our boys back home" ... It was very emotional and these thoughts kept coming back to me during that time in England. No one knew exactly when we were going to go into action and it disturbed me no end to realize that, here I was, a company commander responsible for 120 or 130 men and I didn't know how to look after myself in a battle, let alone look after this number of men.[1]

BERT HOFFMEISTER, 1980

In December 1939, the newly promoted Major Hoffmeister was not prepared for war, and he knew it.[2] Compared to the business training he had received at H.R. MacMillan Export Company, what little he had learned about military matters before setting sail for England seemed wholly inadequate, and things did not improve for the better part of two years. The reasons why are found in the dismal state of the Canadian Army and its training methods at the outset of the war. Hoffmeister found himself in an army unable to give him the technical tools he needed to lead troops in battle. Rapid mobilization, particularly after the summer of 1940, overwhelmed the capabilities of the Permanent Force's cadre of 450 officers and 4,000 troops, most of whom did not know much anyway.

In due course, the Canadian Army got better, but it took time and some guidance from senior British commanders to do so. Five-division armies did not simply sprout up overnight, and Hoffmeister's development paralleled the army's. While the army stumbled from December 1939 to January 1941, his insecurities grew, eventually resulting in a serious nervous crisis. Then, as the army got better, so did Hoffmeister. In fact, a look at Hoffmeister's personal experience between December 1939 and October 1942 reveals much about what was wrong with the formations of the Canadian Army and how they rectified their shortcomings. Conversely, an analysis of army training in the same period illuminates the origins of both Hoffmeister's crisis and his recovery.

Hoffmeister had been led to believe that his training deficiencies would be redressed through a period of intensive training in England. He claimed that he and his fellow soldiers had been told that, on arrival in England, officers and NCOs would be sent on courses in tactics and battle procedure, while the troops would be trained under the supervision of Permanent Force cadres "who knew what it was all about."[3] It never happened. Whatever hopes Hoffmeister may have had for an early resolution to his own training deficiencies evaporated soon after the Seaforths arrived at Aldershot: "There was no organization set up to take us over (for training) as we had been told there would be."[4] For their first two months in England, the battalions of the 1st Canadian Infantry Division (1 CID) were on their own (Figure 3.1 shows the structure of 1 CID and the units within it). In December 1939, the General Officer Commanding (GOC) the division, Major-General A.G.L. McNaughton, issued direction on individual training to be complete by the end of February.[5] Training for soldiers sputtered along in accordance with the GOC's direction, although, looking through the Seaforth War Diary, one

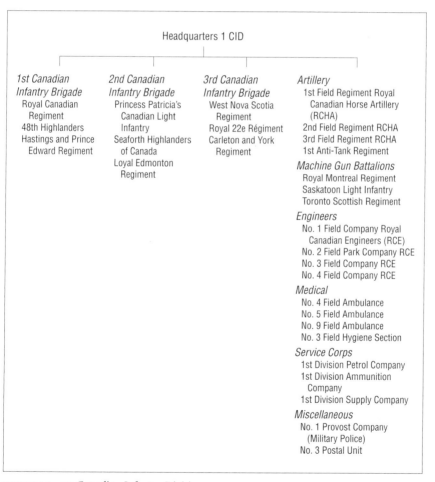

FIGURE 3.1   *1st Canadian Infantry Division, 1940*

is struck by the number of days or half-days spent not training. "No training parades" was a common entry for January 1940.[6] Moreover, most of the training during this period almost invariably took place "under coy [company] arrangements" or "under platoon arrangements," meaning under the supervision of officers and NCOs who themselves knew little. However much that limited training might have benefited soldiers, it did nothing for officers.

Training an officer was different because an officer's job was different.[7] Charged with making tactical decisions in short order and often under stress, officers needed technical knowledge, an understanding of how to make decisions, and guts. The last could not be taught, but the first two could be learned and practised, and that was not happening. To be fair, 2 CIB staff gave a few demonstrations on such things as "tanks in the attack," "principles of the defence," and "the platoon in the attack;"[8] but watching a demonstration in a controlled and uncomplicated environment was no substitute for doing it. Given the training deficiencies of most unit officers, learning exclusively on these lines was not going to produce good results. As one training manual from that period noted, "The most difficult form of command is fighting deployed when the situation is constantly changing, information is hard to obtain, and immediate decisions have to be made. A mere study of the textbooks alone will never prepare an officer to do the right things on such occasions which generally occur at the critical and decisive stage of the battle."[9]

Few Seaforth senior officers had even the fundamentals of tactical decision making, and thus there existed no cadre to develop the rest of the regimental leadership. By the end of March 1940, a mere five of the regiment's officers had passed the Militia Staff Course and only one had attended a Company Commander's Course.[10] These courses, for all of their limitations and shortcomings, were rudimentary building blocks for field-grade officers, and Hoffmeister, like most of his Seaforth peers, had taken neither.[11]

The policy of the Seaforth commanding officer at the time did not help. In 1940, Lieutenant-Colonel J.B. Stevenson refused to release any of his company commanders for out-of-unit training, for fear that the best might be poached by higher commanders in search of officers with potential. Hoffmeister pleaded that he might attend a Company Commander's Course to redress his training deficiencies, but Stevenson demurred.[12] The extent of Hoffmeister's tactical training deficit was evident in this recollection of a field-training exercise in May 1940:

> I didn't have anything by way of a training manual. I went down to Aldershot and into a store, where they sold these things, and bought pamphlets. We had been warned that we were going to be doing an exercise with one of the Guards regiments [the Welsh Guards] ... and that it would be on a company versus company basis ... Well, I hadn't a clue as to what an operation order looked like or how to write one ... The night before the exercise I spent the whole night trying to get it letter perfect so I wouldn't let the regiment down.[13]

He did not even know the proper format for an operation order!

British Army umpires for the exercise assessed that Hoffmeister's company performed quite well, noting the "remarkable ... fieldcraft, morale and spirit" of the soldiers.[14] Making "like cowboys and Indians" may have been enough for a one-day exercise, but a company, a battalion, a brigade could not run solely on the hard work and perseverance of its soldiers.[15] It took skilled leaders to make things work, and Hoffmeister's skills were still wanting. By refusing to send his officers on extra-unit training, Stevenson compounded a serious problem.

The dearth of adequately trained officers and NCOs, a predicament common to most 1 CID units in 1940, severely handicapped any progression in collective training. During their first three months in England, the Seaforths conducted no training at company or battalion level. The 2 CIB staff gave a few lectures and supervised a cloth model exercise or two, but little else.[16] In part, this was due to a training philosophy that espoused that training should progress in separate and distinct phases, beginning with individual skills, moving to single-arm training (infantry only, armour only, and so forth) at the unit level and below, and culminating in all-arms training (infantry, armour, artillery, and engineers working together) at the formation level.[17] That was the 1 CID approach. McNaughton's plan called for the completion of individual training by the end of February (later extended to mid-March), unit training by the end of April, and brigade and division training by the fall.[18] Thus, in March 1940, a typical week of Seaforth training included physical exercise, battle fitness, instruction on the platoon in the defence, compass marches and sports, but no officer or NCO training to prepare leaders for operations above platoon level.[19]

Amazingly, no one in the chain of command noticed the roadblock, least of all the division commander. Following a detailed inspection of the Seaforths in March 1940, McNaughton's staff produced a seven-page report (plus nine annexes) outlining its findings. They made notes on the state of messing arrangements, how many weapons were resting on the ground during rifle drills, and the improper digging of mortar pits, but nowhere was there any identification of officer and NCO training shortfalls.[20] This was entirely in keeping with McNaughton's proclivity to become immersed in matters of national strategy or the equipment and skills of the common soldier, and not much else.

This entire approach was wrong. Lieutenant-General Montgomery, Commander Southeastern Army (November 1941-August 1942), would later rectify many of the 1st Canadian Corps' training deficiencies, knew that officer training had to be concurrent with the individual training of soldiers. It also had to be *the* training priority of commanding officers and formation commanders: "The C.O. [commanding officer] must handle this [training of officers] himself, personally. No one else can do it for him. *He must do it himself.* The best results are obtained when the C.O. has an officers' day once a week. Officers have got to be taught the stage-management of the various operations of war, the technique of movement, the co-operation of all arms in battle, the technique of reconnaissance and de-ployment, administration in the field, and so on."[21] McNaughton, who looked at how mortar pits were built, missed this point entirely.

The problems of the 1 CID contingent went beyond the oversight of officer train-ing. Even if unit commanding officers and brigade commanders had been inclined to address leadership training as an issue in itself, which they were not, too few had the requisite expertise to supervise officer development at the unit level. Hoffmeister's commanding officer, for example, had seen service in the First World War, passed the Militia Staff Course during the interwar period, and attended a Senior Officers' Course at Sheerness in March 1940, but the fifty-three-year-old Stevenson had neither the depth of knowledge nor sufficient appreciation for modern war to give proper guidance to his subordinates.[22] What is more, Stevenson was simply not available to oversee the training of officers. Following attendance on the Senior Officers' Course, and because of the shortage of trained senior offic-ers, Stevenson temporarily replaced Brigadier G.R. Pearkes as commander of 2 CIB. On another occasion, he also stepped in to take acting command of 1 CIB. Such was the training deficit to be overcome in a Canadian Army that was ex-panding rapidly from a Permanent Force strength of 450 officers and 4,000 men before the war to a mobilized force of 76,678 all ranks in March 1940.[23] Even those officers with minimal tactical know-how ascended in a void, leaving battalions without reliable cadres to develop competent officers.

Given the tactical inadequacies of most senior Canadian officers, it should come as no surprise that those charged with readying 1 CID relied heavily on experience – experience that dated back to the previous war. In Hoffmeister's chain of com-mand, for example, the battalion commander (Stevenson), the brigade commander (Pearkes), and the division commander (McNaughton) had all distinguished them-selves in the last war, and they all called on that experience when preparing troops for battle.[24] Thus, when company-level training finally took place, it was patheti-cally dated. On 12 April 1940, Hoffmeister and his company, as part of a division-directed rotation, deployed to the area of Pirbright and occupied an extensive trench system. Over the course of four days, they patrolled no-man's land, con-ducted trench raids, practised chemical defence measures, and fought staged de-fensive battles – activities that were hallmarks of the 1914-1918 war.[25] Hoffmeister's 1980 reflections on the exercise said something about its limited usefulness: "We did our stint in the trenches at Purbright [sic] ... and the thing was done in dead seriousness, in the middle of the night ... stumbling up these communication trenches. It was World War I stuff. First of all the advance party had gone in by daylight. We were shown the gaps in the wire, where the patrols went out and where the patrols came in and this was fun and it was interesting. We didn't know any better."[26] It was a twenty-five year throwback to the First World War, and more of the same was planned for the coming months.[27]

Training for the last war was not a peculiar Canadian proclivity. The British Army was just as prone to the tendency and was equally slow to adapt to the changes of modern warfare. The Trench Warfare Training and Experimental Centre at which the "advanced training" was to take place from May to June, was a British Army establishment. Why were the British and Canadian armies still training for the last war? For historian David Fraser, the roots of the First World War mindset in Second World War training stretched back to the relatively poor state of British Army training between the wars, and to a pervasive sense of caution born of the carnage of 1914-1918.[28] Another prominent British scholar, David French, recently argued many of the same points, while also emphasizing that the immediacy of the German threat in the weeks following the collapse of the French armies in May and June 1940 delayed any radical reappraisals in training methods and doctrine.[29] As a formation of the Fourth British Corps, and lacking any current battle experience, 1 CID followed the British doctrinal lead.[30]

The training lethargy of the so-called Phoney War ended abruptly in the spring and summer of 1940. The shocks that started with the German invasion of Norway in April 1940 and intensified with the fall of France a little over a month later jolted the British and Canadian armies. During this frenetic period, the Canadian division struggled to prepare simultaneously for expeditionary tasks and home defence duties. In mid-April, the Seaforths' sister battalions in 2 CIB, the Princess Patricia's Canadian Light Infantry (PPCLI), and the Edmonton Regiment, scrambled to Scotland in preparation for a raid on the German-occupied coast of Norway, a mission that was fortunately cancelled.[31] Later, in a desperate effort to bolster failing French defences, 1 CIB actually deployed to France on 13 June, only to be withdrawn five days later, without their equipment.

The Seaforth preparations for possible action against the Germans had actually begun on 10 May when the regiment received a warning order for tasks in defence of Great Britain;[32] but that did not mean that training, such as it was, ceased. Between 20 and 25 May, they joined the other battalions of Pearkes' 2 CIB for manoeuvres on Salisbury Plain. Undoubtedly events in France added a sense of urgency to matters; however, given that collective training had barely advanced beyond single-arm training at the company level, this was a classic case of running before walking.

Regarding the May exercise, the Seaforth war diarist recorded an unusual amount of minute-to-minute detail (probably transcribed from the operations log) that reflected both the First World War mindset and the state of training.[33] It started with companies of the brigade's three battalions occupying defensive positions under the covering fire of the carrier platoons. Next came a "night of digging and wiring" to prepare the defensive position, while fighting patrols harassed the enemy. Twenty-four hours after that, Pearkes ordered the Seaforths to prepare a company-size force for "a raid with the support of an artillery barrage." In preparation for that particular assignment, a daylight "rehearsal for the raid was carried out in the rear of the ... [defensive] position." Finally, at 11:00 p.m., the "Raiding Party jumped off [departed]" from the forward line of trenches. It returned ninety minutes later to report that the raid had been a success: "the enemy were bombed out of the trenches." That was just the beginning. Later, the Seaforth carrier platoon "attacked the enemy flank and destroyed 100 ft. of enemy wire" – an accomplishment of dubious tactical significance. When tanks finally entered the battle on 24 May, they moved forward of the friendly trenches, stopped, took up fire positions, and "covered" two advancing companies as they assaulted behind a timed artillery barrage. Fifty-five minutes later, those companies dug in to "consolidate" their gains. No attempt was made to exploit the success of the attack and rout the retreating enemy. That was not part of the prevailing tactical doctrine. Not that different doctrine would have made much difference at this stage; even if Stevenson or Pearkes had been inclined to pursue the enemy, it would have required close coordination of infantry, armour, and artillery, something the immature state of all-arms training simply would not have permitted. In all, the exercise was a pale attempt to replicate the "bite and hold" tactics that had earned the 1st Canadian Corps such fame during the First World War.[34] But that was what Stevenson, Pearkes, and McNaughton knew, and that was how they trained.

Shortly after the evacuation from Dunkirk, the Canadians turned their attention exclusively towards the defence of Great Britain. On 20 June, McNaughton held a conference with all his brigadiers, his staff, and the supporting-arms commanders at Farnborough. He made it clear that the division now had a single operational task: "to move quickly against an enemy invasion, which may be attempted within the next few days." As the General Headquarters (GHQ) Home Forces reserve, 1 CID was to be a centrally located and "hard-hitting mobile force ready to proceed North, South, East or West."[35] "Centrally located" meant the division had to move from its current location near Aldershot to the Oxford area, which it did within days.[36] To constitute a "hard-hitting mobile force," McNaughton opted for a decentralized approach, based on battalion groups. He directed that "battalion groups are to train and operate as complete units; troops of field and anti-tank artillery and sections of engineers are to be under command of the Inf Bns [infantry battalions]."[37] Given the operational requirement to move quickly and destroy enemy incursions, such as parachute assaults, this made sense. Smaller decentralized groups were less cumbersome and quicker to react than larger formations.

Unfortunately, this new operational focus put in abeyance any collective training beyond that which had taken place at Pirbright, or even Salisbury Plain.[38] Not only did that make it difficult to coordinate the movement and employment of all arms at the brigade and division levels, it hobbled the training of the supporting arms in their own right. The division's artillery regiments, for example, had their own collective training eclipsed when their sub-units were placed under command of the battalions.

As the remaining months of 1940 passed, the defence of Great Britain came to mean more than the anti-invasion task, although that definitely was the largest part of it. In addition to numerous counter-parachutist exercises, Seaforth soldiers guarded the British Prime Minister's residence, they defended the southern coastline at Brighton in November, and they paraded for visiting dignitaries.[39] With interruptions due to German air raids, Seaforth soldiers managed to conduct some training in small arms, map reading, physical fitness, and patrolling; but it was all very low-level stuff, and it did little to advance collective skills above section level. To complicate matters further, the turmoil caused by the creation of the 1st Canadian Corps, and the promotions of McNaughton and Pearkes on 17 July to corps and division command respectively, slowed what little training guidance there had been.[40] More often than not, training limped along "under company arrangements." Between July and December 1940, the Seaforths participated in only four half-day exercises with British tanks.[41] That was not enough to identify, let alone address, whatever difficulties lay beyond the section level. Consequently, Hoffmeister and his fellow officers learned very little. But the Battle of Britain beckoned, and tasks in defence of the home islands, rightly it must be said, assumed the highest priority.

Operational imperatives notwithstanding, the second half of 1940 dragged for all ranks because the predominant activities in defence of Britain – providing mobile reaction forces, manning coastal defences, and guarding vital points – primarily involved that most common of military activities: waiting. Meeting these requirements presented its own leadership challenges, and Hoffmeister strove to maintain discipline and keep the soldiers occupied. He arranged what training he could, he route-marched them, he inspected them regularly, and he mercilessly quizzed their section and platoon commanders on their activities and whereabouts. Some of his soldiers even joked about the futility of make-work activities; but, in the main, they liked him and responded well to his leadership.

There were two reasons for this. First, Hoffmeister's soldiers knew nothing of their company commander's insecurities. Given how rare company-level training had been, the soldiers had not really had much opportunity to notice any shortcomings. And second, he looked after his men and did what he could to set an example. He marched with them, he dug his own trenches, he looked after their welfare, and the soldiers respected him for it.[42]

Hoffmeister understood the importance of troop morale; he especially understood that, given the poor state of training during that first year in England, it was something the unit could not afford to lose. He struggled to maintain it from the very beginning. When the Seaforths first arrived in England, they found the accommodations and amenities to be abysmal; billets were unheated and sparsely equipped.[43] Making an unpleasant situation even worse, an influenza epidemic, "bloody awful food," and some inadequate junior leadership exacerbated the malcontent of the rank and file.[44] Early in February 1940, these issues came to a head, as a soldier from Hoffmeister's "B" Company remembered:

These two factors [flu and bad food] plus the alleged incompetence of a couple of the Senior NCOs and officers led to a near riot and a reluctance to go on parade. This lead to Hoffie [Hoffmeister] calling a meeting of the coy [company], less Snr [Senior] NCOs and officers, to thrash out the problems. The result was the removal of one Senior NCO and the posting of an officer ... Some Senior NCOs were quite bitter about his approach to the problem ... However, it did settle things down and ... it did not bother people too much as it got rid of the incompetents ... It also got us a new Regimental Cook. The one who left was a factor in the near riot because of his ... bloody awful mutton stew.[45]

In his unorthodox resolution of this brief morale crisis, Hoffmeister displayed many of the analytical abilities he admired in MacMillan. He appreciated that the situation had the potential to undermine the soldiers' morale and their confidence in the chain of command, that it could not be ignored, and that it had to be re-solved quickly. Accordingly, he gathered the facts to determine what issues had to be fixed and how. There was not much that could be done about accommodations (they were limited) or the influenza.[46] However, on the issue of amenities such as books, games, or newspapers, Hoffmeister and a few of his fellow officers seized the initiative since the chain of command appeared unable to remedy the situa-tion. In London, they called on Bill McAdam, the Agent General of British Colum-bia, who happened to be hosting H.R. MacMillan at the time. Hoffmeister relayed the plight of the regiment to the two influential gentlemen, "and in no time Bill McAdam authorized his people to get soldiers' comforts together and get them down to Aldershot. Then life took on a different meaning entirely."[47] Regarding the problems of inadequate leadership and bad food, Hoffmeister removed two junior leaders from the company and replaced the cook. His remedies worked.

More important than what Hoffmeister did was why and how he did it. He felt compelled to take action because, as he had learned during the Seaboard crisis five years earlier, his future successes would depend on subordinate performance. He believed that content soldiers who had faith in their leaders would perform better. That was why he consulted them – as part of "gathering the facts." The rationale was simple enough: since soldiers were the ones who would have to follow, who better to determine the "followability" of commanders? His litmus test for com-manders always started with the soldiers.[48] And while reaching a few levels lower in the chain of command to find problems may have annoyed junior leaders in between, it strengthened his credibility with the common soldier. It demonstrated his responsiveness to their concerns. It also showed them that he was a commander who could get things done. His credibility flourished, and not just in his own company. It spread by word of mouth to the other companies of the battalion.

Solid as Hoffmeister's human skills may have been, his insecurities mounted during the second half of 1940, while he was "not learning a thing."[49] It was not simply a question of not knowing the format for operation orders; the problem was much greater than that. Hoffmeister realized all too well that his lack of technical knowledge and training impaired his ability to make tactical decisions. In other words, when faced with a tactical problem, he could not gather together the facts to formulate options and develop plans because he did not know what the appropriate facts were. At this stage in his development as an infantry officer, consideration of such factors as enemy force capabilities, time and space, or ground would have been difficult, if not impossible.[50]

The nature of company command only magnified Hoffmeister's worries. At this level, the commander received little assistance for tactical decisions. The structure of the company (see Figure 3.2) gave the company commander some assistance for training, discipline, and logistics: the second in command took care of administration; the company sergeant-major saw to the discipline and training of soldiers; and the company quartermaster sergeant kept the company supplied and fed. But for battlefield decisions, he was on his own.

Another noteworthy characteristic of company command was short decision cycles, which accentuated the essential difficulty. Whereas a sales manager might

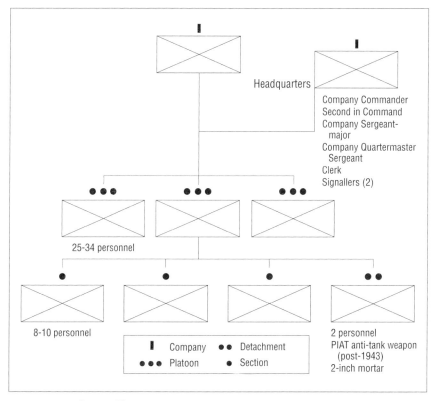

FIGURE 3.2   *Infantry Rifle Company, 1940-45*

have had days in which to gather the facts and make decisions, a company commander in battle often had only minutes. During a dismounted advance, for example, a company commander commonly had to execute a hasty attack within 45
to 60 minutes of coming under enemy fire, and the time for a tactical decision
represented only a fraction of that total.[51] To allow time for preliminary moves and
the passage of subordinate orders, the company commander normally should not
have consumed more than one-third of the total execution time to conduct a quick
battlefield appreciation, devise a plan, and issue his own orders. Roughly speaking, this translated into a decision cycle of 15 to 20 minutes. Given the rapidity
with which decisions had to be made, and the fact that they had to be made with
little assistance, the company commander needed technical knowledge and expertise at his fingertips. Moreover, to keep it at his fingertips, the process had to be
practised regularly, something that had clearly not been happening under
McNaughton's 1940 training regimen. Hoffmeister had enough experience with
the decision-making process at H.R. MacMillan Export Company to realize – as
perhaps other officers did not – that he lacked the tools to do the same in the
military context. The fact that lives, not profits, were now at stake hugely compounded the problem.

By early 1941, Hoffmeister was heading for a nervous crisis that, in retrospect,
appears inevitable. When, as an office boy, he found himself deficient in technical
knowledge, Hoffmeister went back to the mill and learned what was necessary to
perform effectively. In the military, the option of going back did not exist, and
Stevenson's reluctance to sanction attendance on out-of-unit courses further frustrated the young self-starter. In January 1941, Hoffmeister's confidence crisis cli-
maxed: "I had a nervous breakdown. It was brought on by the anxiety of having
responsibility for a hundred men, [being] responsible for their lives, taking them
into battle, and not having the necessary training to ensure I would do a satisfactory job."[52] He first realized the extent of his trouble when he discovered an inexplicable numbness of the left side of his body on 10 January 1941.[53] The next day,
medical authorities admitted him to the Number 1 Neurological Hospital at
Basingstoke for "hysteria."[54] Doctors diagnosed the paresthesia of the left side of
Hoffmeister's body as the physical manifestation of acute anxiety. Specifically,
Hoffmeister's disorder was one of "conversion hysteria," a condition in which "physical symptoms are substituted for symptoms of anxiety."[55]

To cure the condition, neuropsychiatrist Dr. H.H. Hyland tackled the affliction
from the point of view that acute anxiety could be treated with "rest, reassurance
and a 'detailed discussion' of the factors 'causing immediate mental conflict and
tension.'"[56] The treatment, which took place from 13 January to 4 February, went
well. Hyland succeeded in reassuring Hoffmeister that he was capable of fulfilling
his responsibilities, that he could only do his best, and that he should not let his
worries accumulate.[57] When Hoffmeister showed encouraging signs of recovery,
Hyland released his patient, who then proceeded on leave. Within two weeks, how-

ever, Hoffmeister suffered a relapse and returned to Hyland's care.[58] According to one of Hyland's colleagues, Dr. J.C. Richardson, Hyland deliberately decided against repatriating Hoffmeister to Canada for medical reasons, opting instead for another round of psychotherapy. He did so because of an abiding belief in the capacity for psychological recovery in men of "good basic personality."[59] Whatever "good basic personality" meant, Hyland saw it in Hoffmeister, who exhibited sufficient progress to be released a second and final time on 24 February. Outside a limited few in Hoffmeister's regimental chain of command, not many people knew of the episode.[60]

Hoffmeister soon returned to commanding his company, but the experience had affected him profoundly. In a way, it was a catharsis. It reinforced his belief that confidence underpinned command. Inadequate training and experience had so crippled his own confidence, so hindered his ability to perform effectively, that he had eventually suffered a breakdown. Moreover, the crisis sharpened Hoffmeister's understanding of soldiers – people, really – and deepened his conviction that confidence was equally crucial to subordinate performance. He believed that soldiers and officers who were confident in their own abilities, and those of their leaders, performed better. They were easier to lead because they less frequently succumbed to the hesitation of self-doubt; and they were easier to manage because they would be prepared for a wider range of challenges. But confidence took time to develop, and Hoffmeister understood this. He also grasped that the bricks and mortar of confidence were training. Only through adequate training would soldiers acquire the individual and collective skills necessary to complete the tasks assigned them. More than that, the shared experiences of both training and combat built bonds and gave soldiers confidence in the commanders who led them. Regular and mission-oriented training for all ranks: this became a hallmark of Hoffmeister's approach to preparing men for battle, one that lasted the duration of his military career.

Despite his psychological recovery, Hoffmeister's deficiency of technical know-how did not go away, but he did have the good fortune to return to his unit at a time when the shock of the German victories of 1940 was finally beginning to have a positive impact on collective training. With the Battle of Britain won, and the threat of German invasion dissipated somewhat, attention turned to a much more ambitious program of collective training – one that featured more offensively oriented manoeuvres and force-against-force schemes.[61] Exercises such as FOX (February 1941), directed by McNaughton's newly formed corps headquarters, exposed many of the inadequacies of senior Canadian commanders and staffs,[62] but they also provided an opportunity for companies and battalions to work out their own tactical procedures and techniques. During Exercise HARE (9-11 April), for example, the Seaforths made excellent use of intelligence section scouts to reconnoitre routes, select suitable assembly areas, find enemy machine guns, and define attack objectives.[63]

Slowly, the chain of command figured out how to harmonize training activities at all levels, something that had been clearly lacking throughout 1940. But the Canadians did not improve in isolation. As David French has pointed out, the British Army, and especially the Home Forces under which the Canadians served, made many significant improvements in training and organization following the evacuation from Dunkirk.[64] Much of the credit for this went to General Alan Brooke, Commander-in-Chief (C-in-C) Home Forces (July 1940-December 1941). A Great War veteran whose recent experience included the fighting withdrawal of his II Corps from Dunkirk, Brooke made training more realistic and effective. He introduced tactical battle drills, not only to forge a common understanding of tactics at the lower levels of command, but also to improve the tempo of operations.[65] Section and platoon commanders who could react instinctively to tactical situations did not have to be told what to do when faced with the terror and confusion of combat. This sped up operations at the lowest levels, clipping critical minutes and hours off decision cycles higher up the chain of command. Brooke also held longer and larger field-training exercises, which gave commanders above company level greater opportunity to practise their skills against "enemy" forces, outdoors and away from the sterile environment of a classroom.

The 1st Canadian Corps' training gradually fell in line with this new emphasis. The counter-invasion Exercise PAREX (19-20 May 1941), for example, prepared 2 CIB for the much larger Southeastern Command Exercise WATERLOO in June.[66] Moreover, between formation-level exercises and counter-invasion assignments, concurrent training made more efficient use of the available time and better prepared the various components of the battalion for their responsibilities. During one typical week in May 1941, the Seaforth rifle companies alternately conducted range practices or other routine low-level training, the carrier platoon ran its own five-day exercise, the intelligence section took part in a brigade intelligence (reconnaissance) exercise, and the commanding officer attended a Senior Officer's Course.[67] Things were improving.

Things improved for Hoffmeister as well. More frequent field exercises allowed him to practise tactical decision-making and command soldiers.[68] During the first half of the battalion force-on-force Exercise SOCKEYE, his company defended a vital point against the other companies of the unit. Then, when the roles reversed for the second half, his company attacked.[69] In all, Hoffmeister participated in nine such force-on-force exercises between March and November 1941, most of which were preceded with officer training sessions or tactical exercises without troops (TEWTs).[70] By trial, error, and repetition, Hoffmeister's skills and confidence improved. The situation was by no means ideal – he should have received formal training as a company commander first – but it was better than it had been in the months leading up to his breakdown.

December 1941 was a turning point for Hoffmeister. Brigadier A.E. Potts, the commander of 2 CIB at the time, must have seen something he liked in Hoffmeister because he brought the young major to his headquarters as the commander's liaison officer.[71] A lazy commander, Potts preferred social events to hard work.[72] The industrious Hoffmeister suited his purposes nicely. Although initially unenthused about leaving his regiment, Hoffmeister threw himself into his new responsibilities with all the alacrity he had demonstrated as an office boy at the Rat Portage Lumber Company. As a representative of the brigade commander, he coordinated brigade defence plans for the Downs area of southern England with the British Home Guard, the civil authorities, local police forces, and the other brigades of the division.[73] Hoffmeister's new position also afforded him more freedom to seize whatever training opportunities he could, and he did. On 30 January, he slipped away to attend a corps lecture on "the Div [Division] in the approach march."[74] He twice filled in as acting brigade major and, on one occasion, he even conducted a reconnaissance "of the area ... at TRULEIGH HILL *to site new defences,*" a task that should have been completed by the brigade commander.[75] Small wonder that, when Lieutenant-General Montgomery, the General Officer Commanding (GOC) Southeastern Command visited, Hoffmeister hurriedly had to brief both the brigade major and the brigade commander on the detailed disposition of the brigade's forces. Neither knew well the deployment of brigade sub-units because neither had visited the positions.[76] Montgomery saw through it: "[Potts] knows very little of what is going on."[77]

The learning environment might not have been ideal, but it did give Hoffmeister a chance to familiarize himself with a staff that was more or less functionally divided into operations, intelligence, personnel, and logistics (see Figure 3.3). He gathered what he could from the experience and proved himself a quick learner in the process. In February 1942, since he had long been doing the brigade major's job, and then some, Potts made Hoffmeister the G staff learner, an appointment that signalled his selection for further staff training.[78] Working as understudy to Major "Knobby" Clark, whom Hoffmeister described as "one of the laziest buggers I have ever met," cannot have been fun, but it gave Hoffmeister a chance to prove his mettle and make an impression on his superiors that would pay dividends later.[79]

Whereas Hoffmeister's immediate superiors failed to impress him, Montgomery gave him something to emulate. From the time Montgomery took command of the Southeastern Army in November 1941, he made his presence felt.[80] He readjusted defensive plans, rejecting the Maginot-minded approach that demanded "every inch of coastline be defended" in favour of a more flexible defence in depth. Instead, he "pulled the troops back from the beaches and held them ready in compact bodies ... poised for counter attack and for offensive action against the invaders."[81] This impressed Hoffmeister, who, looking back on his time as a company commander on the southern coast of England, recalled: "Not only were we unable to cover our front by manpower, we were unable to cover it by fire. There's no doubt whatsoever in my mind that had the Germans chosen to land anywhere

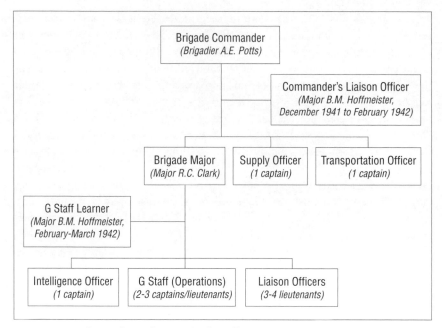

FIGURE 3.3   *2nd Canadian Infantry Brigade staff organization, 1941*

along our sector ... they could have taken it."[82] Montgomery changed that and Hoffmeister respected him for it.

He also recognized in Montgomery a commander who knew how to train soldiers and who expected his subordinate commanders to do the same. In the main, Hoffmeister held a poor opinion of the Canadian chain of command, most of whom, like Clark, were old Permanent Force hands, so he looked "very favourabl[y]" on Montgomery's proverbial housecleaning: "he roared through Southeastern Command ... and just weeded people out all over the place – you go back to Canada ... you're not fit."[83] The 2 CIB War Diary entry on Montgomery's 28 February visit to the brigade hinted at how the army commander's approach caught the Canadians a bit by surprise: "Brig [Brigadier] Arthur E. Potts ... and Major R.C. Clark ... met the Army Comd [commander] General Montgomery prior to a visit to the Seaforth [Highlanders] of C [Canada]. No regular parades were called. Bns [battalions] are to carry on with normal duties. The Army Comd is more interested in meeting the officers and sizing them up."[84]

To Hoffmeister, Montgomery seemed just the man to provide the bricks and mortar of solid training to the flagging Canadians; he weeded out the incompetents, he developed those with potential, and he planned more effective and regular training.[85] Montgomery's December 1941 address to the brigade's officers also struck Hoffmeister for its directness of approach, its exhibition of competence, and its demonstration of unwavering self-confidence.[86] More important, perhaps,

Hoffmeister witnessed how favourably soldiers responded to the man they referred to as "Monty." They respected him not only because they perceived him as competent, but also because they knew him. As Hoffmeister noted: "I think that at some point Montgomery likely saw just about every soldier serving in Southeastern Command."[87] In H.R. MacMillan's parlance, Montgomery effectively "energized" his subordinates. So impressed was Hoffmeister that he later described himself as a "disciple" of Montgomery.[88]

Although Hoffmeister had found his military role model in Montgomery, he still lacked much in the way of military training. In March 1942, he took a huge step towards redressing that deficiency when he returned to Canada for the Canadian Junior War Staff Course (CJWSC). At the time, however, this development annoyed him. He realized all too well the importance of formal training, but Hoffmeister also feared that staff training invariably meant staff employment – and a war away from his regiment and the action.[89] It turned out to be a fortuitous four-month watershed in his military career. The training he received between 30 April and 23 August 1942 better prepared him for battlefield command and did much to restore his confidence. In short, he learned the technical business of what Montgomery described as the "stage management" of battles.

The staff course curriculum sought to convey much.[90] For the first half of the training, Hoffmeister and his fellow students devoted themselves to basic staff skills and procedures. The training progressed logically and in sequenced steps. Since brigade and division staff officers had to know what they had to work with and against, early in the course students learned the characteristics, capabilities, and functions of the various arms and services: armour, artillery, engineers, reconnaissance elements, air assets, and even airborne forces. They needed that body of knowledge for the other predominant topic of the first stage of training: operational staff duties, or how to conduct tactical appreciations, make plans, and disseminate orders. A variety of lectures, syndicate discussions, and command post exercises (CPXs) made the material comprehensible.[91] With those basic skills in hand, students who survived the onerous first half of the course applied themselves to the focal point of the latter portion of the curriculum: tactics. The scope of this training included tactics for the defence, the withdrawal, the advance, the attack, and even combined operations.[92] In this stage, the training focus switched to the practical resolution of problems using CPXs and TEWTs. Directing staff (DS) assigned students to various command and staff appointments and gave them tactical missions – opposed river crossings, deliberate defences, advances, and so on. Then, based on their assigned missions, students conducted appreciations, developed plans, and issued orders, individually and as members of a staff. They determined the object of their mission; they considered all of the factors (friendly forces, enemy forces, ground, weather, time, space) that might influence the outcome; they weighed the various courses of action; and they selected and developed the best plan.[93] Because even the best of plans could collapse without the timely dissemination of information, Hoffmeister and his course mates also mastered "battle procedure," a formalized process by which battle preparations such as road moves and logistical build-ups occurred in tandem with staff planning.[94] Significantly, students spent one-sixth of their time learning how to plan and conduct collective training – how to build the platoons, companies, and battalions needed to execute all those tactical plans. Though not without its shortcomings, CJWSC did what it was designed to do: it gave officers the technical tools they needed to manage battles and prepare their soldiers for combat.[95]

Most of it was new to the candidates, although Hoffmeister saw in it much that reminded him of what he had learned at MacMillan Export. In 1980, William J. McAndrew asked Hoffmeister directly: "Did your civilian experience help at all in coping with the theoretical problems you encountered at the Staff College?" Hoffmeister's response was unequivocal: "Yes, because H.R. MacMillan was a great teacher." As Hoffmeister saw it, the mental processes were essentially the same – "a matter of assembling the facts and then making a decision based on the facts."[96] In a November 1943 letter to MacMillan, Hoffmeister made the tongue-in-cheek remark that "commanding a formation is not unlike running a business. Sound principles and sound thinking give the answers every time whether one is killing Germans or selling lumber."[97] Hoffmeister's humour notwithstanding, the similarities were there, and he took comfort in them.

Staff training steadied Hoffmeister's wavering confidence. Not only did he finally understand what "facts" had to be gathered to solve military problems, and how, he also mastered a more formalized decision-making process than the one he had learned under MacMillan. Less obviously, CJWSC also restored some of his faith in the chain of command. The structured and progressive program was better than any training he had experienced to date. Certainly, it contrasted with the disjointed and ineffectual training sessions of his first year in England. He also thought highly of the directing staff, particularly a handful of British officers who were "fresh from the desert [North Africa] and very knowledgeable."[98] By the end of the course, Hoffmeister was much better equipped to survive in the soldier's environment of abbreviated decision cycles.

Yet for all that the course taught him, it very nearly ruined him. This, however, had more to do with the methodology of the course than the material conveyed. The pace of work was furious. Hoffmeister and his fellow candidates simply had too much work to do in the time available: "I was bewildered a bit by it at the outset. We were loaded up with far more work than it was possible for anyone to do in 24 hours, which was done deliberately, and I put in long hours until 2 and 3 o'clock in the morning. I could feel myself getting more and more exhausted and becoming less and less efficient and losing self-confidence ... I was on a self-destructive course."[99] Fearing he was heading for another nervous crisis, Hoffmeister drew on Dr. Hyland's treatment and did a volte-face: "Finally I just came to the conclusion, early one morning, that this was ridiculous and that I had to change my philosophy. So starting the next morning I went to my DS box [where directing staff left assignments for students] and sorted out the stuff that I thought was important and left the rest of it there. That evening I worked after dinner till 7 or 7:30, then went to a movie ... Everything seemed to fall into place after that."[100]

It certainly did. He attained the highest possible mark on the course, his final course report noting the "excellent progress" he had made from a "below average" beginning. Hoffmeister's course report also described him as a "very capable officer" with outstanding tactical aptitude, commending him for his "strong personality," his ability to "work well in a team," and his "considerat[ion] of other people's views." Perhaps most significantly, it surmised that, by the course's end, Hoffmeister exhibited "all the confidence of real ability."[101]

By the autumn of 1942, Hoffmeister's fortunes were definitely on the upswing. When the course ended, the chain of command presented Major Hoffmeister with his choice of several high-profile staff appointments, or command of the Seaforth Highlanders, which had recently become available due to the illness of the current commanding officer, Lieutenant-Colonel J.M.S. Tait.[102] Hoffmeister jumped at the chance to command his regiment. How things had changed.

Hoffmeister had come a long way in the eighteen months since his nervous breakdown. He had despaired over what he thought was the misfortune of being assigned to a staff position. He had survived the tribulations of Staff College, proving himself to be among the most able of his peers. Now, after having completed the staff course, he had the basic tools for stage-managing battles. He could conduct tactical appreciations and make decisions because he knew what factors had to be weighed and how. He knew better how to manage his time and that of his subordinates. He had a better understanding of how to train soldiers for war. But most of all, he was confident. Battlefield management skills – although far from complete – now complemented his formidable abilities as a leader of men, buttressed them, made them stronger. He was winning again.

4
Battalion Command: Training for War

[A primary objective of collective training is] to afford leaders opportunities of exercising command in the field under warlike conditions. Although under peace conditions the stress and danger of war can never be fully portrayed, collective training affords a wholesome check on theoretical training, and gives some experience as regards the effect of fatigue, the incidence of friction, the factors of time and space, the "fog of war" and uncertainties due to lack of information, ambiguous orders, and messages which are vague, go astray or are received too late.[1]

MILITARY TRAINING PAMPHLET, 1940

From October 1942 to July 1943, Hoffmeister primed himself and his battalion for battle. On a personal level, he honed his technical skills through self-study and participation on numerous field-training exercises. Collectively, he readied his sections, platoons, and companies for the challenges to come, purging them of ineffective leaders and putting them through their paces in mission-oriented manoeuvres. Timing and good luck helped. Improved training methods coincided with a shift in strategic focus, one that saw the Allied armies in Britain switch from defensive to offensive training, following the German invasion of Russia in the summer of 1941. While Hitler looked east, British, American, and Canadian forces got ready for a return to Continental Europe. Thus, high-quality offensive training, sharpened by an impending operational mission, offered a "wholesome check" to "theoretical" learning, and gave Hoffmeister the chance to figure out, as much as training would permit, how best to command an infantry battalion in battle. His human skills were, as always, steady. By the time Hoffmeister set foot on Sicilian soil on 10 July 1943, he was as prepared as any battalion commander could have been, without the benefit of combat experience.

THE CANADIAN ARMY to which Hoffmeister returned in the autumn of 1942 was also much improved. This was mostly the result of General Montgomery's influence on training.[2] Indeed, in the ten months that he commanded the Southeastern Army in England (November 1941-August 1942), Montgomery had made a greater impact on the training of 1st Canadian Corps units than any other officer, including McNaughton and his successor, Harry Crerar.[3] As he did with all formations under his command, Montgomery had jolted the Canadians in two ways: he had taught them how to train, and he had weeded out the weakest commanders.

Montgomery's influence can be gauged with a quick comparison of two Canadian exercises, one before he came to the Southeastern Army and one after he left. McNaughton's 1st Canadian Corps instruction for Exercise HARE in March 1941 allocated only one umpire to each division, brigade, and artillery regiment.[4] Two years later, the 1 CID instruction for Exercise PAST included an appendix that assigned umpires to all staff branches of the division headquarters, two to each brigade headquarters, one to each battalion headquarters, and one to every company or squadron in the division, including the supporting arms.[5] Another annex outlined the duties of umpires, as well as a projected table of exercise events.[6] Montgomery brought structure and systematic supervision to collective training.

Montgomery also visited every unit and formation of the 1st Canadian Corps in February-March 1942. He noted the key deficiency of the previous two years' training in a report to Major-General H.D.G. Crerar, then acting commander of the 1st Canadian Corps: "There is a lack of training ability in the COs [commanding officers] ... Little time is spent in teaching officers *how to train troops.*"[7] Collective training, as a result, was often "haphazard," non-progressive, and usually without any validation of training aims. When planning exercises, commanders made only minimal use of impartial umpires to observe the exercises and offer constructive criticism to commanders and staffs.

"Monty" had also picked up quickly on the poor state of officer training. Because battalion commanders rarely observed or tested their subordinates in the field, company commanders too often conducted their own training and received little feedback on what they did right and what they did wrong. The same applied to staff officers. In a note to Crerar, he remarked that the attention commanders paid to training battalion and headquarters staffs was far too scant.[8] In Montgomery's opinion, commanders at all levels also made too little use of skeleton-force exercises and command post exercises (CPXs) to sharpen the skills of their subordinates and staffs before they went to the field with troops.[9]

Blunt as these observations were, Montgomery passed them to Crerar, but not without dispensing guidance and a framework for redressing the deficiencies, something he did regularly and often. Montgomery planned his army-level validation exercise, TIGER, for the second half of May 1942, and gave guidance to subordinate formations on how to prepare for it. In January, he had suggested and later participated in a 1st Canadian Corps study week to teach the proper coordination of advances, attacks, and defence operations to senior officers and staffs.[10] Montgomery also reviewed the direction that his corps commanders passed down their own chains of command prior to TIGER and closely supervised training to ensure that it proceeded as intended. In general, Montgomery approved of Crerar's program, which was logical and progressive.[11] For example, the skeleton Exercises BEAVER I and BEAVER II (January and February 1942) practised headquarters staffs from battalion to corps level before BEAVER III and BEAVER IV (April and May respectively) tested the divisions of the corps in the operations that had been discussed in the January study week.[12] Montgomery also encouraged a cleaner separation of operational tasks and training. Even after the invasion scare had dissipated with Hitler's march into Russia in June 1941, Canadians had still been in the habit of trying to train and to complete operational tasks concurrently, neither optimally. At Montgomery's suggestion, weeks, not days, became the measure for units engaged in operational tasks or training.[13]

It all made good sense, and it did improve the battle readiness of the corps, but the training also confirmed what Montgomery believed to be a stumbling block to further progress: a paucity of able senior commanders. After observing 1 CID on Beaver III in April 1942, he commented: "It is not the fault of the regimental commanders and men that [1st] Division failed badly. It was the fault of the Divisional Commander."[14] And since he found the division to be made of "very fine material," Montgomery knew that the difficulties began at the top. Too few commanders from battalion to division level had the requisite skills and knowledge to do their jobs effectively. Mostly, the sad state of the interwar army was to blame. Opportunities for low-level training had been rare enough; occasions for learning the "stage-management" of all arms had been non-existent. For this reason, Montgomery distinguished between "teachable" and "useless" commanders. Because he could not fire Canadians directly, however, Montgomery made recommendations to Crerar on who should go, and Crerar obliged in the housecleaning chores.

Two of those shuffled home held positions in Hoffmeister's chain of command: Major-General George Pearkes and Brigadier A.E. Potts. After observing Pearkes in command of the 1st Canadian Infantry Division during Exercise BEAVER III, Montgomery had expressed his misgivings to Crerar: "Pearkes is unable to appreciate the essentials of a military problem and formulate a sound plan ... a gallant soldier without a doubt; but he has no brains."[15] Of the indolent Potts, Montgomery could only conclude that the brigade commander had made a "poor showing ... [and] should go back to Canada."[16] By setting such deadwood adrift, Montgomery made room for younger officers with the potential to learn and the ability to train. In the place of Pearkes, the competent Major-General H.L.M. Salmon took command of the 1 CID in September 1942. Potts' successor in the 2nd Canadian Infantry Brigade (2 CIB) was Brigadier Chris Vokes.

A Permanent Force officer and Royal Military College graduate (1925), the gruff and hot-tempered Vokes had passed through British Army staff college at Camberly in 1935 and had served as general staff officer, 1st class (GSO I), of 1 CID before his appointment to brigade commander.[17] No tactical genius, Vokes was, nonetheless, a "fine fighting brigade commander," who earned the respect of most of his subordinates.[18] His real strength was training troops, and, like most Canadian and British officers, he took his cue from Montgomery in this regard. He planned *and* supervised progressive training, and he provided plenty of feedback to subordinates. Most of all, Vokes did not let faults pass. He was more than willing to make an organization do a task over if he thought it had been blundered the first time, and did so frequently with company and battalion commanders.[19]

During his first meeting with Hoffmeister in October 1942, Vokes let the incoming battalion commanders know that he was displeased with Seaforth performance: "Now you've got a real job of work to do. This battalion [the Seaforths] is a poor third in this Brigade and my orders to you are to bring it up to par with the others. You've got absolutely a free hand. I'll back you up in anything you want to do."[20]

His regimental pride stung, Hoffmeister went back to his unit at Stone Cross to gather the facts, come up with a plan, and take the necessary action. He first conferred with the acting CO, Major Douglas Forin. A pre-war Seaforth and a friend from the Vancouver Rowing Club, Forin "didn't pull any punches."[21] His opinion was that the unit had indeed slipped badly under the leadership of the two previous commanding officers. An arduous two-day exercise on 13-14 October and a series of sub-unit inspections led Hoffmeister to the same conclusion. He found small arms that were dirty and not properly maintained, quarters that were "untidy and slovenly," and too many old and out-of-shape officers and NCOs. Unsatisfied with the state of the unit, Hoffmeister intended to change things: "Not that I had any new and novel ideas or approaches. There was a job of training to be done, consistent with my training in the MacMillan Co., and the principles that I had developed at Staff College."[22]

Fully aware that he could not do it all himself, Hoffmeister set about securing the willing support of all ranks in the battalion. And because he believed that "there was nothing wrong with the men [and that] they were as good as ever," Hoffmeister started at the top, with the officers. Leadership in the battalion, as Vokes had emphasized, cried out for reinvigoration, so Hoffmeister began by tapping their regimental pride.[23] He told his officers that he concurred with Vokes's assessment; the Seaforths lagged behind the other battalions in the brigade. He also emphasized that he expected officers to set a better example for discipline, training, and physical fitness. To do so, they had to be competent, able to enforce training standards, and absolutely passionate about their business. He would do the same. Because he was physically robust, Hoffmeister had no difficulty setting an example in physical fitness,[24] and his diligence spoke for itself. In short, he wanted commitment. Provided officers stayed physically strong, showed a willingness to learn, discharged their duties with enthusiasm, and displayed potential, Hoffmeister, like Montgomery, did what he could to develop them. Also like Montgomery, he had little patience for officers lacking the requisite qualities; those he posted out of the unit.[25]

What Hoffmeister sought most in his officers was the ability to inspire soldiers and make them willing followers, the key to drawing the best possible performance out of each individual. This required competence in both the technical and human dimensions of command. One such officer was Captain S.W. (Syd) Thomson.[26] Physically fit, intelligent, honest, and tactically competent, Thomson was well liked by his soldiers. In the words of Private F.C. Wood, Thomson "was an outstanding man. He had sort of a brash manner about him, but he would walk about with his helmet in his hand. He was clean, tidy, relaxed and always smiling in command – everything was so easy."[27] The perceptive Hoffmeister sensed that soldiers not only liked Thomson on a personal level, they responded favourably to his breezy self-confidence. Because of that, he carefully mentored the young leader, something that meant more than just providing Thomson with solid training before going into action, although he did that as well. It meant preserving the personal and professional confidence that had been built over several years of training.

A telling example of Hoffmeister's patient tutelage occurred during a cross-country night march in September 1943. Tasked with leading the battalion on a night march across the difficult terrain, Thomson got hopelessly disoriented: "It was a dark night, and I got lost with the whole battalion behind me. I felt terrible. When I realized I was lost I sent a message to Bert. He came up [to the front of the column], I apologized." The trek had been gruelling and, like everyone else who marched miles off course, Hoffmeister could not have been pleased. Yet Hoffmeister resisted the impulse to berate the young captain or assign blame. Neither did he embarrass Thomson or do anything to rattle his confidence. Hoffmeister remained composed. He told Thomson: "Syd, I am the CO, I should have been watching too, it is no more your fault than mine." Thomson was surprised: "This impressed me. After we had bedded down for an hour ... Bert said, 'Come on, we will go back and find out where *we* went wrong.'"[28] An insignificant incident perhaps – no enemy fire, no casualties, no great victory – but it illustrated Hoffmeister's acute appreciation for teamwork and subordinate confidence. By his actions, Hoffmeister not only salvaged the sagging self-confidence of a capable young officer who would later distinguish himself as a battalion commander at Ortona, he won the devotion of a loyal follower.[29]

Hoffmeister tried to develop the same sort of willing followership in his soldiers. Having witnessed the impression made by Montgomery, he well understood that only a commander who was known to his soldiers could inspire them. So he made himself known: he led them on marches, he participated in small arms training, and he competed in unit sports. As one former NCO commented, "As soon as Bert came back [to command the battalion], things started jumping and we felt his personality right away ... He was in there all the time, every exercise or scheme, he was in there leading. He'd come around and ask people how they were doing ... He was very good with the troops."[30] Of course, the practice of plumbing soldiers' opinions on training and morale went over well and fostered a feeling that each individual contribution mattered and was appreciated.

Circumstance also favourably disposed Hoffmeister to winning over the soldiers. His predecessor, Lieutenant-Colonel J.M.S. Tait, who reportedly liked to adorn himself with Patton-like pistol holsters, had been neither liked nor respected by the soldiers of the unit, the nickname "Hollywood" attesting to their cynicism regarding his abilities and sincerity.[31] They were receptive to a change, particularly if it came from someone they regarded as a "soldier's officer." Hoffmeister's reputation was certainly that.[32] He had taken good care of his troops as a company commander; his soldiers knew it, and they felt comfortable with him at the helm. As one soldier wrote when Hoffmeister took command: "The battalion could not be in better hands."[33]

Then there were the unit's senior NCOs. During his initial inspections, Hoffmeister formed the opinion that many of them were not doing their jobs – enforcing discipline and maintaining high training standards. Something had to be done. Accordingly, Hoffmeister scheduled a "smartening-up" school for warrant officers and sergeants. Designed to reinvigorate the keepers of unit discipline, the training emphasized drill and instructional technique. More telling of Hoffmeister's approach to the NCO problem, he used the sessions for "sizing up a potential RSM [Regimental Sergeant-Major]."[34] Training and motivating the battalion's NCOs was largely RSM J.J. Nicholson's responsibility, and the poor showing of the unit during Hoffmeister's initial inspections did not reflect well on him. An "Umpire's Report," following an inspection by the division commander (then Major-General H.L.M. Salmon), later confirmed Hoffmeister's misgivings. It severely criticized Nicholson for not exercising sufficient control in and around the battalion headquarters.[35] That was enough for Hoffmeister. On 7 April, he replaced the aging Nicholson with RSM R.H.W. Ireland, one of the youngest RSMs in the Army to that point.[36] Young blood and tough new standards: Hoffmeister's actions gave the corps of NCOs the spark it needed.

An imposed change to the battalion's war establishment also presented Hoffmeister with an opportunity to make some constructive personnel changes. In January 1943, the First Canadian Army reduced the number of rifle companies in infantry battalions from four to three, while increasing the strengths of the rifle platoons from thirty-four men to forty-five men (see Figure 4.1).[37] This change did not affect the total number of soldiers in the unit, but it did trim one company's worth of officers and NCOs from the order of battle, and that allowed Hoffmeister to keep the best leaders and send the "surplus" to holding units.[38] In deciding how to divide the soldiers among the three rifle companies, Hoffmeister displayed a keen understanding of how organizations worked and developed their own values. He disbanded "B" Company and divided its soldiers between the newly named 1, 2, and 3 Companies.[39] This was no random choice. Hoffmeister's old company, "B" Company, still contained soldiers who had served under him during the unit's first two years in England, soldiers with whom his standing was still very good. Scattering them around the battalion could only help secure the loyalty of the unit.

Re-energizing the battalion prepared it to take full advantage of the training opportunities that were offered. In this, the timing of Hoffmeister's arrival was

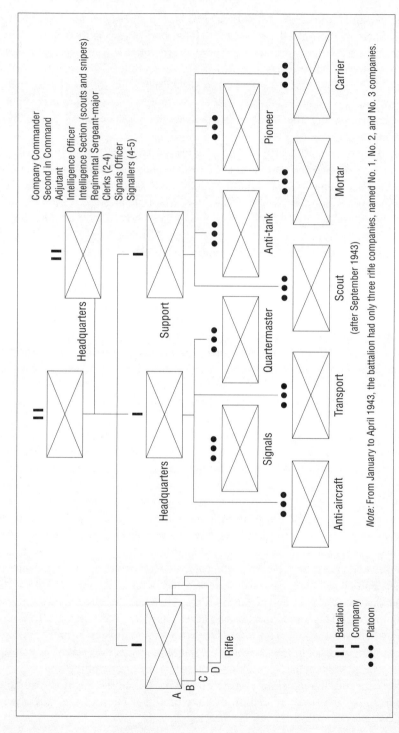

Company Commander
Second in Command
Adjutant
Intelligence Officer
Intelligence Section (scouts and snipers)
Regimental Sergeant-major
Clerks (2-4)
Signals Officer
Signallers (4-5)

Headquarters

Support

Headquarters

Rifle

A
B
C
D

Signals

Transport

Anti-aircraft

Quartermaster

Scout
(after September 1943)

Anti-tank

Mortar

Pioneer

Carrier

II Battalion
I Company
••• Platoon

Note: From January to April 1943, the battalion had only three rifle companies, named No. 1, No. 2, and No. 3 companies.

FIGURE 4.1 Seaforth Highlanders of Canada order of battle, 1943

fortuitous as well. In October 1942, a new training cycle that focused on the coming offensive commenced.[40] This permitted Hoffmeister to assess the skills of his soldiers and build his unit from the ground up. The new regimen started with a declared emphasis on individual training. At the lower levels, rifle company soldiers fired their weapons and practised small-unit tactics and drills, while specialists such as scouts, mortarmen, and anti-tank gunners worked in their own fields, sometimes under brigade direction.[41] Further up the chain of command, the battalion's officers worked on battle procedure and tactics, Hoffmeister not least among them. Using some of what he had learned at Staff College, he designed a skeleton exercise with the object of practising the planning of operations and the dissemination of orders at battalion and company level, timings for mounting and preparing operations, and "meeting unexpected situations."[42] So that Hoffmeister would not know in advance what the events would be, the exercise instruction included an external exercise director and umpires at the company level. This was the sort of concurrent training activity that Montgomery had encouraged all along. That the Canadians now planned exercises this way was one sign of progress. That officers like Hoffmeister and Vokes had the skills and ability to make it happen was another.

Collective training also went back to basics, back to low-level battle drills, a change in direction that was army-wide. In mid-November, Hoffmeister, like so many Canadian officers before and after him, attended a week-long course on battle drill at the General Headquarters Battle School at Barnard Castle, County Durham.[43] Instituted largely at the behest of General Sir Alan Brooke while he was Commander-in-Chief Home Forces, the prescribed battle drills attempted to standardize tactical doctrine, quicken reaction time at section and platoon levels, reduce the tendency towards hesitation in combat, and thereby increase the tempo of operations above company level. As a 1941 Army pamphlet noted, "The need for speed of execution in all offensive operations calls for swiftness of decision and action in all exercises."[44] The rationale was sound; drills for tactical movement or reaction to enemy contact made ponderous decisions unnecessary.[45] At section and platoon levels, where decision cycles were often measured in seconds, doing something was viewed as always better than doing nothing.

The same desire to standardize drills at the section and platoon levels also led to a more deliberate attempt at establishing standing operating procedures for all-arms cooperation. In December 1942, Seaforth platoons and Canadian tank troops participated in a brigade-directed exercise, the aim of which was to "reach a satisfactory standard ... of co-operation" between tanks and infantry at the squadron/company level and below.[46] It began with reciprocal demonstrations of armaments, communications, and drills between infantry and tank troops. Field engineers contributed to the process of cross-pollination by showing the other arms the drill for breaching a minefield. Infantry and armoured troops "tested" methods for intercommunication and target indication – radio, tracer ammunition, coloured smoke, beacon lamps, and flares. The exercise did not exactly yield any groundbreaking doctrinal changes – tanks and infantry still tended to operate separately in the attack, with infantry assaulting and tanks supporting by fire.[47] But the exercise did make solid progress towards coordinating actions at the platoon/troop and company/squadron levels.

Things were getting better. With new leadership and a more systematic approach to training, the Seaforths improved steadily under Hoffmeister's leadership, and Brigadier Vokes was "very pleased" with their progress.[48] By the beginning of 1943, Hoffmeister was well on his way to raising the battalion from its "poor third" position in the brigade. That was a good thing; for unknown to either Hoffmeister or his soldiers, by January 1943, Allied leaders and Canadian politicians were making decisions that would commit 1 CID to the invasion of the Italian island of Sicily within six months.

For reasons of operational security, the soldiers, of course, knew nothing of the high-level negotiations that would lead to the deployment of 1 CID and the 1st Army Tank Brigade to the Mediterranean, but training for offensive operations did give them an indication that a return to the continent was not far off. The advent of combined operations training in February 1943 only amplified rumours that plans for large-scale operations were under way. Soldiers had followed keenly the developments of the war in North Africa, and morale crested at the thought of being part of "the show." That was, after all, why they had volunteered in the first place. So, as the Seaforths boarded trains for Scotland on 14 February, an air of excitement went with them.

The combined operations training at Inverary, Scotland, was progressive and comprehensive, and it did wonders for unit skills and morale. Commencing on 16 February, it benefited everyone in the battalion. For the soldiers, the exercise started with four days of low-level training, which included lectures on amphibious operations, familiarization with landing craft, loading and unloading drills, and live fire range practices. Leaders participated in most of these activities, but their focus was clearly on other things. On 19 February, for instance, Hoffmeister planned and issued orders for his first amphibious operation on Exercise EAGLE I. He had much to learn. Owing to their complexity, amphibious operations were tedious to plan and coordinate. Not only did the commander have to plan the assault once ashore, he had to allocate personnel and equipment to landing craft such that they hit the beach in the configuration he wanted for the assault – who was on the right, who was on the left, and who was in reserve.[49] Working out those details and presenting them in a "landing table" ate up a lot of time, requiring close coordination with both the companies (which knew the numbers and names of the personnel) and naval forces (which piloted the landing craft). For that reason, and because his main concern was the battle after landing ashore, the commander usually gave guidance on the tactical plan but left the task of assigning individuals to landing craft to someone else. Hoffmeister gave this chore to his second in command, Major J.D. Forin. Judging by the extensive ink amendments to the order and landing table dated 18 February, Hoffmeister and his team experienced some growing pains.[50] Nevertheless, Hoffmeister did take his battalion through the four phases of a daylight amphibious assault – road move to the loading site, embarkation, landing, and assault. He made the most of the experience, and so did his companies. Two of them had to repeat their assaults because of miscues.[51]

EAGLE II, conducted on 24 February, presented the same tactical problems as EAGLE I, only it was conducted at night.[52] Hoffmeister's orders differed little from EAGLE I, but the lack of ink amendments and some subtle refinements indicate what he had learned. In the first phase of movement to the loading site, for example, troops boarded trucks according to their "serials" in the landing table, not in their company and platoon configurations. This saved much unnecessary reorganization and confusion after debussing from trucks at the boat-loading site.[53] Then, to maintain control during boarding, Hoffmeister tasked Forin to coordinate loading at the site. But doing things at night was significantly more complicated than doing them in daylight. It demanded more stringent control measures, many of which were still being learned. The Seaforth war diarist captured some of the comedy of the "learning experience":

A few unfortunate mishaps caused several upsets in plans ... As a result, there were no lights [on the beach] with which to usher in the different serials. Landings ... were somehow accomplished in the pitch darkness and the attacks were successful ... Cease Fire was called at 2359 hours and then the battle really began. All troops were safely re-embarked on the one remaining LCT [Landing Craft Tank] jammed together like sardines. For the next three hours LCAs [Landing Craft Assaults] and LCMs [Landing Craft Mechanizeds] were bumping into one another on LOCH FYNE. NAVAL OFFICERS with OXFORD accents were adding to the din of roaring engines with "Port Helm" or, "Port, I said, not Starboard." All troops were safely back in Camp by 0300 hours.[54]

Canadian infantry soldiers were not the only ones who learned from the experience; Royal Navy officers gleaned a thing or two as well.

For the next three days, while the companies participated in range practices and compass marches, Hoffmeister conducted battle procedure for Exercise DALMALLY, a full-scale brigade amphibious assault. His orders for this exercise, some nine detailed pages including landing tables and objective sketches, reflected both the time available for planning and the lessons learned on previous assaults.[55] As a result, the loading of landing craft aboard the Duke of Argyll on the evening of 28 February went well, as did the initial landings at 1:00 a.m. on 1 March. Because he had three immediate objectives to establish a bridgehead, Hoffmeister chose to assault with all three companies forward, attaching a section of pioneers to enhance the mobility of each. That proved handy, because the enemy force attempted to impede movement by destroying the bridges on all the routes leading to the inland objectives. Two of Hoffmeister's companies seized the initiative and forded the frigid waters to capture their objectives. The third company needed the assistance of the engineer troop to get across the river. Repairing the bridge took three hours to complete, but the third company made it to the objective, and the Seaforths accomplished their task of securing the bridgehead by 4:15 a.m.[56]

In all, the training was challenging, interesting, and well conducted. Hoffmeister and his soldiers gained from it. The amphibious phases of the exercises, some of which went better than others, made clear the necessity for detailed planning and coordination in those types of operations. The live enemy force, bent on spoiling action, reminded all ranks of the need to revise plans, to make quick decisions, to improvise. And during DALMALLY Hoffmeister learned an important lesson about command and control – redundancy in communications. As was too often the case with radios, Hoffmeister's failed, and he was unable to communicate directly with his companies. Fortunately, the Intelligence Section scouts attached with the companies relayed the progress of the sub-units to the intelligence officer, co-located with Hoffmeister. It was not ideal, but it worked.[57] These were the sorts of things that no amount of book-learning, TEWTs, or CPXs could teach.

Morale crested with the mission-oriented training. As Hoffmeister noted, "We really thought we were getting somewhere. I had arrived at a time that was opportune because, with this type of training and new blood at the top, the troops sensed that something was about to happen."[58] Hoffmeister correctly assumed that he had the good fortune to take command when the battalion was preparing (unknowingly) for an operational mission. But, by imposing his vision on the regiment, reinvigorating the leadership, and winning the loyalty of the soldiers, he prepared it for the opportunity that beckoned. Quite simply, the soldiers appreciated what he had done; and over the course of the coming months, their affinity for him deepened. One young soldier echoed the feelings of many of his comrades: "I just idolized Hoffie at the time, I think we all did."[59]

The division also trained for operations beyond the beachhead. In the spring of 1943, the advance, the pursuit, and the withdrawal occupied a fair amount of training time. On 22-23 March, Hoffmeister and his company commanders attended TEWTs on withdrawal, mine-clearing, and assault-bridging in preparation for the division Exercise PAST, 30 March-2 April.[60] PAST concentrated on mounted and dismounted advances, and on overcoming the obstacles that might have impeded them; hence the emphasis on bridging and mine-clearing. It was a gruelling test, and PAST revealed a number of deficiencies in drills for relaying information on obstacles, finding bypass routes, and breaching – all of which slowed the advance.[61] To correct these faults, Vokes scheduled battalion exercises for "CROSSING MINEFIELDS" in May.[62] He also directed that his battalion commanders personally instruct their NCOs on battle procedure, orders, and river-crossing operations, which Hoffmeister did on 22 April.[63] Pursuit operations were the focus of a division-run skeleton exercise on 4-10 April. Hoffmeister commanded the brigade during that particular scheme, while his second in command filled in as battalion commander.[64] All ranks kept busy.

And they got busier. On Monday 26 April 1943, the day after the Canadian government gave its approval for 1 CID participation in Operation HUSKY, Lieutenant-Colonel Hoffmeister travelled to London for preliminary orders. Details were sketchy; however, his unit was to prepare to leave its current billets within two weeks and proceed on another period of intense amphibious training. Sometime thereafter, it would be committed to action. The key piece of information that the orders did not disclose was the location of the impending action, and soldiers, as soldiers often do, began speculating on the likely area of operations. The Balkans, Norway, the Low Countries, and North Africa – all were on the list of debated possibilities.[65] While rumours swirled, deployment preparations continued: weapons were zeroed, kit bags were packed, and equipment was checked before the Seaforths left England for the last time on 9 May.[66] But before they went to war they had some final training chores to complete in Scotland.

The sequence and scope of this second round of combined operations training at Inverary did not differ greatly from the training they had conducted in February. Field firing and load/unload drills occupied soldiers for most of the first three days. On the morning of 13 May, Hoffmeister gave orders for a repeat of Exercise EAGLE I, which the battalion executed flawlessly that same afternoon.[67] Most of the scheme was the same as the previous EAGLE I – the terrain, the objectives, the code words. But this time, because of another change to the battalion war establishment, Hoffmeister had four companies instead of three to accomplish his mission, and that meant more tactical flexibility. Hoffmeister chose to use two companies (with pioneers) in the first wave to capture immediate objectives, keeping the other two in reserve to seize objectives in depth or exploit opportunities. It also meant the Seaforths had to start from scratch with the landing tables, which they did without difficulty. The brigade repeated Exercise EAGLE II during the hours of darkness on 14-15 May. It went well, though not perfectly, and a few more refinements to operating procedures took place between battalion and brigade.[68] The learning continued.

All ranks profited from the repetition and quality of the mission-oriented training, Hoffmeister especially. Again, he practised what he had been taught at Staff College. In planning amphibious assaults, Hoffmeister conducted several appreciations: he determined the object or aim of each mission; he considered how such factors as enemy strength, friendly force capabilities, ground, weather, time and space, and communications might affect operations; he developed options aimed at achieving his objectives; he weighed those options for their relative advantages and disadvantages; and he developed plans based on the best course of action. Although the formulation of a ground tactical plan was exclusively Hoffmeister's, he did receive some help from various members of his battalion staff. As discussed,

Forin sorted the nitty-gritty of landing tables. His intelligence officer provided advice on enemy strengths and capabilities, and he controlled the scouts who could gather the information the commanding officer needed. His signals officer made recommendations on communications and tended to an endless stream of troubleshooting tasks for failed or broken equipment. His forward observation officer (FOO), from the battalion's supporting artillery, helped develop indirect fire plans (including naval gunfire) in support of the ground tactical plan. And his liaison officers coordinated with the naval crews that carried the troops ashore. As such, the functional delegation of responsibility for planning and execution, limited though it may have been, was not unlike that which had been instituted at MacMillan Export Company in the late 1930s. It was a team effort.

The training also provided plenty of opportunity to practise a less-deliberate and more abbreviated form of decision making – that which occurs after the operation has been initiated and contact with the enemy has been made. As always, commanders at all levels had to be prepared to make rapid and timely decisions based on changes to the tactical situation, enemy action, or perceived opportunities. Sometimes the requirement to make decisions occurs as a result of unanticipated developments or confusion – what is often referred to as the "fog of war." During Exercise WETSHOD (21-22 May), the "fog" rolled in. Owing to some confusion on the part of the naval task force, the Seaforths and the Princess Patricia's Canadian Light Infantry both landed in the wrong areas.[69] Confused and unsure of where he was, Hoffmeister tasked several reconnaissance patrols to determine the exact location of the battalion. Once assured of the battalion's whereabouts, he quickly altered his plan and issued abbreviated orders. Because the battalion was well trained and, by this point, well drilled, it reacted smoothly to the foul-up, and, in relatively short order, the companies redirected themselves and seized their objectives. It was not a wildly successful exercise, but the Seaforths had not panicked; they had acted deliberately, and they were pleased with their performance. In fact, had it not been for a lengthy six-hour delay at the termination of the exercise, during which soldiers had to wait in the rain, morale was not likely to have been any the worse for wear.

The spring exercises culminated at Troon, Scotland, in the early morning hours of 18 June. Although the troops were not aware of it at the time (except for the usual rumour-mongering), Exercise STYMIE I was a full-scale divisional rehearsal for Operation HUSKY – the invasion of Sicily.[70] As a confidence-building measure, the importance of this exercise, on beaches that were "exactly the same" as those in southeastern Sicily, was crucial.[71] Like the repetition of individual and collective drills, a rehearsal over similar ground, with similar landmarks, and in similar conditions, had the reassuring effect of bringing some familiarity – some points of mental and physical reference – to soldiers. Because HUSKY was the first combat experience for most of the Canadians, that was important; and planners, who had been working on Operation HUSKY for well over a month, appreciated the point: "To ensure that nothing had been overlooked, it was planned to carry out a final 48-hour exercise just before we sailed. Orders for this exercise, based as closely as possible on the actual Husky operation, had been drawn up simultaneously ... Every unit would embark on the same ships it would use for the real invasion, as well as landing in the same type of craft and in the proper formations. Each platoon commander and lorry driver would get to know the boat crews he had to work with and the routine for clearing the beaches on landing."[72] Similar it was. The plan for STYMIE I had the same assault formations and beach code names as HUSKY. In fact, for the HUSKY order, the 2 CIB staff made no changes to the landing table from STYMIE – not even the date.[73]

Unlike Exercise WETSHOD, Exercise STYMIE went without a hitch. The companies landed at "exactly the right time and place," captured their immediate objectives, and then dashed inland to seize their secondary objectives. Drills went well, beach landings were flawless, and the Seaforths gained their objectives through quick and aggressive action. Justifiably, their confidence was soaring when the exercise ended at 11:30 a.m. on 18 June.

When another delay followed the exercise cease-fire, Hoffmeister demonstrated both the premium he placed on morale and his ability to keep it high. After finishing on a high note, the battalion, again, waited hours for trucks to take them back to their billets, a predicament once more made worse by inclement weather and a lack of cover. Sensing that this turn of events had the potential to sap some of the satisfaction the unit had accrued during the exercise, Hoffmeister "obtained some rum from a local pub and a general issue helped offset some of the misery."[74] Apparently, this was just the medicine; "an impromptu concert" followed to while away the hours until the trucks arrived.

The training in Scotland was personally important to Hoffmeister for several reasons. First, numerous exercise missions gave his battlefield management skills the challenge and repetition they needed for fine-tuning. Throughout the arduous manoeuvres, and under occasionally difficult circumstances, he planned and executed complex operations with considerable success. Second, he had the opportunity to determine how he would direct his subordinates in battle. For example, the appropriate size and composition of his tactical headquarters was one such command-and-control matter he managed to work out.[75] Third, his subordinates – particularly his company commanders – performed well. They too had endured difficult conditions and had demonstrated commendable initiative and *esprit de corps* in the completion of their tasks. More important, Hoffmeister had the opportunity to observe them and take note of their strengths and weaknesses. Thus, he had a sound idea of what the capabilities of his people were – a critical prerequisite for the determination and assignment of tasks. Fourth, the exercises had been, for the most part, well orchestrated and ideally suited to coming tasks. This improved Hoffmeister's faith in the chain of command in general, and his immediate superiors in particular. Certainly, his opinion of Chris Vokes – already favourable – deepened during this period: "He was a good trainer. He demanded a pretty high standard in the brigade and he made it his business to see that it was done."[76] Fifth, Hoffmeister's soldiers had a chance to see their boss in action, and he had done well – and not only tactically. He also proved that he had lost none of his concern for their welfare and, despite the sometimes-trying circumstances of the exercises, he was still "a soldiers' officer." Last, and most significantly, the training exorcised most of the self-doubt that had troubled him two years earlier. Although Hoffmeister still did not have everything he needed in the way of skills, knowledge, and tactical ability for success in combat, his solid performance during the training indicates that he had come a long way in addressing those deficiencies. He was adequately prepared for his first test as a battlefield commander.

As the HMT *Circassia* left the United Kingdom in the company of four other transports on 28 June 1943, a palpable sense of excitement gripped the Seaforths. They had no idea of their destination, but they knew they were going to war. So it was with a combination of relief and apprehension that the Seaforths listened to a loudspeaker message the following morning: "A signal [message] has been received from the Admiralty ... 'You are going to the Mediterranean to take part in the biggest Combined Operation the World has ever seen.'"[77] Later that day, Brigadier Vokes informed the officers and senior NCOs aboard *Circassia* that 1 CID would be joining Montgomery's Eighth Army, their task being "one of assault in a landing that will be the first blow in the invasion of the continent."[78] Not until 1 July did Vokes disclose that the target was Sicily.

Immediately on receipt of his orders, Hoffmeister launched into his own battle procedure. Because the area of their intended beachhead was "the same in every respect to TROON BEACH, SCOTLAND,"[79] it was more a matter of sorting the details than conducting another full-blown appreciation.[80] He studied the orders in detail. He examined the many maps, air photographs, and models of the objective area. Then he threw the full weight of his attention to what he believed to be the most important of his pre-battle tasks: "briefing all ranks on the upcoming operation."[81] Wanting to make certain that every soldier fully grasped the plan, the objectives, the terrain, and the enemy, he took it on himself to address every platoon in the battalion: "The briefing took the form of a complete picture of the enemy situation given by the ... Intelligence Officer after which I carried on outlining the broad plan and the details of the Brig[ade] and B[attalio]n plans."[82]

This was an unusual practice, not only for the fact that Hoffmeister did not use the normal chain of command, but also for the information he conveyed. Normally, orders provided "only what the recipient require[d] to know to carry out his task."[83] In practice, this was often interpreted to mean providing information on friendly forces only "two levels up." Thus a private soldier might only be given information on platoon operations, while a platoon commander might only be advised of what was happening at the battalion level. Not in Hoffmeister's battalion; he knew instinctively that the more soldiers understood how all the pieces of the plan fit together, the more comfortable they would be with the operation as a whole. He did not "scale down" orders to give soldiers only what they needed to complete their portion of the task; he told them what they needed to be confident.[84] And confidence, he well appreciated, was important. He told them, all of them, everything he knew.

He also comprehended that, despite their solid state of preparedness for the coming operation, it was important that the troops believe in *him:* "I was a believer in the troops getting to know me and know me well, hoping they would develop some confidence in me and I felt it was important to do this ... Officers, NCOs and other ranks were allowed to ask questions."[85] Hoffmeister, who so harped on the importance of subordinate performance, was different, and his men knew it. The battalion's war diarist noted the effect of Hoffmeister's approach in a 6 July entry: "There is scarcely a man on the ship who is not intimately acquainted with the outline of the Operation and the ... Attack Plan ... The outlook of the men is completely confident."[86] One soldier realistically reflected that it would have been difficult to say that he and his comrades felt "completely safe" with Hoffmeister, but he did believe that they would not be exposed to "any unnecessary risk ... I thought we were well led. It all filtered through him."[87] For troops entering battle for the first time, that was critical.

Clearly, by the time *Circassia* joined the rest of the Allied armada steaming towards Sicily, Hoffmeister had succeeded in the task Vokes had given him the previous October; his battalion was no longer a "poor third." Having endured a period of intensive and effective training, his troops were confident in themselves and in the officers and NCOs that would lead them through their first trials by fire. That is not to say, however, that they were unafraid. In the waning hours of 9 July, as the soldiers loaded themselves into the landing craft, their mood was a bit ambiguous. Apprehension of the unknown mixed with a strange sense of relief at finally getting on with the job they had volunteered to do. Hoffmeister sensed the emotional intensity of the moment. At that point, he knew there was little he could do but make his way about the ship, speak to his men, shake their hands, look into their eyes, and wish them the best of soldier's luck, which he did. These were the sons, husbands, boyfriends, and brothers of all those people who had crowded the Burrard Street Armoury a little over three years earlier and implored him to look after their loved ones. None of the soldiers knew how much the anticipation of this day had troubled him, how close it came to ruining him. He had done his best to prepare them for what followed, and they could tell that he cared. Small gestures at times like these made a difference. During those last few hours aboard *Circassia,* it was not just the soldiers' confidence he sealed; it was their affection as well.[88] In the words of one platoon sergeant who made the same voyage, "They would have gone through hell for him. As a matter of fact, they did."[89]

5
Battalion Command: The Battlefield Test

Don't tell me how tough you are; show me out there where the shells are falling that you have the right stuff.[1]

CORPORAL DIXON RAYMOND,
CAMERON HIGHLANDERS OF OTTAWA, 1942-46

Hoffmeister was remarkably successful in his first battlefield test. But the remarkable thing was not so much that he had the technical skills to do the job; there were plenty of officers who had the knowledge and training to make good tactical decisions. What separated Hoffmeister from his peers, what made him successful, what helped him inspire subordinates, was his ability to do it "out there where the shells are falling." For a man whose nerves had succumbed to self-doubt a little over two years earlier, this was extraordinary. Hoffmeister was already respected by the rank and file, and his ability to think clearly under fire gave him a capacity for tapping human potential that few could match. In his first month of combat, Hoffmeister proved he had the "right stuff."[2]

The operational plan for the invasion of Sicily was relatively straightforward (see Map 1).[3] Supported by aerial and naval bombardment to neutralize enemy air forces and coastal defences, General Sir Harold Alexander concentrated his 15th Army Group for an assault on the southeastern end of the island, with General George S. Patton's Seventh (US) Army on the left and Montgomery's Eighth (British) Army on the right. Following the landings, the main effort of the advance inland was to be with Montgomery's force, which was to drive relentlessly north, through Syracuse and Catania to Messina: 30th Corps inland and 13th Corps along the coast. To destroy the Axis forces and prevent their retreat to the Italian mainland, Montgomery planned to place his emphasis on 13th Corps. As part of 30th British Corps, the 1st Canadian Infantry Division (1 CID) was assigned landing sites to the southwest of Pachino.[4] Major-General Guy Granville Simonds, the 1 CID commander, decided to assault with two brigades in the first wave – 2 CIB left on "Sugar" beach and 1 CIB right on the beach codenamed "Roger" (see Map 1 inset).[5] For his part, Brigadier Vokes also opted for a "two-up" assault formation, with the Princess Patricia's Canadian Light Infantry (PPCLI) on the right and the Seaforths on the left; the Edmonton Regiment would be in reserve, prepared to exploit inland once the brigade's initial objectives had been seized.[6]

Hoffmeister's battalion plan was simple and, like those of his superiors, it reflected the tactical doctrine to which he had been exposed at Staff College and the training he had conducted with both British and Canadian forces.[7] He divided his attack into phases, based on limited objectives and manoeuvre from firm bases.[8] The Seaforths were to assault "Sugar" beach with three companies in the first phase – "C" Company left, "A" Company right, "D" Company in depth. On the successful completion of the first phase, Hoffmeister would commit his reserve, "B" Company, to take the lead in the advance to inland objectives some six miles northwest of the landing sites.

At first, on 10 July, events for the Seaforths transpired according to plan. The first wave, containing "A" and "C" Companies made it to the designated beaches, breached the wire obstacles, and overcame weak Italian resistance to seize their immediate objectives.[9] With the beach landing site secure, at approximately 3:30 a.m., Captain Syd Thomson, the officer commanding "A" Company, sent the signal for the second wave to proceed. With that, Hoffmeister's tactical headquarters moved towards the beach, followed by "B" and "D" Companies, then the rest of the battalion's fighting echelon. Within minutes, as it had during Exercise WETSHOD, the "fog of war" intervened to complicate matters. The naval officer tasked with guiding the various waves to their landing sites furnished the wrong bearing for Hoffmeister and the remainder of his battalion, sending the second wave far off their intended landing site – so far off, in fact, that they landed to the east of the PPCLI. Confusion set in. The beach, the lay of the land, the terrain features – none of it looked familiar to either Hoffmeister or the equally perturbed company commanders of the second wave. They were lost and Hoffmeister was understandably concerned: "I didn't know where we were, I didn't know where my [forward] companies were. I had to get a picture before moving ahead."[10] Calling on the experience of Exercise WETSHOD – which by this point must have seemed all too annoyingly familiar – Hoffmeister tasked Major H.P. Bell-Irving's Support Company with a number of patrols to determine their exact location, and to make contact with flanking units.[11] The patrols successfully determined where they were and, before first light, the second wave conducted some rather delicate night manoeuvres to cross the PPCLI beach landing site and link up with the forward companies.[12] From there, Hoffmeister made a few adjustments, and then struck out to capture objectives on the high ground to the northwest.

It was an inglorious beginning to the campaign, and, had it not been for light Italian opposition, it might have been much worse. Hoffmeister probably should have been in the first wave, with "A" and "C" Companies. Had he done that, he would have been less confused and better able to direct his companies onto his inland objectives. But he had not trained that way, and it was clearly not common practice in the division.[13] Still, Hoffmeister reacted deliberately and rationally, avoiding the impulse to bluster aimlessly forward. What is more, his forward company commanders proved worthy of the faith he placed in them; despite being out of contact with Hoffmeister, both Thomson and Blair used their initiative, seized their immediate objectives, and carried on with the mission. The training in Scotland proved its worth.

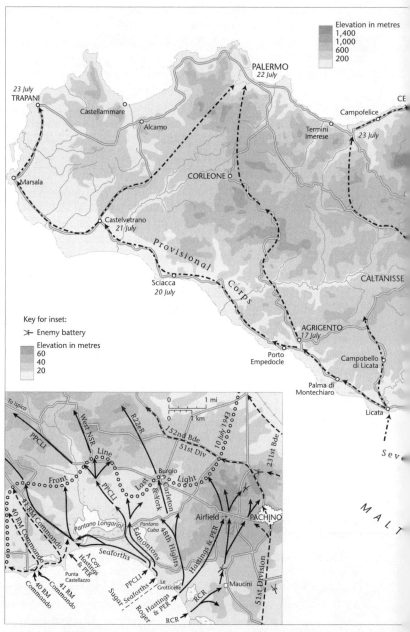

MAP 1   *Sicily, 10 July to 17 August 1943.* Adapted from G.W.L. Nicholson (Lieutenant-Colonel), *The Canadians in Italy, 1943-1945* (Ottawa: Queen's Printer, 1966), map 1, map 2 inset.

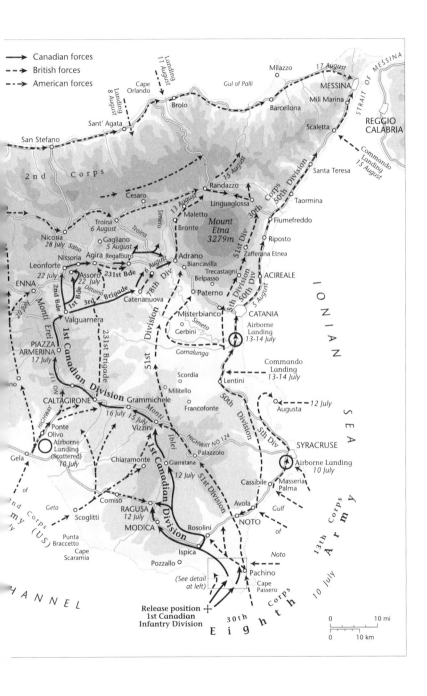

Canadian forces
British forces
American forces

From the time of the initial landings to 19 July, the Seaforths pushed inland through Modica, Ragusa, Grammichele, Caltagirone, and Valguarnera. In the oppressive heat, the battalion covered most of the hilly and rocky terrain on foot.[14] Italian resistance was feeble, but that eventually gave way to determined German delaying action as the enemy attempted to buy time for a withdrawal of its forces from the island.

In a valley near Valguarnera, Hoffmeister came close to marching his entire battalion into a German ambush. Just as he was deploying his companies to the high ground, away from the vulnerable valley floor, the Germans opened fire. Enemy mortars and machines struck Hoffmeister's lead company, immediately felling 18 soldiers. The unit chaplain watched it happen: "Vicious bursts of flame & clouds of dust, dirt and rock flew into the air to the left and right of us ... Wounded were being brought out and I attended the dying. Boys I had known well were among the victims, torn and bleeding beyond all hope of recovery. Mortars continued to drop steadily and with nerve wracking accuracy."[15] Hoffmeister had to figure a way to get the trapped company out of the killing zone.

Scrambling about the battlefield, often dodging bullets, Hoffmeister reconnoitred positions for observation (to find the enemy) and positions for fire (to shoot at the enemy). Once he had found what he was looking for, he directed the action to foil the ambush and get his soldiers out of the murderous crossfire. Neutralizing the German action required the coordination of friendly artillery and mortar fire on the enemy infantry, as well as the forward positioning of the battalion's anti-tank weapons to counter German tanks.[16] By using the tried and true method of firing on the enemy to keep their heads down (and prevent them from firing back) and then manoeuvring when it was safe to move, Hoffmeister eventually extricated his forward company and withdrew them from the enemy's killing zone.[17] In short, he found the enemy, he won the firefight, and he moved his troops to safety. This was more difficult to do than it sounds, but Hoffmeister did it at considerable personal risk. It was not a quick affair either. Several intense and harrowing hours passed before the battalion was able to disengage itself with most of its members – and its morale – still intact.

In the course of the action near Valguarnera, Hoffmeister demonstrated his penchant for being well forward and conducting his own reconnaissance – something that he presumably learned after the frustrations of the Pachino landings. He undoubtedly wanted to get a better appreciation of the situation in order to anticipate problems (such as where the enemy might strike next) and make tactical decisions (such as how to counter the next enemy move). His actions also had another important effect: stiffening the morale of his subordinates. In the course of conducting his own reconnaissance, Hoffmeister narrowly avoided being hit by tank and small arms fire.[18] Lots of soldiers saw Hoffmeister's apparent lack of concern for his own safety and undoubtedly passed their observations on to their mates. One described the impact of his commanding officer's actions in this way:

"Because he was there, I no more thought of running and hiding ... I just felt, 'he'll take care of me.' He's there too. It's just like flying in an airplane; you've got to have confidence in the pilot. If the plane falls, he falls too. You just felt, if he's here I guess I should be too; otherwise I might have crawled under a truck or something."[19] Hoffmeister grasped the effect of a leader's personal courage in war. Syd Thomson, who would later command an infantry battalion under Hoffmeister during the Battle of Ortona, said it best: "During a sticky battle, morale is as important, if not more important than good tactics. On the scale of 1 to 10, morale will go from 4 to 9 just by the appearance of a senior commander in the line when and where the bullets are flying. Bert understood this."[20]

Because he believed this trait to be such a crucial part of officership, Hoffmeister showed no mercy for those in whom it was lacking. Immediately after the engagement at Valguarnera, Hoffmeister relieved a subaltern who had cowered, taking his subordinates with him in hasty retreat. As Hoffmeister saw it, "There was nothing wrong with the men, it was purely a matter of weak leadership."[21] That young officer may very well have been capable of making good tactical decisions; he had probably done so many times in training. But in war it took more than sound management skills, regimental pride, or charisma to make organizations work. It took guts, because sections, platoons, companies, and battalions were comprised of individual soldiers who were subject to the same fears and apprehensions as any other human beings. Yet soldiers in combat had to face those fears more intensely, and more often. Good commanders, like Hoffmeister, carried soldiers beyond their apprehensions and convinced them that they were all on the "same airplane."

Luck also helped. While preparing for an attack on the town of Leonforte on 21 July, several errant artillery shells from the 1 CID preparatory barrage landed in the middle of Hoffmeister's tactical headquarters with devastating results.[22] The Seaforth chaplain described the barrage and its effects:

> Never in my life shall I hear such a terrific sustained roar. For fully half an hour the shells roared over our heads in screaming hordes. Then suddenly I was shaken by an explosion from the ridge I had just left a few minutes before. One of our shells must have fallen short. I soon learnt that this was true and that our adjutant & another officer with whom I had been speaking a few minutes before, had been killed outright & with them two officers were very badly wounded & about five of our men were killed. The colonel [Hoffmeister] had escaped by inches ... [He] was badly shaken by the concussion. He had been standing and talking to the adjutant when the blow fell which had knocked him down and left him senseless for a while. He grieved over the loss of Douglas Strain [the adjutant] who was a close friend of his.[23]

With both Hoffmeister and his second in command dazed by the incident, the Seaforths could not proceed with their planned assault on Leonforte, and Vokes, accordingly, gave the task of capturing the town to the Edmonton Regiment. Hoffmeister realized that the accident had the potential to undermine his soldiers' confidence – confidence in themselves and the artillery that supported them. So did Vokes. That evening, as the Seaforths buried their dead from the incident, he visited them, "to offer his condolence & to assure us of his confidence in us in spite of our inability to carry out the plan [as] conceived before the barrage had been laid down. He was most anxious that we not lose our morale which was based so surely in the reliability of our Artillery. Accidents would happen like this where faulty ammunition or a mixed assortment of shells were sent over."[24]

Saddened though he was over the loss of several soldiers and a close friend, Hoffmeister took a different approach to the situation than Vokes. He chose to get right back into the business of preparing for the next battle: "the less said about it at the time the better."[25] Unlike many less fortunate officers in the Sicilian and Italian Campaigns, Hoffmeister lived to fight another day, and that is precisely what he set out to do.

In the fight for the Sicilian mountain town of Agira, Hoffmeister was the very picture of a battlefield commander rapidly learning his craft. The Seaforths became embroiled in the battle of Agira because, by 21 July, the Eighth Army's drive north had stalled. Strong German resistance north of the Catania Plain had stymied Montgomery's plans for a straight shot north, forcing the army commander to address the unhinging of the German defences at Mount Etna. To set the conditions for a 30th Corps breakthrough west of Etna, Montgomery ordered all Eighth Army formations to adopt a defensive posture (to avoid casualties they could not afford) and tasked the 1 CID "to continue without restraint directed on Adrano."[26] The initial stage of the 1 CID eastward drive saw 1 CIB advance from Leonforte to the eastern edge of Nissoria between 23 and 26 July. From there, 2 CIB took the lead.[27] Vokes's plan was for the PPCLI to capture the first ridgeline, codenamed "Lion," east of the town of Nissoria and advance to the next set of high features, known as "Tiger."[28] Once "Tiger" was secured, the task for the Seaforths was to advance and capture the next set of hill features known as "Grizzly." Artillery concentrations on the immediate objectives and air strikes on the town of Agira in depth provided additional support to weaken German resistance and keep the enemies' heads down (see Map 2).

For his part, Hoffmeister made efficient use of the available time and resources to prepare his battalion for battle. Shortly after receiving his orders from Vokes at 9:00 a.m. on 26 July, he issued a warning order to initiate preparations for battle.[29] He advised his company commanders that they were on two hours' notice to move their sub-units to an assembly area immediately west of Nissoria.[30] In succession, company, platoon, and section commanders passed on the direction, and soldiers shed themselves of all but the essential weapons, supplies, and equipment. While these administrative activities took place, Hoffmeister completed his own tactical appreciation of the mission and formulated his plan. By noon he was ready to give orders.

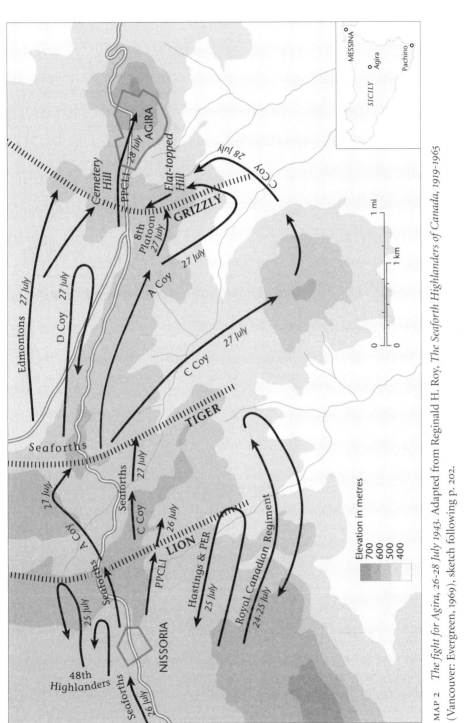

MAP 2 *The fight for Agira, 26-28 July 1943. Adapted from Reginald H. Roy, The Seaforth Highlanders of Canada, 1919-1965* (Vancouver: Evergreen, 1969), sketch following p. 202.

Again, his plan – conveyed by verbal orders – was uncomplicated. Supported by the direct fire of tanks from a firm base on "Tiger," Hoffmeister would advance his battalion with two companies forward; "A" Company (now under command of Major "Budge" Bell-Irving) would be north of the main road, while "C" Company paralleled it to the south. Hoffmeister anticipated that he and his tactical head-quarters would follow right on the heels of the lead companies. Behind him, the reserve companies – "B" and "D" – were to follow, astride the main axis, ready for reinforcing or exploitation tasks.

Battle procedure continued into the afternoon. As Hoffmeister met with Briga-dier Vokes at 3:00 p.m., subordinate orders made their way down the chain of command, from company to platoon to section to individual soldier. On his re-turn, Hoffmeister issued a quick set of confirmatory orders before the battalion left Assoro at 4:00 p.m. It arrived at Nissoria, complete and ready to enter the fight, four hours later.[31] In eleven hours – a short decision cycle by business stand-ards – Hoffmeister had received his orders, formulated a plan, disseminated that plan to a battalion of 700 men, and conducted a four-hour preliminary move in preparation for battle. Concurrent with these activities, companies topped up on ammunition and water, troops ate and took whatever rest they could, and the companies integrated newly arrived reinforcements.[32] Drills for the passage of in-formation and the efficient use of time were slick.

By the time the Seaforths arrived at the western outskirts of Nissoria, the PPCLI was well engaged with the enemy, and Vokes had a difficult decision to make. Early reports indicated that the PPCLI had captured "Lion" and were now advancing on "Tiger."[33] Based on that, Vokes decided to commit the Seaforths to capture "Griz-zly" at 11:00 p.m. Unfortunately, the situation bore no resemblance to what the PPCLI reports had indicated. It was much worse. Not only had the Patricias failed to secure "Tiger," they had not completely cleared "Lion" of enemy, a fact that only became clear to Vokes sometime between his decision to send the Seaforths after "Grizzly" and midnight.[34] Understandably, the incomplete and conflicting reports forced Vokes to rethink briefly his decision to launch the Seaforths into the battle. He did not deliberate long. At midnight, Vokes reconfirmed his bold decision for the Seaforth attack on "Grizzly."

Because Hoffmeister's plan was simple, it required little alteration, despite changes to the tactical situation. Thus, with a minimum of fuss, the Seaforths stepped off, commencing their move through Nissoria at midnight. Once clear of the city's eastern limits, the battalion adopted the advance formation that Hoffmeister had prescribed some twelve hours earlier.[35] But few plans survive first contact with the enemy, and this one was no exception. On the right flank, "C" Company ran into rock-solid resistance and became engaged in a firefight that lasted until daybreak on 27 July. On the left, machine guns and tanks near "Lion" halted Bell-Irving's "A" Company as well. Calmly, and on his own initiative, Bell-Irving decided to use the hours of darkness to bypass the immediate enemy at

"Lion" and carry on to "Tiger" by a more circuitous route.[36] After some initial disorientation, the company eventually fumbled its way onto "Tiger" by first light on 27 July.[37] There, a spirited fight ensued as "A" Company, supported by friendly tank fire from the area of "Lion," cleared the objective of two German tanks and a platoon of infantry.

"A" Company scored a pivotal success. The capture of "Tiger" unhinged the entire German position north of the east-west road, forcing the remaining enemy to withdraw. From atop their objective, Bell-Irving and his soldiers could see a "large number of Bosche infantry ... moving back from the North end of the 'Lion' feature in an East then Northerly direction."[38] Unfortunately, all they could do was observe the retreating Germans because Bell-Irving's force did not at that point have weapons with the range to fire on them. On hearing this, Hoffmeister reinforced the position with the battalion anti-tank platoon, artillery forward observation officers (FOOs), and, later, tanks to bring direct and indirect fire on the enemy fleeing "Tiger." Shortly thereafter, he added another rifle company to consolidate "Tiger" and fend off any enemy counterattack.

There is no evidence that Hoffmeister considered pursuing the retreating enemy at this point, and there are two reasons for this. First, Simonds cast the 1 CID plan in the doctrinal mould that called for attacks in stages, the consolidation of gains, movement only from firm bases, and the use of all available firepower to support any resumption of the advance. This thinking was part of the "bite and hold" approach that bit and held both the Canadian and British Armies. In November 1943, a 21 Army Group publication entitled "The Cooperation of Tanks with Infantry Divisions in Offensive Operations" emphasized the following "Action by the Infantry Battalion Commander on the Capture of an Objective":

(a) Defence against counter attack by tanks.
(b) Defence against counter attack by infantry.
(c) Defence against combined counter attack by both arms.[39]

Objectives were goals in themselves, not necessarily means to ends. Pursuit operations restarted advances; they were not occasions to abandon the deliberate approach and seize opportunities to rout retreating enemy before they could regroup to fight another day.

Second, Hoffmeister was well aware that the division plan called for an air strike on the town of Agira following the capture of "Tiger." For that reason, he sought Vokes's permission to "consolidate [on 'Tiger'] in view of the Aircraft program."[40] Given the friendly fire disaster of Leonforte seven days earlier, this was understandable; pursuing the enemy, in view of the planned air attack, would have exposed the Seaforths to the bombs of the Desert Air Force. Vokes agreed. To allow for the air attack on Agira *and* keep his troops a safe distance from friendly fire, the brigadier established a new "bomb line" and passed it up the chain of command.[41]

At 7:40 a.m. he advised Hoffmeister: "Aircraft will attack Agira. Stay at Tiger until 1200 hrs."[42]

With that, Hoffmeister began planning the next stage of the attack. At mid-morning, he sat on the heights of "Tiger," surveying the ground that led to "Grizzly" and Agira. It was an ideal vantage point from which to make a plan and pass on orders, but before he turned his full attention to those tasks, he ordered that rations be delivered for the tired and hungry soldiers of his rifle companies. The human factors were as important as the technical. Hoffmeister then conducted a quick appreciation of the tactical situation, made his plan, and then held his orders group at 1:00 p.m.[43]

Like his orders for the first stage of the attack, these were simple, and the ability of the company commanders to survey the ground over which they would execute their tasks made the conference a quick affair. Hoffmeister commenced his orders at 1:00 p.m., and the lead companies crossed the start line sixty minutes later; it could not have taken him more than ten or fifteen minutes to pass on his plan.[44] He called for another "two-up" assault. "D" Company, advancing left forward was to capture "cemetery hill" north of Agira. "A" Company, advancing right forward, was to seize the "flat-topped" hill south of the main road. "B" and "C" Companies were to be held in reserve, to reinforce or exploit the efforts of the forward companies, whichever was most appropriate. To support the infantry assaults, artillery and air attacks would soften up the objectives prior to the advance.[45] Then, once the advancing troops commenced their move eastward, the direct fire of machine guns, two squadrons of tanks, and anti-tank weapons on "Tiger" would supplement an artillery barrage to support them.

Again, however, enemy action forced quick revisions to the original plan. Shortly after the troops stepped off, extremely heavy fire from a well-fortified enemy position on "cemetery hill" halted "D" Company. Confirmation of this development only reached Hoffmeister by runner because mortar shrapnel had destroyed the company commander's wireless.[46] Fortunately, such slow means of message passing did not cause any undue delay in decision making. Having watched the tactical situation develop from a series of vantage points, and having witnessed the volume of fire that spat out of "cemetery hill," Hoffmeister had already ascertained that "D" Company's objective was too strong to be taken by a single company. Not wanting to reinforce failure, he ordered Captain E.W. Thomas to withdraw his company and reassigned him to a reserve task. The course of events had, by this point, convinced Hoffmeister to direct his main effort towards the right flank.

Bell-Irving's "A" Company had advanced rapidly to the base of the "Grizzly" feature. Leaving one platoon to provide a firm base, Bell-Irving took his other two platoons to the south, where they scaled an undefended cliff and executed a spectacular right flanking attack that caught the enemy completely by surprise. "A" Company routed the numerically superior German force, killing 75 and taking 14 prisoners.[47] It was a tough fight, but by 5:00 p.m. on 27 July, Bell-Irving had consolidated the 50 remaining men in his company on the southern tip of "Grizzly" and prepared for the inevitable German counterattack.

"A" Company had created an opportunity, and Hoffmeister attempted a repeat of the rapid reinforcement action that had been so successful on "Tiger," but the consolidation of "Grizzly" proved much more difficult. At 3:00 p.m., he ordered "C" Company to outflank "Grizzly" to the south and provide direct fire support to "A" Company with anti-tank weapons. Unfortunately, the going to the south proved difficult and, to make matters worse, radio communications soon failed, eliminating Hoffmeister's ability to quickly redirect "C" Company straight onto "Grizzly." That option out of reach, Hoffmeister turned to his reserve, "B" Company, which he hastily mounted in carriers and launched towards the centre of the objective, but mortar and machine-gun fire stopped it cold.[48] Compounding Hoffmeister's frustration, his fourth manoeuvre element, "D" Company, was still out of radio contact and too far from "A" Company to have an immediate impact on the situation. Thus, it was an understandably anxious Hoffmeister who scurried about the battlefield, attempting to get a better picture of the situation, and trying to reinforce "A" Company. As darkness descended, what he had perceived as an opportunity ripe for exploitation was deteriorating into a problem of just holding on.

Hoffmeister had few cards to play the night of 27-28 July, but he played them with skill. Once communications were re-established with "C" Company, he ordered that sub-unit to continue by way of a southern route to "Grizzly." While the weary troops of "C" Company plodded on by way of a long right hook, Hoffmeister provided what support he could to Bell-Irving's little bridgehead with direct and indirect fire. He personally picked the artillery targets and, at one point, he subjected the northern edge of the "Grizzly" feature to a thirty-minute concentration of mortar fire to rid it of enemy.[49] Mostly, and much to his consternation, he waited.

The next morning, the situation improved. After a night of sporadic German probes and counterattacks, Bell-Irving's beleaguered force was heartened by the arrival of a single and very tired platoon from "C" Company. Bolstered with these reinforcements, "A" Company attacked and cleared the remainder of the "Grizzly" feature, south of the main east-west road. By 8:50 a.m., the Seaforths controlled the objective. Simultaneous with "A" Company's success, the Edmonton Regiment, which Vokes had committed the previous day, took "cemetery hill" from the north. The capture of "Grizzly" cleared the way for the PPCLI to enter Agira on the afternoon of 28 July. The battle for Agira was over.

The assault on Agira was a 2 CIB triumph, but it was Hoffmeister's battalion that played the major part in prying Agira from the enemy. Despite a number of difficulties and strong enemy resistance, the Seaforths had created opportunities – on "Tiger" and on "Grizzly" – and had enjoyed some success in exploiting them, untidy though those victories may have been. Two days after the battle, Hoffmeister marked the regiment's accomplishment when he had the regimental pipe band beat the retreat through the streets of the captured town, an event that was broadcast round the world by the British Broadcasting Corporation. For his part in the battle, Hoffmeister received the Distinguished Service Order, the citation of which reads, "For outstanding leadership which enabled the Seaforth Highlanders of Canada, during two days of fighting on 27-28 July 1943, to reach their objective near AGIRA. During the final battle communications were difficult. With complete disregard for his own safety, this officer made his way from Company to Company, under heavy fire, and personally directed the attack."[50] It should be noted, however, that Hoffmeister's accomplishments at Agira did not come as a result of any tactical innovation or doctrinal departure. In fact, his actions conformed completely to higher plans and reflected the doctrine that had been taught at Staff College and practised in training: he limited his objectives, he operated from firm bases, he sequenced his attacks in phases, and he consolidated his objectives before moving on to exploit his gains. That Hoffmeister did not stray far from established doctrine should come as no surprise. He had been in combat for only just over two weeks. But he was learning fast.

So was the rest of the division. On 4 August, Simonds suggested to Vokes that a "quick blow be struck" against crumbling enemy resistance southwest of Mount Etna.[51] With the British 78th Division safely across the Salso River near Adrano and Vokes's battalions just west of the Troina River, Simonds rightly surmised that a bold eastward advance could seize the high ground on the western bank of the Simeto River and unhinge enemy defences southwest of Mount Etna (see Map 3). Despite the exposed left flank and enemy positions on Mount Revisotto and Mount Seggio, Simonds believed the potential pay-off of uncoupling the German defences dictated that the division could "afford to take bigger chances." Besides, the undulating ground of the Salso River valley afforded good protection against enemy observation and fire from the north. This was a departure from the doctrinal practice of establishing firm bases and securing the flanks before commencing an advance.

So was the organization Simonds proposed for the task. He suggested Vokes assemble a "striking force" of the Three Rivers Regiment, one self-propelled artillery battery, a troop of anti-tank guns, one battalion of infantry, and a reconnaissance squadron. He also suggested that the entire organization be placed under the command of Lieutenant-Colonel E.L. Booth, the commanding officer of the 12th Canadian Tank Regiment (Three Rivers Regiment). Assets such as the squadron from division reconnaissance regiment, the Princess Louise Dragoon Guards (PLDG), would be placed at Vokes's disposal for the operation. In the end, Vokes kept the anti-tank battery and the self-propelled guns to himself and grouped both the Seaforths and the reconnaissance squadron under Booth.

The composition of "Booth Force" made sense and took advantage of the capabilities of the component arms, given the scattered enemy and the nature of the

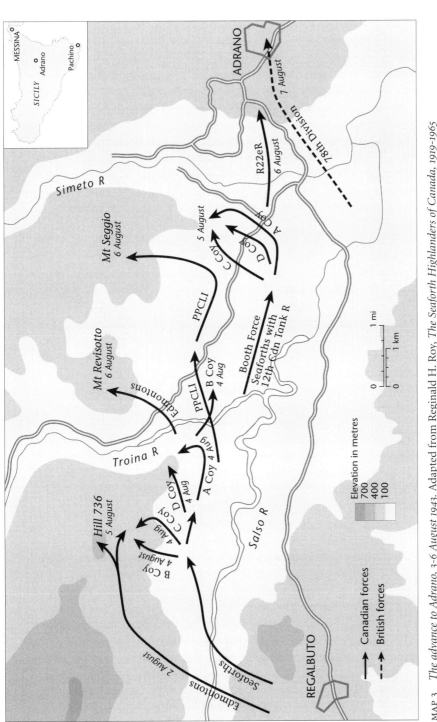

MAP 3   *The advance to Adrano, 3-6 August 1943.* Adapted from Reginald H. Roy, *The Seaforth Highlanders of Canada, 1919-1965* (Vancouver: Evergreen, 1969), sketch following p. 202.

terrain. The carrier-mounted reconnaissance squadron could move quickly in advance of the infantry and armour, scanning the terrain for enemy. Tanks could manoeuvre effectively in the open and undulating country of the Salso River valley, and their firepower could be used to support the assaulting infantry by subduing enemy positions from longer ranges. Infantry troops offered the ability to operate in any type of terrain, thus providing a degree of protection for the tanks, but they moved at the pace of a foot soldier, not an armoured vehicle. Simonds' idea was a good one, but the question of *how* to make it all work still remained.

Booth and Hoffmeister developed practical solutions, and quickly. Hoffmeister received his orders for the operation at 2:00 a.m. on 5 August, only four hours before the lead elements were to cross the start line, the Troina River.[52] To ensure the tanks could support the infantry with direct fire and that the infantry could protect the tanks from anti-tank weapons in close terrain, they took two unorthodox actions. First, Seaforth soldiers rode on the backs of the tanks through close country until they made contact with the enemy. Although the infantry were vulnerable in this mode of movement, it did ensure that armour and infantry stayed together, able to provide mutual support. It also permitted the advance to take place at the pace of tanks, not foot soldiers. Second, they integrated communications to ensure a continuous and reliable exchange of information between infantry and armour. Hoffmeister travelled in Booth's tank while maintaining communications with his rifle companies by way of a radio strapped to the tank, and his own tactical headquarters followed closely behind, in the event that he had to dismount. Company commanders did much the same, travelling with the squadron commanders while remaining "netted in" to their platoons.[53]

These arrangements contributed largely to the success of the operation.[54] After a two-and-a-half-hour delay due to bridging problems at the Troina, Booth Force struck out towards the Simeto River – the reconnaissance squadron leading, followed by "C" and "A" Companies (mounted on tanks), then Hoffmeister's and Booth's headquarters, then "D" and "B" Companies (see Map 3). Through the orange and lemon groves of the Salso River valley, the force crashed ahead at tank speed until it came to a "cement-lined flume filled with water" at around 11:00 a.m.[55] What was impassable to the tanks without some engineering assistance was relatively quick going for the infantry who dismounted and waded across the flume towards their objectives. Hoffmeister sent "C" Company to the southwest side of the high feature that dominated the Simeto. The troops made it across the dangerous valley floor to the slopes of the objective with the support of tanks (sometimes firing over the heads of the advancing infantry) and artillery.[56] Like an artillery barrage, tank fire kept enemy heads down until the infantry scrambled close to the enemy position, but tanks allowed the infantry to get much closer to the enemy than artillery would. Tank rounds were more accurate than artillery shells and presented less of a shrapnel hazard to advancing friendly troops. Moreover, the close communications that existed between squadron and company commanders allowed the infantry to direct the tank fire onto the most dangerous enemy positions. That was how "C" Company made it onto its objective, and much the same cooperation followed when Hoffmeister reinforced "C" Company's success with attacks by "A" and "D" Companies from southeast and south respectively.[57] The support was also mutual. Because the Seaforths had scaled bluffs impassable to tanks and fought an extremely tough battle to clear the objective of enemy, the tanks of Booth Force darted to the Simeto without fear of being engaged from the north.

The tactical arrangements developed by Booth and Hoffmeister were not giant doctrinal departures; some of them had been tried on a limited scale before HUSKY.[58] But they did represent a closer level of all-arms cooperation than had been practised to that point in the Sicilian Campaign. The success of Booth Force so convinced Simonds of the utility of task-organized groups that he later used them extensively during the 1 CID advances in Southern Italy in September 1943. Like his superiors, Hoffmeister, too, was learning much in the summer of 1943. His willingness to try new methods for all-arms cooperation, and the jury-rigging of communications equipment to support them, announced an increased understanding of modern arms as well as a heightened level of comfort with his own abilities.

Hoffmeister's uniqueness lay in his direction and control of the battle. His short, simple, verbal orders furnished enough detail to allow his subordinate commanders to accomplish their tasks, but not so much detail as to stifle their initiative. In short, he told his commanders what to do, not how to do it.[59] As Bell-Irving commented: "T[he] performance [of "A" Company at Agira] depended entirely on absolute freedom of manoeuvre, freedom of time, and delegation of initiative to subordinate officers."[60] Hoffmeister realized that victories in battle, like victories in business, depended to a large degree on the performance of subordinates. At Agira, the key subordinate was Bell-Irving.[61] Hoffmeister also made decisions quickly. Not all his tactical decisions had the desired effect – the failure of "B" and "C" Companies to reinforce "Grizzly," for example – but Hoffmeister's penchant for being well forward allowed him to assess the situation as it developed and take rapid action. In other words, he did not wait for information to come to him before making a key tactical decision; he went to it. This proved all the more crucial when communications failed. Quicker decisions translated into quicker actions. He was a technically sound battlefield manager.

Still, the inevitable question must be asked: What made soldiers fight for thirty-six uninterrupted hours and do extraordinary things? There were many factors: group cohesion, a soldier's aversion to letting down his comrades, and the state of individual training among them.[62] But the very human connection between the leader and the led was also crucial. Consider the case of Corporal Denis Meade, one of Hoffmeister's radio operators during the Battle of Agira. When communications failed at a critical juncture in the battle, on his own initiative and under mortar fire, Meade set up his radio on a high feature between Hoffmeister's headquarters and the companies that were out of radio contact. From there, he relayed messages between parties that could speak to him, but not to each other. At one point, after Meade had re-established communications with Bell-Irving's fatigued force on "Grizzly," Hoffmeister joined Meade in his exposed position so that he could speak directly to the commander of the isolated company.[63] Realizing that the young corporal was alone and scared, Hoffmeister assured Meade that he would send someone forward to stay with him, which he later did. Then, before leaving the radio relay position, Hoffmeister thanked the soldier for his efforts. This affected Meade profoundly. When asked why he took the action that earned him the Military Medal, Meade's response was simple and heartfelt: "I didn't want to let him down."[64] That was the key to Hoffmeister's success as a battalion commander; he made ordinary people do extraordinary things – "out there where the shells are falling."

6
Brigade Command

On the evening of the day of our last battle, "Hoffy" came up and stood amongst us right at the top of the mountain. Here we watched another unit go across the valley ... The unit got well out into the open and then "Jerry" threw his ".88's" and mortars at them. You could see them dropping and hear them yelling, and old "Hoffy's" eyes filled up and he said "Who the hell ever sent those men across there?"[1]

PRIVATE C.A. RIVERS, SEAFORTHS, 6 JULY 1967

Hoffmeister's transition to brigade command was sudden. He received word that he would be taking temporary command of the Second Canadian Infantry Brigade (2 CIB) on 29 September 1943.[2] Five days later, he found himself commanding a brigade group in the advance. Simonds had taken ill with jaundice, and the effects rippled through the chain of command. Vokes replaced Simonds, Hoffmeister replaced Vokes, and Forin replaced Hoffmeister. The changes were immediate. Within hours, literally, Hoffmeister turned over the Seaforths to his second in command and prepared for the brigade's coming tasks.[3]

As a brigade commander, Hoffmeister fought like everyone else in the Eighth Army: he moved deliberately, in limited steps, and with the aid of as much firepower as he could muster. He had mastered Montgomery's method. It was what he did to make it all work that set him apart from his peers. In essence, he did not fight his brigade any differently than he did his battalion. To start, his desire to see the battle kept him farther forward than most Canadian brigadiers, and quicker to make decisions. He also relied more heavily on subordinate initiative than most Canadian commanders. He left the details of administration and logistics completely to his staff, and he continued his practice of telling his subordinates what to do, not how to do it. Subordinate performance was important to Hoffmeister; it always had been. So was subordinate morale. He understood that soldiers needed to win in order to feel good and fight their best. This was the real reason his departures from the doctrinal norm were so few at this stage. An officer with only three months' combat experience when he first took command of his brigade, Hoffmeister understandably stuck with what he knew – best to do that than risk failure, and see troops "dropping" and "yelling" because of it.

BEFORE DISCUSSING HOFFMEISTER's actions on assuming command, it would be best to set the operational context for the early autumn of 1943. In the three weeks following their crossing of the Strait of Messina to the Italian mainland, the Canadians encountered little opposition. Actions higher up the chain of command were the reason why.

After much inter-allied negotiation, General Alexander had assaulted the Italian mainland in two places: the toe of the Italian "boot" and Salerno.[4] With the operational objective of seizing strategic airfields on the Foggia Plain, Alexander placed his main effort with General Mark Clark's Fifth US Army at Salerno on 9 September (see Map 4). To set the conditions for the success of Clark's operations, however, Alexander first landed Montgomery's Eighth Army at Reggio Calabria (Operation BAYTOWN) on 3 September and gave it the task of clearing Southern Italy, from toe to heel. This, Alexander hoped, would draw the Germans away from the Naples sector, thereby making it easier for Clark.

It did not work out that way. The Eighth Army landing at Reggio Calabria went as planned. Lieutenant-General Miles Dempsey's 13th Corps completed the crossing – 1 CID in the south, 5th British Division in the north – but the Germans, under Field-Marshal Albert Kesselring, did not take the bait.[5] They had already decided against holding Southern Italy, opting instead to concentrate their forces further up the Italian boot. That put considerable forces within striking distance of Clark's bridgehead. And strike the Germans did, when 76 Panzer Corps attacked on 13 September. It took four days of vicious fighting, but the Fifth US Army defeated the German counterattack and managed – barely – to hold its bridgehead at Salerno. Not until 20 September did the Eighth Army link up with Clark's forces. To that point, the Canadians, like the rest of Montgomery's Eighth Army, faced only token opposition as they advanced through the eastern portions of Calabria and Lucania.

To keep the pressure on Kesselring's forces, Alexander continued to drive his two armies up the peninsula – Fifth Army in the west and Eighth Army in the east – but problems with the operational plan began to surface. Most critically, Montgomery's force was reaching the limit of its administrative endurance. As he informed Alexander, "the general administrative situation is such that on reaching the line Termoli-Camapabasso-Vinchiaturo, I will have to pause for about 10 to 14 days. I have absolutely no reserve stocks and the whole administrative business in rear is in a bad way and must be tidied up."[6] This was important. Montgomery worried that the Germans were planning stronger and more determined defences, something that would soon necessitate more deliberate and well-staged attacks to break.

Montgomery was right.[7] On 30 September, Hitler gave Kesselring the following direction for the coming months in Italy: "Fight a delaying action only as far as the line Gaeta-Ortona. *This line will be held.* The time necessary for bringing up the infantry divisions will be won by operations forward of the line to be held."[8] This order translated into a series of defensive belts – delaying positions along river obstacles, such as the Volturno and the Biferno, followed by a main defensive line

Gaeta-Cassino-Ortona. That was precisely where Alexander's armies were heading. To complicate matters further, by mid-October the Germans had twenty-four divisions in Italy while the Allies had only fourteen, and both Alexander and Montgomery were aware of it. More and regular supplies of men, ammunition, fuel, and equipment would be needed to blast through the depth of German defences; the ground was too difficult and the Germans too determined for anything less.

Such was the operational situation when Hoffmeister assumed temporary command of 2 CIB. The Eighth Army was to roll back the German delaying positions – 5th Corps on the Adriatic, 13th Corps inland through the Matese Mountains. Hoffmeister's first task as a brigade commander was to provide left flank security for the entire army. While the other two brigades of 1 CID leapfrogged each other from Lucera to Campobasso along Highway 17, Vokes tasked 2 CIB to operate independently on an axis to their south (see Map 5). Since being independent also meant being isolated from the assistance of the rest of the division, Vokes gave Hoffmeister the pieces he needed to support himself: a field regiment of Royal Artillery, one anti-tank battery, a field ambulance company, a machine-gun platoon, an extra mortar platoon, and a reconnaissance squadron of the Princess Louise Dragoon Guards (PLDG). A tank squadron was added later.[9] (The brigade's task organization is shown in Figure 6.1.)

Hoffmeister did not get a lot of direction from Vokes. He and the acting division commander discussed groupings, tentative tasks, and preliminary moves to waiting areas west of Potenza on 29 September, but they did not have another face-to-face meeting before the operation started. Hoffmeister did visit 1 CID headquarters on the morning of 3 October, but Vokes was forward with his tactical headquarters,

FIGURE 6.1   *2nd Canadian Infantry Brigade task organization, October 1943*

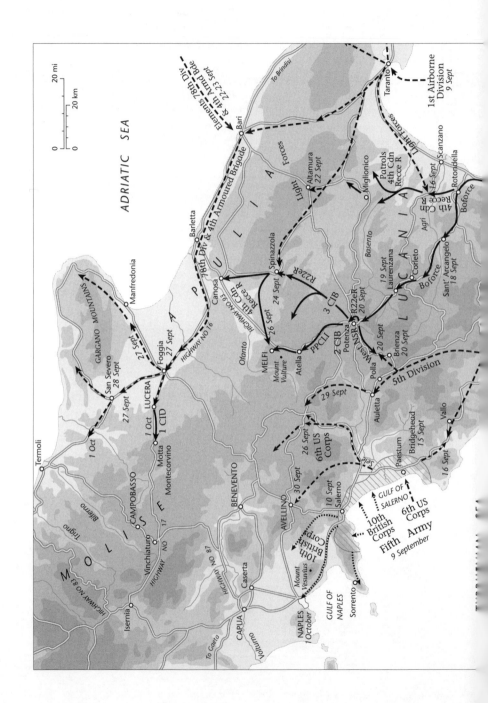

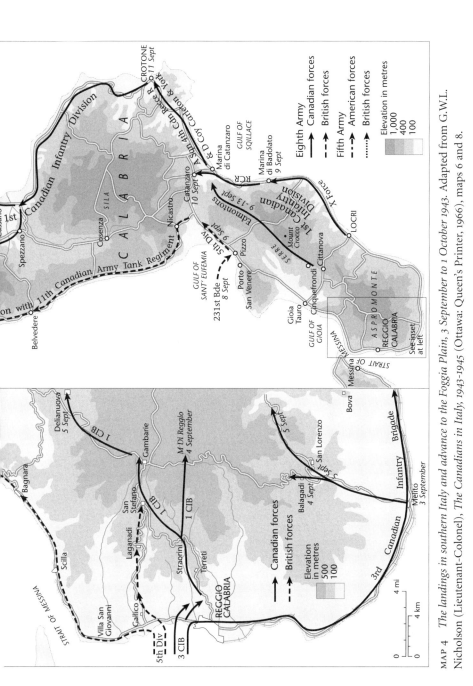

MAP 4 *The landings in southern Italy and advance to the Foggia Plain, 3 September to 1 October 1943. Adapted from G.W.L. Nicholson (Lieutenant-Colonel), The Canadians in Italy, 1943-1945 (Ottawa: Queen's Printer, 1966), maps 6 and 8.*

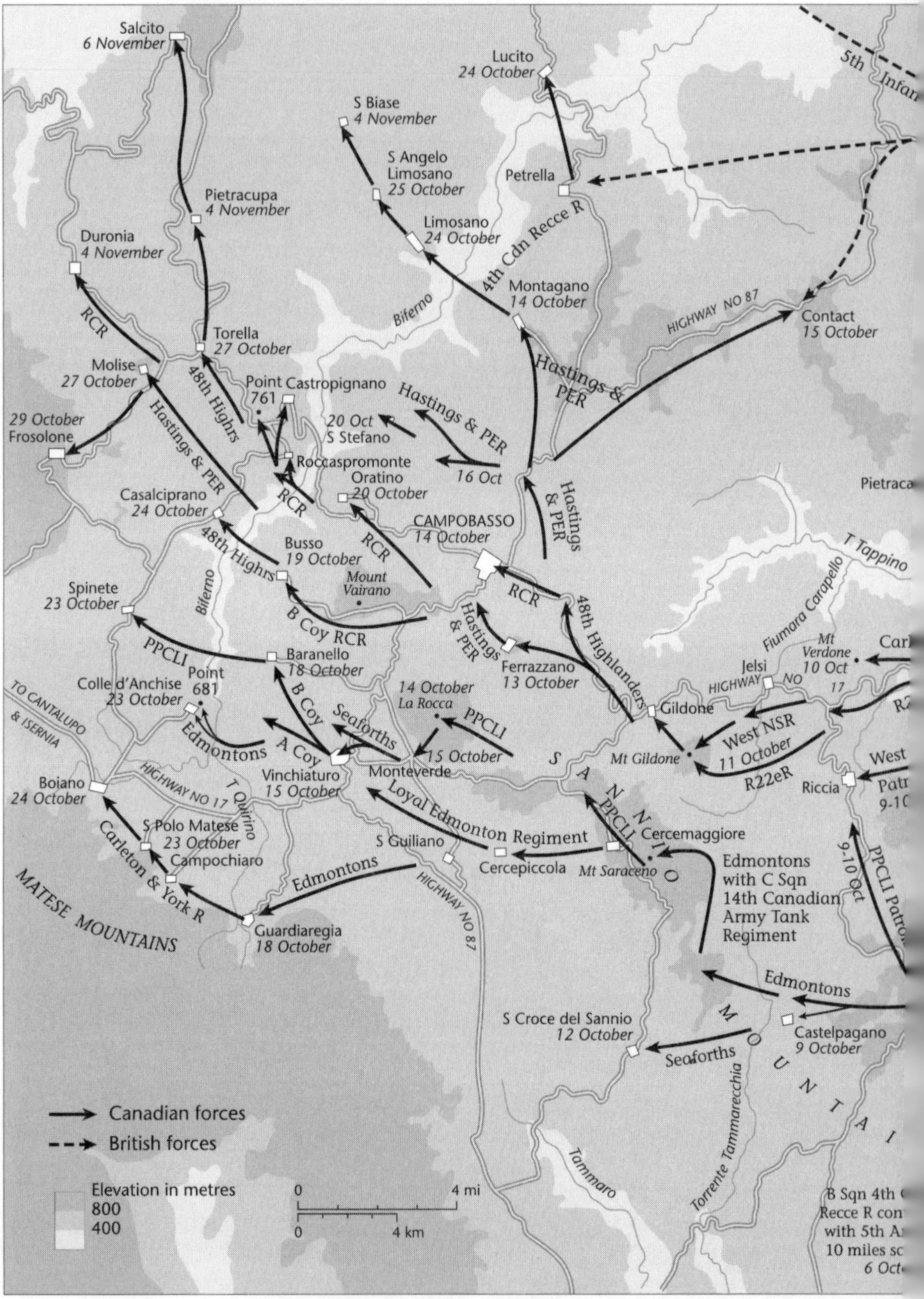

MAP 5   *The fighting on the Upper Fortore and Biferno, 1 October to 6 November 1943.*
Adapted from G.W.L. Nicholson (Lieutenant-Colonel), *The Canadians in Italy, 1943-1945*
(Ottawa: Queen's Printer, 1966), map 9.

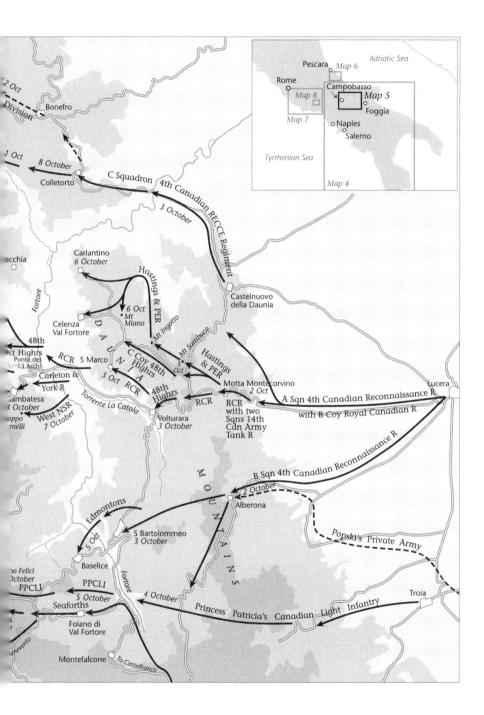

reconnoitring and "teeing-up" details with his other two brigades.[10] In Vokes's absence, Hoffmeister coordinated what he could with the division staff, and then returned to his own headquarters. Vokes must have received word that Hoffmeister had queries, because, as Hoffmeister recalled, "A little later I got a pencilled memo, two or three pages from a small notebook from Chris [Vokes], detailing in very general terms what my task was, and that was it."[11]

The pencilled memo, which Vokes had undoubtedly written at his tactical headquarters and sent via dispatch rider, is worth reproducing in full here, because, despite its brevity, it gave Hoffmeister all the guidance he needed for the next twenty days of operations (see also Map 5):

Comd 2 Cdn inf bde

Dear Bert,

1. You may move 2nd bde [brigade] into the area S. BARTALOMEO – 8506 – rd junct [road junction] 7805 to-morrow morning. I would like you to be established there by to-morrow evening 4 Oct 43 (see para 6)
2. I have in mind then that you move via FOIANO 8106 – CASTELGRANO [Castelpagano] – 6811 S. CROCE 6110 and thence by most feasible means to a firm base covering the road center in vicinity VINCHIATURO 4920
3. I would like you to dispose your bde as follows

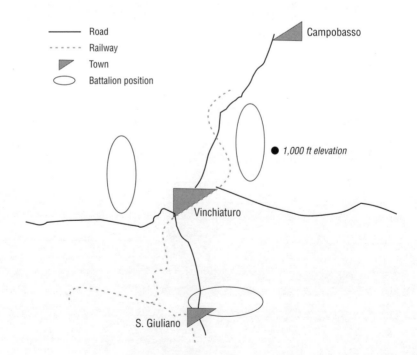

4. Having got the bde in position you can "frig about" [move/deploy] with say one rifle coy [company] from each bn [battalion] with a couple of 6 prs [6 pounder anti-tank weapons] 3" mortars etc. Limit your "frigging" to a radius of 15-20 miles to the NE of VINCHIATURO.

5. 35 TCVs [Troop Carrying Vehicle] will report to you at or about 0700 hrs tomorrow morning. Keep them until the operation is complete or until you cannot use them.

6. On 5 OCT I would like you to "stage" to the area S. CROCE – CASTELGANO [Castelpagano]. And on 6 OCT to commence your move on VINCHIATURO

7. I shall direct the leading bde on main axis to form a firm base at GILDONE and then divert the rear bde towards CAMPOBASSO to form a firm base there.

8. You will be entirely on your own and I can give you no additional help. 5 div [5 British Division] recce [reconnaissance] patrols will be working around or "frigging" about from AVCIANO north and east and may help

9. I may have to restrict your movement to conform with that of the div, but that I can let you know from day to day by [unreadable] or LO [Liaison Officer].

10. When you meet the enemy, which you no doubt will, hit him a hearty good crack for me

1545 hrs   Sincerely
3 Oct 43   Chris Vokes[12]

Vokes gave Hoffmeister his final objective, an axis of advance, and how he saw the battle unfolding – that was it. In Hoffmeister's words, "I was given my objectives and how I got there was strictly up to me."[13] The tone of the note and the independent task it assigned reflected the confidence that Vokes placed in Hoffmeister's judgment – this despite his being the least-experienced brigade commander. Both Brigadier H.D. Graham of 1 CIB and Brigadier H.S. Penhale of 3 CIB had more time in command of their formations, yet Vokes saw fit to stay with Hoffmeister. It would have been relatively easy, for example, to switch 2 CIB for 1 CIB on the southern flank, but Vokes did not do that. He knew his subordinate well, he understood his abilities, and he was comfortable enough to give him the task that was least subject to direct divisional control. For his part, Hoffmeister appreciated Vokes's trust, as his saving of the pencilled memo testified.

When it came to making a plan for the advance, Hoffmeister also appreciated the staff training he had received a year earlier: "I really blessed my staff college training ... because we had done several telephone battles and a couple of exercises precisely along these lines, so it was really putting into practice the things we had actually done at Staff College, which is another plus for the kind of training we got there."[14] He knew his object – get to Vinchiaturo – and he considered the factors that would influence his ability to do so, starting with the ground. Rainfall had rendered much of the mountainous ground impassable to vehicles. As Hoffmeister later reported about capturing one of their objectives, "The ... feature was captured after a difficult advance over rugged country and completely impassable to [vehicles]. Mules were used to get wireless sets, MGs [machine guns] and mortars forward to the objective, while oxen and the bulldozer were the only two means of getting the A/Tk [anti-tank] guns into position."[15] A second key factor – the enemy – complicated matters by blowing all the bridges in the area and mining the routes to retard the Allied advance.

To overcome these difficulties, Hoffmeister concluded that he had to make maximum use of reconnaissance. Having patrols select suitable routes, identify obstacles, and find detours beforehand would permit the main columns to move as far as possible on trucks and at the best possible speed. More important, locating and defining pockets of the enemy early yielded better options for mounting quick attacks, or bypassing German positions. Hoffmeister supplemented the capabilities of the reconnaissance squadron with dismounted patrols from his three infantry battalions to do just that. After the Sicilian Campaign, the battalions of 2 CIB had formed Scout and Sniper Platoons to enhance their reconnaissance capabilities.[16] Hoffmeister put them to good use. Dismounted infantry could operate in areas where reconnaissance squadron carriers could not go. By layering the capabilities of the two arms, he gained a more complete picture of the tactical situation. Hoffmeister still liked seeing things for himself, but a brigade was a bigger organization than a battalion, and he could not be in all places at once. Numerous "eyes and ears" provided him with a steady flow of information and helped him make better decisions.

The nuts and bolts of how Hoffmeister employed his reconnaissance assets during this particular advance warrants some explanation because it set a pattern that he followed to the end of his military career. First, he came to use the reconnaissance squadron on the flanks, reconnoitring lateral routes and maintaining contact with flanking formations. In conditions where carriers were restricted to moving on the main routes, the reconnaissance squadron was simply too vulnerable to operate in advance of the formation – a lesson Hoffmeister learned the hard way on the morning of 6 October:

> We were out of contact with the enemy and I sent them [the reconnaissance squadron] forward ... to establish contact. They allowed their squadron to bunch up on a section of a narrow road [south of the Decorata Crossroads] that was under observation from German positions and German 88 mm guns knocked out the first vehicle, knocked out the last vehicle and just destroyed practically the whole squadron. This depressed me to no end because I heard that this was going on. I got there just at the tail end of it and there wasn't anything left alive. It was just an awful disaster.[17]

From then on, Hoffmeister kept the reconnaissance squadron on the flanks.[18] To the front, he deployed dismounted infantry patrols. Typically, after the lead battalion secured its objective, Hoffmeister sent patrols forward, mostly at night, to find the enemy and report on obstacles.[19] Sometimes small reconnaissance detachments scoured the terrain looking for enemy, speaking to civilians, finding obstacles, or reconnoitring routes. Sometimes full sub-units, up to company-size organizations, assembled for the purpose of fighting for information on enemy identification, strengths, or capabilities. By forcing the enemy to "open up" with their weapons, fighting patrols could quickly obtain important information as to how many Germans were in a given location, and with what weapons. On 9 October, for instance, a Princess Patricia's Canadian Light Infantry (PPCLI) fighting patrol of two platoons engaged an enemy position south of the town of Riccia. As a result of the ensuing firefight, the patrol determined that the outpost consisted of 30 enemy with three machine guns.[20] That information later allowed the PPCLI to plan an attack of appropriate size and strength. Fighting patrols also gained information on German formations by capturing enemy soldiers. As an example, the 2 CIB war diarist noted that the purpose of fighting patrols on 13 October was "NOT only to contact the enemy but also to bring back identifications [of the enemy formations]." This they did; two prisoners of war, snatched by the PPCLI, revealed that the enemy units to the 2 CIB front were from 29 Panzer Grenadier Division.[21] Whatever the nature of the patrol, Hoffmeister placed tremendous emphasis on gathering the facts before driving blindly forward.

As experience enhanced Hoffmeister's understanding of the types of facts that had to be gathered, he gave better direction to his reconnaissance effort. Most often, he issued direction for patrols deliberately in orders; however, the following direction, relayed to the commander of the reconnaissance squadron, was not unusual either: "Move immediately to the area of [Decorata]. On arrival there contact Bde Comd and have patrol stand by to move on Bde Comd[']s order."[22] As the advance progressed, he looked beyond his own resources to collect the information he needed, like what the enemy had in depth, or in reserve. When dismounted patrols and contacts with civilians gave Hoffmeister an indication of enemy artillery concentrations between San Croce and Cercemaggiore, he requested aerial reconnaissance to pinpoint them. That way he could direct his attack on the enemy gun positions, be it from the air or from his own artillery, with greater effect.[23] As had been the case since his landing in Sicily, he hated waiting for the facts to come to him.

There was nothing groundbreaking about Hoffmeister's tactical method of manoeuvre, which can best be described as follows: find the enemy, attack in force, consolidate a firm base, move on. A situation report to division following the capture of San Croce and Cercemaggiore reflected its essence: "[Brigade] Comd's intention to hold pres [present] posn, [send] fighting patrol fwd [then] to capture 1000 feature [La Rocca] tomorrow and continue advance."[24] It may have been deliberate, and sometimes slow, but it suited the tactical situation. Few decent roads snaked their way through the area, and the Canadians needed all of them. Mules may have been useful for moving radios and supplies for the occasional bit of off-road movement, but if the division – the army for that matter – wanted to maintain any momentum for the advance, it needed to move large amounts of men and materiel quickly. That meant roads, and gaining control of the ground that dominated them. Furthermore, because the enemy had the obstacles covered by observation and fire, bridges could not be repaired and rivers could not be crossed until the enemy on the dominating features had been destroyed or forced to withdraw. As Hoffmeister recalled, "As a rule the enemy had all demolitions [blown bridges and road craters, for example] carefully registered by arty [artillery] and mortars and it was necessary to carry out the drill of depriving him of his observation each time through establishing infantry bridgeheads in order to allow the sappers [engineers] to prepare a route [without being fired on] for the supporting arms to get forward."[25]

To accomplish his object *and* save lives, Hoffmeister coordinated his attacks carefully and used *all* of the firepower at his disposal. He did not want to see his men dropping and yelling for lack of a well-coordinated attack in strength, as the chapter epigraph indicates. Thus, when patrols discovered enemy positions en route to Decorata, Hoffmeister launched battalion attacks on Baselice, Mount San Marco, and Toppo Felici. But they were not simultaneous assaults. They were sequential, and that allowed Hoffmeister to give each of his battalion commanders all of the firepower he had to support each of their attacks in turn. Despite having numerous patrols forward, Hoffmeister still insisted on seeing for himself what was happening and conferring with the battalion commanders before their attacks. In this way, he confirmed what they needed and then gave it to them. When the Edmonton Regiment conducted a surprising right-flanking attack on Baselice, they had "a three minute concentration from the 165 Fd Regt (Royal Artillery), which was thickened up by the Bde Sp Grp [Brigade Support Group] 4.2 [inch] Mortars and our own 3" Mortars and 6 Pdrs [anti-tank weapons]."[26] When the Seaforths assaulted up the slopes of Mount San Marco on 6 October, they needed the combined supporting fire of an entire field regiment of artillery, a platoon of 4.2-inch mortars, and a platoon of medium machine guns to subdue the enemy – and they got it.[27] When he could arrange it, Hoffmeister used Desert Air Force (DAF) fighter-bombers to strike enemy positions in depth, to retard enemy counterattacks, and, most importantly, to nullify enemy artillery. For an attack on the Decorata crossroads, he requested and received fighter-bomber strikes on suspected enemy gun positions at Cercemaggiore.[28] When the Seaforths attacked Baranello, the DAF struck the west bank of the Biferno on two successive days – 60 Kittyhawks on 17 October and 72 on 18 October.[29] If it was within range and it could shoot, Hoffmeister used it.

Hoffmeister marched in lockstep with existing doctrine. A Canadian reprint of a 1942 War Office pamphlet on operations underlined the importance of firepower as the first of several principles of tactics: "*Fire* dominates the battlefield. Fire is the chief antagonist of mobility. To retain the power of mobility, it is necessary to overcome the enemy's fire. The use of ground, darkness, or smoke are all means towards the attainment of this object; but in the end, it will nearly always be necessary to neutralize the enemy's fire-producing weapons by the application of superior fire."[30]

Relying on superior firepower was effective, but not without its drawbacks, as the attack on the Decorata crossroads demonstrated.[31] To seize the critical road junction, Hoffmeister called on the PPCLI to execute a deliberate attack. Patrol reports on 7 October indicated that the enemy held the crossroads in force, and Hoffmeister took the time to make sure that the assault force had enough firepower to take it quickly and with minimal casualties. Accordingly, he assigned a field regiment's worth of gunfire in support and placed a newly arrived squadron of the Calgary Regiment under the command of the PPCLI commanding officer, Lieutenant-Colonel Cameron Ware. But the action never happened. First, a shortage of tank fuel forced an unfortunate postponement of the attack from 3:00 p.m. on 8 October to 6:00 a.m. on 9 October. Then patrol reports from the night of 8-9 October revealed that Germans had "once again withdrawn beyond our reach."[32] The Germans had succeeded; they had forced the Canadians to deploy for a deliberate attack and then withdrawn without casualties. That not only bought the German formations the time they needed to prepare their main defensive line from Gaeta to Ortona, it also allowed the delaying troops to fight another day, somewhere else. The Germans conducted similarly successful withdrawals from San Croce (12-13 October) and Cercepiccola (14-15 October). This was the shortfall of a firepower-dependent, deliberate approach.

What Hoffmeister did was one thing; how he made it work was another. Hoffmeister's manner of commanding and controlling departed from the doctrinal template. First, he spent little time in his main headquarters, preferring instead to operate from a tactical headquarters, which consisted of himself, the commanding officer of the supporting artillery regiment, the commander of the brigade support group, a runner, and often the brigade major (see Figure 6.2).[33] Occasionally, he even sent the brigade major to coordinate with the forward battalions or reconnoitre obstacles – both of which were highly unusual tasks for the primary staff coordinator in the brigade headquarters.[34] With both Hoffmeister and the brigade major forward so much of the time, the coordination of logistics and administration fell mostly to the senior staff captain in the main headquarters. Unusual as these arrangements may have been, the brigade functioned reasonably well and Hoffmeister consequently felt little need to meddle in the administrative details. Reflecting on logistic coordination in 2 CIB, Hoffmeister recalled simply, "My staff captain handled that ... We had regular conferences on a brigade level ... just reviewing the thing but we had first class ammunition, food, water, petrol supplies."[35] That arrangement seemed to suit Hoffmeister. He focused on fighting his brigade, not feeding it.

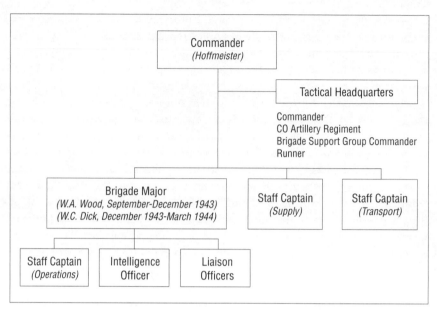

FIGURE 6.2   *2nd Canadian Infantry Brigade headquarters, October-December 1943*

In disseminating direction, he continued (when he could) with what had worked so well at Agira: he brought subordinate commanders forward to see what he could see, and he issued orders from there. By viewing the terrain with his own eyes, Hoffmeister could fill critical gaps in the information he needed, or even confirm what he had learned from patrols before planning his next move. Once he had obtained whatever information he wanted, Hoffmeister quickly formulated a plan (because he had his key advisors with him) then called his battalion commanders forward to give orders. This made good sense. Battalion commanders could view the ground over which they were to operate. More than that, it helped Hoffmeister make absolutely clear his intention – a matter of some importance, given the frequent inaccuracies of the Italian maps.

But doing business that far forward was not without peril or problem. On 14 October, for example, Hoffmeister and the commander of the Brigade Support Group wandered well forward of the lead battalion and stumbled onto an enemy outpost that included tanks. Only after some frantic and undignified scurrying did they make it back to friendly lines unscathed.[36] Later that day, when Hoffmeister attempted to give orders from a forward position, "shelling continued during the 'O' Gp [orders group] which was switched from the original locn [location] to a house at CERCEMAGGIORE from which a good view could be obtained towards CERCEPICCOLA and S. GUILIANO."[37] Hoffmeister cut short another orders group the following day, this one at the crossroads northwest of Cercemaggiore, "due to enemy shelling in that area."[38] The advantages of passing direction in view of the terrain to be traversed obviously had to be balanced with the effect enemy fire might have on the concentration of those receiving the orders.

In the final days of the October advance, Hoffmeister operated with all the skill and confidence of a competent formation commander. Having reached the area around Vinchiaturo, he set about deploying his battalion in accordance with the direction Vokes had issued on 3 October. But he did not stick slavishly to the deployment plan set down by Vokes. He comprehended that the *intent* of the planned pause at the Biferno River was for all Eighth Army formations to reconstitute depleted manpower and replenish supplies before launching a major drive northward, and that meant "frigging about" much more widely than Vokes had originally indicated (see Map 5, p. 76). By 18 October, the Loyal Edmonton Regiment[39] held Guardiaregia, the Seaforths were in Baranello, the PPCLI occupied the high ground around La Rocca and Point 1000, and 2 CIB patrols probed the west bank of the Biferno, but Hoffmeister's brigade still had no respite. As the 2 CIB war diarist noted for 20 October: "Though the Bde is supposed to be in a rest area, the enemy are too close and too active with their shelling to allow much rest."[40]

Plans higher in the chain of command also conspired to postpone any real pause for the Canadians. General Montgomery wanted to punch through to the "Rome Line" with Lieutenant-General Charles Allfrey's 5th Corps on the Adriatic axis towards Pescara. But before that took place, the Eighth Army commander wanted a good strong feint by Dempsey's 13th Corps inland to siphon enemy attention and reserves away from the coastal sector. To do his part, Dempsey intended to have 1 CID establish a bridgehead on the west bank of the Biferno, through which the British 5th Division would advance northward. On 22 October, General Simonds, now back from hospital, outlined his plan, which, to use a boxing analogy, was a "left-right" combination, similar in conception to Montgomery's, only on a smaller scale – 2 CIB first on the left on 23 October, 1 CIB on the right three days later.

Even before Simonds's 22 October conference, Hoffmeister, who remained in acting command of 2 CIB, had anticipated that crossing the Biferno would be necessary, if only to permit a much-needed break. Patrols confirmed that the enemy still had observers in key positions on the west bank of the river. From those vantage points, the Germans could see Hoffmeister's troops and were, therefore, able to spoil the respite with artillery fire. The enemy had to be driven off the western heights of the Biferno, so Hoffmeister made arrangements to strike across the river. Reconnaissance and fighting patrols on 20-22 October defined the objectives of Colle d'Anchise and Spinete and identified routes and crossing sites for two attacks.[41] Hence, by the time Simonds delivered his 22 October orders group, Hoffmeister was well on the way to fulfilling his part of the 1 CID mission.

The 2 CIB plan, which Hoffmeister outlined at an orders group at 11:30 a.m. on 21 October, was sound, well coordinated, and well in line with the Eighth Army tactical template.[42] Before sending the Loyal Edmonton Regiment after Colle d'Anchise and the PPCLI after Spinete, he made sure both flanks were secure. His right required no immediate action; the Seaforths controlled the area around Baranello, and the Royal Canadian Regiment (RCR), of the adjacent 1 CIB, held the town of Busso. To the south, Hoffmeister requested and received from Simonds an extra battalion, the Carleton and York Regiment of 3 CIB, to secure Campochiaro and patrol towards Boiano. Predictably, air and artillery attacks on 21 and 22 October softened up both objectives. Even more predictably, to permit the full concentration of firepower on each objective, Hoffmeister sequenced the attacks for another "left-right" combination – the Loyal Edmonton Regiment starting their attack at 10:30 p.m. on 22 October, the PPCLI stepping off towards Spinete at 2:00 p.m. the following day. But when it came to guiding the actions of his subordinates, Hoffmeister simply told his battalion commanders what they had to do and when they had to do it. As to *how* they accomplished their tasks, he left that to them.

Lieutenant-Colonel J.C. Jefferson of the Loyal Edmonton Regiment and Lieutenant-Colonel "Cammy" Ware of the PPCLI devised markedly different approaches. Jefferson opted to take advantage of the hours of darkness and execute a "silent" attack. Thus, despite the support of tanks and the "on call" fire of the entire artillery regiment, when the Loyal Edmonton Regiment crossed the Biferno, it did so without a large preparatory barrage.[43] Under the guidance of scouts, the lead Edmonton companies sneaked forward on routes identified the previous evening and made it into Colle d'Anchise undetected, achieving total surprise. There were some desperate moments, however. Fending off enemy counterattacks proved difficult when the infantry and the tanks lost each other in the morning mist of the river valley and communications proved inadequate.[44] But in the end, the regiment held on, its objective secured by mid-afternoon on 24 October. In contrast with the silent attack of the Edmontons, the daylight assault by the PPCLI commenced with the artillery regiment firing a combination of smoke (to blind the enemy) and high explosives (to keep their heads down).[45] Since the battalion had to advance in daylight, across open ground and up a long slope towards Spinete, this was the sensible thing to do. Ware's troops seized their objective, without casualties, within two hours.[46] The Patricias executed their attack flawlessly, but the success of the operation owed as much to the actions of the Edmontons in the south as it did to Ware's plan. The capture of Colle d'Anchise only hours earlier had forced the enemy to abandon the small salient at Spinete, thereby permitting the Patricias to enter the town unopposed and to complete the 2 CIB task of establishing a firm base on the far side of the Biferno. Two different approaches to two tactical problems, but they both served a broader plan to pry apart enemy positions.

Hoffmeister drew good performances from his battalion commanders during the October advance. They did what he asked of them and they responded well to his leadership. Ware later described Hoffmeister as the best brigadier he ever served.[47] But at this early stage in his tenure as a brigade commander, whatever impression he made on them, he made by his actions, not by talking about actions. The advance to the Biferno had started too soon after his appointment to acting command for "chalk talks." With the coming of the November pause, Hoffmeister used the opportunity to digest whatever lessons he had learned and to set his commanders and staff straight on how he intended to operate in the future. This was an opportunity to incorporate into the existing doctrine what had been learned about the enemy, the terrain, weapons, and equipment. When his brigade entered the 1 CID rest area at Campobasso, the newly promoted Brigadier Hoffmeister did just that.[48]

On his own initiative, Hoffmeister arranged two ten-day training courses, the first for members of his brigade staff and liaison officers (LOs), the second for all company commanders in his brigade.[49] The first of these started on 4 November with Hoffmeister delivering opening remarks that emphasized "the value of all officers knowing the duties and responsibilities of the various departments at Div [division] and Bde [brigade] level."[50] The liaison officers' course curriculum was accordingly designed to forge a common understanding of doctrine and procedure – the axle on which operations of the brigade turned. For example, to standardize the dissemination of orders, as well as the monitoring and reporting of personnel and equipment strengths, Hoffmeister's brigade major lectured on staff procedures particular to 2 CIB and 1 CID.[51] To make sure liaison and staff officers could communicate effectively, an officer from the brigade signals organization taught classes on communication equipment and procedures, sessions that included hands-on demonstrations. To foster a greater understanding of what existed outside the brigade, Hoffmeister also invited a number of guest experts to speak. From 1 CID, a variety of subject-matter experts taught lessons on the organization and employment of divisional artillery, divisional engineers, the personnel-replacement system, logistics, intelligence, and even public relations. From 13th Corps, a staff officer explained what air support was available and how to get it. The comprehensive training package, which followed the method of the first few weeks of the Canadian Junior War Staff Course, taught Hoffmeister's staff and liaison officers not only "how we make things work" but "what we have, how it works, and who to contact when you need it" – essential information for anyone working in a headquarters.

The other ten-day course, which started on 17 November, Hoffmeister designed to establish "how we fight." Making all the pieces move his way meant placing his stamp on the chain of command. He had already done that with his battalion commanders; for this training, Hoffmeister reached deeper into the chain of command – down to the level of company commanders. Following Montgomery's principle that a commander must personally train the officers in his charge,[52] Hoffmeister delivered the most important lectures himself. The notes of a Seaforth officer who attended the training survive and offer much insight into Hoffmeister's philosophy of command and his tactical method at this stage. Lieutenant W.H.

Melhuish recorded that the first of Hoffmeister's opening remarks was a blunt statement on why the training was important: because it was "not now [a matter of dollars and cents], but men's lives" that were at stake.[53] Once he had grabbed their attention, Hoffmeister expanded on what he expected from company commanders in his brigade. He expected them to be an "example to [the] troops," to show enthusiasm at all times, to foster team spirit, to demonstrate "loyalty [to the chain of command] irrespective of [their] own opinion of [the] plan or arrangement." Anything less would undermine the confidence of the rank and file. He also passed on a few observations based on recent experience – the importance of thorough reconnaissance before committing to action, and the necessity of soldiers at all levels knowing the proper succession of command in the event that a leader is "knocked out," to cite just a couple. Interestingly, Hoffmeister also offered company commanders advice that he seldom heeded: "[Company commanders] should not lead [in the attack and risk] jeopardizing the leadership of [the] Coy." For the most part, though, he confined his opening remarks to telling company commanders why they were attending the training, and why it was important.

Articulation of Hoffmeister's tactical method came later, in his lectures on the advance and the attack, both of which were exhibitions of common sense, based on doctrine and tempered by experience. For the advance, he emphasized the importance of arranging the columns of fighting troops and supporting arms such that they would be roughly disposed as they would be required for an attack, or to fend off an enemy counterattack.[54] He stressed the necessity of dispersing supporting arms, such as artillery and anti-tank assets, so as not to present a lucrative target to enemy air forces. He also offered a couple of rules of thumb; a commander "may commit up to 33½% of his force without reference to a higher commander. If he commits more than this, [he] may involve higher groups [of troops and arms] & endanger the higher plan." When attacked or ambushed while in the advance, Hoffmeister advised his audience to "grab neighbouring high ground [that] may be needed for [a] firm base later." These were rational points, designed to minimize hesitant decisions, and based on the premise that even imperfect decisions are better than no decisions. But the bulk of Hoffmeister's talk on the advance dealt with an activity that minimized the need for making such heat-of-the-moment calls: reconnaissance. For battalions, he counselled that their scout platoons should be "really well ahead, up to 2 miles depending on the [ground] etc., of leading [troops], so as to have lots of time to recce [reconnoitre]." For the brigade reconnaissance squadron, he recounted the experience of the PLDG at Decorata to make the point that, even though reconnaissance squadron scout cars would be in front of the lead battalions, it would usually be necessary to have "infantry first on foot," especially when contact with the enemy was imminent. At times, "when speed or info are essential," the reconnaissance squadron could lead. In most cases, however, he stated his preference for using reconnaissance squadron carriers "as flank and/or rear protection."

His lecture on the attack was pure Eighth Army, pure Montgomery. As Melhuish noted, Hoffmeister preferred the use of "all possible" fire support.[55] The brigadier then cited the example of the PPCLI attack on Spinete as the ideal sequence and combination of firepower for an attack: air bombardment, followed by air strafing, followed by an artillery barrage, followed by the machine-gun, mortar, and anti-tank fire from Brigade Support Group weapons, followed closely by infantry assault. Firepower was central to the Canadian and British way of doing business, and Hoffmeister went on to state plainly the axiom of that approach: an assaulting force "must not move beyond the range of its [supporting] arms," most importantly, its artillery. But that did not mean that he interpreted all operations as simple matters of attrition. He did not, for example, advocate using all available firepower to destroy the *strongest* enemy positions. Quite the contrary, regarding where to direct the attack and the firepower that supported it, Hoffmeister offered the following guidance: "Choose that objective which will cause the utmost dislocation to the enemy." In other words, given the choice, he favoured attacking those objectives that were most likely to unhinge an enemy defensive position, not driving straight into the teeth of German defences. More often than not, that meant attacking weaker positions and gaining advantageous ground that made enemy defences in other areas untenable. With his comments, as with his actions, Hoffmeister left little doubt that he was an Eighth Army soldier, through and through. And though he need not have stated it, he still made a point of emphasizing that he considered himself a "disciple of Monty."

The training sessions were not just about how to do things. They were also about building confidence. Hoffmeister wanted subordinates to have faith in him. That much had not changed since he first took command of a rifle company in 1939. What had changed was the target audience of his personal appeal. Having risen higher in the chain of command, Hoffmeister's ability to make face-to-face contact with every soldier in his command was now much more difficult. But he could make a definite mark on the battalion and company commanders who would lead those soldiers in battle. That was why he delivered *all* of the lectures on tactics himself. He also sought to build a broader confidence – one based on the competence of the Eighth Army, its commanders and staffs at all levels, and its equipment. To that end, the training included a number of topics not immediately applicable to the commander of a hundred or so soldiers: brigade and division staff procedures, Army intelligence, air photography, and the organization and employment of an armoured division among them.[56] Having officers from division and corps speak on their specific areas of expertise reassured the trainees. Lectures such as the one on "Pieces & Uses" of artillery were designed as much to convey general knowledge as to say, "We have the right equipment for the job ahead of us. The people who own that equipment know what they are doing. All you have to do is think about how to use it, and ask for it." Hoffmeister reconfirmed his conviction that the more subordinates knew about what was happening, the more they understood that there *was* a plan and a competent organization to run it, the more confident they would be, and, therefore, the better they would fight. This was the same approach he had taken when briefing every platoon in his battalion about the division-level plan for the invasion of Sicily.

Meanwhile, the Germans did not buy the 13th Corps's feint. As Hoffmeister and his brigade rested and recuperated at Campobasso, Dempsey's corps failed to draw the German reserves to the Eighth Army's inland axis. Far from it, the Germans, sensing that Montgomery's main thrust was to be along the coastal axis, reinforced their positions in front of Sir Charles Allfrey's 5th Corps. Kesselring bolstered 76 Panzer Corps with three additional divisions: 26th Panzer, 90th Panzer Grenadier, and the 1st Fallschirmjaeger (Parachute).[57] In effect, these actions made the ratio of defenders to attackers roughly one-to-one along the Eighth Army front. This left Montgomery's attackers a far cry from the three-to-one advantage they preferred. Moreover, foul weather and the broken terrain tipped the scale in favour of the defenders. The rain-swelled Sangro, Feltrino, Moro, and Riccio rivers cut across the Anglo-Canadian axes of advance, forming natural obstacles that the skilled German defenders fully exploited with mines and the judicious selection of defended localities. Bad weather nullified any advantage that the weight of the Desert Air Force might have added. Most important, however, unlike the ground the Canadians had covered in their October advance (the space between Potenza and Campobasso), the area from the Sangro to the Arielli rivers was no network of delaying positions. It was a main defensive line that Hitler wanted held throughout the winter months, one that made a rapid Anglo-Canadian breakthrough unlikely.[58]

Still, Montgomery remained cautiously, though unduly, optimistic that the "Rome Line" could be reached by the end of December – provided the weather held. On 18 November, he wrote to General Alan Brooke, now Chief of the Imperial General Staff: "I will hit the Bosche a crack that will be heard all over Italy. I have lined up three divisions on my right: 78 DIV, 8 [Indian] DIV, 2 [New Zealand] DIV, with 400 tanks and the whole of my air power ... I have now to wait for fine weather."[59] But the weather he wanted never came. Rain continued to drench the Italian countryside, making the breaching of water obstacles tedious, rendering the off-road movement of vehicles impossible, and keeping Allied air forces on the ground. Roads covered in "chocolate sauce" were barely passable.[60] As Montgomery's Chief of Staff, Major-General Francis de Guingand commented in retrospect, "Mud, that arch enemy of the offensive soldier, however, soon showed us how wrong we were."[61] Even before the Germans fully reinforced the coastal sector, it took Allfrey's 5th Corps four days of heavy fighting (19-22 November) just to gain a lodgement on the north side of the Sangro. The weather, the broken terrain, the washed-out roads, the unfavourable attack ratios: it all conspired to force Montgomery to do the only thing he could – concentrate his forces for some yard-by-yard, inch-by-inch pounding to blast through the German defences. Another letter to Brooke explained the difficulty: "I am fighting a hell of a battle here. The

right wing of my Army on the Adriatic side consists of three divisions. I am opposed there by 3½ divisions; this combined with the mud makes it not too easy. I
am now going to move troops over to my right, from my left – I am sending 5 Div
over."[62]

But before Montgomery moved 5th Division to the Adriatic, he had the Canadians take the place of the battered 78th Division. By early December, although he
had adjusted his objectives from achieving an operational breakthrough to simply
reaching the Rome-Pescara line and waiting for spring to resume the advance,
Montgomery was still curiously sanguine. In a letter to Dempsey, he commented,
"I am bringing 1 Canadian Div round to the Coastal Axis; they will replace 78 Div
who must have a rest. We will now see the Canadians and the New Zealanders
competing as to which division can first get to the Pescara River; quite a good
contest!!"[63] Or perhaps he just wanted to sound sanguine with his subordinate.
Whatever the motivation, Montgomery shuffled the Canadians to the Adriatic coast
at the beginning of December.

Allfrey ordered Vokes to get his division across the Moro as quickly as possible.
Accordingly, between 1 December and 4 December, Vokes brought his division
(less 3 CIB, which had yet to be relieved in the area north of Campobasso) across
the Sangro to relieve the spent units of 78 Division and then close to the east bank
of the Moro River (see Map 6).[64] Hoffmeister's 2 CIB moved to the Moro, opposite
Villa Rogatti and San Leonardo on 4 December.[65] A day later, 1 CIB took over the
terrain stretching from San Leonardo to the coast. Previous attempts to cross the
Moro had failed due to the strength and determination of enemy defences, so
Vokes used what little time he had to send patrols, with engineers, to reconnoitre
"three main crossing places – coast rd [road], main axis [i.e., the road that led to
San Leonardo], and ROATTI [sic]."[66] At this point, Vokes's main effort was in the
centre, at San Leonardo, the attacks on the coast and on Rogatti being diversions
intended to draw enemy away from the main axis and so clear the way for a thrust
to the crossroads (code-named "Cider") two miles southwest of Ortona. As Vokes
recalled, "My object was to establish one of my brigades in the area of the ["Cider"] X rds at the earliest moment with a view to a subsequent move, first on
TOLLO and then on ORTONA."[67] That estimate was overly optimistic, probably
based too much on the experience of the relatively easy October march to the
Biferno, when the division advanced forty miles in two weeks. The Moro and
Ortona-Orsogna Line were different: the Germans intended to *hold* these positions, not simply use them to *delay*. As noted earlier, Vokes had plenty of company
in his hopefulness; Montgomery and Allfrey shared the same view.

On 5 December, after he had digested the information provided by the previous
night's patrols, Hoffmeister outlined his plan for crossing the Moro at 2:45 p.m.[68]
Despite the tremendous firepower he had at his disposal – all of 1 CID's guns, the
fire of part of 1 Army Group Royal Artillery and two battalions of tanks from 4
(British) Armoured Brigade – Hoffmeister opted for a silent attack; that is, "there

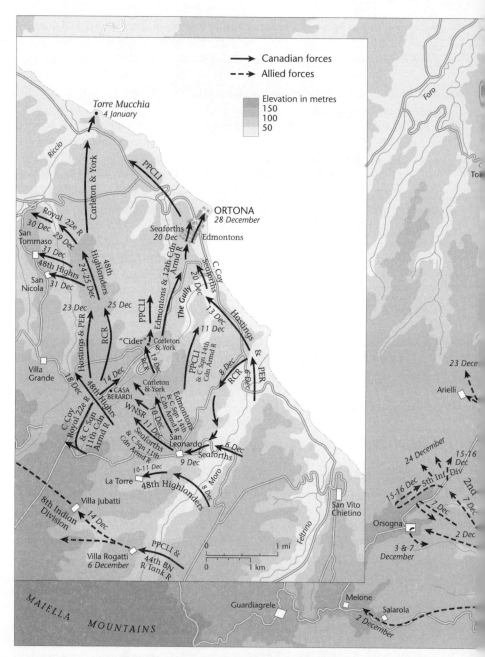

MAP 6   *The Adriatic sector, 28 November 1943 to 4 January 1944.* Adapted from G.W.L. Nicholson (Lieutenant-Colonel), *The Canadians in Italy, 1943-1945* (Ottawa: Queen's Printer, 1966), map 11.

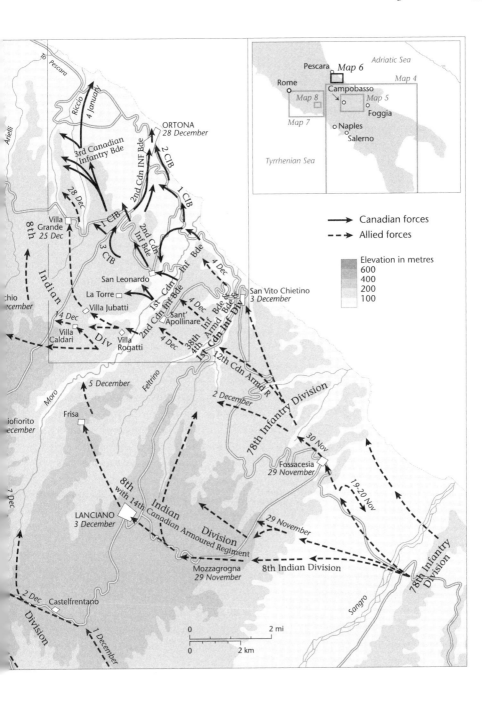

was no barrage or preliminary concentration to lessen the surprise effect of [the] attack."[69] The plan called for the Loyal Edmonton Regiment to form a firm base on the east side of the river while the other two battalions simultaneously secured bridgeheads on the far side – the Seaforths on the main road leading to San Leonardo, the PPCLI at Villa Rogatti. Once the two lodgements had been gained, Hoffmeister wanted to bolster the strength of the two bridgeheads by moving the two battalions of tanks (one to each bridgehead) and anti-tank weapons across the river at first light on the morning of 6 December. Depth artillery strikes – on the "Cider" crossroads and the town of Tollo – pounded suspected enemy artillery positions and reserve concentrations. Finally, to assist Hoffmeister's brigade, Vokes arranged a diversionary attack by 1 CIB along the coast two hours prior to the 2 CIB crossings. The hope was that this action would draw enemy attention away from the main effort at San Leonardo.

The assault across the river unfolded as planned. Moving along an unguarded mule track that their reconnaissance patrols discovered the previous evening, the Patricias slipped silently to the outskirts of Villa Rogatti before encountering any enemy.[70] Catching the Germans completely by surprise, Ware's troops blasted through the perimeter defences, and then cleared the village of its defenders.[71] It was not long, however, before the enemy realized the extent of the penetration and counterattacked in force. On the morning of 6 December, the infantry of 90 Panzer Grenadier Division, supported by artillery and mortar fire, assaulted the precarious PPCLI foothold. In an action that earned him the Distinguished Service Order, Ware reorganized his companies for the defence of the town, moving from company to company, often under mortar and machine-gun fire, to tie down his position. After the PPCLI absorbed the first onslaught, eight tanks and a mule train with much-needed ammunition arrived at 9:30 a.m. and saved the day. Soggy ground and the now chewed-up state of the mule track prevented any more of the supporting tanks from making it up the Moro escarpment, but those that did slog their way to Ware's position were instrumental in stopping the enemy counter-attack cold. Four more such counterattacks, all of which included tanks, failed to destroy the lodgement. Hoffmeister ordered Ware to consolidate his position and hold.

Difficulties with the Seaforth attack on the division main axis rendered the PPCLI foothold at Rogatti all the more important. Lieutenant-Colonel Douglas Forin's companies did make it across the river unscathed, but once they tried to advance up the slopes towards their objective, extremely heavy fire from enemy mortars and machine guns pinned them down.[72] The road junction at San Leonardo was critical to the defensive line along the Moro, and the Germans intended to hold it. They used machine guns, they used mortars, and they used tanks to drive the attackers back. The Seaforths clung to their tiny toehold on the west bank, but only with the help of artillery and the direct fire of tanks and anti-tank weapons from the east bank. When efforts to push tanks and anti-tank weapons across the river proved impossible, so too did the prospect of expanding the bridgehead. As Forin later reflected, "The weakness of the plan of course, was that no prospects existed of getting the tanks across the stream that day or night, nor as a matter of fact, the next day if the Germans controlled the bridge crossing with their arty [artillery] fire in the same volume as the previous night [which prevented engineers from putting in a bridge for the tanks], and an excellent tank run existed ... for the Germans [to move forward and fire on advancing infantry]."[73] Hoffmeister, who had watched the day's developments from his tactical headquarters on the high ground immediately northeast of the Seaforth crossing site, recognized the problem and re-adjusted his plan.[74]

Because his plan to reinforce the PPCLI success at Rogatti would mean shifting the division's main axis to the west, Hoffmeister sought Vokes's permission to abandon the thrust on San Leonardo.[75] Vokes agreed, and Hoffmeister gave orders on the evening of 6 December for the Seaforths to withdraw from their bridgehead on the west bank, which they did early on 7 December. The Edmontons then moved to a position across the river from Rogatti. From there, with the assistance of tanks, they would cross the river, expand the PPCLI lodgement, and strike out to cut the Ortona-Orsogna lateral. By this action, Hoffmeister intended to outflank the enemy in the area of San Leonardo. Had it been accomplished, this move might also have turned enemy defences in a feature known as the "Gully," one mile south of Ortona.

But the action never took place, for two reasons. The first was best explained by Vokes: "The route which the PPCLI and their tanks had followed would not do to build and sustain an attack in strength. Feasibilty [sic] would hinge on whether the demolished road bridge could be restored with a Bailey Bridge."[76] Unfortunately, Canadian engineers proved incapable of erecting a bridge at the proposed site. They assessed – incorrectly as it turned out – that the banks of the river were so steep that they rendered the launching of a Bailey bridge "impossible."[77] Second, the corps commander, Charles Allfrey, believed that the attacks had petered out, not due to the appalling condition of the rain-soaked ground, but due to the division being too widely dispersed, and insufficiently supported by the concentrated fire of a "proper" artillery barrage. Accordingly, he narrowed Vokes's frontage, restricting the Canadian division to the space between Sant' Apollinare and the coast, and ordered the Canadians to try again, this time with a stronger, more-concentrated set-piece attack.[78]

Allfrey, an artillery officer by training, showed a very poor appreciation for arms other than his own. Getting a foothold on the enemy side of the obstacle was not the problem; holding it was. Whether by stealth or by fire, infantry could gain lodgement. But because the Germans always counterattacked, usually with armour, the rapid build-up of friendly tanks or anti-tank weapons was crucial. Without a bridgehead, there could be no breakout; without anti-tank weapons, there could be no bridgehead; without solid bridges, tanks and anti-tank weapons could not make it to the bridgehead. It was at once that simple, and that difficult.

At noon on 7 December, Hoffmeister warned his battalion commanders of the change in plans. That allowed for preliminary moves, including the relief of the PPCLI at Rogatti by a unit from 8th Indian Division. He gave formal orders at 8:30 a.m. the following morning, explaining the plan of his superiors in detail. This was important, especially to Ware, whose battalion had suffered eight killed and sixty-nine missing or wounded in the fight for Rogatti, only to turn over the town to a unit from another formation. More than ever, that battalion needed to believe it was fighting for a purpose. Hoffmeister understood that without faith in a higher plan, PPCLI morale would plummet. Accordingly, he explained that the entire operation was to be supported by massive fire: all 1 CID artillery, 8th Indian Division artillery, 1 Army Group Royal Artillery, thirteen squadrons of Kittyhawk bombers, two cruisers, and six destroyers.[79] With the support of that fire, the division scheme of manoeuvre called for 1 CIB to consolidate the bridgehead – the Royal Canadian Regiment (RCR) attacking laterally from a tiny 1 CIB foothold near the coast to San Leonardo, the 48th Highlanders striking across the Moro to San Leonardo from the southwest. Once 1 CIB had secured the bridgehead, Vokes wanted 2 CIB to break out and grab the "Cider" crossroads.

To do that, Hoffmeister conceived a three-phase operation. First, he tasked the Seaforths with securing the left flank by seizing the high ground northwest of San Leonardo, and he gave them a squadron of the Calgary Tank Regiment to do it. In the second phase, he gave the Loyal Edmonton Regiment and its supporting tanks the job of capturing the "Cider" crossroads. In the last phase, he envisioned either the PPCLI or the Seaforths, with tank support, exploiting to Ortona. Perhaps drawing on his early-August experience with Booth Force, he also directed that, "one tk [tank] will be made available to each bn comd [battalion commander] for comd purposes."[80] In all phases, Hoffmeister held a second tank battalion, the Ontario Regiment, in reserve.

As was often the case, not everything went according to plan, and quick changes had to be made. The 1 CIB attacks of 8 December failed to secure the entire bridgehead. The 48th Highlanders managed to capture their immediate objective across the river without too much difficulty, but enemy machine guns, artillery, and counterattacks stopped the RCR short of San Leonardo, despite the heavy weight of indirect fire support. At this stage, because 3 CIB had still not rejoined the division, Vokes had little choice but to commit 2 CIB (his breakout force) to complete the task of securing the bridgehead. Hoffmeister, who had co-located his tactical headquarters with that of the 1 Canadian Armoured Brigade (the parent formation of the Calgary Tanks and the Ontario Regiment), adjusted his plan accordingly, and called his battalion commanders forward to convey the changes.[81] Instead of securing the left flank, he assigned the Seaforths, now supported by a full regiment of tanks, the task of assaulting San Leonardo from the front and capturing the town. The Edmontons were to occupy a position in the bridgehead line south of San Leonardo, and the PPCLI was to commit one company to the immediate defence of the bridgehead site, while its other three companies remained in reserve on the east bank. Before these assaults, which Hoffmeister scheduled to begin at first light on 9 December, engineers worked furiously to make the crossing site suitable for tanks.[82]

It was not an easy fight, but the next day's events went according to plan, due in large part to close cooperation between the combat arms in Hoffmeister's brigade. When the Seaforths crossed the Moro, they did so with one company mounted on the lead squadron of tanks.[83] In accordance with Hoffmeister's direction, their commanding officer travelled in a B Squadron vehicle with his battalion "18 set" radio and its operator on board.[84] Much as Hoffmeister had done in the Salso River valley, Forin effectively arranged for himself the means to stay in immediate contact with both the tanks *and* the infantry under his command. And because Hoffmeister was similarly co-located with Brigadier R.A. Wyman, the commander of the armoured brigade, infantry-tank cooperation was complete at company, battalion, and brigade levels. From an observation post overlooking the bridge, the two brigadiers watched the operation unfold, issuing direction to their units as required.[85] Artillery cooperation was also woven in. Forward observation officers (FOOs) travelled with the leading companies and squadrons. The artillery representative to the Seaforth commanding officer had a tank/18-set arrangement identical to Forin's. Hoffmeister's tactical headquarters, as it always had, included the commanding officer of the supporting artillery regiment. Close infantry-armour-artillery cooperation contributed largely to 2 CIB capturing all of its objectives by nightfall on 9 December.

With 1 CIB dispersed along the length of the Moro escarpment and 3 CIB still en route from the Campobasso area, Vokes had little choice but to order Hoffmeister's brigade to break out of its own bridgehead. Hoffmeister's plan to do that called for the Edmontons and a squadron of tanks to seize the "Cider" crossroads, an action that was to be followed by the exploitation of the PPCLI towards Ortona. The Seaforths, much in line with the original plan, would secure the left flank in the west. At first, the Edmontons' advance appeared to be going well. In fact, at 10:00 a.m. they reported, "We are now proceeding on final objective."[86] Based on that report, Hoffmeister, from the same observation post he had occupied the previous day, told the PPCLI to get ready for a move through the Loyal Edmonton Regiment and an advance on Ortona. But the Edmontons were nowhere near the "Cider" crossroads. They were still nearly a mile south of Ortona – something that Jefferson, who stayed with his headquarters, could not confirm.[87]

Heavy fire from the Edmonton right flank, from a terrain feature known as the Gully, stunned Jefferson's soldiers and abruptly halted their advance (see Map 6, p. 92). With a width that ranged from 200 yards at the Adriatic to 80 yards where it met the road that joined San Leonardo to the Ortona-Orsogna lateral, the 200-yard deep Gully was ideally suited to the defence (see Figure 6.3). German positions sited at the bottom of both slopes provided not only excellent locations from

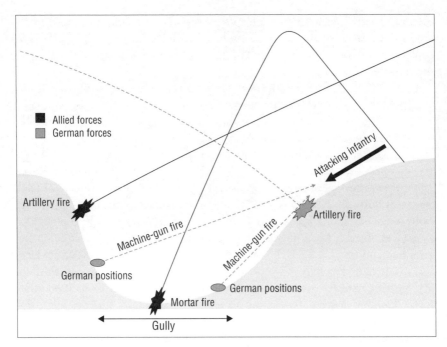

FIGURE 6.3 *The reverse slope defensive position*

which to ambush any would-be attackers that crested the lip of the ravine, they protected the German defenders from artillery fire, the trajectory of which carried rounds safely over their heads to the western slopes behind them. Vineyards also provided covered approaches for German infantry to move onto the eastern lip of the great trench and rake the plateau known as Vino Ridge. These were the tactical problems the Gully presented. That was why it took the Canadians nearly ten days to breach it.

Neither Hoffmeister nor Vokes appreciated fully the strength of this position.[88] Intelligence reports had indicated that enemy intentions were to impose delay, then abandon the Ortona sector for defences on the next set of river obstacles – the Riccio or the Arielli.[89] So when the Edmonton Regiment bumped into the Gully defences, they treated it as just another delaying position, Vokes ordering 2 CIB to clear the length of the position. Hoffmeister stayed with his original plan of manoeuvre – driving the Edmontons straight ahead, bringing the Seaforths up on the left flank, and sending the PPCLI to the northeast along Vino Ridge, but nothing worked. Heavy artillery support failed to affect the enemy sheltered on the reverse slope of the Gully. The high-angle fire of mortars was able to hit some enemy positions, but not in sufficient weight to dislodge the German infantry from their trenches. Mines and mud impeded the movement of the supporting tanks. And enemy machine guns and artillery exacted a terrible toll on the advancing infantry.

The entire enterprise at the Gully was a departure from the Eighth Army manner of doing business – mostly due to haste. Montgomery harried Allfrey; Allfrey harried Vokes; and Vokes harried Hoffmeister into attacking without the benefit of extensive reconnaissance – all at a time when they had run into a position the Germans intended to hold. Attacks went in without sufficient knowledge of how many enemy were there and how they were defending. Thus, Hoffmeister dissipated his combat power in what amounted to three concurrent but separate battalion attacks, the supporting artillery forced to support three attacks at once. At a time when he needed to concentrate his combat power, haste made him drive blindly forward.[90] Moreover, with all three battalions engaged, he had little flexibility for the timely reinforcement of whatever successes may have occurred. Why he did this is unclear. Perhaps his intention was to use his battalion attacks as reconnaissance in force, to determine enemy strengths, identity, and intentions. But it is more likely that he believed he had hit another in a series of delaying positions that would be conceded when pressed, a perception that took several days to prove wrong. Four days after the Edmontons had banged into the Gully defences, the 2 CIB war diarist captured how rapidly the situation could change: "The enemy picture has now become somewhat clearer since Nos 2 and 3 bns, 3 Para Regt [Parachute Regiment] have been identified by PW [prisoner of war] on our front ... It is apparent that the enemy having committed all available tps [troops] of 90 PG [Panzer Grenadier] Div incl the Recce [reconnaissance] Unit, Engrs [Engineers] and the "Kitchen Sink". He has now given depth to his def by reinforcing them with the Para Regt."[91] The Germans threw more guns into the sector as well, tripling the number of artillery batteries from 26 to 76 between 8 December and 10 December.[92] These were definite indications of the enemy's intention to hold the line. By the time this all became clear, however, 2 CIB had launched several unsuccessful assaults on the Gully and sustained very heavy casualties. It hurt. In the PPCLI, for example, "'C' Coy has been so weakened by casualties – they are now down to a strength of thirty all ranks and it is no longer practical to work on a four company basis. 'C' and 'B' coys are therefore to combine under the title 'B' Coy."[93] Bashing ahead blindly cost the Canadians dearly.

This makes Vokes's persistence all the more incomprehensible. After numerous battalion attacks had failed to capture "Cider," Vokes sent the newly arrived 3 CIB straight into the fray. In effect, Vokes reinforced failure with a just-one-more-push approach to breaching the Gully. Even after the blunting of the 2 CIB attacks, and the realization that the defences had been reinforced with troops from a German parachute division, Vokes ordered four separate battalion attacks on the same defensive line between 13 and 15 December. Eventually, after sustaining appalling casualties, 3 CIB gained a foothold at Casa Berardi, which helped turn enemy defences. Following that grim success, 1 CIB launched several attacks towards

"Cider" and Villa Grande on 18 December, attacks that finally forced the enemy to give up the Gully. Later that day, with the position in the Gully turned, Allfrey "ordered Vokes to put the RCR on to their objective [the "Cider" crossroads] with a fire plan, afterwards to exert full pressure with Hoffmeister towards Ortona."[94]

No one questioned the wisdom of assaulting into the streets of the town, least of all Hoffmeister: "At the time I was given my orders for Ortona, it [the town] was represented to me as being a vital spot that would play a most important role in Eighth Army communications and supply, in that there was a rail center and a port where ships could operate, and that it was most important in the administrative scheme of things. I never questioned it at any time. I was given my orders and we got on with it."[95] Ortona never turned into the administrative centre that division and corps staffs had hoped it would become. Eight days of fighting eventually reduced the town and its facilities to rubble. It hardly justified the cost. Not until after the battle did anyone ask, "Would it not have been better to bypass Ortona completely?"[96] Reflecting on what was gained, Syd Thomson, the man who commanded the Seaforths during the battle of Ortona, stated simply, "In hindsight, it [Ortona] was not important; we should have bypassed it."[97]

The limited operational utility of Ortona notwithstanding, few thought much about how the town should be taken either. Fighting inside the town would almost have been easier if the enemy had been denied the ability to reinforce and resupply positions inside it. Simply put, Ortona should have been cut off by a left hook behind the town before it was assaulted frontally. Halfway through the battle, the Loyal Edmonton Regiment would hit on the reason why: "[The] enemy does NOT show any sign of weakening. Interrogation of wounded PW [prisoners of war] we discovered that 40 to 50 of them arrived in town at 2200 hrs last night to reinforce this position. They came from some fwd camp 3–5 kms NORTH of ORTONA."[98] Allowing the enemy the luxury to relieve tired troops and reinforce defensive positions at will led to tougher fighting for the Canadians – much tougher.

At the time, however, no one saw the need to isolate Ortona before entering the town because no one anticipated how tenaciously the Germans would hold it. As noted previously, intelligence sources anticipated that the loss of the Gully would force an enemy withdrawal to the Arielli River, three miles north of the town. A 5th Corps intelligence summary, dated 18 December, sheds some light on what commanders from Allfrey to Hoffmeister expected: "ARIELLI however is strongly held as is ORSOGNA, both places by parachutists. Indeed the parachutists having temporarily stopped the gaps at various points along the front are now holding key positions in order to cover the withdrawal of formations which might not otherwise be able to extricate themselves."[99] Normally, soldiers assigned to covering withdrawals did not stay long, just long enough to let the retiring force pass through. According to this line of logic, the German paratroopers should have withdrawn to positions north of Ortona. That was the intelligence prediction, but that was not what happened. By 21 December, the fresh 1st German Parachute

Division had taken over the coastal sector. They stayed and tenaciously contested the seaside town. In fact, their reinforcement of the area would probably have required the concentrated effort of Allfrey's entire 5th Corps to drill a hole through the German line west of Ortona, but that was not clear at the time. Thus, the idea of "cutting the coast rd [road] NORTH of ORTONA and forc [forcing] the enemy to withdraw the strong def of the town" did not occur to anyone until well after 2 CIB was engaged in a house-to-house fight with German paratroopers.[100]

None of this was obvious when, on 20 December, Hoffmeister assaulted Ortona with the support of a tank regiment (the Three Rivers Regiment), an anti-tank battery, and the full weight of divisional artillery (see Map 6, inset). He assaulted from two directions, the main attack coming from the Loyal Edmonton Regiment, which advanced closely behind a timed artillery barrage, from "Cider" to Ortona.[101] The Seaforths, who had relieved the Hastings and Prince Edward Regiment along the coastal road south of Ortona, drove towards the town from the south. Concurrent with these two actions, the PPCLI moved to the north side of the Gully to protect the brigade's left flank from enemy counterattack.

Hoffmeister, as was his custom, controlled things from his tactical headquarters. However, unlike past operations, this time the tactical headquarters was never static. At first, he located himself "about 2000 yards short [south] of Ortona," a position from which he had a "marvelous view" of the battle.[102] He could see the Edmontons and the Seaforths converging on the town; at one point, he intervened to prevent the units from firing on each other as they simultaneously reached southern approaches.[103] Shortly after the battalions poured into the town and out of sight, Hoffmeister moved his tactical headquarters to the outskirts of Ortona.[104] Because the buildings and rubble of the town limited fields of observation to a hundred yards or less, no single position could give Hoffmeister the view he needed to get an adequate feel for the battle. That made it necessary to keep moving about. One member of the tactical headquarters described Hoffmeister's routine: "During the morning the Brigadier [Hoffmeister] breezed into town, right up to the forward troops and very nearly got hit. He did this every morning during the ORTONA fighting."[105] A dangerous way of doing business, but it suited the tactical situation.

Ortona was a different kind of battle, one fought in the streets of a town of 10,000 people. As Syd Thomson, the commanding officer of the Seaforth Highlanders explained, an urban operation was relatively easy to plan: "It was very simple. Actually, it's probably the simplest of any kind of operation, town-fighting ... because the [terrain] features were sitting right there on the map in front of you, or the [air] photos, and we could say we own this house and not that one. Next day we'd decide to take this one or that street, and so on."[106] That was essentially how Hoffmeister made his plan and assigned sectors to his battalions. When he determined that a single battalion would not be able to take the town, he simply divided the town along the Ortona-Orsogna lateral, which ran roughly north-south.

The Seaforths took the western half, leaving the Edmontons to clear the eastern portion of the town. The PPCLI remained in reserve. The difficulty of the fight owed to the nature of urban fighting and the advantages it offered the skilled German defender. A 1 CID after-action report described the challenge the attackers faced at Ortona: "All roads, except those leading into the pre-selected 'killing grounds,' were blocked by demolished houses which formed admirable barricades. These piles of rubble were in such a position that they could be covered [by machine-gun fire] from above and from the rear, as well as from the front ... The rubble would normally be liberally sowed with mines and booby traps ... Houses, which were not occupied, were booby trapped ... The main tank approaches, naturally limited to streets, were covered by A Tk [anti-tank] guns sited to fire at short range."[107]

The effect on attacking forces was obvious: "Except under the best conditions tps did not work along the streets, but worked their way from house to house. In some cases 'mouse-holing' [blowing holes through walls of connected buildings] was necessary, which generally being done by hand, took some time."[108] Add to this the ability of the German defenders to reinforce and re-supply their positions at will, and the problem of ousting the enemy from Ortona became even more daunting.

From a technical standpoint, beyond the allocation of battalion sectors and deciding when to commit his reserve, Hoffmeister had minimal ability to influence the battle. This was no battle for the massed use of firepower he had come to favour. That only created more rubble, enhanced the obstacles, and made vehicle movement more difficult. To compound the problem, foul weather prevented the Desert Air Force from bombing enemy concentrations north of Ortona.[109] It was no battle of manoeuvre either. Hoffmeister did not have the troops to assault the town *and* cut it off; even Vokes had difficulty mustering the strength to drive a force west of the town to sever the main German supply route from the north. Instead, Hoffmeister's battalions fought a very decentralized fight, one in which single tanks inched forward to blast away at enemy anti-tank guns while handfuls of soldiers moved from house to house, rooting the enemy out of their strong points.

This was a battle of wills – a human struggle that exacted a high human cost – and it presented Hoffmeister with some of his greatest challenges as a commander. In the period 20-29 December, 2 CIB sustained a total of 305 killed, missing, or wounded.[110] That total combined with the brigade's 438 casualties at the Moro and the Gully amounted to a sum greater than the strength of an entire battalion.[111] But those aggregates only tell part of the story. Most of the casualties came from the three infantry battalions, most of them from the main fighting elements of the battalions, the rifle companies. Worse still, a large percentage of the killed and wounded were non-commissioned officers and officers. Reinforcements arrived on 23 December, but by that time 2 CIB was feeling the weight of the losses. On 21

December, the Loyal Edmonton Regiment had to reorganize from a battalion of four companies to a three-company order of battle. The loss of so many leaders also had an impact on morale. One soldier reminisced that during the fighting he had no desire to advance beyond the rank of private because the normal progression was "private, lance-corporal, corporal, corpse!"[112] Realizing that the December casualties had the ability to bleed his brigade of its fighting spirit, Hoffmeister directed the greater part of his command effort to maintaining morale.

With soldiers fast figuring the odds of getting killed or wounded, keeping men motivated meant being well forward and sharing their risks. Hoffmeister did that, and often, to good effect. The recollection of Jock Gibson, a rifle company sergeant-major with the Seaforth Highlanders, who came across Hoffmeister at a forward location during the Ortona battle, makes the point: "I just couldn't believe my eyes – seeing a brigadier in the middle of a battle."[113] Hoffmeister had ventured ahead of the Seaforth battalion headquarters to get a better appreciation of what was happening. He knew Gibson, who had served in his company in England, and he half-jokingly jibed at the scruffy and tired sergeant-major, "You didn't shave today, did you Jock?" Gibson responded, "No Sir, I've been a bit busy."[114] It was soldier's sarcasm, a bit of humour between two individuals in the middle of much death and destruction; but it perked up Gibson's morale. Gibson has recounted this story many times, but never has he failed to mention that the brigadier addressed him not by his rank, but by his nickname – something that Hoffmeister rarely did.[115] At a time when Gibson needed it, Hoffmeister connected with him on a personal level and demonstrated that they were in it together. Gibson went back to fighting. So did Syd Thomson, who described how one particular visit from the brigadier affected him. Thomson was exhausted and Hoffmeister had come forward, ostensibly to gather information on the progress in the battle, but there was more to it than that: "On this particular day, Bert came into Ortona and said, "Great show, Syd, terrific show, you are doing great." He patted me on the back when all I wanted to say was, "For Christ's sake Bert, can't I have a rest[?]" There was no way I could say that to him. He was so great that way ... I was so impressed with the way he inspired and put so much spirit into people. You couldn't say no to him."[116]

Hoffmeister thought about the human factor. He thought about it a lot. On 23 December he visited a field hospital at San Vito Chietino.[117] There he found medics and army surgeons working round the clock to repair the wounded in an abandoned school. But the wounded were many – they crowded the rooms and hallways – and the medical personnel could only do so much. This disturbed Hoffmeister: "They still had the original blood from their wounds on their faces and their hands." Given the circumstances, this was understandable, but Hoffmeister knew that a wounded soldier, if he was to survive, not only needed medical treatment for his injuries, he needed the will to go on – something made more difficult by a foreboding sense of abandonment. He needed to be washed, spoken to, and reassured, and that was clearly beyond the capabilities of the overburdened medical staff. Hoffmeister also knew that the soldiers still fighting needed to believe that they would be well looked after, if ever they fell. Without that sense of security, tapping what Montgomery called those "great emotional forces" would have been difficult. After discussing the issue with one of the surgeons, Hoffmeister sent a request through the medical chain of command for nursing volunteers to come forward and provide comfort for the wounded. Regulations precluded women from being that close to the fighting, but these were extenuating circumstances and there was no shortage of volunteers. The next day, a contingent of British nursing sisters arrived from a medical facility south of the Sangro River. "Working under shell fire and within range of long-range German mortars,"[118] these nurses helped to an extent that would have been impossible to measure.

In battle, soldiers not only wanted to know their leaders cared about them; they also wanted to know what was going on. Hoffmeister knew that. He had long believed that adequate information could mitigate the fear of the unknown. The 2 CIB Intelligence Log recorded the passage of many situation reports from Hoffmeister's headquarters on current enemy identifications and dispositions, the movement of civilians, and the progress of flanking formations.[119] On 22 December, for instance, the following message went to all units in the brigade group: "Bde Comd directs [that] all ranks be warned of German TELLER MINES and BOOBY TRAPS in rubble in and around ORTONA."[120] On 24 December, another situation report advised the brigade of 1 CIB's attempt to outflank Ortona to the west. Hope was important too. How much of the information made it to individual soldiers cannot be known for certain. But, based on Hoffmeister's well-established practice of passing as much information as possible to as low a level as possible, the intent was clear: Hoffmeister wanted to assure his subordinates that he was on top of things, and that those above him were as well.

Understanding that victories, however difficult, were crucial to morale, Hoffmeister opted to continue the battle for Ortona, even after Vokes had offered to call it off. After nearly a week of fighting and sustaining heavy casualties, it was an agonizing decision: having to choose between sending even more men to the hospital at San Vito or conceding defeat and admitting that those who had fallen to that point had done so in vain. But Hoffmeister had his reasons:

> I began to see a glimmer of hope; I could see light at the end of the tunnel. Chris Vokes asked me if I would like to quit, and I said "absolutely not, to quit at this time would be letting the brigade down and the effect on the morale of the brigade would be such that it would be just shocking." Furthermore the objective was represented to me as being *extremely* important, one that Eighth Army just must have, and I said nothing has changed as far as 2nd Brigade is concerned[;] we'll see it through, which we did.[121]

Sound as his reasoning may have been, it did not make the decision any easier.

The battle for Ortona proper ended on 28 December. Early that morning, after patrols reported that the enemy had vacated the town, Hoffmeister cancelled his plan to pass the PPCLI through the dwindling ranks of the Loyal Edmonton Regiment.[122] Instead, he moved the PPCLI around the left flank to cut the coastal road north of Ortona. By this time, 1 CIB was preparing to attack San Nicola and San Tommaso, and Vokes was developing plans to send 3 CIB through 1 CIB towards Torre Mucchia on the coast (see Map 6, p. 92).[123]

These actions essentially closed the Adriatic offensive. Montgomery had long since decided to abandon the drive northward, the original goal of which had been to reach Pescara. The weather was too bad, the casualties too many, and the gains too few to continue.[124] The Eighth Army needed an operational pause to rest and reconstitute before restarting offensive operations when the weather cleared. This was certainly true for 1 CID. On 2 January 1944, Allfrey visited 1 CID "and found Chris Vokes writing me a letter, the gist of which is that his division, owing to loss of leaders, casualties, no specialists and the high sickness rate, has made it desirable for the division to go right out of the line and retrain."[125] Having suffered nearly 50 percent casualties in the strength of its rifle companies, Vokes correctly determined that his division "was temporarily unfitted for offensive operations."[126] Most of Allfrey's divisions were similarly depleted. So it was that, by the end of the first week in January 1944, nearly all the formations of the Eighth Army, Hoffmeister's brigade included, adopted a defensive posture to wait out the winter months, integrate reinforcements, and build up supplies before recommencing major offensive operations in the spring.

HOFFMEISTER served another three months as a brigadier, most of it commanding his brigade in a static defence, but the bulk of his fighting experience had come during those first three months with 2 CIB. Technically, he had made only minor adjustments to his modus operandi as he transitioned from battalion to brigade command. For the most part, however, he fought his brigade as he had fought his battalion. He still ran "the show" from a small tactical headquarters, leaving matters of administration to the staff officers in his headquarters. He still operated well forward, where he could see for himself what was happening, and where he could be seen by as many of his men as possible. This particular aspect of his command method earned him a Bar to his Distinguished Service Order: "For coolness, courage and leadership during the period 9/12 December, when his brigade advanced through the MORO bridgehead against heavy enemy resistance. His continued presence in forward positions, under heavy fire, was an inspiration to all his men."[127]

He still preferred to pass on orders from locations where commanders could see the ground over which they would have to operate. And he still stuck to the doctrine he knew. From a human standpoint, the battles of December 1943, if anything, left him even more inclined to do what he could to minimize the loss of life. He was not yet ready to wander far outside the doctrinal template.

Only after the battle was there any indication of how the losses affected him. While visiting the Seaforths early in the new year, he gathered together a few officers, a few "old hands" whom he had known since Vancouver, to toast the dead and pay tribute to their sacrifice. It was an emotional event, as such things invariably were. Hoffmeister said a few words, but they were difficult – because he was crying.[128]

Major-General B.M. Hoffmeister in the turret of his command tank, "Vancouver." Finding the tank too cumbersome to be an effective command-and-control platform, Hoffmeister abandoned it for a scout car midway through the Liri Valley offensive in May 1944. LAC PA20455

Lieutenant-Colonel B.M. Hoffmeister, commanding officer, Seaforth High- landers of Canada. This photograph was taken in August 1943, at the end of the Sicilian Campaign. Within eight months, he would be commanding an armoured division. LAC PA132779

One of Hoffmeister's Seaforth protegés, Syd Thomson, recovers in a North African hospital from wounds sustained during the invasion of Sicily in July 1943. Six months after this picture was taken, Thomson commanded the Seaforths during the Battle of Ortona. LAC e002107552

Commander of the Eighth Army, General Sir Bernard Law Montgomery pins the Military Medal on Corporal Denis Meade of the Seaforth Highlanders. As one of Hoffmeister's radio operators during the Battle of Agira, Meade had set up a radio installation, under fire, so that Hoffmeister could relay messages to his forward companies. "I didn't want to let him down," was Meade's response to why he placed himself in such danger. LAC e002107554

After his battalion won the 2nd Canadian Infantry Brigade sports competition in August 1943, Hoffmeister accepted the "Shell-Casing Cup" from Brigadier Chris Vokes. Hoffmeister admired Vokes, whom he considered a solid soldier and a friend. LAC e002107553

Hoffmeister brings Minister of National Defence Colonel J.L. Ralston to visit the graves of three of his fallen soldiers near Casaeiprano in November 1943. LAC e002107558

TOP *Hoffmeister's Seaforth "Home Boys." Left to right: Captain F.H. Bonnel, Lieutenant-Colonel H.P. "Budge" Bell-Irving, Lieutenant-Colonel Douglas Forin, and Major Syd Thomson. This picture was taken in October 1943, shortly after Hoffmeister had been promoted to command 2nd Canadian Infantry Brigade. LAC e002107557*

RIGHT *Brigadier Hoffmeister, Commander 2nd Canadian Infantry Brigade, discusses combined infantry-tank assaults at the Moro River with the commander of the 1st Canadian Armoured Brigade, Brigadier R.A. Wyman. December 1943. LAC e002107556*

Hoffmeister's superiors: General Sir Oliver Leese, Commander Eighth Army, and Lieutenant-General "Tommy" Burns, Commander 1st Canadian Corps. LAC e002113660

Lieutenant-Colonel Harry Angle (centre) was Hoffmeister's first GSO I at 5th Canadian Armoured Division. He went on to command the British Columbia Dragoons in September 1944. On the left is Lieutenant-Colonel "Chip" Drury. Lieutenant-Colonel Lord Tweedsmuir, Canadian liaison officer to Headquarters Eighth Army, is on the right. LAC e002113661

The division commander briefs his officers, from major to brigadier, on the coming Liri Valley offensive. Hoffmeister was a big believer in "selling" his plan to as wide an audience of subordinates as possible. LAC PA189920

Making sure everyone *is ready. Hoffmeister inspects a military policeman from the 5th Canadian Provost Company.* LAC e002113663

Brigadier Eric Snow (left) commanded 11 Canadian Infantry Brigade during the battles of the Liri Valley. A difficult subordinate, Hoffmeister had him sacked shortly after the offensive ended. Here Snow chats with Lieutenant-Colonel C.W. Gilchrist (centre) and Brigadier J.P.E. Bernatchez (right). LAC e002113662

Hoffmeister poses with two of his key staff officers: Lieutenant-Colonel C.H. "Chip" Drury (centre) and Lieutenant-Colonel W.C. "Clem" Dick (right). Drury served as Hoffmeister's AA and QMG at 5th Canadian Armoured Division. Dick worked for Hoffmeister twice: once as brigade major in the 2nd Canadian Infantry Brigade, and once as GSO I at 5th Canadian Armoured Division. LAC e002107559

Brigadier Desmond Smith, a career armoured officer who commanded 5th Canadian Armoured Brigade under Hoffmeister during the Liri Valley offensive. LAC PA173706

Hoffmeister believed that his success depended on the collective performance of individual soldiers like this one, Private K.O. Earle of the Perth Regiment. Here, Private Earle pauses in the forest north of Arnhem during the 5th Canadian Armoured Division breakout on Operation CLEANSER, an action that won Hoffmeister admittance as a Companion to the Order of Bath. LAC PA166368

Planning the moves of an armoured brigade. Brigadier Ian Cumberland, Commander 5th Canadian Armoured Brigade (left), discusses the final moves of Operation CLEANSER with the commanding officer of his mounted infantry battalion, Lieutenant-Colonel G.C. Corbould, and the commanding officer of the 8th New Brunswick Hussars, Lieutenant-Colonel Jack Eaton, 18 April 1945. LAC PA131033

The face of the enemy. A German prisoner of war captured on 17 April 1945 by the 5th Canadian Armoured Division at Otterloo, Holland. LAC PA166369

Major-General Hoffmeister relaxes with his favourite brigadier, Ian Johnston, in Holland, May 1945. LAC e002107561

A great admirer of Field-Marshal Montgomery, Hoffmeister considered himself a "disciple" of the 21st Army Group Commander. In this photograph, taken after VE Day, Hoffmeister (third from left) poses with "Monty" and other key commanders and staff. To Montgomery's immediate left are Lieutenant-General Charles Foulkes, Commander 1st Canadian Corps, and Brigadier Ian Johnston, Commander 11 Canadian Infantry Brigade. LAC e002107560

5th Canadian Armoured Division tanks lined up at Eelde airport for Exercise FINALE on 23 May 1945. Hoffmeister wanted the soldiers of his division to realize they had been part of something big, so he assembled every part of it in one place. Lord Strathcona's Horse (Royal Canadians) are in the foreground. LAC PA130489

7
Division Command and the Liri Valley

When an army is fighting, the problem of selecting commanders tends to solve itself; success is the criterion.[1]

COLONEL C.P. STACEY, *SIX YEARS OF WAR*, 1966

Things move quickly in war. Success in battle propelled Hoffmeister from battalion to division command in six short months. Then, sixty-eight days after assuming command of the 5th Canadian Armoured Division (5 CAD), he took the untried formation into battle. Two months was not a long time in which to prepare for battle. It may have been longer than the four days he had before leading the 2nd Canadian Infantry Brigade (2 CIB) in combat, but an armoured division was a much more complicated organization than an infantry brigade. It was bigger, it had more pieces, and it had different strengths and weaknesses. The modus operandi that had worked so well at battalion and brigade levels proved less reliable in the more complicated world of armoured division operations, something Hoffmeister learned the hard way in the Liri Valley. In fact, had it not been for his exceptional grasp of the human factors, he might have failed completely. He needed time to adjust to his new environment, to determine what worked for command and control and what did not. He might have done that in training if he had been given more time, but in the spring of 1944, time was in short supply. As had been the case so often in his eleven months of fighting before the Liri Valley offensive, Hoffmeister had to learn his craft on the battlefield.

ON 20 JANUARY 1944, 5th Corps's commander, Lieutenant-General Charles Allfrey suggested to Vokes "that he should go on leave and hand over to Hoffmeister."[2] Having fought steadily since the invasion of Sicily in July, Vokes needed a break. Allfrey recognized that. He also recognized that, of the 1st Canadian Infantry Division's (1 CID's) three brigade commanders, Hoffmeister was the most able officer to steward the formation in Vokes's absence.[3] Vokes knew it too. The Canadian army had not been fighting long to that point, and it was difficult to find Hoffmeister's match in experience and ability among the ranks of Canadian senior officers.

Still, Hoffmeister was not the first choice for command of an armoured division in early 1944. Neither was he second or third. Wanting to plot the succession for Canada's two armoured divisions, 5 CAD and 4th Canadian Armoured Division

(4 CAD), Canadian Military Headquarters (CMHQ) in London sought the counsel of the 1st Canadian Corps commander, Lieutenant-General H.D.G. Crerar. By this point, Crerar knew that he had been earmarked as the successor to A.G.L. McNaughton as commander of the First Canadian Army. He also knew that the man likely to succeed him as corps commander was Major-General E.L.M. Burns, then General Officer Commanding (GOC) 5 CAD. Thus it was only logical that Crerar, in turn, asked Burns for his input on prospective commanders for the divisions in question: "As it may well be that you will inherit the results ... I consider that I must take your views fully into account before a final decision is reached concerning certain very important appointments."[4] Crerar outlined "the 'slates' as I see them" for command of an armoured division in the following priority: Brigadier R.A. Wyman (currently commanding 1st Canadian Armoured Brigade), Brigadier J.D.B. Smith (currently commanding 4th Canadian Armoured Brigade in England), Brigadier G. Kitching (currently commanding 11 Canadian Infantry Brigade), Hoffmeister, and then Brigadier T.G. Gibson. Crerar also added that Lieutenant-General G.G. Simonds, whose advice he had also sought, was "not happy about this" and had suggested that friend and former chief of staff, Kitching, should be first in line. Simonds also suggested "Hofmeister" as the next suitable candidate.

Burns disagreed with Crerar's slate. His 7 February response to Crerar's query was straightforward. Like Simonds, he thought Kitching was most deserving "because of active experience."[5] As his second choice, Burns nominated the ex-Permanent Force armoured officer, Smith. "Hofmeister" and Gibson, he thought, were equally deserving, but third in priority. Interestingly, Burns placed Wyman, the most experienced armoured officer of the lot, last because, as he put it: "I don't think [his] judgment is very sound ... I think [he] could be left where he is for the present." Because neither Burns nor Crerar had fought with Hoffmeister under their command, they had to rely on what they had heard from those who had – Simonds and Vokes.

In the end, it was Hoffmeister's reputation as a fighter that got him the nod for 5 CAD. Kitching went back to England to command 4 CAD and Wyman stayed with 1 CAB a while longer, but Hoffmeister remained in Italy to lead Canada's second armoured division. His eight months of continuous combat experience outweighed Smith's armoured corps background and several months commanding an armoured brigade in training. Being an Eighth Army alumnus did not hurt either. Montgomery's successor in command of Eighth Army, General Sir Oliver Leese told Crerar he would welcome Hoffmeister's appointment. Like his predecessor, Leese was not fond of "outsiders." Crerar's 3 March message to CMHQ hinted at such a course of discussion: "After full discussion with BURNS [I] recommend HOFFMEISTER for comd [of] 5 cdn armd div with acting rank major general. Comd 8 army accepts with approval."[6] Shortly thereafter, Crerar advised Hoffmeister of the coming appointment. Hoffmeister recalled:

I got a signal from the Corps Commander, General Crerar, asking me to meet him at a particular map reference which turned out to be the center of a bridge. As my jeep drew up at one end his drew up at the other and we walked out to the center of the bridge, the two of us, and I saluted. He put out his hand and we shook hands and we sat on the railing of the bridge, and right away he said 'How would you like to take over command of the 5th Canadian Armoured Division.' I said, 'I would sir, when do I take over[?]' ... He said this would be effective immediately, so I made arrangements to move into 5th Armoured Div HQ right away.[7]

Hoffmeister may have been quick to seize the opportunity, but his feelings were undoubtedly mixed. The competitor in him relished the challenge that the new assignment offered, as well as what it said about his success as a battlefield commander to that point. And being selected ahead of a number of ex-Permanent Force soldiers must have made the appointment all the more pleasing. But the sentimentalist in him also found it difficult to leave 2 CIB, the formation in which he had served since leaving Canada in December 1939. It was there that he had learned how to be an officer, and it was there that he had endured nearly nine months of combat. He knew the organization, its leaders, its men, and he liked them. So it was with much sadness that he "said a tearful goodbye to 2nd Brigade and went over to take command of 5th Canadian Armoured Division."[8]

From the time of its November 1943 arrival in Italy to the time that Hoffmeister took command, 5 CAD had spent most of its time just getting organized. It had started with equipment. The nettled negotiations that had preceded the October 1943 decision to send the division and 1st Canadian Corps Headquarters to the Mediterranean had also produced a plan to equip the incoming Canadians with equipment left behind by British units returning to the United Kingdom. The equipment proved inadequate, and efforts to bring new equipment to the Canadians did not produce results until January 1944. Without tanks, armoured units cannot train, let alone fight. There had also been a "revolving door" of commanders. In November 1943, Guy Simonds had replaced Major-General C.R.S. Stein, who medical authorities declared unfit for duty. Simonds was Canada's most able and experienced commander, but he had spent most of his short tenure as GOC sorting out equipment issues. At the end of January 1944, Major-General E.L.M. Burns had succeeded Simonds. Burns had just started into a progressive training program when he was promoted to assume command of 1st Canadian Corps in March. Recently equipped, unexercised, and subjected to several command changes in a short period, the division that Hoffmeister inherited was a very inexperienced one indeed.

Needless to say, taking command of 5 CAD entailed more than the formality of occupying the desk of the outgoing GOC on 21 March 1944. To start, Hoffmeister knew few of the personalities. He knew the general staff officer (GSO) I, Lieutenant-Colonel Harry Angle, who happened to be a pre-war Seaforth, but the remainder of his staff was new to him. More than that, most of his senior staff members were either ex-Permanent Force or RMC graduates. The commander Royal Artillery (CRA), H.A. Sparling, the commander Royal Signals (CR Sigs), A.E. Wrinch, the commander of 5th Canadian Armoured Brigade (5 CAB), J.D.B. Smith, and the commander of 11 CIB, Eric Snow, were all ex-Permanent Force, all RMC graduates. The commander Royal Engineers (CRE), J.D. Christian and the assistant adjutant and quartermaster general (AA & QMG), C.H. Drury, although they were not Permanent Force in the pre-war period, had both graduated from RMC. Hoffmeister walked into an unfamiliar and potentially uncomfortable environment. He also lacked armoured experience and training. As an infantry officer, although he had worked with squadrons and regiments of tanks, he had never commanded them directly, and he had never seen a full armoured brigade, let alone an armoured division, in action. His credibility would definitely be questioned, at least privately. As the senior signals officer for 5 CAD recalled, Hoffmeister's appointment as GOC "came as bit of a surprise because so far as we knew, he hadn't had any armoured experience."[9] These were the human and technical gaps that had to be bridged before the divisional commander could forge his new team into a fighting formation.

Hoffmeister realized that winning over the staff and key commanders of his division was a necessary precursor to whipping his division into fighting form. He needed them, so he avoided rocking his new boat when stepping on board. He accepted the staff as it was, and he accepted the training program that the staff had coordinated prior to his arrival. This allowed him to take the time to identify the strengths and weaknesses of his people. It also helped him steer clear of making the off-putting impression, "Everything you have done to this point is wrong! I would know, because I know best." He took much the same approach with key commanders. During his first meeting with the commander of the 5 CAB, Brigadier J.D.B. (Des) Smith, Hoffmeister confessed, "Des, I know bugger all about armour and I'm going to depend on you."[10] This was a calculated move on Hoffmeister's part. Smith, an ex-Permanent Force armoured officer, and one of the contenders for command of the division, had to have been disappointed that the assignment had gone to Hoffmeister. He needed to be soothed. Hoffmeister might have tried to put Smith in his place, emphasizing his own combat experience to enhance his own credibility. But an I've-been-in-combat-and-I-know-better approach would have been counterproductive. Hoffmeister chose instead to boost the subordinate's credibility and gain a willing follower.

Hoffmeister's approach contrasted sharply with that of another successful Canadian general, Guy Simonds. On assuming command of 2nd Canadian Corps in January 1944, Simonds met with his key staff and stated quite plainly, "Good morning gentlemen. There are some of you in whom I have not much confidence. I will see you all individually the next day and tell you why."[11] He then proceeded to relieve a number of key staff officers and replace them with his own hand-picked individuals. To be fair, Simonds had his reasons. He believed that Canadian soldiers – whom he considered to be the world's best – deserved the most competent commanders and staffs to lead them. And Simonds had neither the patience nor the personality to tolerate those in whom he had "not much confidence." But that was not always how those that worked for him interpreted it. J.D. Christian, who served both Simonds and Hoffmeister as the senior engineer officer in 5 CAD summed up the difference in command styles: "You did a better job for Hoffmeister than you did for [Simonds] because you could talk to him, convince him or concede to him; you couldn't with [Simonds] who knew so much more than everyone else."[12] As Christian noted in his diary for 23 March, "Spent morning preparing note for GOC [Hoffmeister] on existing Engineer problems. Discussed this with him in afternoon and he agrees entirely and is going to try and take immediate action after reference to Corps."[13] Simonds used fear; Hoffmeister built teams.

Also in his favour, Hoffmeister had a well-known reputation as "a very gallant soldier with the Seaforths and 2nd Brigade."[14] Soldiers in 5 CAD may not have known Hoffmeister personally, but they had heard positive things about him. "I knew he had taken over 2 Brigade from Chris Vokes in [1] Div, but he was just a name to me, although I knew him as a good Brigade Commander," was how one member of the 5 CAD staff remembered it. The rank and file had heard of him too. A subaltern in a 5 CAB armoured regiment also testified, "we all knew about his great success with the Seaforths and his long walks [marches] through [Southern] Italy with the Regiment."[15]

First among Hoffmeister's reported qualities was his abundance of that most crucial of soldierly qualities – guts – and he wasted little time in demonstrating that his reputation in that regard had been well earned. On 22 March, less than twenty-four hours after his arrival at 5 CAD, Hoffmeister accompanied the lead infantry companies of 11 CIB as they advanced behind a "creeping" artillery barrage during a live fire exercise. At that point, he had barely conferred with any of his key staff, but he brought most of them along to witness the event. One of them, Lieutenant-Colonel A.E. Wrinch, recalled the exercise and the impression it left on the division:

> The day after Bert arrived, all the Div staff officers and a lot of observers from Corps and various places were going out to an OP [observation post] to observe this exercise. It was due to start and there was no sign of the GOC [Hoffmeister] ... Well the exercise went on, the artillery started on various targets, and the barrages began lifting in timed stages with the infantry behind them. The one person we saw with the black beret leading the troops was Bert Hoffmeister, the brand new GOC. His ADC [aide-de-camp] was with him and Bert was right up behind the barrage ... Bert led the advance all the way, immediately behind the artillery. Obviously that went around the division like a flash; everybody knew that the new GOC really knew what he was doing and was not afraid to show the boys how to do it regardless of the danger. I

really think that that one episode in that little series of exercises had a fantastic effect on the division.[16]

The man who oversaw the artillery shoot for the exercise, Brigadier H.A. Sparling, also commented on the impact of Hoffmeister's actions: "That took 5 Div and their morale just went straight up; a divisional commander who would give that example, going with the lead elements to show them the need to keep close to their supporting fire ... It certainly impressed me; I don't know how many other people would have thought of it."[17] It was not just the commander's example for the infantry that impressed Sparling; it was the faith that Hoffmeister placed in him and all his gunners: "This [type of artillery barrage] is always difficult for a gunner because one always has to be conscious of the possibility of dropping rounds short [onto friendly troops]. There are times when this can happen, an error with one gun, or a troop, or faulty ammunition."[18]

One such mishap happened while Hoffmeister was conducting the exercise. Hoffmeister recounted with humour and humility:

> I'll never forget one of my most embarrassing moments, having given my usual spiel, and having told them [the infantry troops] how important it was to keep right up close to the shell bursts, that the first shell bursts were all forward and there was absolutely no danger. In keeping up, you got to the German positions before they got their heads up, it reduced casualties and so on. There was one company of Cape Breton Highlanders; the barrage was being fired and just tapering off when one round landed behind us. We were all flat on the ground, of course, and ... the hot stuff was flying all around the place, but every soldier in that company looked around at me as if to say, 'OK wise guy, what have you got to say about this?'[19]

Fortunately, no one was injured. Hoffmeister knew the risks, and the fact that accidents could, and did, happen. But he also wanted Sparling and all of his gunners to know that he trusted them – with his life. That kind of thing wins over soldiers and makes them work harder, be they Permanent Force, militia, RMC graduates, whatever.

Of course, the first purpose of that particular exercise was not to present the new GOC with an opportunity to impress his staff, although that was a useful by-product. The staff had designed it to prepare elements of 5 CAD for battle. At the time, the division consisted of only two brigades, one infantry and one armoured (see Figure 7.1). Of the two, only 11 CIB had seen action, and that had not gone well.

On 17 January, 11 CIB had taken part in a "limited" offensive operation as part of a wider effort to hold German forces in the Adriatic sector and prevent their redeployment to the Cassino sector where Alexander, switching his main effort to the west, had hoped to break through the Gustav Line of defences.[20] Far from being an

Commander

Headquarters
(See Figure 7.2)

11 Canadian Infantry Brigade
Perth Regiment
Cape Breton Highlanders
Irish Regiment of Canada

5 Canadian Armoured Brigade
Lord Strathcona's Horse
8th New Brunswick Hussars
British Columbia Dragoons
Westminster Regiment
(Motorized)

Combat Support

Reconnaissance
Governor General's Horse Guards

Artillery
HQ Royal Canadian Artillery 5 CAD
17 Field Regiment
8 Canadian Field Regiment (SP)
4 Canadian Anti-Tank Regiment
5 Canadian Light Anti-Aircraft
Regiment

Engineers
10 Canadian Field Squadron
4 Canadian Field Squadron
5 CAD Bridging Troop

Signals
5 CAD Signals Regiment

Combat Service Support

Supply and Transport
HQ Royal Canadian Army Service Corps 5 CAD
5 CAB Company
5 CAD Division Troops Company

Medical
7 Canadian Light Field Ambulance
13 Canadian Field Dental Services
11 Canadian Field Hygiene Section

Ordnance
5 Canadian Mobile Laundry and Bath Unit
5 CAD Ordnance Field Park

Electrical and Mechanical Engineers
5 CAB Workshop
5 CAD Troops Workshop

Miscellaneous
5 Canadian Provost Company
5 Canadian Field Cash Office
7 Canadian Field Service (Intelligence)
5 CAD Postal Unit
1 Canadian Corps Mule Transport Instructors
Cadre
5 CAD Section Reinforcement Camp

FIGURE 7.1   *5th Canadian Armoured Division, May 1944*

easy introduction to combat for the green brigade, the "Arielli Show," as the action came to be called by the troops, had been a dismal and dispiriting failure.[21] Despite a carefully coordinated artillery fire plan, one that Lieutenant-General Charles Allfrey personally intervened to "put right," the attackers had failed to reach their objectives and suffered 157 casualties while a further 28 had been taken prisoner.[22] Inexperienced troops had attacked seasoned German paratroopers across an open valley and in broad daylight, only to make minimal gains and be withdrawn within hours. One Perth Regiment soldier describes how he and his comrades felt: "It was quite clear to most of us that our glorious attack wasn't going at all well ... Hardly had the echo of the last shell's arrival on their positions faded when they came up out of their dugouts, and popped out of their slit trenches with guns blazing ... Nine hours had gone by and we hadn't done anything worth bragging about. Most of those hours had been spent either hugging the half-frozen ground, or ducking in a slit trench while all hell was going on around us."[23] The effect of the terrifying experience was obvious to this young soldier: "One thing for certain, morale was also taking a beating. It was about as low as it could go. One quick look around at the faces of the guys around me and I could see how low it was."[24] Two months later, after Hoffmeister had assumed command of 5 CAD, the incoming division commander assessed that the Perths had not adequately recovered from the experience.

The Arielli Show had been a disaster, and Hoffmeister "appreciated right away that [his] big task was to rebuild 11 Brigade."[25] Fortunately, the framework for a sound and progressive training program had been put in place in January when 1st Canadian Corps became operational.[26] It was not a perfect program – the business of fighting a war and restricted timelines interrupted the training progression too often for that – but it did follow the now familiar sequence of collective training: a study period, followed by tactical exercises without troops (TEWTs), followed by field exercises.[27] The 5 CAD study period, which Simonds held 3-7 January, was largely a coming together for officers of the various arms of the division, most of whom had not had opportunity to work together prior to that time. The material presented was basic. The organization and roles of the various units, the conduct of an armoured division advance, and attacking across a defended obstacle (like a river) were among the subjects of discussion. But the training sputtered along unevenly as rotations through the line – periods that entailed manning defensive positions and patrolling no-man's land – prevented progression beyond company/squadron level.

By 15 March, however, 5 CAD was out of the line, in reserve, and preparing itself for the much-anticipated 15 Army Group spring drive on Rome. Things had to be done quickly. As a 5 CAD training instruction emphasized, "It is stressed that TIME IS SHORT and all phases of [training] as outlined must be completed by the 2 Apr."[28] The instruction also gave direction on rectifying, quickly, weaknesses within the various units, and on attendance at obstacle breaching and assault river-crossings schools, but the emphasis was unquestionably on all-arms cooperation at the battalion/regimental level and below. Unfamiliarity between infantry, armour, and artillery had been blamed for the debacle at the Arielli in January. Accordingly, the division had its armoured brigade arrange a TEWT designed to improve cooperation between infantry, armour, and artillery. The idea was that officers from tank squadrons and infantry companies would get together with representatives from the supporting artillery regiments to plan attacks, and then test those plans on live-fire exercises.[29]

The result was the SLUGGEM series of exercises. Beginning with a TEWT, rifle company and tank squadron officers worked together in eight- to ten-man syndicates to plan and execute attacks.[30] To test those plans, dry runs involving all of the troops and vehicles from the sub-units concerned followed the TEWTs. Then a live-fire execution of the attack plans, supported by artillery, mortars, anti-tank weapons, and machine guns provided the final validation.[31] The purpose of the SLUGGEM exercises was to develop sound procedures for infantry-tank cooperation, which meant working on methods for communication, command and control, target indication, and battle procedure. Also, because the time available for training was so restricted, the exercise planners deliberately grouped companies and squadrons according to forecasted affiliations. As much as practicable, Perth Regiment companies worked with the Lord Strathcona's Horse, while the Irish Regiment of Canada started an affiliation with the British Columbia Dragoons, and the 8th New Brunswick Hussars and the Cape Breton Highlanders did likewise.[32] The exercises generally went well and did much to mend the morale of 11 CIB's battered battalions.

Hoffmeister inherited this training regimen, but he did supervise the conduct of the exercises closely. He also shoehorned a brainchild of his own into the crammed timetable: a division exercise. With 11 CIB scheduled to depart on 9 April for a month in the line with 2 New Zealand Division near Cassino, he could only arrange for a quick two-day shakeout. Still, Exercise THRUSTER, set for 7-8 April, was an ambitious enterprise with an ambitious scope, designed to ready the division for its part in the coming offensive. Among the activities to be practised were the deployment of infantry and tanks in a set-piece attack, the conduct of joint reconnaissance by infantry and armoured commanders, movement between concentration areas and assembly areas, movement from assembly areas to forming-up places (FUPs), the marrying-up of infantry and armour with supporting arms, such as engineers and anti-tank assets, and the passage of information during the battle.[33] These stated objectives of THRUSTER reflected a logical understanding of what was required for a successful attack: getting all the pieces of the division to the right place, at the right time, and without being seen; ensuring that all those pieces knew how to plan and work together; and making sure that the commander got the information he needed to make good decisions.

In an organization as large as an armoured division, this was not a simple affair. For that reason, it had to be practised and practised again. Getting all the pieces where they were needed required the careful coordination of road movement, which, in turn, meant routes had to be allocated, timings adhered to, and a system for traffic control established. In this regard, the division performed unevenly on THRUSTER. Division and brigade staffs produced solid movement tables to conform to the established routes and timings, but the execution of road movements proved less successful. An umpire's report accused the provost corpsmen (military policemen), those principally responsible for traffic control, of "bad directing."[34] Their "hand signals were "indefinite and confusing" to drivers. But it was not completely their fault. In some instances, they had not received adequate information on which convoys would pass a given checkpoint and when. Obviously, information did not always make it down to the lowest levels in the chain of command, and not just in the provost corps. The umpires reported that many drivers "did not know their destination" either. Predictably, traffic jams ensued, in one case even before the unit had left the concentration area. Lessons were learned, noted, disseminated. Some corrective measures, like 5 CAB's direction that detailed Route Cards be issued on a scale of one per vehicle, helped.[35] But the problem of traffic control stemmed from organizational deficiencies: there were simply not enough provost corpsmen. With little more than 100 men in the divisional provost company – not all of whom could be allocated to traffic control – things could easily go awry, and later did.[36]

Given the time and effort spent on all-arms cooperation during the SLUGGEM exercises, the results of THRUSTER were disappointing. "No marrying-up [between infantry and tanks] noticed" was a common comment in umpire reports.[37] Tanks and infantry did not plan together or establish effective means of intercommunication before the attacks. Thus, during some attacks there was, "no apparent attempt at communication" between tanks and infantry at the company/squadron level.[38] To Hoffmeister and those who planned the training, it must have been maddening. But this was a new formation, and one in which the various arms had not had extensive opportunities to work together. Working together was not yet second nature. It would take more than a few days of field exercises, no matter how good, to build solid combined-arms teams. Only more time in training or the crucible of combat could do that.

For Hoffmeister and his headquarters, the THRUSTER exercise was the only real opportunity to exercise command and control of all 5 CAD formations in the field before the spring offensive. Staff planning, a relatively sterile process, can be practised anytime or anywhere, but testing real command and control requires the full participation of troops – troops that get sleepy, cold, and hungry.

Hoffmeister tried to get the most from his two-day training opportunity. First, the division conducted a preliminary move to a forward assembly area. Next, Hoffmeister gathered his commanders and key staff to give orders for the attack in his usual manner – verbally and in a location from which the ground to be traversed could be viewed. His plan called for 11 CIB to break in to the enemy defences, followed by a 5 CAB exploitation against an enemy force arranged in depth.[39]

The attack portion of the exercise went reasonably well, but THRUSTER, like most of 5 CAD's pre-battle training, was too short. Hoffmeister had barely enough time to identify command and control difficulties, let alone rectify them. Planning the movements and operations of an armoured division is one thing, but doing them is another. Hoffmeister fully intended to continue his practice of running the show from a small and highly mobile tactical headquarters (see Figure 7.2) that included himself, his aide-de-camp (ADC), his senior artillery officer (CRA), a GSO III (captain) staff officer, and occasionally his senior engineer (CRE). The Division Main Headquarters, which consisted of "40-50 vehicles and signals group with a dozen or so more" monitored the battle.[40] The Division Rear Headquarters, containing mostly administrative elements, coordinated the logistical requirements of the formation. A week after THRUSTER, during a smaller scale exercise, TALLYHO, Hoffmeister had two umpires attached to his tactical headquarters and two assigned to the main. But it too was a brief affair, two days in duration, and relatively uncomplicated. The headquarters hardly had opportunity to master the simplest procedures for planning, coordinating, and monitoring operations. Knowing what to do when things went wrong was still a long way off.

If THRUSTER and TALLYHO demonstrated anything, it was that Hoffmeister's division needed more time to train. True, matters would have been much worse had the exercises not taken place, but time constraints forced the quantum leap from company/squadron level training on SLUGGEM to divisional training on THRUSTER. Battalion and brigade training got short shrift. 5 CAB did have one more opportunity (Exercise TALLYHO 14-18 April) to ready itself before preparations for the Liri Valley offensive commenced in earnest, but 11 CIB left for the Cassino sector the day after THRUSTER ended and did not return until 9 May. Soldiers, commanders, and staffs still had much to learn.

In spite of certain technical deficiencies that only time and more training could cure, 5 CAD made significant progress in the human dimension. Soldiers in the brigade liked the training they did in the spring of 1944. After a winter of sitting in trenches and patrolling no-man's land, they welcomed the opportunity to attend the assault river-crossing school or take part in mountain-warfare training: "The stagnant period of static front duty had sapped the strength and stamina we had acquired in a year of intensive training. It wasn't far from the truth to say that we'd become soft after living a good part of the time like gophers in damp, cramped dugouts, unable to stretch or flex our limbs. Only a daily regimen of route marches in the hilly countryside, along with some hard training on schemes would bring us back."[41] Hoffmeister capitalized on that sentiment. The divisional exercise, for all of its difficulties, had to have impressed the soldiers, most of whom had never experienced training at that level. For Hoffmeister, that was a key point:

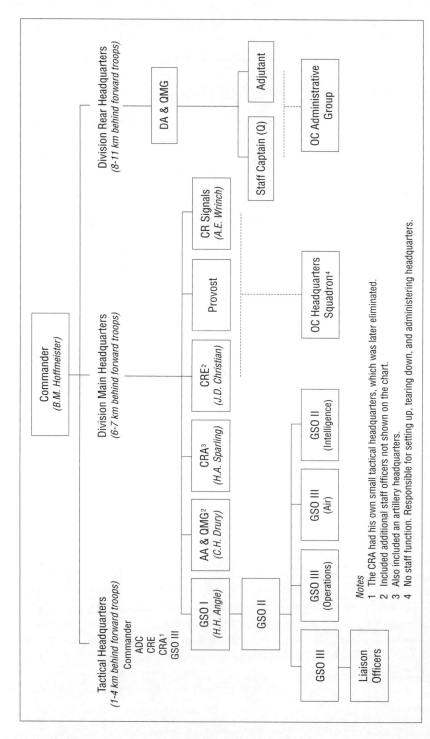

FIGURE 7.2 *5th Canadian Armoured Division headquarters, May 1944*

One thing that would help get the division battle worthy ... was to have a divisional exercise and let them see first hand the formation of which they were a part. The fact that there were these hundreds of tanks there to support them, a SP [self-propelled artillery] regiment, we had tractor-drawn guns, we had the Westminster motor battalion, the Governor General's Horse Guards, the armoured recce regiment. The punch, the clout this division had, was just tremendous, and no person, private soldier, NCO, or officer could fail to be impressed by this."[42]

To bolster morale further, Hoffmeister also spent considerable time visiting units, talking to officers, NCOs, and soldiers.[43] As one commanding officer remembered, "He knew what was going on, he didn't sit back somewhere and wait for news to come."[44] This, in addition to his participation in live-fire training, both surprised and pleased the soldiers. In one soldier's recollection, "There was something about the look on his face, his physical appearance, and the air of confidence he carried with him at all times that told me as it told all of the others that we had a winner here. And when he gave us a short introductory speech, I was convinced then and there that he was a born leader of men."[45] It helped. Soldiers of all ranks and arms soon began to identify with their division, which they coined the "Mighty Maroon Machine" after the colour of the division's square shoulder patch.

But Hoffmeister still worried about the state of one battalion in 11 CIB: the Perth Regiment. The Perths had suffered most heavily in the January Arielli Show and, based on his observations, Hoffmeister concluded that they had not adequately recovered. He wanted to know why. He asked the brigade commander, Eric Snow, to identify the malady and prescribe a remedy, but neither he nor the Perth commanding officer, Lieutenant-Colonel W.S. Rutherford, were capable of doing so. Frustrated, Hoffmeister gave the two officers 48 hours to find a solution, and, when none came, he took matters into his own hands: "I sent out a signal to the regiment saying that at 9 o'clock on a certain morning, in a certain place, I wanted two representatives from each platoon ... not over the rank of lance corporal, and they're to be in that room ready to meet me. I do not want [an] officer there, or NCO, or anyone else. I will be there by myself and I am going to stay there with these men until I find out what the trouble is."[46]

When the selected soldiers finally met with Hoffmeister, there was some understandable hesitation, and perhaps a bit of bewilderment at the unorthodox approach. But after assurances that nothing they said would be recorded, and that the information they offered would help ready the unit for battle, the soldiers began to speak. According to Hoffmeister's recollection, they identified several officers and NCOs who had performed poorly in the Arielli Show and in whom they had "absolutely no confidence." Hoffmeister had those individuals reassigned.[47] Not for the first time, Hoffmeister reached down the chain of command, seeking the counsel of soldiers concerning problems in their unit – he had done it as a Seaforth company commander in England. This was a highly unusual practice, one that most senior officers would have scorned because it circumvented the normal chain of command and potentially undermined the levels in between. But Hoffmeister had long believed in the ability of soldiers to distinguish good leaders from bad. They must have prescribed the right medicine, because the Perths fought gallantly in the weeks and months ahead.

By the second week of May, 15th Army Group was ready for its next major offensive, which Alexander had scheduled "to force the enemy to commit the maximum number of divisions to operations in Italy at the time Overlord [the Allied invasion of Northern France] is launched."[48] That required threatening the Germans with a major breakthrough or the capture of a political prize, like Rome. The stalemate of operations on the Adriatic front, combined with the repeated failure of the Allied Armies to take Cassino, convinced Alexander that only a concentrated drive in the west would break the Gustav and Adolf Hitler lines and give the Allied armies an open run at Rome (see Map 7).[49] His plan was to drive the Fifth US Army towards Gaeta and Terracina, while forces in the Anzio bridgehead stuck out towards Valmontone several days later. The Eighth Army, the bulk of which he shifted south, was to assault in the area of Cassino and advance along the Liri River valley. Allied air forces, which enjoyed a six-to-one superiority, would support these thrusts with interdiction tasks to isolate the battlefield, cutting rail and resupply routes to key German positions.

Leese prepared extensively for the operation. First, he turned over his entire sector to Allfrey and his 5th Corps, which then came under direct command of Alexander's army group headquarters. Then, he moved his army south, painstakingly and with the utmost care assigned to concealing the redeployments from the enemy. Vehicles only moved in the hours of darkness, and Leese also employed an elaborate deception plan, supported by dummy radio traffic and some troop movement, to confuse the Germans as to the disposition and intentions of Eighth Army forces.[50] For the main assault, Leese concentrated heavily on his left flank – the Polish Corps on Cassino and the British 13th Corps on the Liri Valley. 10th Corps, employed in a holding task, occupied a broader and more thinly defended front on the army right. Because he did not have much faith in the untried 1st Canadian Corps headquarters or its commander, E.L.M. Burns, Leese held the Canadians in reserve.

As the army reserve, the Canadians had no specific task, but they had a pretty good idea of what they would be asked to do. A 5 May corps directive stated, "It is practically certain that at some stage it will be necessary to break through an extensive and strongly fortified enemy line."[51] Anticipating that 13th Corps would successfully breach the Gustav Line, Canadian commanders down to unit level studied maps, air photographs, and intelligence reports of the Hitler Line defences (and the Liri Valley approaches to them) at corps and divisional study periods 10-11 May.[52] Of course, the specific site of the Canadian assault could not be determined for certain; that depended on the success or failure of the 13th Corps, or even the

Polish Corps, assaults. But the Canadians looked into the most likely assault areas and tried to anticipate problems. They were not far off their mark.

When the fire of some 2,000 guns announced the start of the offensive on the evening of 11 May, the officers and men of the 1st Canadian Corps were "in Army res [reserve], positioned behind 13th Corps facing the Liri Valley,"[53] waiting for the moment they would be committed to the fight. At first, the 13th Corps assaults did not go well.[54] The assault boat crossings of the Gari River proved difficult, the launching of tank-bearing bridges even more so. However, by 15 May, after much difficult fighting, the 8th Indian Division had established a bridgehead that extended to the town of Pignataro. With two of 13th Corps' divisions blunted by the assaults on the Gustav Line, Leese decided to commit the Canadians to the battle, but he did not give the 1st Canadian Corps sole responsibility for the advance to the Hitler Line. Instead of placing 13th Corp's remaining division (the 78th) under command of the Canadians, he split the advance frontage between the two corps, forcing them to share the available space for movement – and routes. That caused problems in the coming days.

The intricacies of route and terrain management require some comment. In battle, close coordination of the use of available routes was critical for the movement of troops, fighting vehicles, and ammunition – especially in an operational theatre like Italy where serviceable roads were at a premium. For this reason, their use had to be carefully managed from the highest levels. Unnecessary traffic could not be permitted to impede the forward movement of artillery ammunition, for example. But, in order for "unnecessary traffic" to get off the routes, those units had to have places to go. That meant the assignment of assembly areas, off-road, which was not a simple task. The closer one got to the front, the more crowded the terrain became. Guns that were positioned forward to be in range of their targets took up a tremendous amount of space. So too did units in contact with the enemy, and those waiting to take up the advance. The Eighth Army did not manage routes or space well. On 19 May, Burns noted in his diary, "There has been a great deal of difficulty in the last two days over the use of [the] route ... called HEART by Cdn Corps and SPADE by 13 Corps. This is the only practicable route by which to reach the RIGHT bde sector of 1 Cdn [Infantry] Div and also the left sector immediately RIGHT of FORME D'AQUINO of the 13 Corps. [A] conference was held at Tactical [Eighth] Army HQ at which time the route was allocated to 13 Corps."[55]

Stuffing two corps into a corridor with only enough routes to service one corps properly was unwise. That the same route, which was used by two different corps, should have two different names shows that a bad decision was compounded by a lack of Army-level coordination. The coordination conundrum continued down the chain of command. At the corps level, Burns's headquarters permitted 25 British Armoured Brigade to move rearward for refuelling as 5 CAD attempted to move forward and take up the lead in the advance.[56] Since both formations were using the same route, the results should have been predictable and avoidable. One

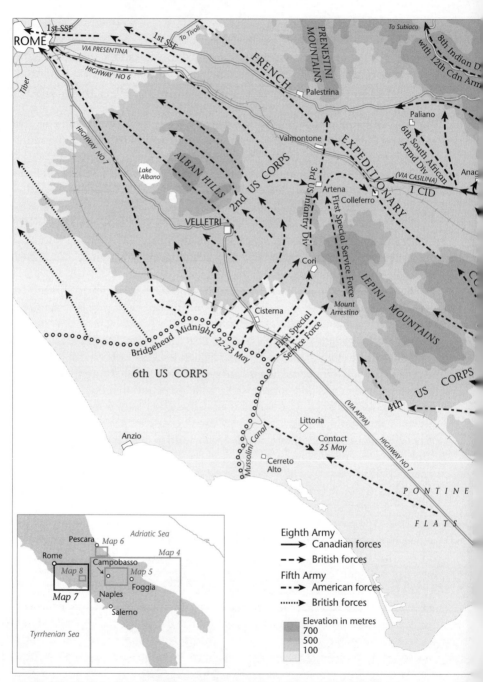

MAP 7   *The battle for Rome, 11 May to 4 June 1944.* Adapted from G.W.L. Nicholson (Lieutenant-Colonel), *The Canadians in Italy, 1943-1945* (Ottawa: Queen's Printer, 1966), map 15.

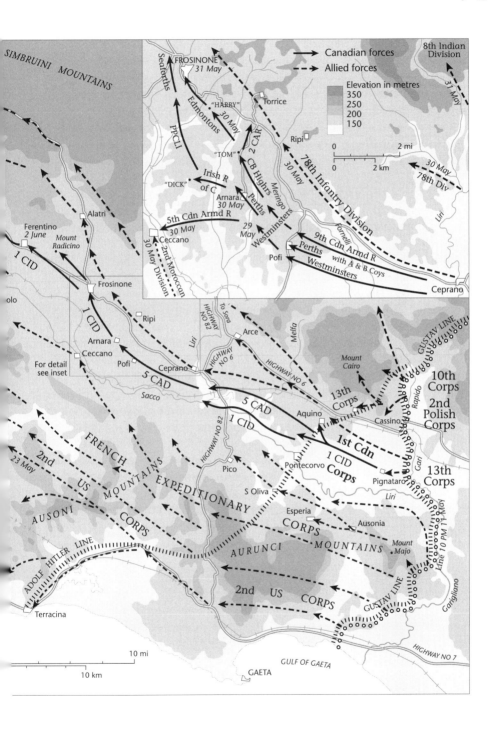

SIMBRUINI MOUNTAINS

8th Indian Division

Canadian forces
Allied forces

Elevation in metres
350
250
200
150

0   2 mi
0   2 km

FROSINONE
31 May

Seaforths

Torrice

"HARRY"
30 May

Edmontons

Ripi

30 May
78th Div

PPCLI

"TOM"

2 CAR

CB Highrs

78th Infantry Division

Liri

"DICK"

Irish R
of C

Perths

Arnara
30 May

Meringo

30 May

5th Cdn Armd R
30 May

29
May

Westminsters

Ceccano

2nd Moroccan
30 May Division

Pofi

9th Cdn Armd R
with A & B Coys

Perths
Westminsters

Tornell

Ceprano

Ferentino
2 June

Mount
Radicino

Alatri

1 CID

Frosinone

1 CID

Ripi

Arnara

Ceccano

Pofi

Ceprano

Liri

olo

For detail
see inset

5 CAD

Sacco

HIGHWAY NO 82

To Sora

Arce

Melfa

HIGHWAY NO 6

HIGHWAY NO 6

Mount
Cairo

10th
Corps

2nd
Polish
Corps

Rapido

FRENCH

2nd
23 May

US

MOUNTAINS

EXPEDITIONARY

5 CAD

1 CID

5 CAD

Aquino

13th
Corps

Cassino

1st Cdn

1 CID
Corps

13th
Corps

HIGHWAY NO 82

Pico

Pontecorvo

Pignataro

Gari

AUSONI

CORPS

S Oliva

Liri

Esperia

Ausonia

CORPS

MOUNTAINS

Mount
Majo

Line 10 PM 11 May

ADOLF HITLER LINE

AURUNCI

2nd   US   CORPS

GUSTAV LINE

Garigliano

Terracina

GUSTAV LINE

10 mi

10 km

GULF OF GAETA

GAETA

HIGHWAY NO 7

formation was coming from the battle, the other going to it. The one about to join the fight should have had priority on the route, and that was clearly not the case. Not that Hoffmeister's staff was above such oversights. The Lord Strathcona's Horse after-action report noted, "on the night of 18/19 May HEART route was jammed with vehs while CLUB route scarcely a mile away was clear."[57]

Despite the mistakes and oversights, Burns committed Vokes's 1 CID to the battle on 16 May. The corps commander intended for Vokes to advance from the bridgehead at Pignataro to the Hitler Line. But the day after Vokes commenced his advance, Burns issued orders for him to keep going and plow into that line of defences. The corps would "breach the HITLER Line and exploit towards Frosinone" – 1 CID to pierce the German defences between Pontecorvo and Aquino, and Hoffmeister's 5 CAD to break through.[58] So that his division would be ready when the time came, Hoffmeister and his staff tried to coordinate routes and assembly areas west of the Gari River. As ever, this was more easily said than done. The distance between the Gustav and Hitler lines spanned no more than six miles in length, while the distance between the boundary with 13 Corps (on the right) and the Liri River (on the left) measured only three to four miles across. Crammed into that limited space were an infantry division and an armoured brigade, both with their supporting guns and ammunition carriers – all ahead of Hoffmeister's leading elements. On top of that, 5 CAD had to orchestrate the entire affair without the benefit of the best route in the area, HEART Route (Highway no. 6).

Hoffmeister spent a lot of time at Vokes's headquarters, attempting to find assembly areas and routes forward of the Gari, but squeezing his division into the limited space available was a tedious, incremental process. He moved what he could, when he could, but he did it in balanced bits. Burns wanted Hoffmeister to have a brigade group poised behind 1 CID, ready to take over the advance or exploit any break in the German defences. Anticipating that he might be ordered to take over the break-in fight at the Hitler Line, should 1 CID be spent by the time it got there, Hoffmeister moved his infantry brigade first. At a 16 May orders group, he outlined his plan to move 11 CIB, reinforced with the British Columbia Dragoons and other supporting arms to an assembly area east of the Gari River.[59] This was a sensible grouping. Because it had infantry and other arms, this particular brigade group would have been capable of breaking into the Hitler Line. Because it had armour, it could have been used for the breakout as well. When, on 19 May, it became apparent that 5 CAD would be used for the breakout after all, Hoffmeister was able to inform Burns that he had a task force comprised of the Irish Regiment, an armoured regiment (the British Columbia Dragoons), a regiment of self-propelled artillery, a battery of self-propelled anti-tank guns, and a reconnaissance squadron ready to exploit any breach by 1 CID on short notice.[60] The Dragoon/Irish battle group might not have possessed the full hitting power of a brigade, but, in the short term, the task force could move and shoot without outside help, and it was part of what Hoffmeister moved first when crossing the

Gari – better to have a small balanced force now than a full brigade of infantry waiting for its supporting arms.[61] Considering the road movement difficulties, the delays associated with bringing forward the rest of the armour, and the need to keep the enemy on the run, this was essential.

As it turned out, Hoffmeister need not have hurried too much. The 1 CID advance was slow, only reaching the Hitler Line on 18 May.[62] After an attempt to breach that line of defences failed on 19 May, Leese instructed Burns to plan for a set-piece attack in "about 48 hrs time." As the 1st Canadian Corps attack between Pontecorvo and Aquino was to be the Eighth Army main effort at the Hitler Line, Leese provided the fire of all available army artillery (500-600 guns) and whatever air support he could muster. The Canadians needed it; in that portion of the line, they faced five German battalions, including a battalion of German paratroopers at Aquino. 13th Corps was to execute a holding attack on the right to keep the defenders at Aquino from interfering with the Canadian assault.

The 1st Canadian Corps plan, which Burns explained to Leese on the morning of 20 May and passed to his divisional commanders later that afternoon, essentially mirrored the one that Burns had anticipated and discussed in the study periods leading up to the offensive.[63] In very simple terms, Burns's plan for Operation CHESTERFIELD was a break-in/break-out operation – the break-in being conducted by 1 CID with the support of the British 25th Army Tank Brigade and the Three Rivers Regiment, and the break-out towards the town of Ceprano being executed by Hoffmeister's division through whatever "hole" 1 CID made.[64]

For the most part, that was how events transpired. 1 CID accomplished its task. Vokes had to make some readjustments to his plan, and the costs were heavy (880 men killed, missing, or wounded), but he did succeed in "breaking in."[65] He made a hole. By the late afternoon of 23 May, less than 12 hours after the start of the battle, his third brigade had penetrated the Hitler Line midway between Pontecorvo and Aquino, and Hoffmeister was there when it happened: "I was in Chris Vokes' headquarters right up to the time we moved off and I'll never forget the moment when Chris turned to me and said, 'Bert this is the best we can do, there is not much of a hole, good luck to you.'"[66] At 5:30 p.m., Hoffmeister telephoned Burns and advised him "the situation was favourable for the 5 Cdn Armd Div to adv [advance]."[67] Burns agreed and gave Hoffmeister the order to move.

With characteristic simplicity, Hoffmeister based his break-out plan on the seizure of three successive objectives, suitably based on the terrain and likely enemy positions – a crossing over the Melfa River, a crossing over the Liri River at the town of Ceprano, and the capture of the village of Frosinone (see Maps 7 and 8).[68] To his armoured brigade, 5 CAB, went the task of breaking out of the Hitler Line and capturing the first crossing site at the Melfa. Once a bridgehead had been established, his infantry brigade, 11 CIB, would then pass through 5 CAB and advance on Ceprano. Again, Hoffmeister did not deviate far from established doctrine.[69] Advancing in limited steps, securing firm bases before moving on, and

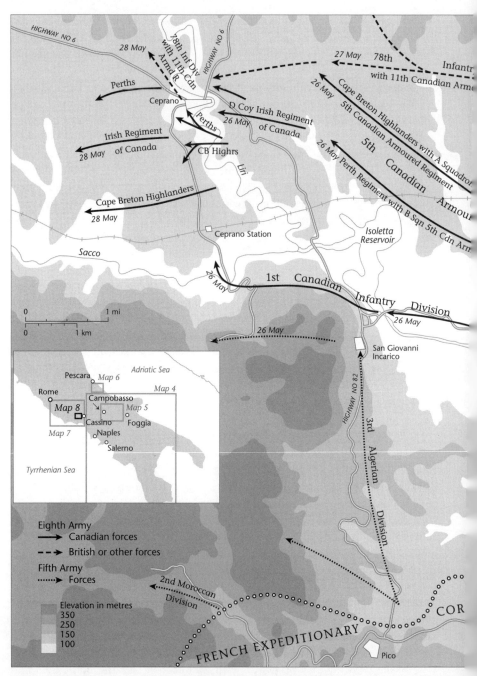

MAP 8   *The breakout from the Hitler Line, 24-28 May 1944.* Adapted from G.W.L. Nicholson (Lieutenant-Colonel), *The Canadians in Italy, 1943-1945* (Ottawa: Queen's Printer, 1966), map 14.

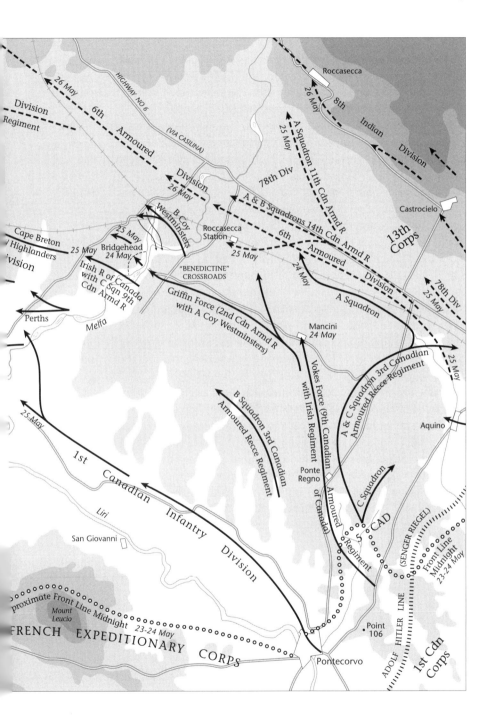

not getting beyond the range of supporting artillery; this was the Eighth Army way of doing things. Hoffmeister fought that way, and so did his brigade commanders. Brigadier Smith, commander of 5 CAB, planned three successive phases for his objective – one to Mancini, one to the Melfa River, and one to exploit towards Ceprano if the opportunity presented itself.[70]

How Hoffmeister organized his forces for the operation was not as orthodox as his tactics. Since the Seaforth/Three Rivers Regiment attack in the Salso River valley the previous August, he had believed strongly in combined-arms teams. He had used them in 2 CIB (although occasions to do so were rare) and he stressed the importance of infantry-tank-artillery training on SLUGGEM and THRUSTER. For the pursuit beyond the Hitler Line, Hoffmeister grouped his brigades by phases to provide maximum flexibility. In the first phase – the advance to the Melfa – he placed under command of 5 CAB a regiment of artillery (self-propelled), two batteries of anti-tank guns (self-propelled), a field squadron of engineers, a field ambulance unit, two reconnaissance squadrons of the Governor General's Horse Guards (GGHG), and an infantry battalion (the Irish Regiment).[71] To ensure that the infantry battalion could keep pace with all the tanks and motorized elements of the brigade, Hoffmeister stripped every unit in the division of its bren gun carriers, assigning the vehicles to the Irish. In all, he cobbled together enough carriers to ferry two companies of infantry; the remaining two companies would ride on the back decks of the reserve squadron tanks. All of this was in addition to the brigade's normal complement of three armoured regiments and one battalion of motorized infantry (the Westminsters). Here was a force that could move, shoot, breach obstacles, kill tanks, care for its wounded, protect its own flanks, and occupy ground – quickly and without immediate recourse to higher authority. For the second phase, he regrouped slightly, hiving off the 8th New Brunswick Hussars from 5 CAB and reassigning them to 11 CIB for the advance to Ceprano.

At the brigade level, Smith similarly combined his elements into task forces.[72] "Vokes Force," named for the commanding officer of the British Columbia Dragoons, Lieutenant-Colonel F.A. Vokes (Chris Vokes's younger brother), was based on the armoured regiment, the Irish Regiment, and a battery of self-propelled anti-tank guns. To it went 5 CAB's first-phase task of advancing to Mancini. "Griffin Force," similarly named for the Strathcona commanding officer, Lieutenant-Colonel P.G. "Paddy" Griffin, consisted of the Lord Strathcona's Horse, one company of Westminsters (motorized), two scout platoons, one battery of self-propelled anti-tank guns, and one battery of self-propelled artillery. Its task was to advance to the Melfa. The third task force, Smith's reserve, combined the 8th New Brunswick Hussars with the remainder of the Westminsters and various supporting arms.

The first phases of the breakout went well, though far from perfectly.[73] Poor road conditions, rain, reduced visibility, insufficient space, and enemy shelling hampered 5 CAB's movement to a forward assembly immediately behind 3 CIB during the evening of 23 May. Consequently, the advance that was supposed to start at 6:00 a.m. was delayed by two hours. Vokes Force rumbled ahead with two tank squadrons forward, each followed by a company of carrier-mounted infantry from the Irish Regiment, and then the remaining two companies mounted on reserve squadron tanks. Reaching Mancini in the face of relatively light opposition at 10:30 a.m., it took until mid-afternoon to clear the objective of enemy. At a cost of four Dragoon tanks destroyed and twenty-eight Irish Regiment soldiers killed or wounded, Vokes Force knocked out three German tanks, killed eighty-nine enemy soldiers, and took fifty prisoners. Cooperation between the arms was surprisingly good.

Knowing that speed was essential, Smith did not wait for Vokes to complete the consolidation of Mancini before calling forward Griffin Force. He ordered them to move at 11:30 a.m.[74] Griffin Force, still east of the San Martino River at this point, took a full two hours to wind its way forward to Mancini.[75] With its own reconnaissance troop leading and a divisional reconnaissance squadron on each flank, the task force then advanced from Mancini with one squadron forward, closely followed by the motorized Westminster company. The remaining two squadrons brought up the rear. Owing to bad roads, restricted terrain, and poor visibility, the going was difficult. Griffin noted the effects in his "Report on Operations": "The country proved to be very close with visibility limited in places to 20 yds. Fire and [movement] was impossible and sqns frequently moved in line ahead" – not exactly tank country.[76] But restricted fields of fire and visibility could, and did, work against the defender as well – the Strathcona reconnaissance troop managed to make it unscathed to the Melfa in remarkably quick time.[77]

It made even quicker time securing a small bridgehead. Within twenty minutes of their 3:00 p.m. arrival at the river, the troop managed to place three of their Stuart tanks on the west bank. But the bridgehead was isolated and in a precarious position. The tank squadrons that the reconnaissance troop had left behind in its rapid advance became embroiled in several tank-on-tank fights that cost the regiment 17 tanks. And when the remaining Sherman tanks did reach the river, owing to their size and the steepness of the Melfa's banks, they could not cross. Until a solid bridge spanned the river, those tanks had to provide what support they could from the near bank.

Help for the beleaguered troop finally came at 5:00 p.m. when the motorized Westminster company arrived at the bridgehead.[78] In fairly short order, the company waded across the river, and the reconnaissance troop held the tiny bridgehead against a German counterattack at dusk on 24 May. Two more Westminster companies crossed the river later that evening, one to the left, the other to the right of the bridgehead. That strengthened the foothold, hardening it enough to withstand successive German counterattacks throughout the night.

Due to a dearth of information from 5 CAD, Burns knew little of these developments as they occurred. His diary entry for 24 May hints at his frustration: "From about 1500 hrs, only very fragmentary news was received from 5 Cdn Armd Div, until about 2110 hrs when a reasonably complete report was received, from which it appeared that the Div [5 CAD] had been able to get reasonably well placed to resume its adv the following morning."[79] Hoffmeister, who had been following the lead elements of 5 CAB in his command tank found communications "a little difficult" – difficult to the corps and difficult to his own headquarters as well.[80] On the morning of 25 May, Burns visited the 5 CAD Main Headquarters and "asked" Hoffmeister's GSO I to have Hoffmeister "make arrangements for getting back [information]" on his intentions and intelligence.[81]

The immediate result of that shot in the arm was a handwritten situation report, which Hoffmeister dictated to his ADC at 10:00 a.m. on 25 May and passed to 1st Canadian Corps headquarters by way of a dispatch rider.[82] It described the state of the bridgehead and the deployments of all 5 CAD's fighting elements. The Westminsters were across the Melfa. Overlooking them from the east bank were the three LdSH tank squadrons, which were later joined by the Irish Regiment, which Smith brought forward from Mancini, and a reconnaissance squadron of the Governor General's Horse Guards. Two miles east of the river, Hoffmeister's tactical headquarters passed the night near Mancini with 5 CAB headquarters, 11 CIB main headquarters, the British Columbia Dragoons, the Perth Regiment, and a field regiment of artillery. The Cape Breton Highlanders and the 8th New Brunswick Hussars huddled in an assembly area north of Pontecorvo. All the fighting elements of 5 CAD were west of the Hitler Line.

Hoffmeister also outlined his intentions for 25 May. They were first to expand the bridgehead with an attack by the Westminsters, then to launch 11 CIB on the second phase of his plan, the drive to Ceprano. Early on the morning of 25 May, Hoffmeister also learned of elements of 1 CID reaching the Melfa one and a half miles to the southwest. His left flank was secure. His right flank, however, was a different story. 13th Corps had not yet moved beyond Aquino, and Hoffmeister was worried about enemy counterattack from the north. Thus, first among his priorities for 25 May was to send a reconnaissance squadron to patrol along his exposed right flank (beyond the boundary with 13th Corps) to determine "the enemy situation along Hwy 6 and in the Aquino sector of the HITLER Line ... This patrol is necessary because we are in complete ignorance of the sit [situation] on our right flank and cannot obtain the info from 13th Corps."[83]

Unknown to Hoffmeister, Leese had plans for 13th Corps that would affect his operations in the coming days. Just as Griffin Force was striking towards the Melfa, Leese made another terrible decision. At 12:30 p.m. on 24 May, he and the commander of 13th Corps, Lieutenant-General S.C. Kirkman, visited Burns's headquarters to request "that HEART route [Highway 6] should be cleared as soon as possible for the 6 Brit Armd Div to pass through, in order that they could mov fwd on the RIGHT of 5 Cdn Armd Div and help to mop up the enemy in the CASTROCIELO and ROCCASECCA area, thus securing the RIGHT flank of 5

Cdn Armd Div for the move fwd."[84] The idea was for Kirkman to skirt the town of Aquino, using one of the few good crossing sites to the south, instead of attacking the now weakened German defences frontally, or from the north.

Why Leese chose this time to cram two armoured divisions into a corridor only fit for one is difficult to discern. In a draft autobiography, he stated simply that his "plan was to pass 6th [British] Armoured Division and 5th Canadian Armoured Division through the leading infantry, whilst the 8th Indian Division advanced in the hills north of Highway 6 and the Poles cleared M. Cairo and Piedmonte."[85] But there was no need for two armoured divisions at this point. The 5 CAD breakout, only a few hours old when Leese directed Burns to clear the only good route, may not have been lightning fast, but it was succeeding against weakening opposition.

Part of the reason for his inexplicable decision may have been the uneven flow of information. On the night of 23-24 May, 13th Corps patrols into Aquino reported "no opposition."[86] Owing to the scarcity of information from 5 CAD, however, corroborating evidence to complete the picture that "some [enemy] are now perhaps back on the MELFA while others are probably desperately trying to reach it" did not reach the Eighth Army until 25 May.[87] But even at that, the wider operational situation should have clued Leese to the fact that enemy resistance south of Rome was crumbling. The 6th US Corps had started its breakout from the Anzio bridgehead, and the French Expeditionary Corps was several miles ahead of the Eighth Army to the south. Thus, with Canadian troops through the Hitler Line and behind the enemy to the west, and Allied advances proceeding at a good pace to the south, it should have been clear that 5 CAD would not be facing much opposition on the way to Ceprano – provided the enemy was not given opportunity to regroup. In a 24 May letter to his wife, Leese expressed his uneasiness: "I don't know what the Bosches will do tonight as we are all around him & yet he is ... hanging on in parts of the Adolf Hitler Line. I hope we may get on again tomorrow as we want to keep him on the run. He is very rattled at the moment & has his units and formations all over the place."[88] But squeezing two corps onto one main axis had the opposite effect. As he later admitted, "This proved too difficult an operation with the poor roads and rainy weather on a narrow front; and there was great congestion and consequently serious delay. The enemy, as ever ready to take advantage of the slightest relaxation of pressure, reorganized quickly and opposed us strongly with stout rearguards. As a result, the leading units of the Armoured Divisions [5 CAD and 6 British] made slow progress and we lost the advantages gained by our break into the enemy defences."[89]

The decision to send 6 Armoured Division around Aquino dramatically affected Hoffmeister's operations, for several reasons. First, it occurred just as he was preparing to pass 11 CIB through 5 CAB's bridgehead for the second phase of his plan. Having to clear the routes for the 6 Armoured Division made the forward passage of fighting troops and their supporting arms difficult. Traffic held up

Smith's supporting artillery, forcing him to delay the Irish Regiment attack for the expansion of the Melfa bridgehead from first light to mid-morning on 25 May. At 10:05 that morning, Hoffmeister advised 1st Canadian Corps headquarters that the presence of 6 Armoured Division vehicles on a 5 CAD route were seriously hampering 5 CAD operations. "Request you get them off it" was his frustrated demand. The corps complied, but it took several hours to reroute the traffic.[90] Poor road conditions and traffic also prevented echelons from moving forward to resupply and replenish depleted stores of ammunition and fuel for the fighting troops. As an example, midway through the 11 CIB breakout towards Ceprano on 26 May, the leading battalions were, for a while, without the support of their armoured squadrons, because the tanks had to pause and refuel. Why? "It had been impossible to get [petrol] fwd during the night 25/26 May."[91] Tanks could not run indefinitely without fuel, and fuel trucks did not do well bounding cross-country.

The other thing that slowed the advance to Ceprano was the excessive cautiousness of the 11 CIB commander, Brigadier Eric Snow. Ponderous and deliberate, Snow was not one for anticipating requirements and issuing preliminary orders from which to make quick adjustments depending on the tactical situation. Take, for example, how he prepared for the breakout from the Melfa bridgehead. Early on 25 May, Hoffmeister ordered Snow to attack at noon and seize the high ground 500 yards to the west of the bridgehead.[92] It was a straightforward task, yet it took until 10:30 a.m. for Snow even to summon subordinate commanders to his headquarters for an orders group, a gathering that finally assembled at noon. Hoffmeister's intended timing for the start of the assault lapsed, and his subordinate had not even given direction to his units. The delays did not stop there.[93] Orders for the attack, which was to be conducted by the Cape Breton Highlanders with the full support of the 8th New Brunswick Hussars, had yet to be issued. Because the Cape Breton commanding officer waited for the arrival of his artillery representative (he was late due to traffic) to coordinate the indirect fire plan, the delays continued. Not until 3:00 p.m. did Lieutenant-Colonel Weir finally issue his orders, and he took forty-five minutes to do it. As a direct result, squadron and company commanders had precious little time to scramble back to their own sub-units and hastily pass on orders before moving off at 4:20 p.m. Predictably, "O gps [orders groups] were very hurried and the plan did not get below [tank] crew comds unless crews were briefed on the move."[94] Making matters worse, failure to conduct adequate preliminary moves meant that the Cape Bretons and the Hussars were still in separate assembly areas while the orders were being passed. It was 4:15 p.m. before tank squadron commanders linked up with their infantry counterparts to "marry-up" and "net-in" radios, but that was too late; most of "the inf were already on the move."[95]

The Cape Bretons reached their intended objectives before dusk, but a day had been wasted due to poor battle procedure. Unlike Smith, Snow did not have a simple, yet flexible, plan from which to adjust; he started from scratch each time.

Moreover, Snow compounded a difficult situation by bringing battalion command-ers back to his headquarters on 25 May – this at a time when routes were jammed and the bulk of the planning for that day's operations had to be done by the com-manding officer of the Cape Bretons. He inexcusably ate up precious time. The example he set for his unit commanders was not a good one either. Like their boss, the battalion commanders in 11 CIB were painfully slow, and Snow was not the man to push them. In the words of the 11 CIB brigade major at the time, Snow was simply "too nice."[96]

This was a stressful period for Hoffmeister. At a time when the pace of the advance slowed considerably, he was also being criticized for the performance of his headquarters. Burns had already rebuked him for not keeping his higher headquarters adequately informed, and it was no secret that the Eighth Army was not happy with 5 CAD's poor reporting procedures.[97] There was some merit in these criticisms. In the advance, corps and armies had to plan operations days, not hours, in advance. When to commit the reserve division, where to commit it, how to get it there: such decisions required not only timely and accurate in-formation, but sound projections as well. Handwritten situation reports con-taining twelve-hour-old information simply did not suffice, as Hoffmeister was beginning to realize.

Hoffmeister's small tactical headquarters compounded the problem. He liked doing his own liaison, liked being well forward, liked seeing the battle area for himself. For those reasons, he had opted to operate from a small tactical head-quarters. It was a good idea in theory, but, unfortunately, the communications infrastructure of the division could not support it. Hoffmeister's CRA, who also operated from a small tactical headquarters and who often co-located with his commander, explained the problem: "We made a mistake – Bert and all of us – in forming a tac headquarters and going forward ... Bert and I each had a command tank ... But we were away from the focal point of communications. I tried to operate on the wireless, and this was all right up to a point, but the real crunch came when it got dark ... Wireless at night was very difficult."[98] Field telephones, connected by landline, from headquarters to headquarters, were more reliable, as were the more powerful radios in each of the command hubs. At the division level, wireless was essential to commanding and controlling the battle. Gone were Hoffmeister's days of walking up to a subordinate commander, tapping him on the shoulder, and telling him what to do. A division was too big, and the distances too far for that to be the primary means of controlling the battle. The central difficulty was that Hoffmeister spent very little time in his main headquarters, often outpacing radio and landline. The officer in charge of 5 CAD signal explained, "One of our problems in the Hitler Line was the fact that Bert was up with the forward troops all the time and I caught hell personally for communications be-cause the divisional commander every now and then was out of touch ... and I couldn't catch him."[99]

This, combined with Hoffmeister's habit of not returning to the main division headquarters at night, often left his staff guessing about what would happen next.[100] Staffs needed to know a commander's intentions well in advance if they were to support the operations – arranging for route clearance, bringing ammunition forward, moving bridging equipment to proposed crossing sites. Because of its fighting vehicles, the armoured division had a much larger administrative "tail" than an infantry division, and managing that tail required a fair amount of number crunching, most of it done by logistic planners in Division Rear Headquarters, to determine how many fuel and ammunition carriers would be required to keep the division's 300-plus tanks, 200 guns, and 2,500 infantry troops fuelled, fed, and fighting. Once those determinations were made, routes – and timings on routes – had to be allocated such that the supplies reached those who needed them, when they needed them. In the Liri Valley, where formations had to share routes, division headquarters staffs had to "bid" for route timings based on their projected administrative requirements. The main divisional headquarters also had to have enough information to keep the next level of command advised on their commander's intentions. That way, higher commanders could make sounder decisions. It required commanders to think ahead. It also required good communications so that staffs could set to their tasks in a timely manner. With communications between Hoffmeister's tactical headquarters and his main headquarters as erratic as they were, this did not always happen. That was the nub of the problem.

Having a subordinate who was slow to make plans, and even slower to make changes, only made matters worse. Hoffmeister had to watch over Snow's every move. For a commander used to giving subordinates a fair amount of latitude, this was an unwanted distraction. Snow did not like it either. In his after-action report, he complained that Hoffmeister "was continually urging that we get on, that the adv was too slow, that something must be done."[101] Commander and subordinate, in this case, could not have been more dissimilar. Whereas Snow saw the risks of advancing in the dark with an exposed right flank, Hoffmeister saw the risk of not keeping the retreating Germans on the run: they could prepare another line of defence, probably on the Liri, and fight another day. The Moro and the Gully had taught him that. Thus, when the tanks supporting the Perths and the Cape Bretons stalled for lack of fuel on 26 May, Hoffmeister told Snow to get the infantry moving again – with or without tanks. Snow would rather have had his infantry adopt a defensive posture. A few hours later, when Snow realized that he would not be able to reach the Liri River before dark, and decided, again, to deploy his battalions for a hasty defence, Hoffmeister fumed and demanded that 11 CIB immediately seize the crossing sites on the river. By that time it was all too late. The enemy that had been on the run since the breaking of the Hitler Line now moved back in an orderly withdrawal. Two Irish Regiment companies, the two that Snow had dispatched to the Liri on Hoffmeister's order, reached the river on the night of 26-27 May only to find the bridges blown and the town of Ceprano abandoned.

Meanwhile, in a ridiculous pause, the remainder of Snow's brigade dug a hasty defensive position two miles to the east. One Perth Regiment soldier, Stanley Scislowski, recalled the inexplicable pause in typical soldier's language: "The advance went along unimpeded either by mines or fire of any sort when smack in the middle of this wide-open stretch of meadowland we were told to dig in ... What a way to fight a war – sitting here in the hot sun, fingers up our ass, while Jerry's up ahead somewhere probably building himself another Hitler Line."[102] Snow, who spent little time forward, was in no position to assess just how little opposition stood between the lead battalions and Ceprano.

But Hoffmeister, who hated waiting for information to come to him, knew what was happening. As Private Scislowski dug into the open field east of Ceprano, he witnessed one of Hoffmeister's forward forays first-hand. When an approaching cloud of dust cleared, Hoffmeister's scout car had halted fifteen yards from the front-line soldier's trench:

> Hoffmeister put his field glasses to his eyes and scanned the terrain in the direction of Ceprano. I took it that he came up here to see what the hell the bloody holdup was ... It took the [German] mortar crews only a minute or so to zero in on the target ... The first salvo dropped short of [Hoffmeister's] scout car, close enough to give even the bravest a good scare. But dammit, Hoffmeister didn't so much as blink an eye – just stood there with those big glasses scanning the terrain ahead ...
>
> I could only imagine what happened when he got back to his command post ... Whatever happened, it sure got results. Less than a half-hour later we were up and on our way.[103]

Hoffmeister eventually found Snow, but his patience had worn thin: "At a time when I could ill-afford the time to go out and hunt for Eric Snow, I was obliged to ... I ultimately found him in a bit of a cul-de-sac, without adequate knowledge of what was going on and in no position to control the battle."[104] Hoffmeister was fighting two battles – his and his lead brigade's.

Getting over the Liri with enough force to strike out towards Pofi and Frosinone presented Hoffmeister with a difficult problem. As always, a foothold had to be established on the enemy side of the river, far enough back to allow engineers to build a bridge capable of putting tanks across. Hoffmeister ordered Snow to cross the Liri and establish a bridgehead 500 yards beyond Ceprano. The Perth Regiment moved off in assault boats at 9:00 a.m. on 27 May. They entered the city at 9:30 a.m., and by mid-afternoon they had all four rifle companies on the west bank. To harden the bridgehead, anti-tank weapons and mortars then crossed the river on rafts; however, the enemy repulsed an attempt to capture the high ground 600 yards northwest of the town.[105] This was a vital piece of terrain, for from its heights the enemy could observe the area of the crossing site and adjust mortar and artillery fire on engineers trying to build a bridge. That was why Hoffmeister had directed that the bridgehead line be pushed beyond it. But Snow, ever cautious, decided to wait until his second battalion, the Cape Bretons, crossed before having the Perths try a second time.[106]

That did not happen quickly. At 11:00 a.m. Snow ordered the Cape Breton Highlanders to cross behind the Perths and take up a position on the left (or southern end) of the bridgehead. Once more, the Cape Breton commander, Weir, proved unbelievably slow getting his unit into action; five and a half hours later, his companies had still not moved.[107] This was too much for even a "nice guy" like Snow, who summoned Weir to his headquarters and "granted [him] 72 hours rest."[108] In other words, Snow fired Weir. Not that getting rid of Weir immediately sped things up. The Cape Bretons still took until 7:10 p.m. to cross the river, only attaining their final objectives just before midnight.

While 11 CIB secured the bridgehead, Hoffmeister made a few adjustments to how he exerted command and control over his subordinate formations, no doubt based upon earlier discussions with Burns. For one thing, he spent more time at his "stripped down" main headquarters, where the communications were reliable, and where all the essential artillery, engineer, and signals representatives gathered as well.[109] On the night of 27-28 May, Hoffmeister met with his staff principals and put together a simple plan to take the 5 CAD advance to Frosinone. They did so based on orders from 1st Canadian Corps, map study, and the most recent developments in the tactical situation (see Map 7, inset, p. 134). Still not one to bring subordinate commanders back for time-consuming conferences, Hoffmeister sent a one and one-half page written order and graphic forward.[110] With subordinates, he preferred doing business "eyeball-to-eyeball," but given the circumstances – traffic jams, poor roads, widely dispersed units – that was simply impractical. The graphic, typical of British and Canadian doctrine, delineated routes and bounds, based on the terrain and suspected enemy delaying positions. The written order tasked 11 CIB with the expansion of the Ceprano bridgehead on 27-28 May. That was to be followed by a 5 CAB breakout, on two routes, not later than 12:00 noon on 28 May.

Hoffmeister sent the order to subordinate, higher, and flanking formations via signals dispatch riders (on motorcycles) at 2:35 a.m. on 28 May. In so doing, he was addressing the problem of keeping all pertinent formations informed of his intentions while making most efficient use of the time available. Smith had sufficient time, for example, to issue his own warning order and move his fighting units from an assembly area east of the Melfa River to a concentration area immediately east of Ceprano – all before holding a more detailed orders group at 7:00 a.m.

Unforeseen difficulties caused problems. At the only crossing site suitable for tanks, the bridge south of Ceprano collapsed at 7:30 a.m. Poor passage of information in 11 CIB resulted in hurried and faulty construction that, unfortunately, doomed the bridge. Later that morning, at the request of Lieutenant-General Kirkman, whose 13th Corps had stalled in the face of stubborn resistance from

German paratroopers at the town of Arce, Leese assigned priority on the bridge to 78 Division in order that it might skirt the source of its troubles.[111] This was yet another incomprehensible move by Leese; not only was 5 CAD already positioned to break out of the bridgehead, another colossal traffic jam ensued. "Things were in quite a flap as two Divs were virtually lined up on the rd waiting to get across one [bridge]," as Hoffmeister's chief engineer noted in his diary.[112] It took longer to reconstruct the bridge than first projected. Estimated times for completion regressed steadily from 11:30 a.m., to 3:00 p.m., to 4:00 p.m. Engineers finally finished at 5:15 p.m., but the delay had already forced a change of plans.[113] Less than thirty minutes earlier, Burns had directed Hoffmeister to make use of bridges over the Liri and the Sacco in the 1 CID sector. Accordingly, Hoffmeister sent a battle group, based on the British Columbia Dragoons and the Westminster Regiment, by way of the long circuitous route around the Isoletta Reservoir, then north to where 1 CID had bridged the Sacco River. From there, the battle group drove north into the 11 CIB bridgehead, where they arrived at 9:00 p.m. The fallen bridge at Ceprano, coupled with the decision to give 78 Division priority on the crossing site, imposed a huge delay on Hoffmeister's plans.

The solution – sending 5 CAB elements to the south – took a seemingly long time to dawn on Canadian commanders. Certainly Burns was self-critical in retrospect: "I was not quick enough to appreciate the point that while there was no tank crossing available on the right, there was a crossing on the left."[114] He might even have done better to have 1 CID take over the advance from their bridgehead in the south. Hoffmeister, on the other hand, had weighed the idea of diverting 5 CAB to the south, even before the bridge collapsed. The 5 CAD Operations Log shows that he advised 5 CAB at 11:25 p.m. on 27 May that he would "make a decision whether to use the 1 Cdn Div bridge by 0400 tomorrow."[115] However, he preferred this option least, for obvious reasons; the route was long, the roads poor, and the traffic unpredictable. Those factors, combined with unduly optimistic engineer projections, probably caused him to do everything he could to avoid heading south. Instead, he coordinated the passage of 5 CAB immediately after the lead brigade from 78 Division had crossed the bridge.[116] As much as possible, he stuck to his original plan.

The problem was that the plan had flaws. The ground between Ceprano and Frosinone was unsuited for an armoured breakout. When the British Columbia Dragoons and the Westminsters advanced on Pofi, they did so using the two routes that Hoffmeister had designated in his 28 May written order.[117] However, as the advance moved beyond the Liri Valley to the north, the ground became hilly and broken, more so than anything they had seen to date, and the enemy added to the difficulty with mines and well-sited anti-tank weapons.[118] Boggy ground and anti-tank fire claimed numerous Dragoon tanks and delayed the arrival of the regiment at Pofi until 7:15 p.m. The motorized Westminster companies hobbled along behind them and formed a firm base overlooking Arnara at around the same time.

This was infantry country, and the infantry brigade probably should have led from the start. Having 11 CIB break out of its own bridgehead also would have avoided the day-long delay associated with the reconstruction of the bridge. But with Snow at the helm, nobody was going anywhere in a hurry, and Hoffmeister probably wanted the more reliable Smith to take the lead.

Not long after the British Columbia Dragoons started their advance on 29 May, Hoffmeister realized the necessity for infantry to lead in the close country and adjusted his plan accordingly. Snow groused that Hoffmeister had just recently advised him that he "would probably remain in [his] present [bridgehead] position for about 36 hours [while 5 CAB broke out]," but pushing 11 CIB forward was the only sensible thing to do.[119] Soon after telling Snow to send a battalion to mop up enemy that had been bypassed in Pofi, Hoffmeister redirected the brigadier to advance with his entire brigade and capture key terrain between Pofi and Arnara by first light on 30 May. Once Snow had secured those objectives, Hoffmeister wanted 5 CAB to strike out towards objectives "TOM," "DICK," and "HARRY," using the same two routes mapped on the 28 May order (Map 7, inset, p. 134). 5 CAB's armoured regiments would, in turn, be relieved by battalions from Snow's brigade to complete the mopping up and form firm bases for 2 CIB (now under command of 5 CAD) to advance on Frosinone.[120] The division reconnaissance regiment, the Governor General's Horse Guards, protected the still-exposed right flank. With Frosinone in hand, 5 CAD could hand over the lead to 1 CID.

The plan to have the armoured brigade lead on to the objectives, followed by the battalions of the infantry brigade, never worked. The terrain impeded nearly all tank movement. On the way to "DICK," the Hussar tanks "completely bogged down within a few hundred yds of their start line so the Inf Bns went without them."[121] In fact, on the far left, once 5 CAB confirmed that no adequate, northbound vehicle route existed, Hoffmeister directed Smith to send the Hussars and two motorized Westminster companies to Ceccano, where they later linked up with the French Expeditionary Corps. Back on 27-28 May, Hoffmeister had selected the routes based on a map study, but he had not yet viewed them with his own eyes. And because those routes had not been reconnoitred by reconnaissance patrols either, he had no reliable confirmation that they were actually tracks. Here was evidence of a harried commander trying to balance the often-conflicting requirements of maintaining momentum in the advance, controlling the battle, and gathering reliable information from which to make decisions.

In part, this was due to his having risen so quickly from battalion to division command. He was not looking far enough in advance. A division commander's decisions were based less on what was happening immediately to his front than what lay several miles beyond it. He needed reliable information on the ground and the enemy that his troops would face a day or two ahead of time, not what they would face in three hours' time. That information might have been obtained from aerial reconnaissance, his own reconnaissance patrols, prisoners of war, local civilians – a number of sources. Just as operations had to be planned, so too did reconnaissance. Clearly, when he made his plan for the advance to Frosinone, he had not adequately tapped those sources. The on-the-spot reconnaissance direction that had worked during the 2 CIB advance to the Biferno did not yield results early enough for a division commander. Thus, while Hoffmeister had the right idea for conveying his orders – pushing them forward with a simple graphic – owing to inadequate information, his plan was deficient in its conception.

On the right flank, the actions of the Strathconas and the Cape Breton Highlanders highlighted another problem with the plan: unclear command relationships. Shortly after the Cape Bretons had captured "TOM" (without the support of tanks that found the going too difficult), "an urgent message from Div [5 CAD] ordered the LSH [Lord Strathcona's Horse] to move with all possible speed ... with a view to cutting off enemy tks which were known to be withdrawing along Highway 6."[122] The Strathcona squadrons made for the crossroads northeast of "TOM," but they did so without the support of any infantry because the Cape Bretons, who were not under command of the tanks, had orders to stay on "TOM." The Strathconas could have used their help. The armoured regiment took five tank casualties from enemy sniping tanks and anti-tank weapons that the Cape Bretons might have ferreted out of the close country. The Strathcona after-action report testified to the frustration: "During this time frequent requests were made for inf sp [support] on the objective ... As darkness fell, without this sp arriving, the adv sqn was faced with the possibility of having to abandon tks if the enemy inf became active."[123] How much easier it would have been had the infantry battalion been *under command* of the tanks. That way, infantry support could have been directed, not requested. But Hoffmeister's concept of operations precluded that. What was essentially two brigade operations layered on top of each other – the armoured brigade leading onto the objectives, the infantry following up – left no scope for this. And only a division commander could direct a brigade commander to hand over a battalion to another formation. The entire concept of operations was curious, considering that the bulk of pre-Liri Valley training had dealt with tank-infantry cooperation – the same type of cooperation that had been evident in the first phase of the 5 CAD breakout from the Hitler Line, when the tanks of 5 CAB had advanced to the Melfa with the Irish Regiment under command. Leaving too much to people on the ground led to bickering and confusion. That events unfolded this way was also a sign of all levels of command being rushed and tired.

The 5 CAD battle for the Liri Valley ended on 31 May, Hoffmeister's last real command decision being the committal of 2 CIB to the capture of "HARRY" on the afternoon of 30 May. As planned, that set the stage for 1 CID to lead the 1st Canadian Corps advance to Ferentino and Valmontone (see Map 7, p. 134). Three days later, Leese stopped the Canadian advance, passing command of the Canadian sector to the 6th South African Armoured Division, which in turn came under command of 13th Corps to continue the advance northeast of Rome. When

General Mark Clark's Fifth US Army entered Rome on 5 June, the battle for the ancient capital ended for all the Allied Armies in Italy.

Hoffmeister's battlefield decisions may have ended on 31 May, but his command responsibilities, as he saw them, did not end there. A divisional commander's opportunities to make *his* mark on the rank and file were rare, but Hoffmeister did it better than most. He visited them, spoke with them, and shared some of their risks under fire. His forays forward made their mark on those who witnessed them. And when battles were done, he went to see his wounded. This pained him tremendously. No commander relished the idea of sending men to injury or death, Hoffmeister especially. The thought of their suffering had contributed to his breakdown in 1941. Seeing it was even worse:

> It demoralised me quite a bit ... I had been around to visit the fellows who had bandages over their eyes, fellows who had been blown up in tanks, all of whom were convinced they were going to be blind forever, regardless of how much hope the doctors held out. They were terribly depressed as a group, so I just stayed with them and told them about the battle, how well the unit had done and how important it was[, and] without which we couldn't have won the whole thing. I put a lot of myself into those visits and walked out of the hospital feeling like a dishrag.[124]

After the Liri Valley, he had to discontinue his post-battle hospital calls: "I really had to give up these hospital visits because it could affect my judgement in planning an attack."[125] Being with the troops when they were under artillery fire was one thing; seeing them broken and depressed was another. A commander needed clear, rational, unemotional judgment. In Hoffmeister's case, that meant eliminating hospital visits.

IN SPITE OF ALL the difficulties, Hoffmeister's division had achieved all of its objectives in May 1944. Hoffmeister won a second bar for his Distinguished Service Order: "As Commander of an Armoured Division which had never before been in action as a whole, [Hoffmeister] led it with greatest determination and success. By his constant presence in forward areas under shell and small arms fire, he inspired confidence and a fine offensive spirit in all. Between 24 and 30 May, the Division broke out of the Hitler Line, forced the crossings of the MELFA and LIRI rivers, captured three villages, destroyed large quantities of enemy equipment, took many prisoners and advanced 35 kilometers."[126]

The day the battle for Rome ended, the Eighth Army commander sent letters of congratulations to his formation commanders. The one addressed to the "GOC 5 Cdn Armd Div" expressed Leese's appreciation for the efforts of the division and its soldiers: "You ... advanced with great dash to the Melfa Line, where brilliant actions were fought; in particular by the Governor General's Horse Guards, Strathcona's Horse, and the Westminster Regt. After that you had considerable fighting with your infantry brigade, culminating in the passage by swimming and boating, under fire, by The Irish Regiment of Canada and The Perth Regiment, at Ceprano ... I am very proud to have the 5th Canadian Armoured Division in the Eighth Army."[127]

Leese was right; Canadian soldiers had fought well. In one week Hoffmeister's troops advanced twenty-two miles over extremely difficult ground, and in the face of determined German delaying action. As the Eighth Army commander noted in a letter to the War Office: "The Canadian troops themselves have been quite excellent; their fighting has been beyond praise."[128] But it could have been better. As Leese explained: "One's problem, therefore, is to train commanders and staff to make better use of the excellent material at their disposal."[129] In a second letter to Hoffmeister, this one addressed to "My dear Bert" and obviously intended for division commander's personal consumption, Leese indicated that commanders and staffs had a lot of work to do:

> I would like to write a short line to tell you how pleased I am to be able to let you have a short spell [in army reserve] to digest the lessons of your last fighting.
>
> As you know, there is a great deal to learn in the system of command, staff organization and intercommunication in an Armoured Division. I talked about this a lot to your Corps Commander, and I know that you both know how much there is to be done on the organization side in a short time. Traffic Control and sapper [engineer] work are two further essentials ...
>
> I shall look forward to the return of your Division to active operations in the Army.[130]

Hoffmeister did not disagree with Leese's assessment. In fact, he had already begun the process of introspection.

8
The Lessons from Liri

Their Armoured Division did an excellent small operation in the MELFA area and showed great dash. Hoffmeister, their General, is always in the forefront of the battle – so much so that he seldom remembers about his staff duties and movement technique, and his inter-communication to the rear. But he has that inestimable asset, the will to get on at all costs.[1]

LIEUTENANT-GENERAL SIR OLIVER LEESE, 26 MAY 1944

The lessons of the Liri Valley experience had to be distilled, disseminated, and absorbed into existing organization and procedures. From the commander, who made things work by force of his "will to get on at all costs," to the staff and subordinate commanders he forced, the 5th Canadian Armoured Division (5 CAD) chain of command had much to do in the summer of 1944. Although they had done everything asked of them in the spring offensive, widespread inexperience and some inefficiencies meant that Hoffmeister had been forced to exert an extraordinary personal effort just to keep the formation moving forward. By the end of the offensive, he was physically and mentally exhausted. That, combined with the first significant criticism of his military career, resurrected some self-doubt and temporarily unsettled his self-confidence. Still, he managed to focus on gleaning what lessons he could from the spring offensive, making adjustments accordingly. Technically, Hoffmeister and his staff examined their procedures for command and control to determine what had worked and what had not. Based on their findings, they reshaped organizations and rewrote procedures to make things function more smoothly in the future. They also replaced several key personnel. But the systematic self-analysis was not exclusive to 5 CAD; to improve future operations, every headquarters in the Canadian corps sifted through the experience of the drive for Rome, looking for the appropriate lessons. They found them.

AND IT WAS NOT JUST the Canadians who had a hard look back at the Liri Valley operations. Everyone in the Eighth Army chain of command strove to make the most of the experience gained in the recent offensive, starting with the army commander. On the morning of 5 June, Sir Oliver Leese met with E.L.M. Burns for "a long discussion" on such matters as "staff work, engineering org [organization] and control and the technique of comd [command]."[2] He wanted these issues addressed during the month or so that the Canadian corps would spend in reserve.

Burns took the criticism well and soon set to the task of finding the problems and fixing them.

They also discussed personalities within the Canadian corps. Much of what they discussed Burns restated two days later in a letter to the commander of the First Canadian Army, General H.D.G. Crerar. Leese believed that most of the Canadian corps's staff failings stemmed from weakness at the top of the staff chain, starting with a "poor B.G.S. [brigadier general staff]."[3] He recommended replacing Brigadier G.A. McCarter. Given the Eighth Army manner of doing business and McCarter's inability to make things work in action, Burns agreed that his senior staff officer had to go: "As you know, they like to operate on the 'Montgomery System,' which involves the Comd being forward during the day, and seeing subordinate comds. This necessitates a 'Chief of Staff' staying at HQ, to see that the battle is going according to intention when the Comd has got his fingers on it. Now, in view of what has happened, I felt that Nick [McCarter] had not shown the requisite grasp of the business to operate under this system."[4]

Burns found a suitable replacement in Brigadier J.D.B. Smith, the talented and adroit commander of 5th Canadian Armoured Brigade (CAB), who took over as BGS on 7 June.[5] Also on Leese's recommendation, Burns fired his chief engineer, who had not "gone down well with the CE [Chief Engineer] Army."[6] Regarding Burns's divisional commanders, however, Leese had mostly good things to say. Vokes "did very well, with a little direction and an occasional prod" – the army commander was convinced that the infantry division commander's performance had improved considerably.[7] As for Hoffmeister, both Burns and Leese believed that he "did an excellent job, and fought his green division with all the drive we expected of him."[8] Probably more than either Burns or Vokes, Hoffmeister *tried* to use the "Montgomery System" – being forward, making decisions, and leaving the staff to work out the details and monitor the battle. Leese liked that.

Burns failed to mention one important matter in his letter to Crerar – how dissatisfied Leese was with Burns's performance as a corps commander. To be fair to Burns, this may have been because Leese was less than direct in his criticism. Despite Leese's claim of having been "quite candid" during their 5 June meeting, the army commander left Burns with the impression that command of the Canadian corps would remain unchanged.[9] Leese had no such intention. To the War Office, he complained that Burns lacked "personality, initiative, tactical sense and power of command," and he actively pursued either the disbandment of the 1st Canadian Corps Headquarters, or the replacement of Burns by a British corps commander. This was unfair. Burns may have been a somewhat dour and uninspiring leader, but the blame for the slowness of the Eighth Army advance in the Liri Valley should not have landed on his shoulders alone. It was Leese's idea to jam two corps into a corridor with only enough serviceable routes to keep one corps going. It was Leese who created a problem that proved too difficult for the "green" Canadian formations to handle. And it was Leese who was looking for a scapegoat. Right or wrong, Leese continued to criticize Burns, something that eventually led to the Canadian being replaced by Lieutenant-General C. Foulkes in October 1944.

In the meantime, the Canadian corps had to incorporate the lessons of the recent fighting and prepare for its next battles. In 5 CAD, Hoffmeister had already begun to address a number of problems, even before his formation left the line for the training area near Volturno. During the first week of June 1944, as the remainder of the Eighth Army pressed on to Florence, the 1st Canadian Corps advance wound down, giving Hoffmeister a chance to reflect on the previous fortnight's operations. He wanted all his staff and commanders to do the same. On 1 June, he held a conference, attended by brigade commanders and key staff, at which he outlined "future intentions and trg [training] policy," and he directed all of the attendees "to have written reports of [the] parts played by their fmns [formations] [on recent operations] submitted ... by 1200 hrs 3 Jun."[10]

While that was being done, Hoffmeister and his staff went to work on the most glaring deficiencies of the recent campaign: communications, control, and the passage of information. As a first step, they instituted organizational changes in the headquarters (see Figure 8.1). Gone was the separate tactical headquarters that Hoffmeister had used at the outset of the operation. That had proven too difficult and too unreliable to exert effective command and control. As Hoffmeister's synopsis of the Liri Valley lessons noted: "Ops [operations] over a three day period with Tac [tactical] HQ separated from Main HQ showed that this was not a practical way of operating."[11] Instead, a smaller main headquarters became the focal point for command and control. From there, Hoffmeister could venture forward in a jeep, accompanied, always, by his GSO II (an operations staff officer in the rank of major). That arrangement he found to be much more practical than the slow and lumbering tank that he had used at the outset of the Liri operation. And when he was away from the headquarters, the GSO I had greater responsibility for controlling the battle. No longer one of several staff principals, the GSO I was now *the* senior man in the headquarters. In this arrangement, the GSO I did not have to wait for the commander's direction on everything (as had been the case in Liri). When the commander was away from the headquarters or out of radio contact, the GSO I took action in accordance with the commander's established intent. This was, in essence, "Chief of Staff System" or the "Montgomery System," an arrangement that "an experienced GSO I," sent by Eighth Army to "assist" 5 CAD on 29 May, undoubtedly had counselled.[12] Hoffmeister later added his own caravan, equipped with map boards and landline communication, to the main headquarters. In it, he could plan and reflect on operations.[13] His apparatus for commanding and controlling the battle were changing for the better.

The signals exercise STOP PRESS, which took place on 5 June, tested the changes.[14] Reorganized as it was, the headquarters worked efficiently. In the new format, the technical limitations of the wireless radios were less of an issue because, without

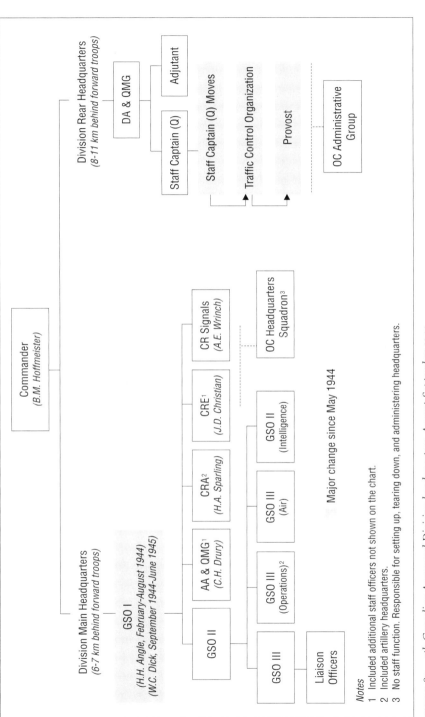

FIGURE 8.1   *5th Canadian Armoured Division headquarters, August–September 1944*

Commander
(*B.M. Hoffmeister*)

Division Main Headquarters
(*6-7 km behind forward troops*)

GSO I
(*H.H. Angle, February-August 1944*)
(*W.C. Dick, September 1944-June 1945*)

GSO II

AA & QMG[1]
(*C.H. Drury*)

CRA[2]
(*H.A. Sparling*)

CRE[1]
(*J.D. Christian*)

CR Signals
(*A.E. Wrinch*)

GSO III

GSO III
(Operations)[2]

GSO III
(Air)

GSO II
(Intelligence)

OC Headquarters
Squadron[3]

Liaison
Officers

Division Rear Headquarters
(*8-11 km behind forward troops*)

DA & QMG

Staff Captain (Q)

Adjutant

Staff Captain (Q) Moves

Traffic Control Organization

Provost

OC Administrative
Group

Major change since May 1944

Notes
1   Included additional staff officers not shown on the chart.
2   Included artillery headquarters.
3   No staff function. Responsible for setting up, tearing down, and administering headquarters.

the tactical headquarters, the commander could only outpace his means of communication for very short periods. And when he was away from the headquarters, the GSO I looked after the battle. Exercise observers commented that "Sig [Signals] comms [communications] within the div are adequate and work well when used correctly," although they did identify the requirement for alternative forms of controlling operations when wireless transmissions failed.[15] Changing the organization of the headquarters, changing its modus operandi, confirming the communications infrastructure: these were important steps – ones that would prove beneficial in the months to come.

After his meeting with Leese, Burns resolved to iron out all the rough spots in his corps. On 7 June, he met with Hoffmeister and Vokes to give them guidance on training for the period that 1st Canadian Corps was scheduled to be in reserve.[16] Training was to be conducted with the following objects foremost in mind:

(a) To enable the corps to carry out [the] pursuit of a retiring enemy more speedily and effectively.
(b) To be able to break through an organized posn [position] of the type of the HITLER Line.[17]

Burns also gave guidance on the specific skills required to meet these aims. To speed up pursuit operations, infantry companies had to be more proficient in "quick attack[s] against hastily prepared posns, such as those encountered in the recent delaying action by the Germans." And, to avoid the time-consuming deployment of engineers every time units encountered man-made obstacles, Burns wanted "special trg ... in the recognition of German anti-pers [personnel] mines and booby traps together with methods for dealing with the same."

This initial guidance provided a good framework for moving forward, but it was just a framework. Further guidance had to be based on a more in-depth analysis of the May offensive. Accordingly, Burns scheduled a conference of corps officers, down to the rank of lieutenant-colonel, to ensure that the training fully incorporated the lessons that had been learned.[18] Seven pages of meeting minutes recorded what was a thorough, structured, and well-informed discussion.[19] In accordance with a promulgated agenda, the 1 CID staff led the open dialogue on matters pertaining to the break-in battle, while the armoured division expanded on lessons for the breakout. For the break-in, how to select crossing sites, the need for at least two crossings per division (to avoid unnecessary bottlenecks of traffic), the use of smoke to blind enemy on the far bank during the initial assaults, and the importance of eliminating enemy artillery observers before commencing bridging operations were among the lessons brought forward. For the breakout, because that phase of operations had proved most difficult, discussions were more wide-ranging. 5 CAD representatives talked about equipment, especially the need for "lighter and more manoeuvrable vehs [vehicles]" for the division reconnaissance regiment.

They expanded on the lamentable dearth of "usable battlefield information," the necessity of proper liaison with flanking formations, and the importance of regular reports. They also discussed two key organizational shortfalls – the requirement for additional infantry in the hilly and broken Italian terrain, and the critical deficiency of engineering assets in the armoured division.

Most important, they discussed how they fought, and how they would fight in the future. Because "isolated pockets" of enemy resistance had imposed delay too easily on the corps' advance from the Gustav Line to Frosinone, methods for speeding up the pursuit became a central theme of the conference. Along those lines, the conferees observed that, although nearly all German delaying positions were located "on or near the most suitable axis of adv [advance]," few of them actually "offered serious or determined resistance" for fear of being quickly overrun: "Considering the degree of resistance afforded by these pockets, it was found quicker to clean them out with leading tps [troops] rather than to attempt to by-pass them and leave the clearing up to others. If, however, these pockets are on the flank of the axis and can be bypassed, they will probably clear out when they are flanked."[20] This was exactly what Burns had in mind when he directed his divisional commanders to train for "quick attacks" at the company level – clearing the enemy quickly and aggressively, then moving on.

Related to speeding up the pursuit, there was also some nuanced dialogue about firm bases. So far as planning and controlling the battle was concerned, the conference participants made some subtle, and useful, distinctions between "bounds" and "firm bases." Whereas a "firm base was defined as a def [defensive] area designed for a specific purpose and to remain after the relieving troops passed through," a bound was "a posn on which consolidation and reorg [reorganization] may take place, but which dissolves as soon as other tps pass through." When planning an advance, bounds were necessary. Firm bases were not: "The firm base is, therefore, required on bde [brigade] or higher level in the breakthrough battle as long as the enemy is known to have res [reserves] and the threat of counter-attack is considerable. In the pursuit of a disorganized enemy, firm basis [sic] slow up the pursuit."[21] Snow's order for 11 CIB to dig in to the east of Ceprano, in spite of there being no enemy to his immediate front, was a perfect example of a firm base unnecessarily delaying the pursuit. At least the Canadians learned from their mistakes.

In all, the productive forum identified problems and crafted solid framework solutions for the corps's training, without having to wait for the detailed written after-action reports. Based on conference findings, for example, the corps issued a training instruction on the pursuit within two days of the 16 June conference.[22] It incorporated what had been learned and gave guidance to reconnaissance, armour, artillery, infantry, and engineers on their respective roles in pursuit of a retiring enemy, and on how to prepare for such operations.[23] Further down the chain of command, 5 CAD held a study period on the pursuit for all officers down to company squadron level. They discussed firm bases, bounds, intercommunications, the use of scouts in the advance, maintaining contact with the enemy, traffic control, and a host of other issues aimed at quickening the tempo of the advance.[24] Subsequent to the study periods, 5 CAD tasked 11 CIB with devising and conducting a series of field exercises to practise armour and infantry cooperation in situations when the enemy anti-tank weapons attempt to impose delay.[25] Repeated manoeuvres against a delaying enemy, it was hoped, would enhance all-arms cooperation and, therefore, speed up the tempo of operations. Exercise FRAME-UP, which took place 24-28 July, did just that. Full battalions advanced with the support of a squadron of tanks each. To improve the flow of "useful" information, liaison officers (LOs) received special training to ensure they gathered and relayed appropriate information.[26] To hasten the breaching of minor man-made obstacles, sappers from 10 Canadian Field Squadron trained division officers "in use of explosives as an expedient in clearing obstacles impeding the adv."[27] To hone intercommunication skills, staff and commanders from company to corps level participated in several signals exercises.[28] The point to be made here is this: had Burns waited for the completion of all the written after-action reports (which were completed in the third week of June) this training could not have been arranged and completed in the timely manner that it was.[29]

The interesting thing about the 16 June conference that set so much of this training in motion was that Hoffmeister missed it. He was on leave in Cairo – sixteen days of rest and relaxation that started on 12 June.[30] While nearly two and one-half weeks might have seemed excessive at such a critical juncture, mid-June presented Hoffmeister with the best opportunity for a much needed break. Since landing in Sicily, he had only had one other period of leave, eight days in early February.[31] Most of the training in June, with the exception of a few signals exercises, focused on individual and small-unit skills – not the sort of thing that made his presence critical. Besides, during the first three weeks of June, the highest priorities within the corps were the integration of reinforcements and the resting of the "old hands." As the 5 CAD historical officer recorded: "Every effort is being made to get all ranks away on seven days' leave ... It has been laid down that no large scale exercises are to be held in this area and training, for the most part, be carried out on a Regtl [Regimental] or Sqn/Coy basis."[32] Everyone in the Canadian corps needed some respite. Hoffmeister was no exception.

Before he left for his own period of rest and relaxation, however, Hoffmeister tied up a number of loose ends. And, as had always been his custom, he tended to the human factor first. Not wanting to miss an opportunity to build bonds on the combat experience that he and his soldiers now shared, Hoffmeister made his way from unit to unit. During the slowest period of training in early June,

> the GOC availed himself of the opportunity of visiting all units and HQ's [sic] of the Div and speaking to both officers and men. It is Gen Hoffmeister's practice not to keep troops standing in the sun during these talks but to break them off and have

them seat themselves comfortably in the shade, himself standing in the center of the group talking to them in the friendliest and most informal manner. The gist of most of these talks was an expression of appreciation for the loyal cooperation of all ranks in the operation. He took pains to point out to the members of Div and Bde HQ's [sic], and to other troops who do not themselves have the opportunity of killing Germans, that their job of communications and the numerous other services was of no less importance than that of the men who actually fire the weapons.[33]

Hoffmeister knew that the upcoming period of training would require the patience and effort of all ranks. Road movement exercises, for example, mostly bored the soldiers, there being little for them to do but follow along and wonder why they were there. At least now, having seen Hoffmeister, and having listened to him, they might have been more inclined to think, "Well, he didn't make us stand in the sun when he spoke to us; he probably wouldn't run an exercise like this just to annoy us. There must be a good reason for it." Thanking the troops did not hurt either. Every soldier – be he sapper or staff officer, machine gunner or mechanic – needed to believe that his contribution was both important and appreciated; that was key to eliciting the best individual effort. Hoffmeister had made it work for Corporal Meade at Agira. Ten months later, he was doing the same, albeit with a larger audience.

He also knew what had to be done to address the technical difficulties of the Liri Valley offensive, and he ensured that his people had the necessary guidance to make things happen during his period of leave. By 5 June, he had compiled and sifted through all the after-action reports from his brigades, staff principals, and supporting arms. He also had the comments of two outside observers, staff officers from the Directorate of Military Training, Allied Armies Italy, who briefed him on their findings on 9 June.[34] Based on such input and his own observations, he outlined a training program for the remainder of the month at a 10 June conference. To make certain that he would be well represented at Burns's 16 June conference, Hoffmeister briefed his temporary replacement, Brigadier H.A. Sparling in some detail. And last, Hoffmeister paused to brief the corps commander on his findings and intentions before embarking for Cairo. Actually, Hoffmeister was "ordered to attend a conference with the Corps Comd" on 11 June. Burns must have wanted to make sure everything in 5 CAD was well in hand before Hoffmeister left.[35] Evidently it was.

In spite of the logical manner in which Hoffmeister tackled the problem of resting and retraining his division, a sense of desperation pervades the documentation concerning his departure on leave. To be fully appreciated, however, Hoffmeister's need to get away must be considered in the context of what was happening at the time, starting with the operation just completed. While not a failure, the 5 CAD breakout from the Hitler Line interrupted for Hoffmeister a two-year run of unqualified successes. Both the corps and army commanders criticized some aspect of his performance, and that of his headquarters; and however gently they may have done so, that had to have bothered the competitive young division commander who had become so accustomed to success and the praise that came with it. There was also the fact that they were right; there were times when Hoffmeister was not able to exert the sort of control he wanted over the battle. That had frustrated him immensely.

Having to deal with an unresponsive subordinate only compounded Hoffmeister's stresses, and Snow's thorn in Hoffmeister's side continued to be an irritant even after the Liri Valley battles. In an after-action report, which Snow circulated to the corps commander, among others, before Hoffmeister had reviewed it, the brigadier implicitly criticized his division commander.[36] He complained, for example, that "it was terribly confusing to the junior officers to have plans changed as many times as they were during the campaign."[37] And his backhanded statement, "I must not hound my Bn Comds while they are conducting their battle even though I am being pressed by my own comd," was a barely veiled shot at Hoffmeister's supervision during the battle. That did it. If Hoffmeister had been at all inclined to tolerate Snow, and perhaps work with the brigade commander to improve his performance, the report dissipated any sympathy there may have been. The day Hoffmeister read the report and realized its extended circulation, he wrote an adverse "Officer's Confidential Report" on Snow, suggesting a "change of employment."[38] Hoffmeister was direct: "This offr [officer] has made a good effort but does not possess the strength of character or ability to comd an inf bde in active ops." He recommended Snow for employment as a colonel in command of an infantry training establishment. Snow protested to both Burns and Crerar, but the two senior commanders supported Hoffmeister's recommendation, and Brigadier Ian Johnston replaced Snow as commander of 11 CIB on 24 June.[39] Hoffmeister found the experience singularly trying.

Even with the issue of Snow resolved in his favour, a combination of stress and physical exhaustion continued to weary Hoffmeister. The 5 CAD War Diary for 6 June shows that he "spent a very quiet day in the HQ area" – no doubt mulling over Snow's report and writing the confidential report that led to the brigadier's dismissal.[40] The next day was much the same. Mixed praise from above and criticism from below undermined the confidence that had been on the mend since his 1941 nervous crisis. The visits to units and the informal talks with soldiers that started on 8 June were not only intended to bolster the morale of the rank and file, they were also a form of refuge – a safe place where Hoffmeister's currency was still extremely good. He was seriously fatigued – so seriously, in fact, that sixteen days of leave did not solve the problem. A little over two weeks after his leave, Hoffmeister checked into 15 General Hospital.[41] Because his medical records are still restricted, and because Hoffmeister never discussed his physical or mental condition during this period, it is impossible to determine, for certain, the diagnosis and the treatment that followed. He may have been heading for another nervous crisis. He may simply have been physically and mentally worn-out. Or, he may have been suffering from a combination of ailments, to which he had become susceptible as a result of fatigue. Whatever the affliction, the 5 CAD war diarist recorded that the four-day stay in hospital did much to improve both his demeanour and his appearance: "The GOC returned from hosp [hospital] looking and feeling very much better than he did when he left on Sunday last."[42]

It was fortunate that Hoffmeister tended to his personal health when he did, because there was still much work to be done before his division re-entered the battle. During the period 23-24 July, he and his headquarters received an excellent shake-out on Exercise VITAL. Designed by 1st Canadian Corps "to exercise Corps and Div Staff with particular reference to liaison between GS [General Staff], RCA [Royal Canadian Artillery] and RCE [Royal Canadian Engineers]," the exercise addressed the uneven flow of information that had characterized the planning and conduct of operations in the Liri Valley.[43] The exercise planners conceived a useful training program to that end. Both 1 CID and 5 CAD had the task of advancing "with best possible speed," breaking into an enemy defensive area, capturing key terrain, and exploiting beyond the main defences. For planning purposes, the corps staff provided the divisions with information from a myriad of sources, including air photographs, intelligence summaries, and patrol reports, to name a few. Umpires at each headquarters – eight at each division, and ten at Corps – observed how information was processed, passed, and used to plan the various phases of operations. This was the sort of exercise that the 5 CAD staff had missed in the weeks preceding the Liri Valley offensive. It proved so useful, in fact, that 5 CAD conducted two more such headquarters shakeouts during the second week of August.[44]

The corps also needed to improve its road movement and traffic control. Every one of the after-action reports, from brigade to corps, mentioned the traffic problems that had afflicted the Canadians during May and early June. Specifically, "the present resources of Corps and Div Pro [Provost] coys are not sufficient adequately to control the movement of traffic within the corps area."[45] Hoffmeister made an alarming, though unintentionally humorous, observation that gave some insight to just how deeply the problem of traffic control affected – and derailed – the function of his headquarters: "It is not practicable to send SC [Staff Captains] on TC [Traffic Control] duty ... Every SC has a particular task and the efficient running of the HQ demands that they remain at the HQ."[46] A system of traffic control that required staff planners to act as traffic cops was not a system that worked well.

At the corps level, Burns addressed the shortage of provost corpsmen by converting the 254-man 35 Light Anti-Aircraft Battery into a Traffic Control unit. The decision made good sense. The elimination of the threat in Italy rendered the existence of the air defence unit a luxury, even superfluous. In addition, the unit had, in its current war establishment, the communication infrastructure to control traffic effectively and respond to changes on short notice. Following Burn's example,

Hoffmeister did the same with 5 Light Anti-Aircraft Regiment in his division. On 1 July, the 5 CAD Exercise WORK-OUT tested the new organization's four traffic control points (TCPs) and traffic control office. Further, officers specifically designated to handle moves joined corps and division "Q" staffs to assist with road-movement planning (see Figure 8.1, p. 157). The corps Exercise TIME OUT practised all the new organizations by making them plan and execute the movement of most of the corps' vehicles.[47] The new system was a vast improvement over the ad hoc system that had sent staff captains to act as traffic cops.

Other organizational changes took place in July and August. By this stage in the Italian Campaign, all Eighth Army formation commanders realized the armoured division organization for battle, based as it was on lessons learned in the North African desert, was unsuited to the olive groves and mountains of the Italian peninsula. As Sir Oliver Leese remarked in an 8 June letter to the War Office: "The armoured division with one infantry brigade is no good in this type of fighting."[48] It did not have enough infantry. Consequently, Leese reorganized armoured divisions in the Eighth Army based on an establishment of one armoured brigade and two infantry brigades. The British 6th Armoured Division and the 6th South African Armoured Division converted to this format in early June, and Leese hoped that the Canadians would send another infantry brigade to Italy so that 5 CAD could do the same. But the priority assigned to operations in Northwest Europe precluded the dispatch of an additional brigade to what was now a subsidiary theatre.[49] Based on that, Leese suggested to Burns on 2 July that he "submit proposals" for organizing "another inf bde for 5 Cdn Armd Div" from units already within 1st Canadian Corps.[50] On 12 July, Burns received authorization from CMHQ to organize 12 Canadian Infantry Brigade by removing the Westminster Regiment (motorized) from 5 CAB, converting 1 CID's reconnaissance regiment, the Princess Louise Dragoon Guards (PLDG), to infantry, and changing the 1st Light Anti-Aircraft Regiment to infantry (later redesignating it as the Lanark and Renfrew Scottish Regiment). By these sensible actions, 5 CAD made up a notable deficiency at minimal cost. The corps lost its reconnaissance regiment when it assigned the Royal Canadian Dragoons (1st Canadian Armoured Car Regiment) to 1 CID as a replacement for the PLDG. The corps's second light anti-aircraft regiment also disappeared, but, as has been mentioned, the absence of a significant enemy air threat justified the conversion. And 5 CAB lost its motorized infantry battalion (the Westminsters), but that was a shortfall that could be easily made up with a quick regrouping. A new brigade staff and the addition of various support services rounded out the 12 CIB order of battle.

The task of readying the new formation for battle went to Brigadier D.C. Spry. It was an enormous undertaking. Not only did the two "non-infantry" battalions have to be reorganized and retrained, they had to be equipped as well. Staffs struggled to find sufficient rifles, mortars, and machine guns for the units to fulfill their new roles, and early enough to allow them time to become proficient. Sorting out all the war establishment and equipment issues took well over a month; however, by the end of July and early August, the battalions had enough weapons for their soldiers to conduct range practices while officers and non-commissioned officers attended study periods on such relevant topics as the "battalion in the advance," "the company and the platoon in the attack," and "break-in" and "breakthrough" battles.[51] To make certain that the training fully integrated the lessons the corps had learned in May, Brigadier Spry, and after 13 August, Brigadier J.S. Lind issued direction on training and operating procedures by way of a numbered memoranda system.[52]

Hoffmeister, whose health and spirits improved steadily following his brief hospital stay, monitored closely the preparations of 12 CIB, often intervening to give advice and make changes. He also had a hand in selecting battle-experienced commanders for the new units. For example, to command the Lanark and Renfrew Regiment and turn them into infantry, he appointed Lieutenant-Colonel W. Clement Dick, who had formerly been his brigade major in 2 CIB and whom he trusted completely.[53] Near the end of July, he began planning a brigade-level exercise to build on the progress 11 CIB had made on Exercise FRAME-UP (24-28 July) and validate the state of his newest formation.[54] Exercise CANYON, which took place not far from the division area near Foligno (75 miles northeast of Rome) was actually two exercises designed to practise

(a) Bde consolidation on a permanent feature;
(b) A deliberate attack across an obstacle with the final objective some 4000 yds from the obstacle and an intermediate objective between the two.[55]

11 CIB went first and experienced few difficulties. Then, on 16-17 August, 12 CIB took to the field, supported by an armoured regiment, an engineer field squadron, a field regiment of artillery, two anti-tank batteries, and two sections of provost corpsmen for traffic control. Hoffmeister carefully watched the progress of the 12 CIB manoeuvres, which, despite being initiated in great haste, went well. That the brigade managed to give a reasonable account of itself was remarkable, given the inexperience of the new brigade staff and two of the infantry units.

But it would have been foolish to expect that 12 CIB could perform as well as a battle-experienced brigade. They had made real progress in a little over a month, but it was not so long ago that 11 CIB, a brigade of infantry that had been training together for months, took a terrible beating on the Arielli. Hoffmeister remembered. However well 12 CIB may have done on Exercise CANYON, he was well aware how green the formation really was to battle. In the back of his mind, he knew that, for the coming operation, he would have to parcel out tasks judiciously.

Still, like all the units and formations in the Canadian corps, Hoffmeister's division had come a long way in three short months. Organizationally, procedurally, and technically, the Canadians in Italy were better in August 1944 than they were in May. They had taken the experience of the spring offensive, pored over its lessons, and made the necessary changes. How much they had improved would be demonstrated in their next major operation – the assault on the Gothic Line.

HOFFMEISTER LEARNED much from his first operation as a divisional commander – most of it technical. Tapping into the human dimension never had been a problem. He impressed soldiers at all levels of command with his physical courage, his perseverance, his sincerity, and his sense of concern. But when he found himself deficient in technical knowledge, his capacity for battlefield management faltered, and so did his confidence. That was what had led to his 1941 nervous crisis, and it very nearly happened again in 1944. Six months was a very short period in which to advance from battalion to division command, even in wartime. It was certainly not enough time to master – beyond the book-learning of the staff college environment – how to manage all the intricate pieces in an armoured division. The Liri Valley battles changed that. Cruel as that learning environment may have been, Hoffmeister gained immeasurably from the experience. He learned how to think ahead, gather information, and plan operations at the divisional level. Concerning his control of the battle, the coordination of his staff, and the passage of direction to subordinate formations, he received much valuable guidance from corps and army, guidance that he put into practice during the summer pause. Thus, although it severely tried him, Hoffmeister emerged from the Liri Valley experience a technically capable divisional commander, and he never looked back.

Gothic Line to the End in Italy

Hoffmeister would never tell me how to do a job; he would tell me what had to be done but he wouldn't tell me what troops to use or anything like that.[1]

BRIGADIER IAN S. JOHNSTON,
COMMANDER 11 CANADIAN INFANTRY BRIGADE

Hoffmeister's human and technical skills continued their ascent throughout the remainder of the Italian Campaign. With the trials of his first divisional battle behind him, he forged a formidable fighting force out of the 5th Canadian Armoured Division, drawing on the fullest talents of its commanders, staffs, and soldiers. The ability to elicit the best from his people complemented his hard-earned technical skills – thinking ahead in battle, orchestrating the efforts of his all-arms team, and guiding the activities of his staff and subordinates. In all, his "Mighty Maroon Machine" fought five more major engagements before leaving the Italian peninsula for Northwest Europe in February 1945, beginning with its spectacular assault on the Gothic Line.

As THE ALLIED ARMIES in Italy slugged their way past Rome and on to Florence from June to August in 1944, Field-Marshal Kesselring's forces traded space for time to complete their next significant line of defence in Italy – the Gothic Line. Cracking the defensive network that ran from Pesaro on the Adriatic to just south of Lucca on the west coast was a significant problem for General Alexander and his Allied planners (see Map 9).[2] To start, several divisions departed the Fifth US Army for operations in Southern France. This left General Clark with only five divisions – four infantry and one armoured – with which to conduct operations in a theatre that the Combined Chiefs of Staff now considered secondary. Kesselring realized the weakened state of Clark's forces and, despite the fact that the deteriorating German situation in France had forced him to send away four divisions of his own, he shifted enough forces away from the anaemic Fifth Army front to retard the main Allied effort north of Florence. The strength of German defences in the mountainous centre of the peninsula, combined with the Eighth Army's lack of trained mountain troops, led Leese to convince Alexander that the main effort of the Allied offensive should be switched to the Adriatic coast, where better use could be made of Allied superiority in artillery, armour, and air forces.[3] Not that attacking along the coast would be easy – a series of watercourses ran across the intended line of advance between Pesaro and Ravenna – but Leese believed it to be the best way to break into the Po River valley, where he hoped his armour could really be effective. Alexander agreed, modifying his strategy to one of a "two-handed punch," threatening both Bologna and Ravenna with the hope of forcing the enemy either to split reserves, or, better yet, to commit the majority to stop the subsidiary thrust – now in the centre. The army group commander had to bolster the weakened Fifth Army with 13th (British) Corps and employ an elaborate deception plan to make the Germans take the bait in the Florence sector, but it worked. In early August, the bulk of the Eighth Army moved to the Adriatic sector undetected, and lined up behind the Metauro River – 2nd Polish Corps right, 1st Canadian Corps in the centre, 5th (British) Corps left. Kesselring, still fixed on Florence, kept the majority of his forces in the centre of the peninsula.

The lessons of the Liri Valley still fresh, Leese sought to break through with best possible speed, exploit to the valley of the Po River, and drive on towards Venice. On 11 August, at a conference attended by the commanders of 1st Canadian, 5th British, and 2nd Polish Corps, and their staffs, he outlined his plan for Operation OLIVE. Leese emphasized the importance of security – keeping the enemy convinced that the main attack would be in the area north of Florence – and its relation to achieving surprise, but his notes for the offensive highlighted the central tenet of the operation: speed.[4] Speed was what had been missing in the Liri operations, and Leese wanted to ensure that opportunities for the pursuit did not slip away again. He was convinced that the traffic difficulties that the army experienced in the spring offensive stemmed from the commitment of pursuit forces (1st Canadian Corps then 6th South African Armoured Division) onto routes they did not control. The solution? Place the pursuit force under the command of the principal assaulting corps, which would also control the routes.[5] Thus Leese entrusted the British 1st Armoured Division to Lieutenant-General Charles Keightley's 5th Corps. With this arrangement, the army commander hoped that the pursuit force could be committed with a minimum of fuss and coordination whenever the opportunity for a breakthrough occurred.

But there was a problem with Leese's plan – not so much with *how* he grouped his formations as *where* he employed them. Keightley's heavily weighted corps, which consisted of four infantry divisions, one armoured division, and two armoured brigades, had for its axis of advance the inland route, the one with the most mountainous terrain, the one that most restricted the movement of armour. The best ground for tanks was in the centre, where the Canadians were to attack with only two divisions and a British armoured brigade. This was where the heaviest corps, whether Keightley's or Burns's, should have been committed. In this inexplicably bad tactical oversight, Leese's poor opinion of Burns undoubtedly clouded his judgment. A 25 July letter to the War Office spelled out the reason Leese chose not to place the pursuit force, or any other divisions for that matter, under Canadian command: "I am ... confronted with the problem of trying to

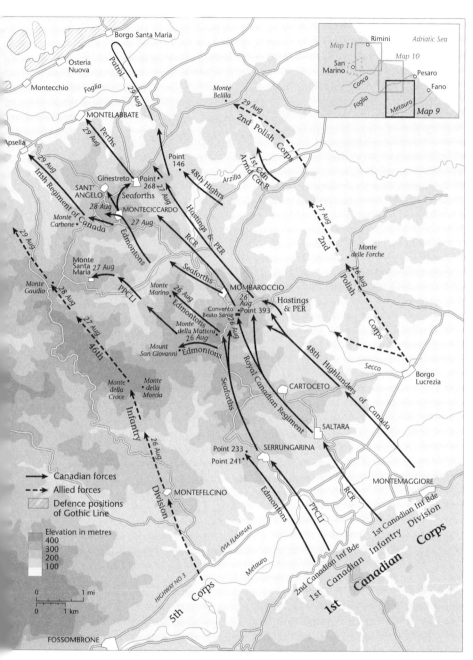

MAP 9   *The advance to the Gothic Line, 26-29 August 1944.* Adapted from G.W.L.
Nicholson (Lieutenant-Colonel), *The Canadians in Italy, 1943-1945* (Ottawa: Queen's
Printer, 1966), map 18.

fight the Canadian Corps under a Corps Commander in whom I do not believe, and under whose command I would not put the additional divisions necessary for any normal Corps operation."[6] Leese's reservations aside, he made a bad tactical decision that would have a detrimental impact on the battles of August and September.

Problems with the army plan notwithstanding, Burns turned his attention to the tactical problem of penetrating the Gothic Line. In support of the army commander's aim of breaking into the Po valley, Burns' stated intentions were to "destroy the enemy facing us on the [River] METAURO," "penetrate the GOTHIC LINE," and "exploit to RIMINI."[7] To do that, he divided his task into four phases (see Maps 9 and 10):

> PHASE I – The assault across the [River] METAURO and [the establishment] of brheads [bridgeheads] and crossings.
> PHASE II – The [advance] from [River] METAURO to the [River] FOGLIA.
> PHASE III – The breakthrough of the GOTHIC LINE.
> PHASE IV – Exploitation to RIMINI.[8]

Although the phased operation reflected the deliberate nature of Canadian and British doctrine, these stages of the attack were not rigid. Burns understood Leese's desire to seize the initiative, put the enemy on the run, and keep him running; and he built a plan flexible enough to take advantages of any such opportunities. While the first two phases were set – Vokes's division would assault across the Metauro and advance to the Foglia – the third offered "alternatives." As the 21 August order noted,

> There are two alternative situations which may be met on reaching the Gothic Line:
>
> (a) The enemy may be completely disorganised and thereby forced to man his prepared posns [positions] with only lt [light] forces.
> (b) The enemy may have been able to man his prepared posns in considerable str [strength] which will require a full scale attack.
>
> In the case of (a), speed will be the first consideration in order to take full advantage of his [enemy] surprise on finding the [strength] of [friendly] forces opposing him.[9]

If 1 CID found the enemy at the Foglia unprepared, it would "push [forward] with all speed and break through the GOTHIC LINE without waiting for the arrival of 5 Cdn Armd Div." At that point, 5 CAD, which was the corps reserve, would be "called fwd to exploit through the GOTHIC LINE." In the event that the enemy had prepared and manned defences in strength, 1 CID would advance to the Foglia, and then wait for 5 CAD and the subsequent launching of a set-piece corps attack. Once his corps had pierced the Gothic Line, Burns planned to drive though Cattolica to Rimini by way of the coastal axis.

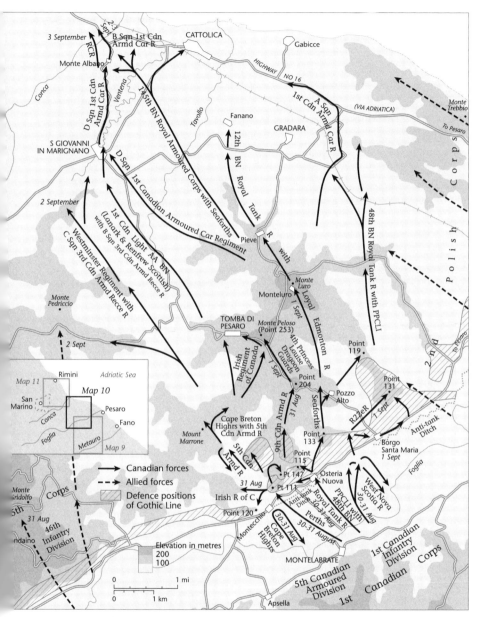

MAP 10 *The breaking of the Gothic Line, 30 August to 3 September 1944.* Adapted from G.W.L. Nicholson (Lieutenant-Colonel), *The Canadians in Italy, 1943-1945* (Ottawa: Queen's Printer, 1966), map 19.

Building that much flexibility into the plan required a tremendous amount of coordination and reconnaissance. Between the time he received his orders for Operation OLIVE on 11 August and the time that he issued his own orders on 21 August, for example, Burns had five meetings with Vokes, four with Hoffmeister, five with the army commander, and two with each of the commanders of the British and Polish corps on the flanks.[10] These meetings with flanking, subordinate, and higher formations continued into the operation. He also conducted two aerial overflights to look at the terrain and assess the strength of the German defences.[11] It helped: boundaries were adjusted, assembly areas assigned, and routes reserved, as Burns and his division commanders fine-tuned their plans.

To Hoffmeister, the task seemed particularly daunting. He first received word of Operation OLIVE while his infantry brigades were practising assault river crossings on Exercise CANYON. Within hours of Leese's 11 August orders, Burns visited 5 CAD headquarters "and gave [Hoffmeister] a brief outline of the proposed ops [operations]."[12] Hoffmeister remembered how Burns presented the problem: "The Gothic Line was represented to me to be a particularly heavily fortified line, possibly more so than even the Hitler Line, with a huge anti-tank ditch running across the front of the entire thing, and the ground rising up and forming an ideal defensive position. It really had great opportunities for mutual support, ending in Coriano Ridge way at the back ... It was [built] in great depth."[13]

It was extensive: 9,800 yards (8,944 metres) of anti-tank ditches, 72,517 anti-tank mines, 23,172 anti-personnel mines, and 128,000 yards (117,370 metres) of wire obstacles bolstered a line of defences that included 3,604 dugouts, 2,375 machine-gun posts, and 479 anti-tank gun positions. Impressive as those figures may sound, in August 1944 large sections of the Gothic Line still remained incomplete.[14] Although the Germans had begun constructing the coast-to-coast line of defences in the autumn of 1943, the priority they had assigned to the Hitler and Gustav Lines (for obvious reasons) had consumed the lion's share of dwindling manpower and materiel in the early months of 1944. In June, as the Hitler Line was crumbling under the weight of Eighth Army assaults, Kesselring's forces had been forced to conscript Italian civilians for service in labour battalions just to make the Gothic Line defensible. Most important, however, in mid-August, fighting troops had yet to occupy its trenches. Hoffmeister knew nothing of the weaknesses of the Gothic Line defences, however, when he was warned of the impending operation; he assumed the worst and immediately set to planning what he figured was sure to be a set-piece attack on a prepared defensive position.

Burns went over the plan in greater detail with Hoffmeister on the afternoon of 12 August, leaving the division commander with some planning notes and some maps with which to commence his own tactical appreciation. Hoffmeister spent most of 13 August reviewing the notes and doing a detailed map study of the proposed area of operations. Five days later, after he had watched his infantry brigades on Exercise CANYON, and after the division had conducted an efficient road move to an assembly area south of the Metauro River, he briefed Burns on his initial plan of action. This might seem an undue amount of time to keep a corps commander waiting, but for Hoffmeister, seeing what his brigades were capable of doing – especially the newly formed 12 CIB – was crucial. Without that knowledge, it would have been difficult to assign tasks commensurate with the capabilities of all his formations. Hoffmeister "felt it would be necessary to attack MONTECCIO [sic] frontally during darkness, as this was the key to the enemy posn in his sector and no adv [advance] could be effected until it was reduced."[15] This was true (see Map 10, p. 171). Because the German positions on Points 120 and 111 dominated the open approaches from Montelabbate to Montecchio, they had to be captured before tanks could move. Similarly, if tanks were to move beyond the gap between Points 120 and 111, towards Mount Marrone and Tomba di Pesaro, enemy fire from Point 147 at least had to be neutralized. Long before tanks put the run to anyone, this was to be an infantry fight.

But it was no job for an untested brigade, populated with soldiers only recently converted to infantry. Hoffmeister rightly picked 11 CIB for the first stage of the Gothic Line operation. By the autumn of 1944, it was the most experienced brigade in 5 CAD. The problems of the Arielli Show were well behind it; its soldiers had proven their mettle in the Liri Valley. Equally important, it had a talented new brigadier, Ian S. Johnston. An RMC graduate from the class of 1930, Johnston became a lawyer and had served in the interwar Non-Permanent Active Militia with the 48th Highlanders of Toronto. Having started the war as a captain, he rose to command his regiment from May 1943 to June 1944, after which time he replaced Snow in 11 CIB. He was experienced – he had been fighting steadily since the invasion of Sicily – intelligent, and thorough. Hoffmeister knew he was just the man to look at cracking the first crust of the German defences.

Johnston's written appreciation for dismembering the Montecchio positions, besides being an exceptional and concise piece of staffwork, offers some insight into the modus operandi in Hoffmeister's division.[16] Hoffmeister gave Johnston his object – "to breach the GOTHIC LINE in the MONTECCHIO area" – during a 13 August conference. The division commander also passed on some planning parameters, some basic assumptions: that the enemy would be able to man the Gothic Line and force the corps to mount a set-piece attack, and that Johnston's brigade would be task-organized with four infantry battalions, one regiment of tanks under command, and all the engineering assets of the division.[17] Other than that, Hoffmeister left the determination of *how* to achieve the object to Johnston. For his part, Johnston looked first at the enemy, considering that members of the 3rd Parachute Regiment, then resting at Tomba di Pesaro, would probably garrison the line. Based on his experience fighting paratroopers, he also considered that, although the enemy would be relatively "thin on the ground," they would be equipped with a "large number of automatic weapons" – weapons that were deadly during the day, but which could "only fire on fixed lines at night." Consequently, he favoured a night attack on the forward positions. Regarding the ground, he concurred with Hoffmeister's assessment: the forward positions that dominated the tank approaches had to be captured by infantry before any armoured exploitation could begin. Johnston also had an in-depth look at breaching the anti-tank ditch and the minefields, which he thought would be difficult, but not impossible.

In the end, Johnston selected a night attack by two infantry battalions, each supported by a squadron of tanks, as the best course of action. The Perth Regiment would assault Point 111 on the right and then drive to Point 115 and Point 147. The Cape Breton Highlanders would attack Point 120 on the left, later exploiting to a position 500 yards beyond it. While those initial attacks were taking place, engineers would clear the usable routes and make gaps in the minefields for the subsequent passage of the remaining tanks, anti-tank guns, and the two reserve battalions. For a fire plan, Johnston recommended holding the fire of the guns until two battalions had reached the minefield. After that, he proposed that artillery should commence to neutralize the forward positions, especially Point 120. Thinking about the pursuit, Johnston also wanted the mortars of the Brigade Support Group to move forward of the Foglia River so that they would be in range to support any opportunity to strike deep towards Mount Marrone.

Johnston's well-considered first cut at the problem of breaching the Gothic Line served Hoffmeister well. When he briefed Burns on 18 August, he based much of what he had to say on Johnston's preliminary analysis and discussions he had had with the brigadier. As will be seen, the battle did not unfold exactly according to Johnston's recommended course of action, but having the brigade commander carefully think through the numerous options for the attack – the sort of detailed consideration that time would not permit a division commander – paid dividends later. For example, although it was not his preferred option, Johnston did believe that Point 120 could be captured from behind – a possibility that later became reality.[18] Hoffmeister relied heavily on Johnston to work through the details of the break-in battle, but it had long been his practice to give his subordinates a large share of responsibility for planning and controlling a portion of the battle: "I was always ready to take advice from my gunners, my sappers, and for that matter from my brigadiers. When I asked my brigadiers if they had any questions or suggestions, I meant it and they knew I meant it ... I was looking for the best idea and if, in the planning stage someone had a better idea, that was fine with me."[19] He had done much the same with Smith's 5 CAB during the breakout from the Hitler Line and, before that, he had done it with Bell-Irving at Agira. It made sense. The breakthrough of the Gothic Line was only one phase (the third) of the corps operation, and Hoffmeister, as the division commander, had to think about *all* phases.

Beyond reaching Mount Marrone and Tomba di Pesaro, Hoffmeister deliberated on how he would get to Cattolica and thence to Rimini – the fourth phase of the corps operation. He rightly figured that the capture of Tomba di Pesaro and Mount Peloso were key to blunting the counterattacks the Germans were sure to hurl at any Canadian bridgehead. Once he had those positions secure, he could launch 5 CAB, with the Westminster Regiment under command, to Cattolica and the Conca River. The next logical bound, as Hoffmeister saw it, was for 12 CIB to pick up the two battalions it had detached to the other brigades and chase the withdrawing enemy to Rimini.[20] Having carved the operation into successive brigade tasks, he had each of his brigadiers scrutinize their respective portions. With his brigade commanders giving their full attention to those issues, Hoffmeister was free to consider what the enemy might do: "I thought it was important for me to have this period ... during which I would put myself in the position of the enemy commander and figure out what he might do and then take the necessary steps to counteract him."[21] In this way, potential problems could be identified for staffs to resolve in advance of the operation, not during it. That Hoffmeister was now looking at events days beyond the start of the operation was a clear indication of his maturation as a divisional commander.

Turning ideas into action required the toil of many staff officers, and the process of staff coordination in 5 CAD warrants some comment. Because so much of it was done in person or on the telephone, documentation on this is scant, but memoir accounts and interviews, when combined with log references, permit the piecing together of a reasonable picture of how things were done. First, the division did not stick to a rigid forum – regularly scheduled conferences or meetings – for sorting administrative arrangements based on operational requirements. As Hoffmeister's primary logistic planner, the assistant adjutant and quartermaster general (AA & QMG) remembered, "It wasn't always the same but according to the situation. Sometimes you got together directly, at others you called people in for a conference, at others you sent a liaison officer out. A lot of work was done directly or on the telephone."[22] In other words, how the coordination took place mattered less than knowing who was responsible for making sure it was done. Typically, on returning from visits with subordinate commanders, Hoffmeister relayed the tentative plans to his GSO I so that the necessary staff coordination could be initiated (see Figure 8.1, p. 157, for the organization of Hoffmeister's headquarters).[23] As the chief of staff, it was the responsibility of the GSO I to ensure the chain of actions was connected – getting the ammunition, finding the trucks to transport it, gaining access on the routes to move it, and securing a location to dump it – so that the rounds reached the troops who needed them, when they needed them.[24] The detailed coordination of these actions devolved to the AA & QMG, whose staff officers would do the logistic staff checks and make the necessary arrangements. Most of that activity took place under the DA (deputy adjutant) & QMG at Division Rear Headquarters, the hub of logistical and road-movement planning. Organizational changes in the 5 CAD headquarters following the Liri Valley operations made matters much easier.

In Hoffmeister's modus operandi, coordination figured as prominently as weighing tactical options. From the time he issued his initial warning order on

13 August, his basic plan of manoeuvre – 11 CIB breaking in as far as Tomba di Pesaro, 5 CAB exploiting to the Conca River, followed by 12 CIB advancing on Rimini – stayed the same. It was a solid plan, simple enough and flexible enough to permit two weeks' worth of tweaking the details. And who better to examine the details of the various stages of the fight than the commanders principally responsible for fighting them? The brigade commanders and the staff put the flesh on Hoffmeister's skeleton. From the time he issued his initial direction, he was more conduit than creator – conferring with his brigadiers and then relaying their recommendations to his staff to make things happen. For the 5 CAD staff, its sweat went into dovetailing the various phases of the plan and making sure the various elements had the administrative support they needed.

In this regard, Hoffmeister emulated many of the senior British officers under whom he served. It was not that they were uninterested in details; they just did not think that they should be the ones to dig for them. As Hoffmeister recalled, they conferred with subordinates to see what was needed for a particular operation, then got it:

> Leese, Dempsey, Allfry [sic], McCreery, particularly the first three, were great people with whom to work. They *always* came up to my H.Q. and together we made a recce [reconnaissance] of the ground. The orders were verbal, informal and never firm until my opinions were given and considered. I recall so clearly on one occasion [in October 1943 when Hoffmeister was acting commander of 2 CIB] when the subject of additional support was raised. Dempsey turned to Kit Huxley, his B.G.S. [Brigadier General Staff], and said, "Kit, do what you can [to] get guns [artillery] and air [support] for Bert." ... The result – we had 2 Medium [artillery] regts & 1 heavy [artillery regiment] ... medium bomber as well as fighter-bomber direct support.[25]

This manner of doing business worked well in the Eighth Army. From their subordinates, commanders obtained well-considered analyses for each stage of a given operation – the sort of analyses they could not do on their own – and that, in turn, ensured a thorough and proper examination of the tactical problem. It also fostered what Hoffmeister called the "great mutual confidence" that he enjoyed with British commanders in the Eighth Army.[26] Being a part of the planning process gave Hoffmeister a stake in the plan.

In contrast, Canadian generals, with the exception of Vokes and, to a lesser extent, Burns, tended towards a more top-down approach. Simonds, for example, made the plan himself, let his staff coordinate the details, then passed on orders – no questions.[27] Crerar, although he allowed his staff to develop courses of action for his consideration, passed on the selected option with little input from subordinate commanders.[28] Keeping subordinate input to a minimum had the effect of minimizing the subordinate share in the plan, and that was not good for morale. Hoffmeister recognized this. He had known it since his experience with all those "miserable little mill" owners during the Seaboard lumber crisis of 1935. That was why he made such an effort to bring people on board, make them feel part of the team, and tap into the talent he had below him. With Simonds, the plan was his and his alone. With Crerar, the plan was the staff's. With Hoffmeister, the plan belonged to everyone – commander, subordinate, and staff. That was the essential difference.

Personality mattered. Here again, Hoffmeister followed the lead of the British generals. More dynamic than their Canadian contemporaries, British commanders placed more emphasis on making a personal impression on subordinates – at all levels. As a battalion commander, Hoffmeister had marvelled at how Montgomery could manipulate the emotions of soldiers crowded around his jeep in Sicily:

> He was quite a bit of a showman, but he was a darned good psychologist at the same time ... Monty drove up in his jeep and I reported to him. He addressed me by my first name, said he was glad to see me, and said what a good job the Seaforths had done, etc ... Then he said, "I don't like to talk to my soldiers so far away, come around," and the whole blinking battalion just surged out and around the jeep in a great solid mass. Monty then looked them all over and smiled in a benign way and said, "Well who have we here" and a great roar answered, "Seaforths". [Montgomery then said,] "Well of course my Seaforths"; just as corny as all get up, but the troops loved it ... Monty in typical style said, "You recall my order of the day when I said, that by such and such a time we would have Sicily in our hands; well we have, and now I tell you that we're going into Italy and across the straits of Messina and that Rome will be in our hands by a certain date. If I say it will be, then you can depend on it" ... And you know that this is the sort of stuff the troops wanted. It just built them up, their tails were vertical.[29]

"Monty" had a knack for mining the emotions of soldiers. Hoffmeister also admired Leese, who, for all his technical foibles, was good at this sort of thing as well. He saved the letter that Leese sent to all ranks of the Eighth Army before the Liri Valley offensive, on which he pencilled a marginal note that reads, "A very inspiring message from our much loved and respected army comdr."[30] Leese was definitely better with words than he was with route planning. On 22 August 1944, the army commander addressed every 1st Canadian Corps officer above the rank of major. In an eighty-minute speech on the upcoming operation, Leese emphasized that "the essential for success was to drive ruthlessly on, leaving pockets of resistance to be cleaned up by the troops following up."[31] Everyone present got the message. It was an impressive performance in public speaking, one that led Canada's official historian of the Italian Campaign to record, "Sir Oliver's racy informality, the clarity of his presentation, the scope of his discourse, and his abounding confidence made an impression that his audience were unlikely to forget."[32]

Few of Hoffmeister's Canadian bosses could do the same. Crerar was stodgy – a stickler for details and dress discipline who seemed oddly out of step with the informality of the Eighth Army. Simonds was technically brilliant, but Hoffmeister did not like him at all. Although Simonds tried to follow Montgomery's example, he was too "cold blooded" and aloof to pay attention to the "psychology of the situation."[33] And Burns, while Hoffmeister admired him for his "guts" and his willingness to go "well forward to 'read' the battle," "lacked the poise and charisma of his British counter-parts."[34] Hoffmeister summed up the problem of Burns's personality succinctly: "He moved slowly, gave orders in a monotone [manner] and lacked [the] enthusiasm and personality to 'sell' the plan."[35] Soldiers believed that "Monty" would give them victories. With Burns, no one was sure.

Hoffmeister had only one Canadian commander with the ability to impress subordinates with strength of personality: Chris Vokes. Tellingly, although Hoffmeister saved correspondence from every British general he served, Vokes is the only Canadian with personal letters in the Hoffmeister Collection. One, an eight-line note that Vokes wrote on leaving Italy to take command of the 4th Canadian Armoured Division in Northwest Europe, was a simple soldier's farewell. Vokes wished his friend well and praised him for turning 5 CAD into a "magnificent fighting machine." He then closed with, "It has given me always a great deal of pleasure to have had your military career associated with mine. I look forward to meeting up with you again at some future date."[36] Not a long note, but it was sincere, and Hoffmeister obviously appreciated that Vokes had taken the time to write it. Vokes affected Hoffmeister in a way that the other Canadians could not. For that reason, he looked to "the Brits" for role models.

Following the example of his British bosses, Hoffmeister gave formal orders on the morning of 25 August, with a view to selling his plan for the breaking of the Gothic Line. So much consultation and coordination had taken place in the previous twelve days that there were no surprises. A written order, signed by Hoffmeister's GSO I on 21 August, had already parroted the corps order of the same day, emphasizing the four phases of the corps plan, including the option of gate-crashing the Gothic Line should 1 CID find it to be undefended.[37] As always, Hoffmeister kept his orders brief; two hours from the start of the division commander's conference, Johnston was back at 11 CIB headquarters delivering his.[38] Everyone read from the same sheet of music, and believed in the score, long before the conductor struck up the band.

When the Eighth Army offensive started at one minute short of midnight on 25 August, it initially caught the enemy by surprise.[39] All of the efforts to conceal the movement of 5th Corps and 1st Canadian Corps to the Adriatic worked, leaving the enemy convinced that the main Allied attack would come in the centre. As a result, the lead battalions of the three advancing corps met no resistance at the Metauro and managed to thrust some three to five miles beyond it by first light on 26 August (see Map 9, p. 169). In the Canadian sector, as in the British and Polish sectors, the battalions of the 1 CID waded across the thigh-deep Metauro and pressed forward against what amounted to a few German observation posts overlooking the river. Those observation posts formed the first part of a twelve-mile-deep security zone in front of the Gothic Line, the purpose of which was to impose delay and give the German defenders enough warning of impending attack to man the main defensive area in force. Collapsing that security zone quickly was the key to catching the enemy by surprise, and Vokes pushed on to the next set of delay positions – at Monte della Morcia, Monte della Croce and Monte della Mattera – to do just that. But the German defenders did not make it easy. They shelled the advancing infantry and delayed the progress of the division's supporting tanks with blown bridges, craters, and mines. Vokes still hurled his lead brigades onward (without tank support until noon), reaching Monte Marino by midnight on 26 August. Beyond those heights, the enemy had one more delay position, one anchored on the hill town of Monteciccardo, before the Gothic Line. The Canadians crossed the Arzilla River on 27 August with the intention of closing with the Foglia River as quickly as possible, but a combination of difficult terrain, obstacles, and increasingly stubborn opposition kept Vokes's forces occupied for two more days.

By this point, the Germans had determined that the main Allied thrust was indeed in the Adriatic sector. On 27 August, Kesselring transferred two divisions from his Fourteenth Army, in front of the Fifth US Army in the west, to the Tenth Army facing Leese's forces in the east. A race was on.[40] The Germans were concerned that Eighth Army, particularly the Canadians, would reach the Gothic Line at the same time as, or even before, the reinforcements; hence the stubborn resistance west of the Arzilla River – to buy time.

On 28 August, gate-crashing seemed a remote possibility. During a flyover the previous day, Burns had noted "no activity visible" beyond the Foglia, but when he had asked Vokes if there were "any likelihood of reaching the Foglia by morning?" Vokes replied pessimistically, "Seems unlikely."[41] With that, Burns decided on a set-piece attack and brought 5 CAD forward to execute that option. He followed the original third phase plan that he had coordinated in the weeks before the operation, with only one alteration: he opted to "reduce the frontage of the attack on the GOTHIC LINE [for 5 CAD and 1 CID] ... enabling a stronger [concentration] of [artillery] to be effected."[42] On 29 August, Leese concurred with Burns's recommendations and made arrangements to bring an additional six regiments of artillery to support the 1st Canadian Corps attack, which Burns thought would take two days to "tee up."[43] While the artillery moved forward, and planners at corps and army coordinated an aerial bombardment of the Gothic Line position, Burns ordered both his divisions to patrol aggressively across the Foglia, the intent being to identify suitable crossing sites and potential routes through minefields.

To that point, Hoffmeister had done his best to keep current with the tactical situation and anticipate requirements. On 26 August, he had conducted an air reconnaissance to look at the area beyond the Metauro, but "visibility was poor and the trip did not prove a success."[44] The following day, with his three brigade commanders and his GSO II in tow, he visited 1 CID headquarters to conduct some coordination for the move forward of 5 CAD and to study a detailed "model of the terrain that lies in front of us."[45] This was a perfectly sound idea. The brigade commanders knew best what sort of assembly areas they needed for the forces under their command. Johnston, for example, personally arranged for his battalions to relieve Vokes's left forward brigade, 2 CIB.[46] It also did not hurt to have them familiarize themselves, even further, with the ground over which they would operate. More important, it was a continuation of Hoffmeister's team approach to planning; the brigadiers liked having their say, and in doing so, their stake in the success of the plan increased. Finally, because the GSO II was there to document what had been discussed, a written record of decisions came back to the GSO I for staff action.

The result was a smooth move forward of 5 CAD. Johnston's brigade group crossed the Metauro without incident the following morning, establishing itself at an assembly area at Monte della Mattera. Hoffmeister and a "reduced Main Div HQ" followed close behind. After these initial moves, the division commander then went back to 1 CID headquarters to gather the most current tactical information and be with Vokes to sort out any problems that should arise. Johnston did the same, co-locating with 2 CIB headquarters. By first light on 29 August, the Perth Regiment had relieved the Seaforths near Ginestreto, the Cape Breton Highlanders had taken over for the Loyal Edmonton Regiment at Monteciccardo, and the Irish Regiment replaced the PPCLI at Monte Santa Maria – all without any serious difficulty.

Preparations for the corps set-piece attack – 5 CAD left, 1 CID right – unfolded according to plan, until the Canadians had a closer look at the Gothic Line defences. Patrols went forward to identify the best routes and crossing sites, and Hoffmeister, as had always been his practice, moved forward to analyze the situation for himself. With his CRA and his GSO II, he met Johnston and the commanding officer of the Irish Regiment, Lieutenant-Colonel R.C. Clark – the "lazy" brigade major for whom Hoffmeister had worked in early 1942. From a very good observation post on Monte Santa Maria, "the Foglia R [River] and the GOTHIC LINE could be clearly seen."[47] What Hoffmeister saw surprised him:

> We could look right down on the anti-tank ditch and a lot of open ground between where we were and the GOTHIC line, and the Montecchio feature ... behind the anti-tank ditch, just a real fortress in itself, this great rocky thing, with good approaches to it from the back. We could by careful examination pick out the odd concrete gun emplacement, and we could see the barbed wire, and we saw the minefields; *but there was no life around the place at all.* I didn't expect to see German officers to be swanking up and down but the whole thing looked terribly quiet ... I remember turning to

Ian Johnston and saying that there's just something wrong with this whole picture, it just doesn't sit right with me ... So I reported back to the Corps Commander that I'd had a look at it and suggested that we do some patrolling as soon as we got organised."[48]

They did not see anything because the remnants of the two enemy divisions that 1 CID had been facing – 71st Infantry and the 1st Parachute divisions had withdrawn across the Foglia only hours before, and the two reserve divisions from 14th Army were still on their way, and not expected to be operational until 30 August. But the small reconnaissance party atop Monte Santa Maria did not know that. Maybe it was just good camouflage. Maybe the Germans were just waiting for the predictable set-piece artillery barrage to announce the start of the attack before they manned their positions.

Hoffmeister recognized a potential opportunity to gate-crash, and deployed his forces accordingly. That might not have been his primary consideration during the planning stages of the operation – 1 CID was supposed to do it alone if opportunity offered – but he did identify the chance to exploit rapidly into the German defences. He was conditioned for it. Indeed, Leese had harped on it. So had Burns. Not surprisingly, Hoffmeister and every commander down to battalion level had been looking for it. But they proceeded cautiously, grabbing two firm bases first. Hoffmeister had Johnston move the Irish Regiment forward to Apsella, since they could see no enemy between that location and the one they were on. In addition, a company from Johnston's reserve battalion, the Princess Louise Dragoon Guards, occupied a high feature near Montelabbate. From these two positions, patrols from the Cape Breton Highlanders and the Perth Regiment would move forward on the night of 29-30 August.[49] If these reconnaissance parties found their objectives undefended, a company from each battalion would immediately move forward and seize the key terrain. It was only a slight variation on the plan that Johnston and Hoffmeister had been discussing for two weeks; the objectives were the same, but it was a compromise – a compromise between deploying to seize an opportunity and avoiding a potential trap. Essentially, the deployment amounted to echeloning two battalion columns, each unit proceeding first with a section (8 men), followed by platoon (25 men), followed by a company (80 men), followed by the remainder of the battalion (400 men) and a squadron of supporting tanks.[50] Lead elements, with engineer support, could pick their way through minefields and call each successive echelon forward, all without sending a battalion headlong into an ambush. This innovative tactic suited the situation perfectly – highly unorthodox and not at all within the parameters of the Eighth Army method.

No wonder everyone took credit for it. In his draft autobiography, Leese claimed that, on 30 August, he ordered "strong detachments of infantry and tanks to seize the high ground north of the Gothic Line."[51] Burns did the same. In his diary, he wrote that he directed "both divs to push fwd with Coys [companies] followed by bns [battalions] and endeavour to effect a lodgement in the line while it was still unmanned."[52] In spite of those claims, the method, without a doubt, came about as a result of discussions between Hoffmeister and Johnston during their reconnaissance the previous day. In fact, they had been prepared to gate-crash on the night of 29-30 August. The Cape Bretons and the Perths each had held one company on "stand-to," ready to rush forward and capture key terrain if patrols had returned by 2:00 a.m. with an indication that the line was unmanned. However, when patrols returned, just before daylight, reporting that they had encountered mines and some enemy activity in the Montecchio area, the rush forward was cancelled.[53] It made no sense to lurch forward in broad daylight, especially with enemy in the area. While this was taking place, Burns was still arranging to narrow the frontage for a stronger artillery concentration and "ask[ing] for the maximum air effort on the GOTHIC Line from BORGO S[ANTA] MARIA ... to MONTECCHIO ... all day 30 August."[54] The aerial bombardment actually interrupted the patrol plan for the morning of 30 August and delayed any further probing until midday. Burns was going ahead with plans for a set-piece attack on the night of 1-2 September, not preparing to gate-crash.[55]

But patrols did cross the Foglia on the morning of 30 August – quite by fortuitous mistake. At 10:45 a.m., 5 CAD had informed 11 CIB that "under no circumstances [would] troops cross R [River] FOGLIA today because of hy [heavy] bombing programme."[56] That caution came too late. At 12:20 p.m., the Cape Breton Highlanders advised the brigade, "One patrol got out before being warned of air programme."[57] Some frantic coordination ensued, and the errant patrol was stopped and turned back to its parent battalion, where it arrived at 1:00 p.m. During the quick patrol debriefing that followed, the soldiers reported that they had "actually moved along the lateral road [between Montecchio and Point 120] in the open, in broad daylight and drew no fire."[58] The area around Montecchio was deserted, and the Cape Bretons relayed that information up the chain of command.[59] Johnston knew what to do: he "informed Gen [General] Hoffmeister of the result of this patrol and immediately the set-piece attack previously arranged was teed up."[60] The news stunned corps staff, which had been busy making arrangements for a set-piece attack on 1-2 September. The 5 CAD operations log recorded their dumbfounded response: "MONTECCHIO clear [and] bn being put through. Is this correct?"[61]

It was. Hoffmeister put into motion the same outline plan that had been in the works for weeks, with a few minor modifications. Instead of executing a full frontal assault, 11 CIB would advance with two battalions – the Perths to Point 111, the Cape Bretons to Point 120 – in the echeloned formation that Hoffmeister and Johnston had wanted to use the previous day. Moreover, there was to be no large preparatory artillery bombardment to tell the Germans they were coming either: "Everything was planned on the basis of achieving surprise."[62] All of the artillery targets that Sparling and his gunners had worked out in preparation for the set-piece attack would still be registered, but they would be "on call," meaning the guns would be fired only if there was a need to neutralize an enemy position for the protection of attacking troops.[63] At this stage, the tasks for 5 CAB and 12 CIB remained the same. The simplicity and soundness of the original plan permitted Hoffmeister and his subordinate commanders to initiate a surprise attack with very little fuss.

Still, many actions had to be synchronized. Shortly after receiving Burns's permission to gate-crash, Hoffmeister told 5 CAB to have one armoured regiment on standby, prepared to exploit any significant breaches in the German line; then he called an orders group at his Division Main Headquarters for 4:00 p.m. All his key players attended, with the exception of Johnston, who was preparing to cross the start line at 5:00 p.m. Hoffmeister's staff made arrangements to transfer extra mortars and ammunition from 12 CIB to 11 CIB, in case Johnston's people needed the extra support.[64] Significantly, the traffic control organization efficiently disentangled a few traffic difficulties at the Metauro River. All the cogs in the machine functioned as they should have done.

With his verbal orders completed, Hoffmeister then moved to the place he most liked to be during a battle – forward. Thirty minutes after the lead battalions crossed the Foglia, he arrived at Johnston's tactical headquarters, an excellent observation position at Sant' Angelo, where he remained until early the following day.[65] For two hours, until last light, he watched the progress of Johnston's lead battalions and anticipated when to bring forward his armour. After dark, when he could no longer see for himself what was happening, he relied on reports as they came into Johnston's headquarters to help him look ahead.

The plan, as devised by Hoffmeister and Johnston, worked, but not without some setbacks and hard fighting. The Canadians caught the Germans unprepared; however, the defenders did manage to man their positions and give battle. Enemy had occupied Point 120 and were in the process of manning the other forward positions of the line. Prisoners taken by the Cape Breton Highlanders later that day revealed that elements of 26 Panzer Division had arrived only hours before, without their tanks, to relieve the depleted elements of 76 Panzer Corps and plug the gap.[66] This enemy stopped the lead platoon of the Cape Breton Highlanders suddenly, as it reached the outskirts of Montecchio itself. Their commanding officer, Lieutenant-Colonel R.B. Somerville tried to silence the German defenders with mortar, tank, and machine-gun fire in an effort to manoeuvre follow-on companies around Point 120, but nothing worked. The enemy on and behind Point 120 were too well protected in their defiladed positions, their machine guns too effective. With Johnston's concurrence, he called off the attack and decided to regroup before trying again. At 00:45 a.m. the next morning, Somerville attempted to blast the enemy out of their positions with a tremendous artillery concentration, supplemented by the fire of the supporting tanks and the machine guns of the Brigade Support Group.[67] Again, however, reverse-slope positions protected the defenders in their trenches, and when the barrage lifted, they raised their heads and resumed the fire that retarded Somerville's second attempt to take Point 120 from the front.

Fortunately, as the Cape Bretons struggled in front of Point 120, the Perths captured Points 111 and 147.[68] A Perth patrol earlier that day had discovered a road bridge across the anti-tank ditch still intact.[69] Johnston and the Perth commanding officer, Lieutenant-Colonel W.W. Reid, wanted to grab the crossing site intact, before German engineers demolished it. The ability to move tanks and anti-tank weapons forward without having to wait for the construction of a new bridge would rapidly strengthen the bridgehead before the inevitable German counterattacks. However, when the same patrol attempted to bring the lead platoon of the lead company to that location, mortar and machine-gun fire ripped into the ranks, causing many casualties and preventing any further advance. Fortunately, if such a word may be used, the echeloned method of advance meant that only one company was caught in the fire. The remainder regrouped and recommenced the advance after dark. And darkness, as Johnston had predicted, proved to the advantage of the attackers. When the second company approached the site, they realized that the German machine guns firing across the bridge were doing so on fixed lines (pre-arranged targets) and at fixed intervals – because the machine gunners could not see their targets in the dark.[70] During the lulls, perceptive, quick-minded, and decisive leadership on the part of Perth NCOs and officers propelled the attacking soldiers across that bullet-swept bridge and to the base of the Point 111 feature.

The Perths took only a few hours to drill a hole in the Gothic Line. By 10:00 p.m. they had captured Point 111, and one hour later they had consolidated on Point 147 as well. It all appeared so simple in retrospect, but battles were never as clinical or clear as all that – not to the soldiers fighting them. The human factor, could be, and often was, decisive. Fifty yards shy of the Point 111 defences, when machine-gun bullets ripped into the Perth company, the attack faltered. A soldier's memoir captured the actions that followed:

> With some couple hundred bullets zipping through the air less than two feet over our prone bodies, I couldn't see us doing much about putting that gun out of action. In effect, we froze. Nobody moved a muscle.
>
> ... Only a sudden uncontrollable impulse would stir me to heroic action. That impulse never came ... I felt so inadequate, so helpless ...
>
> ... Someone had to make the first move. I tried. Lord God Almighty how I tried! But I couldn't bring myself to get up and go. And then it happened. From close behind us I heard [the company commander Captain] Sammy Ridge give out a bellow of orders. I couldn't make out exactly what he was hootin' and hollerin' about but it sounded like, "Come on Dog Company, up and at 'em, what the hell are you waiting for?" I raised my head high enough to see someone off to my right a short ways stand up. And then right next to him somebody else got up. And then, as if by magic the

whole company was up and moving. No one now had to tell us what our job was. "Take the high ground."[71]

Screaming like banshees and firing from the hip, the soldiers of that Perth company annihilated the German machine-gun position and captured a critical piece of ground. Elation at the capture of Point 111 bounded up the chain of command, right up to the army commander. At 11:20 p.m., Leese relayed a message to Hoffmeister: "Well done on your chaps to-day. Very important to push as far as you can tonight."[72]

Leadership like that exhibited by Captain Ridge on Point 111 made the difference between success and failure in battle. Good planning and tactical manoeuvre got his company to the base of the objective, but it took more than that to seal the victory. It took guts and solid leadership at the company level to move those soldiers the last fifty yards and overwhelm the German defenders. Hoffmeister knew that courage was contagious. So was cowardice. That had been part of his rationale for taking the recommendations of Perth soldiers and replacing a number of officers and NCOs back in May. Whatever problems that unit had experienced on the Arielli River in January, they were behind them now. Whether Hoffmeister's personnel changes directly affected the Perth turnaround is impossible to say for certain. But, by his actions, Hoffmeister did demonstrate an acute understanding of the value of good low-level leadership in battle. And the Perths were now a very well-led unit.

The gallant actions of one Perth company pried open a portion of the Gothic Line, fortuitously setting the stage for a full-scale breakthrough. Although the failure of the second Cape Breton attack disappointed Johnston, he had already thought through that possibility. His tactical appreciation proved prescient – Point 120 did afford the enemy good defiladed positions, which could only be captured by an attack from the rear. Even as the Cape Bretons prepared to assault up the slopes towards Montecchio shortly after midnight, he warned the Irish Regiment they might have to pass through the Perth objective on Point 111 and assault Point 120 from the northeast.[73] At 3:15 a.m., when the Cape Breton attack finally faltered, Johnston ordered the Irish to execute the rear envelopment. Johnston knew how to think ahead and plan accordingly.

So did his boss. To that point, Hoffmeister had been co-located with Johnston at 11 CIB headquarters, gleaning what he could and planning his next moves.[74] This might seem an unusual arrangement – most people do not like working with their bosses looking over their shoulder – but Johnston did not seem to have minded. The brigadier recalled, in general terms, how the relationship worked: "He would say I would like you to do this, I would say maybe that. Certainly I was doing what he told me to do. He would make the decisions and I would carry them out. Unlike some commanders he would not tell me which units I should use in which positions and so on."[75] It might have been different if Johnston had not been fighting his brigade so adroitly. Unlike his predecessor, Eric Snow, Johnston fought aggressively and intelligently. In this case, Hoffmeister had no need to fight his subordinate's battle (something he did not like doing), and that allowed him to focus on the "bigger picture." Immediately on hearing that the Perths had taken their objectives, he directed his headquarters "to get our armd units across the river if possible tonight."[76]

The 8th New Brunswick Hussars, being under command of 11 CIB, already had tanks across the Foglia River – one squadron was assisting the Cape Bretons, a second was with the Perths, and a third later went with the Irish Regiment to Point 111. That was fine, but Hoffmeister wanted to be poised to penetrate beyond the initial crust of the Gothic Line defences with the full power of his armoured brigade, even before his left flank was secure. That meant having tanks on the far side of the river, not bottled-up on the friendly bank waiting to rumble across a bridge, one at a time. To get the remainder of 5 CAB's tanks on the other side of the Foglia quickly, Hoffmeister halted the move forward of his reconnaissance regiment, the Governor General's Horse Guards, and sent them to a harbour near San Angelo. Because the Horse Guards were to provide flank security to the west, he accepted some risk on his left flank. He still isolated his battlefield on the other sides, however. To make sure that the crossing of the armoured regiments took place with a minimum of interference, he directed that 11 CIB keep Point 120 "under constant HF [Harassing Fire]." In addition, he ordered that "smok[e] be used on [the] feature as soon as it becomes light" to keep the enemy from seeing the tanks pouring across the bridge sites.[77] Later in the morning, to isolate further the breach through which he wanted to shove his armour, he arranged for an air attack on Tomba di Pesaro, where enemy reserves were thought to be gathering. Finally, thanks to the 1 CID capture of Points 115 and 133, by first light on 31 August, his right flank was secure.

At this point, however, the immediate battle was still very much Johnston's fight. Point 204 and Tomba di Pesaro still had to be subdued before tanks could race to the Conca River. Hoffmeister might have had his armoured brigade take up the lead at this point; but leapfrogging a brigade into the battle, onto ground with which it was unfamiliar, was certain to slow the tempo of operations. Better to give Johnston what he needed to complete the task he had long prepared to do. Accordingly, Hoffmeister handed 11 CIB an additional armoured regiment, the British Columbia Dragoons, to attack Point 204 with the Perth Regiment under command. To free the Perths for the assault, Hoffmeister detached the Princess Louise Dragoon Guards (PLDG) from 12 CIB and assigned them to Johnston for the defence of Points 111 and 147. The division commander then forecasted the action that would follow the capture of Point 204. In preparation for a possible advance on Tomba di Pesaro, Hoffmeister ordered Brigadier Ian Cumberland, the 5 CAB commander, to detach his remaining armoured regiment, the Lord Strathcona's Horse, and its accompanying infantry, the Westminster Regiment, and send it to a waiting area near Point 147.[78] That battle group would be ready when Johnston needed it.

To avoid unnecessary delays when opportunity came, Hoffmeister squeezed everything he could into the bridgehead, but not everything went flawlessly. Bringing the Irish from the left flank to Point 111 crossed several units and muddled matters somewhat. That action, coupled with the problem of units moving on the wrong routes caused traffic jams to form at the Foglia crossings. Three months earlier, this might have been a disaster, but the new traffic control organization proved capable of disentangling the foul-ups, thereby permitting Hoffmeister to execute his plans without too much difficulty.[79]

After coordinating most of these actions with his own staff in his own headquarters, Hoffmeister returned to the 11 CIB tactical headquarters to monitor the current battle and confer with Johnston.[80] There he kept abreast of the Irish assault on Point 120, an attack that was almost four hours old and proceeding relatively well. As the tanks attached to the Cape Breton Highlanders fired from south of Point 120, and the Brigade Support Group lobbed mortars onto the enemy position, the Irish advanced.[81] At 1:25 p.m., they were on their objective and in the process of netting 117 prisoners.[82] By stealth and by first-class fieldcraft, they had outmanoeuvred the enemy. Hoffmeister was pleased and relieved. As Johnston relayed to the Irish commanding officer, "Sunray [Hoffmeister] is prostrate with joy."[83] He had reason to celebrate; he now had a solid door-jam in the entrance of the Gothic Line.

But there was no time to relax, as the Cape Breton Highlanders found out. Enemy counterattacks, as always, were expected, and the penetration had to be expanded. Within moments of the Irish Regiment's capture of Point 120, Johnston sent the following direction to the Cape Bretons: "My Sunray [Johnston] and his Sunray [Hoffmeister] congratulate [you] for a very brave show last night. Have instructions for you now. You will take all arms now supporting you [tanks and anti-tank weapons] and move to [Mount Marrone]. Enemy tanks reported [Tomba di Pesaro] ... Liaise with Sunray Irish on your way through. Report when you start and when you arrive."[84]

After a few pauses in which the Cape Bretons – in fact the entire 11 CIB – stopped and braced themselves for enemy counterattacks that never materialized, the battalion trundled towards Mount Marrone at around 5:00 p.m. Having had no sleep in over twenty-four hours, and having left sixty-three dead and wounded comrades on the slopes south of Point 120, this was a difficult time for the Cape Bretons, but they persevered diligently; by 6:00 a.m. on 1 September, they had consolidated on the heights of Mount Marrone.[85] With their tanks and their commanding view of the approaches from Tomba di Pesaro and the northwest, the Cape Bretons held a strong left shoulder in the division bridgehead. Sensing that the door-jam had gotten wider, the Germans hammered the exposed hilltop position with intermittent mortar and artillery fire for another twelve hours.

Securing the right shoulder of the 5 CAD bridgehead depended on the capture of Point 204 by the British Columbia Dragoons.[86] That too was a costly fight, mostly because of bad decisions by the Dragoon commanding officer, Lieutenant-Colonel F.A. Vokes. By late morning, he had grown impatient waiting for the Perths to link up with his tanks and decided to go without his infantry support. This was an impetuous decision – tanks without infantry to ferret out enemy infantry in a main defensive position were vulnerable to anti-tank weapons. But even more egregious was Vokes's failure to have artillery fire neutralize the German anti-tank guns on the ridge that ran from Mount Marrone to Tomba di Pesaro. Because the Cape Bretons had yet to start their advance on Mount Marrone, unmolested German anti-tank guns in that area had clear shots at the Dragoons as they raced along the spine of the feature that led to Point 204. Vokes's gauntlet run across the open, although it did succeed in reaching Point 204 shortly after noon, devastated his regiment. Some tanks had fallen victim to anti-tank fire, while others that had tried to escape the enfilading anti-tank fire on the reverse slope of the ridge slipped tracks and tumbled down the south side of the hill. The action cost the Dragoons twenty-seven wounded and twenty-two killed, including the commanding officer.[87]

The survivors that did make it to Point 204 had to hold the position for four hours without infantry before any relief arrived. Only after 1 CID had destroyed the enemy on Point 115 could the Perths and one squadron of Strathconas fight their way to the isolated Dragoon position. During the night of 31 August-1 September, the Perths took many casualties, but they held the objective against repeated and desperate counterattacks by soldiers of the 4th Parachute Regiment. The capture of Point 204 did not come cheap.

With his bridgehead in the Gothic Line firmly established, Hoffmeister considered the big picture before deciding his next move. To his right, 1 CID had a tenuous toehold centred on Points 115 and 133. At the army level, early on 31 August, Leese abandoned all plans for a set-piece attack in favour of a quick drive to the two key features of the Gothic Line in the east.[88] Monte Luro, to be attacked jointly by 1 CID and the 3rd Carpathian Division of the Polish Corps was one; Tomba di Pesaro, a little over a mile in front of Hoffmeister's leading elements, was the other. Shortly after the army commander's decision trickled down the chain of command, Hoffmeister announced his intentions for operations in the next couple of days. First, in anticipation of enemy counterattack, all units would "consolidate [for the] night 31/1 [their] present posns." Then, "at first light 11 Cdn Inf Bde [was] to attack pt [Point] 253 ... and TOMBA DI PESARO." Last, "after this attack succeeds 5 Cdn Armd Brigade will exploit through S. GIOVANNI and seize crossings on the [River] CONCA."[89] While Johnston was fighting for Point 204 and Mount Marrone, Hoffmeister made the preliminary moves to support subsequent operations. He rushed the remainder of 5 CAB (which at this point was just the headquarters and the Westminster Regiment) across the Foglia and concentrated it in the area of Point 147, where it would be poised for its coming tasks. Then, to make sure that his depth brigade commander would be in the picture and available for consultation, he directed Brigadier J.S. Lind to move his tactical headquarters to Sant' Angelo, where Hoffmeister had co-located with 11 CIB tactical headquarters. In terms of the basic scheme of manoeuvre, Hoffmeister deviated little from his original plan. He was simply lining up the various components so that he could use them when he needed them.

Hoffmeister left the determination of *how* to take Point 253 and Tomba di Pesaro to Johnston. For the attack on Point 253, Johnston had originally intended to use the Perths with the tanks of the Strathconas under command, but they were spent. After the assaults on Points 111, 147, and 204, the regiment had sustained more than ninety combat casualties, including their commanding officer, and numerous cases of battle exhaustion. Those who were still fit to fight were exhausted; even before the recent fighting, they had endured two excruciating days of approach marches just to reach the Foglia.[90] Simply put, the Perths needed rest. Consequently, Johnston, somewhat reluctantly, handed the task to the still-untested Princess Louise Dragoon Guards.

For a unit that had been raised as a reconnaissance regiment, and having just converted to infantry, the PLDG demonstrated tremendous courage and tenacity in their first infantry battle. Even before the assault began, they endured enemy mortar fire as they made their way from Point 111 to Point 204, an attack that left the unit shaken, and that delayed the start of the operation until after midday. The advance, along the spine of the feature leading to Point 253 was a miserable one. Mortars, machine guns, and anti-tank fire cut into the PLDG and the Strathconas as they scampered across the ridgeline, but they pressed relentlessly on, eventually forcing the enemy to withdraw towards Tomba di Pesaro. Over 130 men killed or wounded – that was what it cost the PLDG and the Strathconas to push the enemy off Point 253.[91] However, the victory was signal; it effectively sealed the fate of the Gothic Line. Because the objective dominated Tomba di Pesaro, the enemy put up little resistance in holding the town; when the Irish Regiment entered it later that day, it did so unopposed. 5 CAD had broken the Gothic Line.

For his part in the victory, Hoffmeister won admittance as a Commander into the Most Excellent Order of the British Empire: "For fine leadership, untiring energy and drive, which enabled the 5 Canadian Armoured Division to effect the initial break in the GOTHIC Line and capture the key position of MONTECCHIO."[92] It remained to be seen whether or not anyone else could make the most of the breakthrough.

Unfortunately, the Eighth Army could not capitalize on 5 CAD's spectacular success. When the Germans concluded that the Gothic Line had been irreparably ruptured, they commenced a phased withdrawal. With that withdrawal came a magnificent opportunity to trap the bulk of the 1st German Parachute Division, then retiring by way of the coastal route to the next line of defences on the Conca River. Success, of course, depended on whether or not Leese could get a suitably large pursuit force into action quickly. His flawed plan, however, precluded such action.[93] Because of the manner in which the army commander had grouped and assigned his forces for this operation, 1st Canadian Corps did not have a fresh division that it could fling into the pursuit. Of Burns's two divisions, Hoffmeister's was too far off for quick action, and 1 CID, after seven days of fighting, was nearly spent. On the Eighth Army left, even further away than Hoffmeister, and in mountainous terrain, Keightley had two divisions (1st Armoured and 4th Infantry) and two brigades (7th Armoured and 25th Tank) yet uncommitted. They were the right forces for the job, but not at the right place or the right time.

Still, the opportunity was too good to pass up, and Leese had to settle for what Burns could put together. The only formation capable of rapid action was 1 CID, so Burns in turn ordered Vokes to cobble together a force capable of striking eastward to the coast. For the assignment, Vokes called on Brigadier D. Dawnay's 21st (British) Tank Brigade, the formation that had been giving Vokes tank support since the crossing of the Metauro. To beef up the tank brigade, Vokes gave Dawnay 2 CIB complete, the Royal Canadian Dragoons (armoured car regiment), and two companies of the Royal 22e Regiment from 3 CIB.

Dawnay's force made good progress, but it was not good enough. With the support of the 12th Royal Tank Regiment, the Loyal Edmonton Regiment took Monte Luro without too much difficulty at 8:00 p.m. on 1 September and captured Fanano early the following day. On Dawnay's right flank, the 48th Royal Tank Regiment, with the assistance of the PPCLI, made it to the area just southeast of the strongly held fortress Gradara – a position that fell when the capture of Pieve threatened its flank. Squadrons of the Royal Canadian Dragoons also pressed the enemy – to San Giovanni in the northwest, and along Highway 16 in the east. But when the Seaforths reached Cattolica on 2 September, they found the town abandoned. The enemy had escaped again. The Canadian official history noted that, in the 1st Parachute Division's withdrawal, "the 4th Parachute Regiment reported casualties of more than 70 percent, and there were admitted losses of a number of anti-tank and heavy anti-aircraft guns left behind with the dead."[94] But the truth of the matter was that the German paratroopers withdrew in fairly good order. Both the 1st and 3rd Regiments made it across the Conca River unscathed, another opportunity lost to "put the enemy in the bag."[95] However well Dawnay fought his brigade group, he simply did not have the combat power to roll over the enemy covering the withdrawal. It all came back to Leese's plan. At a time when the pursuit needed a fresh division, Burns did not have one. As a result, operational victory did not follow 5 CAD's tactical success.

While Dawnay attempted to pursue the retreating Germans, Hoffmeister adjusted his plan to reach the Conca. By 1 September, 11 CIB held a bridgehead a mile and a half wide that extended to Tomba di Pesaro. Hoffmeister had wanted to race 5 CAB to the Conca, but he had been forced to feed 5 CAB's armoured regiments into the 11 CIB fight, and it had cost them dearly. Cumberland's armoured brigade needed at least one day to refit or replace the tanks that had been lost in the previous three days of fighting.[96] They were in no position to thrust towards the Conca as planned. As a result, at 4:00 p.m. on 1 September, Hoffmeister turned to 12 CIB.[97] He directed Lind to take his two remaining battalions – the Westminsters and the Lanark and Renfrew Scottish – and drive from Tomba di Pesaro to the Conca. In support, Lind would also have a field regiment of artillery and two tank squadrons of the Governor General's Horse Guards.[98] This was an unusual task for the division's reconnaissance regiment, but the Horse Guards were equipped with tanks, and Hoffmeister did not have another armoured unit that was fit to fight at this stage.

The ad hoc force did its job. In its first combat action, and against stiff enemy delaying action, 12 CIB took San Giovanni in Marignano by 6:30 p.m. on 2 September. A Desert Air Force attack on enemy positions immediately west of the Conca temporarily delayed any exploitation towards the river; however, shortly after dark, Hoffmeister ordered Lind to send a "combat group" to cut the Highway 16 withdrawal route over the Conca. He believed "the time was ripe for a rapid thrust" to trap the withdrawing enemy. Much to the division commander's disappointment, it was already too late. The Royal Canadian Dragoons were already in Monte Albano, they too having arrived after the enemy had escaped. It would have been a triumph to trap the withdrawing enemy, but that was not Hoffmeister's main concern. His task was to pursue the enemy across the Conca. To that end, he told Lind to hold his current position, while the now-refitted 5 CAB came forward to take up the advance towards Rimini.

From this point, the momentum of the offensive started seriously to wane. Hoffmeister tried to press 5 CAB forward, but the Germans held desperately to the ground on the Conca and Marano rivers. And for good reason – reinforcements were arriving from the centre of the peninsula. To stop the haemorrhage on the 1st Canadian Corps front, the 29th Panzer Grenadier division and some elements from the 98th Infantry Division moved into the gap between the 26th Panzer and 1st Parachute divisions, strengthening the line that ran from Coriano to the sea. That effectively checked the Canadians, and the British to their left, and put paid to any notions of reaching Vienna any time soon.[99]

By 6 September, Leese had little choice but to readjust his plan and get over, or at least ignore temporarily, his misgivings about Burns. The dominating position at Coriano, which was in 5th Corps' area, prevented the Canadians from advancing west of the Besanigo and Melo rivers (see Map 11).[100] To deal with this, Burns met with Hoffmeister, Johnston, and the commander of the flanking British 1st Armoured Division. Together, they hashed out tentative plans for 12 CIB to assault Coriano Ridge, provided the army commander approved the necessary westward shift in the Canadian boundary.[101] Leese had other ideas. He placed four formations under Canadian command – the 4th Infantry Division, the 2nd New Zealand Division, the 25th Army Tank Brigade, and the 3rd Greek Mountain Brigade –

and tasked Burns with getting across the Marano River. Keightley's 5th Corps would clear the enemy from Coriano to Gemmano. The set-piece attack by two assaulting corps took nearly a week to prepare. Artillery ammunition had to be brought forward, an undertaking made all the more important by the absence of the Desert Air Force, the bulk of which was then supporting Clark's Fifth US Army near Florence. Eventually agreeing to the boundary shift proposed by Burns, Leese announced his plan to push the Eighth Army to Ravenna on 9 September. Keightley's corps would protect the left flank with the 46th and 56th divisions in the mountains. With the new inter-corps boundary passing between Coriano and Passano, the Canadian corps would take Coriano Ridge after all, while 5th Corps would assault Passano from the south. In the next phase, Burns would move the 4th Infantry Division past Coriano Ridge to the near bank of the Marano River. Keightley would do the same with 1st Armoured Division. From there, the Canadians were to seize the high ground at San Martino, break through the Rimini Line, then cross the Marecchia into the Lombard Plain, where it was anticipated that armour could be used to sweep across the flatlands.

The initial task, clearing Coriano Ridge, went to Hoffmeister.[102] The division commander had been studying the problem and discussing it with Burns, his own brigadiers, and the flanking formations for a week, so he fully appreciated the difficulty of the task. Getting across the Besanigo and seizing the ridge was an infantry task, at least initially. Bringing up the tanks and anti-tank weapons would have to await the preparation of suitable crossing sites, something that would take time. Once again, Hoffmeister leaned on his most experienced brigadier, Johnston. He beefed up 11 CIB, placing under Johnston's command a regiment of tanks, the Westminsters, and two batteries of anti-tank guns.[103] Also supporting the assault would be eighteen regiments of artillery. Although it would take place at night, this would not be a silent attack; patrols in the days leading up to the assault had encountered too many enemy in the Coriano area for that.

The attack highlighted the level of all-arms cooperation that had developed between armour, infantry, artillery, and engineers within the division. At 1:00 a.m., with the British attack at Passano two-hours old and making good progress, Johnston's lead battalions "leaned on the barrage," following the intense artillery fire onto their initial objective.[104] The Cape Bretons took the north end of the ridge by 4:00 a.m., the Perths capturing the southern tip a half-hour later. Difficult though the German reverse-slope positions were to crack, Hoffmeister realized that the initial assaults were less precarious than what came next: "the key to the whole thing was getting a bridge across [the] river that would enable us to get our tanks up to support the infantry."[105] Thus, immediately behind the lead battalions, the engineers, under mortar and small arms fire, worked through the hours of darkness to prepare the necessary crossing sites, while Hoffmeister and Johnston waited anxiously for word that the bridges were ready.

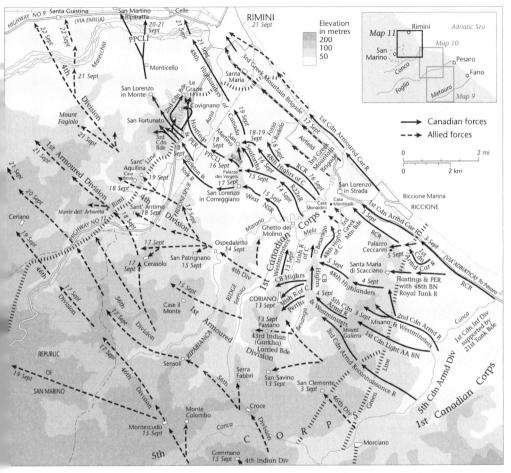

MAP 11   *The advance to Rimini, 3-22 September 1944.* Adapted from G.W.L. Nicholson (Lieutenant-Colonel), *The Canadians in Italy, 1943-1945* (Ottawa: Queen's Printer, 1966), map 20.

Finally, shortly after first light, crossing sites for both wheeled and tracked vehicles were ready. Immediately, the Irish Regiment and a squadron of tanks passed through the lead battalions and cleared the centre of the objective, which included the village of Coriano. At noon, the Westminsters and a squadron of Strathconas rolled past the Cape Bretons to secure the remainder of the ridge to the northeast. But, because the enemy was still active on the north side of the Fornaci River, an artillery smokescreen protected the Westminster/Strathcona left flank as they darted towards the junction of the Fornaci, Melo, and Besanigo rivers. There would be no repeat of the Point 204 gauntlet-run here. Hoffmeister also squeezed the remainder of the Strathconas into the bridgehead, both to harden it against enemy counterattacks and to provide direct fire support to the units of the 4th Infantry Division as they prepared to cross the Fornaci and force the Marano. At 3:00 p.m., even before the Westminsters had fully cleared the ridge, Hoffmeister advised the 4th Division commander that 5 CAD was ready to support his move forward and fire him onto his first set of objectives. It had cost the Mighty Maroon Machine 210 casualties, but the attack had gone remarkably well.[106] Artillery supporting infantry onto an objective, followed by engineers building bridges to move tanks in support of infantry on the objective, followed by artillery firing a smokescreen to protect an infantry-amour assault – all within fourteen hours: this was a solid all-arms team.

The battles of the Gothic Line and Coriano Ridge had been some of the toughest of the Italian Campaign, and things would only get tougher. Hard slogging: that was the story of the rest of the Italian Campaign for the Canadians. The open tank battles that many, Leese foremost among them, had anticipated for the flat Po River valley never happened because, as Hoffmeister pointed out, "the whole plain was 'just one more river to cross.'"[107] Even if the rivers were narrow, as many of them were, crossing them was always difficult. Tanks could seldom get across without bridging, and the Germans always had the best bridging sites covered by machine-gun, mortar, and artillery fire. Making matters worse, by late September, heavy rains covered the countryside in the same "chocolate sauce" that had slowed the Eighth Army at the Moro River the previous December. What was more, the Allied Armies in Italy had no great advantage in arms. Alexander had only twenty-two Allied and two Italian divisions compared to Kesselring's twenty-eight divisions.[108] True, the German divisions were under-strength and the Allies had complete superiority in aircraft and artillery; but this hardly yielded the three-to-one ratio that attackers normally needed to dislodge defenders, especially in the difficult Italian terrain. That Alexander's armies managed to knock the German defenders backwards at all was an accomplishment in itself. Small wonder though, that, in the week that followed the capture of Coriano Ridge, the Eighth Army had an average daily casualty rate of 145 killed and 600 wounded.[109]

Hoffmeister first experienced the gut-wrenching disappointment of the Po valley when his division attempted a rapid breakout from the Marecchia bridgehead in late September (see Map 12).[110] Having driven 11 CIB hard in the past month, Hoffmeister hoped to use Lind's green 12 CIB to spearhead his push to Fiumicino, from which point he hoped to drive 11 CIB and some supporting tanks towards the Savio River. Accordingly, he directed Lind to move as quickly as possible, "bypassing and picketing centres of resistance, leaving 11 Cdn Inf Bde to mop up as they catch up."[111] With an armoured regiment, two anti-tank batteries, a field company of engineers, and most of the corps' artillery in support, Lind thought he might be able to clip quickly through three quick phases – the PLDG to the Uso River, the Westminsters to the Salto River, and the 1st Light Anti-Aircraft Regiment (Lanark and Renfrew Scottish) to the Fiumicino. However, from the time his troops stepped out of the 4th Infantry Division bridgehead at 9:00 a.m. 23 September, they encountered problems. Enemy from 29 Panzer Grenadier Division occupied strong points at Casale and Variano that stopped the PLDG, literally, in their tracks. Mortar and machine-gun fire felled six officers and seventy-one troops, causing considerable confusion and breaking up the attack.[112] Making matters worse, vine-rows restricted what tank crews could see and, therefore, prevented the armour from suppressing the machine guns that were cutting up the PLDG companies. Sensing that his lead battalion could do little more in the short term than dig in and attempt to regroup, Lind ordered the Westminsters and a squadron of Strathconas to execute a right flanking manoeuvre to the east of Variano, aimed on San Vito. Commencing their attack at 3:00 p.m., the Westminsters fared only slightly better than the PLDG. Although they managed to push to within one mile of San Vito, it took until first light on 24 September to take the town, and it cost the supporting tank squadron seven tanks, two of which had become bogged in the off-road mud, and five of which had been immobilized by anti-tank mines. At noon, Lind tried a second right hook with his reserve battalion, the 1st Light Anti-Aircraft Battalion, but that too failed in the face of heavy enemy fire. In fact, the lone bright spot of the day came when the PLDG finally consolidated the strong points of Casale and Variano. By this point though, Lind had already realized there was little else he could do beyond securing a bridgehead across the Uso; he would not get to the Salto, let alone the Fiumicino.

Hoffmeister realized it too and adjusted his plan accordingly. As Lind pulled up to the Uso, Hoffmeister brought his reconnaissance regiment, the Governor General's Horse Guards, forward to fill the gap between his division and the 2nd New Zealand Division to the northeast. With the breakout proceeding as slowly as it was, he did not want to present the enemy with an opportunity to exploit the gap and slam into his right flank. He also brought Johnston's brigade forward to finish the job of closing to Fiumicino, which it did after 12 CIB had slogged through the mud and rain to create a bridgehead over the Uso on 26 September. Johnston sent two regiments across the Salto, without tanks because the banks of the stream (now a torrent) were too steep and the bridges blown. Both the Cape Bretons and the Irish advanced across the river in one-company-up advance formation. This

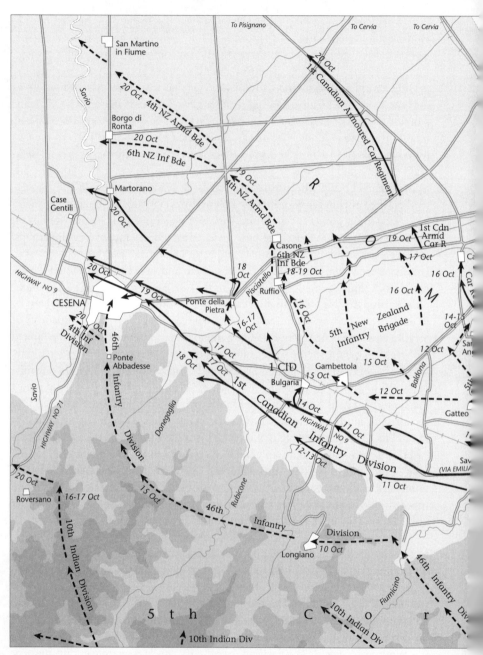

MAP 12 *Into the Romagna, 22 September to 20 October 1944.* Adapted from G.W.L. Nicholson (Lieutenant-Colonel), *The Canadians in Italy, 1943-1945* (Ottawa: Queen's Printer, 1966), map 21.

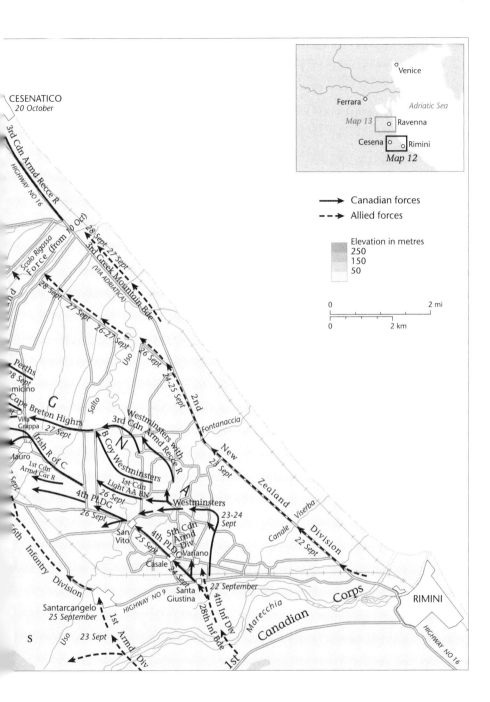

CESENATICO
20 October

3rd Cdn Armd Recce R

HIGHWAY NO 16

Scolo Rigossa
Force (from 10 Oct)

28 Sept 27 Sept
3rd Greek Mountain Bde
(VIA ADRIATICA)

28 Sept 27 Sept

26 Sept

26-27 Sept

Uso

24-25 Sept

2nd

Perths
28 Sept
micino

G

Cape Breton Highrs
Villa
Grappa   27 Sept

Irish R of C

Mauro
1st Cdn
Armd Car R

N

Salto

Westminsters with
3rd Cdn Recce R

B Coy Westminsters

1st Cdn
Light AA BN

4th PLDG

26 Sept

26 Sept

A

Westminsters

San
Vito   25 Sept

4th PLDG

Casale   24 Sept

Santa
Giustina

Santarcangelo
25 September

S

Uso   23 Sept

1st Armd Div

HIGHWAY NO 9

6th Infantry Division

5th Cdn
Armd
Div

Variano

23-24
Sept

22 Sept

22 September

Fontanaccia

New

23 Sept

Zealand

Canale

Viserba

Division

4th Inf Div

28th Inf Bde

Marecchia

Canadian

1st

Corps

RIMINI

HIGHWAY NO 16

Venice

Ferrara

Adriatic Sea

Map 13   Ravenna

Cesena   Rimini

Map 12

→ Canadian forces

--→ Allied forces

Elevation in metres
250
150
50

0   2 mi

0   2 km

sort of echeloned advance had worked well in grabbing key terrain at the Gothic Line against an unprepared enemy. This time, things were different. "A" Company of the Irish Regiment got caught. After sneaking across the Salto shortly after last light on 27 September, the Irish soldiers bumped into a superior – and ready – enemy force near San Mauro. Outnumbered and outgunned, and after suffering nine killed and one wounded, fifty-three Irish Regiment soldiers surrendered.[113] The lone consolation could only have been that the cautious echeloned advance had prevented the loss of the entire battalion. Upset though he was by the loss, the next day Johnston ordered the remaining companies of the Irish Regiment to skirt east of San Mauro, while Cape Bretons moved past Villa Grappa to Fiumicino. One mile north of that, Johnston launched the Perths on a long right hook to capture a crossing opposite Sant' Angelo. As these movements indicate, it had been his intention to proceed with a three-battalions-up assault river crossing of the Fiumicino, but events behind him precluded that next step. Rains had washed away bridges and ford sites over the Marecchia and the Uso rivers. Even if Johnston had established a bridgehead, neither Hoffmeister nor Burns would have been able to bring forward sufficient forces for a breakout. Operations were halted accordingly. Such were the depressing conditions of the Po River valley in late September 1944.

And matters did not improve much as autumn wore into winter. After passing two fairly uneventful months in October and November, it took Hoffmeister eleven dreary December days to shove his brigades over five diked waterways within a space of four short miles (see Map 13).[114] The Battle of the Rivers started just after last light on 10 December when 11 CIB, with no artillery preparation, paddled across the Lamone River in assault boats, as 12 CIB on their left and 5 CAB on their right opened up with every weapon they could to draw the enemy's attention away from the main crossing. The plan had the desired effect; it took the enemy a good half-hour to figure out what was happening. Before the enemy could initiate any spoiling action, the Perths had pounced on their objective at Borgo di Villanova and the Cape Bretons had done likewise at Villanova. Johnston then put through the Irish, who captured a bridge intact at the Fosso Vetro, then ploughed ahead to the demolished bridge at the Fosso Vecchio. The next morning, quite fortuitously, the brigadier committed the Westminsters, temporarily under his command, to the right flank, where they foiled a German counterattack that included fifteen to twenty tanks.

Getting beyond the Fosso Vecchio proved extremely difficult, as 12 CIB found out when it took up the lead on the night of 12 December. Both the Lanark and Renfrews and the PLDG had difficulty assaulting the twenty-foot embankments on the Canale Naviglio, especially since it had taken until mid-morning on 13 December for engineers to prepare enough tank crossings for the British Columbia Dragoons to move forward and provide direct fire support from eight-foot mounds of the Fosso Vecchio. Later that day, acknowledging the futility of another costly assault over the machine-gun-swept earth walls of the Canale Naviglio, Hoffmeister devised a plan with the new Canadian corps commander, Lieutenant-General Charles Foulkes, to send a battle group over a crossing site that 1 CID had established further south.[115] Early on 14 December, the Westminsters, supported by a squadron of Strathconas, crossed the Canale Naviglio in the 1 CID sector and successfully cleared northward along the Via del Canale.

An assault across the Fosso Munio did not take place until four days later, after a 1 CID attempt to break through south of Bagnacavallo had failed. When the assault did go in, flame-throwers helped secure the crossing sites over the Munio, and Johnston's brigade bolted over the embankments just after dark on 19 December, but movement beyond their initial objectives stalled because of the difficulty in getting tanks forward to silence enemy machine guns. It was past midday on 20 December when a squadron of Strathconas at last reached a Perth foothold at Casa della Congregatione to ensure the integrity of the bridgehead. After intense fighting and vicious counterattacks, the German commander finally withdrew his troops behind the safety of the Senio River. One miserable water crossing after another; that had been the Battle of the Rivers.

Fights such as these along the Eighth Army front, convinced Leese's successor, Lieutenant-General Sir Richard McCreery, to abandon offensive operations and adopt defensive posture for the winter.[116] The hard-slogging of late 1944 had depleted ammunition and personnel to such an extant that McCreery convinced the new army group commander, General Mark Clark, to forget about plans for a renewed offensive and dig in at Ravenna in the east to an area twenty-five miles north of Pisa in the west.[117] This operational pause would allow for the replenishment of ammunition and manpower prior to another major army group assault in the spring. Clark agreed, and McCreery went to work stabilizing his line along the most defensible ground. Thus, although major offensive operations ceased as of 30 December, minor actions took place in preparation for the long winter wait.

One of those chores went to the 5th Canadian Armoured Division (see Map 13 and inset). As part of the 1st Canadian Corps, which anchored the Eighth Army's eastern flank from Porto Corsini on the Adriatic to Cotignola on the Senio in the west, Hoffmeister's division (less 12 CIB, which held a position between Alfonsine to Fusignano) had the task of clearing the enemy from a four-mile-deep stretch of ground between the southern banks of the Valli di Comacchio and the Lamone River.[118] In that area, the German 73rd Korps had its 114th Jaeger Division, with the 721st Regiment dug in along the Lamone and the 741st Regiment centred on Sant' Alberto in depth. The enemy's hold on this chunk of terrain was menacing. The German reinforcement of Alfonsine and strong offensive actions in the Fifth Army area convinced Eighth Army planners of the need to clear the south bank of the Valli di Comacchio – to eliminate any plans the Germans may have had for using their position to threaten road and rail communications extending out of Ravenna only six miles to the south. This was the situation when, on 27 December,

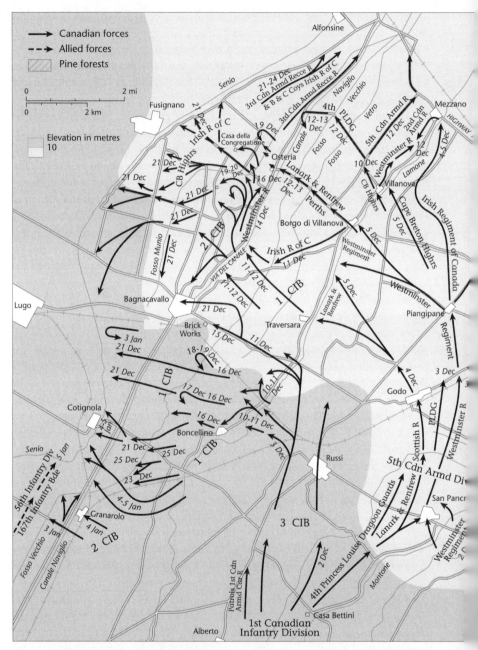

MAP 13   *From the Montone to the Senio, 2 December 1944 to 5 January 1945.* Adapted from G.W.L. Nicholson (Lieutenant-Colonel), *The Canadians in Italy, 1943-1945* (Ottawa: Queen's Printer, 1966), map 25.

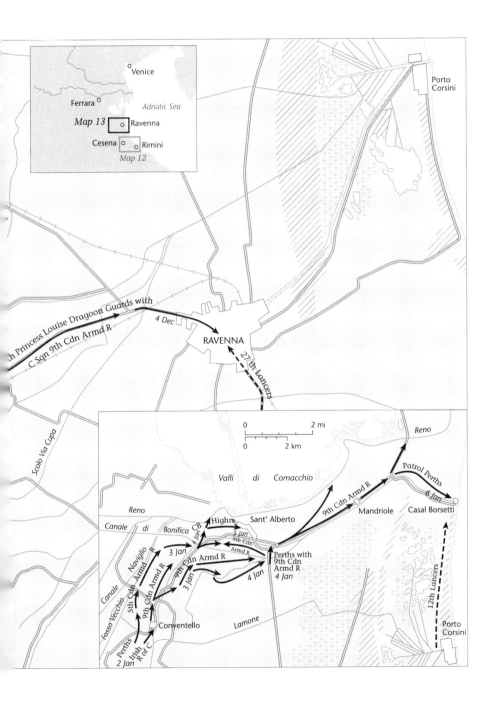

Hoffmeister received orders to rid the sector of Germans from Sant' Alberto to the Adriatic.

In planning Operation SYRIA, Hoffmeister undoubtedly took into account experience of his division during the Battle of the Rivers only weeks earlier. Battering against those positions, one after the other, had proven costly in terms of casualties and ammunition, especially since the diked canals kept tanks from rolling forward and supporting the infantry assaults. In consultation with his brigadiers, Hoffmeister decided to use his infantry to break into the enemy's first line of defences along the Lamone, then use his armour to thrust, as much as possible, parallel to the line of waterways, not across them. Some situational factors permitted this bold right turn to Sant' Alberto. First, the cold December weather had frozen the ground that only weeks before had been rain-soaked and impassable to tanks. And second, the Valli di Comacchio was a huge water obstacle that partially protected his left flank against armoured counterattack as he made the eastward turn. There had been no such safeguard at the Senio earlier that month. Hoffmeister also considered that the timing of the assault was also critical for control: "We made a plan cracking off at first light and getting the element of surprise. Since tanks were heavily involved, daylight was necessary in order that the rest of the operation would be carried out in an orderly manner."[119] With these considerations in mind, Hoffmeister settled on a characteristically simple two-phased plan – an 11 CIB assault on Conventello to destroy the enemy's forward defences and "make a hole" through which the tanks of 5 CAB could pass on their way to clearing the area to the north and east.

It was a solid plan, but not without oversights that soon revealed themselves. The attack started at 5:00 a.m. on 2 January with one heavy and three field artillery regiments pounding enemy positions around Conventello and dropping counter-battery rounds on 114th Division's artillery in depth. On the 11 CIB left, the Perths reached their first objectives within an hour.[120] On the right, tank and anti-tank fire held up the Irish until "air support was called down and CONVENTELLO was bombed strafed," enabling the battalion to reach its first objectives by 9:00 a.m.[121] By 2:00 p.m., 11 CIB was ready to assist the forward passage of the armoured brigade and its supporting infantry, the Cape Breton Highlanders. While this was happening, Hoffmeister, who was forward with Johnston, had another close look at the map: "I was looking at my map this morning and again had the feeling in the back of my head that there was something wrong with the whole thing ... Finally, it occurred to me, and it should have occurred to me earlier, that there was this vulnerable hinge; we had to do a right turn ... while we were advancing on a fairly wide front. Consequently, we were exposed at this point."[122]

He was right. Once the Cape Bretons had gone past with the Hussars, there would only be the Perths to defend a four-mile stretch along the Vecchio and Vetro canals. Although he had the Irish Regiment complete at Conventello, Hoffmeister was still one battalion short for blocking any enemy penetration from the west. He and Johnston had both missed it, despite their deliberations, and it had to be corrected. To harden that vulnerable hinge, Hoffmeister spoke to Foulkes and arranged to have the Westminster Regiment transferred from 12 CIB to Johnston's brigade, but that would take a day to make happen. In the short term, the Irish and the Perths repositioned themselves to defend against a counterattack from the west, as did the Cape Bretons, who stopped near the junction of the Bonifica and Vecchio. Hoffmeister even took a squadron away from the Hussars to bolster Johnston's hasty defensive posture; this gave the brigadier a small mobile reserve to plug any enemy penetrations. These small adjustments proved their worth the next morning when the enemy launched a two-company attack, supported by machine guns and mortars, on the Perth positions. That particular enemy attempt to wreck Hoffmeister's bridgehead failed, as did a battalion attack that landed on the Cape Bretons a few hours later. Midway through the afternoon, the Westminsters arrived in the bridgehead to relieve the Perths, who shifted north, allowing the Cape Bretons to carry on in support of the 5 CAB advance. Hoffmeister personally briefed the Westminster commanding officer, Lieutenant-Colonel Gordon Corbould, on his tasks in defence against enemy counterattack from the west and north. This also proved prescient. The next morning a battalion of the 36th SS Panzer Grenadier Regiment slammed into the Westminster positions.[123] While the enemy tanks had difficulty getting across the Fosso Vecchio, the SS infantry poured into the Canadian killing zones, only to be annihilated by the Westminsters and Johnston's reserve combat team, a squadron of Hussars and a company of Irish. In all, the Westminsters killed twenty-four, wounded sixty, and took forty-four prisoners while only sustaining seven casualties of their own.[124] The bridgehead held. Hoffmeister had made a nice recovery from a dangerous oversight.

With Johnston's brigade holding the hinge in the west, Ian Cumberland's two lead regiments made good progress, closing in on Sant' Alberto from two directions. By last light on 3 January, the Hussars had advanced to the Canale di Bonifica, a little over a mile West of Sant' Alberto. Although they found the bridge blown, the Hussars pushed two of their dismounted Cape Breton companies across the canal on 4 January as engineers worked to make the crossing site suitable for tanks.[125] Fortunately, south of Sant' Alberto, an action was taking place that would ensure the success of both thrusts on the town. The British Columbia Dragoons, having negotiated their way over the abandoned canal, had raced to the Bonifica, where an intrepid squadron commander, Major R.B. Sellars, dismounted from his tank and, under fire, neutralized the demolitions that had been set to blow the bridge.[126] Shortly thereafter, when two companies of Perths met up with the Dragoons, Lieutenant-Colonel Harry Angle, Hoffmeister's former GSO I, and now the Dragoon commanding officer, wasted little time in putting them across to the north side. There they coordinated the defence of the bridgehead with "B" Squadron's tanks. On hearing of the Dragoon success in the south, Hoffmeister ordered Cumberland to send a tank squadron across the bridge and along the north side of the canal to the Cape Breton bridgehead. Without a bridge to move tanks and anti-tank weapons, and with ice rendering the rafting of anti-tank weapons difficult, the infantry-only toehold was vulnerable to counterattack; the addition of the Dragoon squadron on the afternoon of 4 January guaranteed its survival.

Early the next morning, Cumberland's brigade made efficient use of both bridgeheads. At daybreak, the Cape Bretons and "C" Squadron of the Dragoons burst out of theirs, reaching the Sant' Alberto at 10:00 a.m., only to find the streets clear of enemy, the remnants of 114th Division having withdrawn hours earlier. From the southern crossing site, a simultaneous sweep to Mandriole by Angle's remaining two squadrons and the two Perth companies resulted in minor clashes with withdrawing enemy and the capture of 47 enemy prisoners.[127] Patrols to the Reno and Casal Borsetti on 6 January closed a highly successful operation in which 5 CAD inflicted over 1,000 casualties on the enemy, while suffering less than 200 of its own.[128]

IN THEIR LAST major operation before leaving Italy, Hoffmeister's troops had shown themselves to be a truly skilled all-arms team. From the commander whose leadership both guided and inspired, to the staffs that crunched the numbers and fine-tuned administrative details, to the officers and NCOs that transformed direction into action, to the soldiers who did the shooting, they had all learned to fight the hard way – by fighting. In the seven or so months since the 5th Canadian Armoured Division had first stepped into the Liri Valley, Hoffmeister and his troops gained much in the way of experience, know-how, and comradeship. But they had lost much too. Hundreds of their comrades would not make the journey to Northwest Europe. Hundreds of them still rest in Italian soil. So it was with a mix of sadness and relief that officers, NCOs, and soldiers of the 5th Canadian Armoured Division left their fallen friends, the Italian Peninsula, and the army in which they had seen and done so much.

The army commander was sorry to see them go. On learning that the 1st Canadian Corps would be leaving the Eighth Army for Northwest Europe, McCreery expressed his gratitude in a personal letter to Hoffmeister:

> I was delighted that your Division finished up in this country with such a successful operation in January, when you commanded the Division with great skill. It was very satisfactory that you were able to use tanks in mid-winter in such unpromising country.
>
> You have a splendid Division, and I know that you will take a great part in the final big battles, unless the Russians produce a big collapse before you get going!
>
> All good wishes, I shall always follow your fortunes with the very greatest of interest.[129]

Northwest Europe and After

We had a feeling that the Canadian Army would be completely different ... Things were stuffier and more formal than they were working with the Brits.[1]

BERT HOFFMEISTER, 1980

Within one week of being notified of the impending move to Northwest Europe, the 20,000 troops, 450 tanks, 5,600 wheeled vehicles, and 320 carriers of Hoffmeister's division had crossed the Italian Peninsula from Ravenna to the port of Leghorn.[2] From there, they moved via a combination of LSTs (Landing Ship Tank) and troop ships to Marseilles in the south of France, from which point road and rail carried them the last leg of their journey to Dixmude, Belgium, where the division assembled at the end of February.

The move was largely an administrative affair, one mostly for logistics and administrative staffs, and Hoffmeister attempted to use the opportunity for some rest and relaxation at a villa that Chris Vokes had previously established as a leave centre on the Sorrento Peninsula, south of Naples: "I went down there with my chief of staff and ADC [aide-de-camp] and we were having a very pleasant and relaxed time ... I had everything set up as far as the move to North-West Europe was concerned and there wasn't a thing for me to do beyond what I had already done. I got regular reports as to how things were going."[3]

But the respite did not last long: "Then after the first week Charles [Foulkes] sent an LO down and insisted that I come back. When I came back I told him that I thought it was an unreasonable request, that everything was under control, and my return was completely unnecessary, and that I didn't see any reason why I shouldn't go back and finish my leave. He said, 'Oh no, I'll just feel better if you are around' ... He was a bit of a nit-picker at times in that way."[4] It may only have been a minor annoyance, but it portended a new working atmosphere for the division commander and his staff.

They were leaving the professional informality of the Eighth Army for the meticulousness of the less-experienced First Canadian Army. Charles Foulkes, who had commanded the 2nd Canadian Infantry Division (2 CID) from January to November 1944, knew what to expect and was probably feeling the pressure already. Brigadier A.E. Wrinch, who was promoted out of Hoffmeister's division to an appointment as the chief signals officer at Foulkes's 1st Canadian Corps Headquarters noted the contrast and the uncomfortable adjustments that followed:

"When we got there [Belgium], Charles [Foulkes] said to us 'Now we have to start planning our next operation; we have to get out an operation order.' Well this took us by surprise, as we were not used to preparing written orders in Italy ... There was none of the informality there had been in the Italian theatre; you had to get right down to producing written orders which may or may not be used."[5]

In General Harry Crerar's army, written orders and formal conferences were de rigueur, not one-on-one consultations and verbal direction. The affect of the new command climate rippled down the chain of command. Hoffmeister, a self-professed admirer of the Eighth Army modus operandi, had to adjust to the new environment, but it was not easy: "I didn't feel nearly as comfortable in North-West Europe as I had done in Italy where there was such great rapport and mutual respect and we knew each other so well."[6] Still, unpleasant though the new working atmosphere may have been, Hoffmeister and his staff adapted to the increased flow in paperwork and got down to business. There was, after all, still some fighting to be done.

WHILE THE NEW COMMAND climate may have brought challenges, the terrain of Northwest Europe offered opportunities – for armour. Unlike the cramped corridors of the Liri Valley or the river-laced Lombard Plain, Holland had areas – areas that were not flooded, that is – where tanks could spread out and manoeuvre. The enemy situation differed from Italy as well. At this late stage in the war, with the Germans on the run and so close to final defeat, campaigns were no longer a series of infantry-intensive break-in battles against extensive defensive lines; the Germans tended to husband their dwindling resources in strong points and carefully selected localities. For these reasons, shortly after its arrival in Belgium, Hoffmeister's second infantry brigade, the 12th Canadian Infantry Brigade (12 CIB), was disbanded, its units reverting to their original roles. The Westminsters went back to the 5th Canadian Armoured Brigade (5 CAB). The Princess Louise Dragoon Guards (PLDG) happily resumed reconnaissance duties in the 1st Canadian Infantry Division (1 CID), and the Lanark and Renfrew Scottish became anti-aircraft gunners again. As a result, 5 CAD adopted its old order of battle based on one armoured brigade and an infantry brigade – the same configuration with which it had entered the Liri Valley ten months earlier.

Operationally, the enemy facing the Canadians in the early spring of 1945 were also cut off. On 23 March, General Montgomery's 21st Army Group had crossed the Rhine River. With General Sir Miles Dempsey's Second British Army on the left and the US Ninth Army on the right, Monty had bolted across the great river between Wesel and Emmerich.[7] For Operation PLUNDER, Dempsey had been given Lieutenant-General Guy Simonds's 2nd Canadian Corps to expand the bridgehead towards Emmerich, which it did by 1 April, as the remainder of the Second Army drove westward and straight into Germany. While this was happening, Crerar's First Canadian Army, which at this point only consisted of the newly arrived 1st Canadian Corps and the British 49th West Riding (WR) Division, held the "left shoulder" from Emmerich, along the Maas and Waal rivers to the sea.

This is when Hoffmeister's troops entered the battle for Northwest Europe in earnest. Elements of 11 Canadian Infantry Brigade (11 CIB) moved forward to the Nijmegen sector on 21 March, at first being placed under command of the 49th WR Division, and then eventually passing back to 5 CAD as the division took control of its own sector west of Oosterhout on 31 March (see Map 14).[8] In accordance with Crerar's instructions, they held their ground until after 2nd Corps had captured objectives four miles northeast of Emmerich on 1 April.[9] The army commander then wanted Simonds's corps to drive towards the North Sea, on the east side of the Ijssel River, while Foulkes' 1st Canadian Corps seized the high ground between Arnhem and Apeldoorn in preparation for the clearing of western Holland. Foulkes achieved his goal in three stages. First, in an operation codenamed DESTROYER, the 49th WR Division and 5 CAD cleared the flooded area between the Waal and Neder Rijn rivers. This they accomplished in the face of negligible resistance on 2-3 April, both division commanders assigning the sweeps across soggy ground to their infantry brigades. The next operation – crossing the Neder Rijn and establishing a bridgehead at or near Arnhem – had to be coordinated with the action of the 2nd Canadian Corps west of the Ijssel River and was delayed until 11 April when 1st Canadian Infantry Division (1 CID) struck westward across the Ijssel between Deventer and Zutphen. Temporarily under command of the 2nd Canadian Corps, Major-General Harry Foster's forces crashed across the river and advanced steadily on Apeldoorn. With the enemy fixated on 1 CID in the north, the way was clear for 49th WR Division to cross the Neder Rijn and secure Arnhem, a task that was completed by 13 April. The job of breaking out of the Arnhem bridgehead and clearing the area between the Ijssel River and the Grebbe Line fell to Hoffmeister's division.

Foulkes visited Hoffmeister's main headquarters, now concentrated at Didam, late on the afternoon of 13 April to discuss the 5 CAD breakout, starting with the enemy situation.[10] Two weak German divisions opposed 1st Canadian Corps – 361st Volksgrenadier Division opposed 1 CID on the Apeldoorn front, while 346th Infantry Division held the Arnhem sector. The intelligence assessment that the corps commander passed to Hoffmeister surmised that the enemy had only two battalions that it could "throw against our drive Northward" – 1/858 Grenadier Battalion and the 346 Engineer Battalion – although both would first have to be disengaged from their current positions along the Ijssel River.[11] Civilians had also reported the presence of "small and weak" reserves, believed to be a hodgepodge of anti-aircraft units and other ancillary troops, between Apeldoorn and Amersfoort. Everything, it seemed, was up front and facing east, trying to stop the haemorrhage along the Apeldoorn-Arnhem line. Just as important, what little the enemy had to resist a 5 CAD breakout could not be moved quickly. German tanks were in short supply, the armoured threat considered "not a serious one." The Canadians

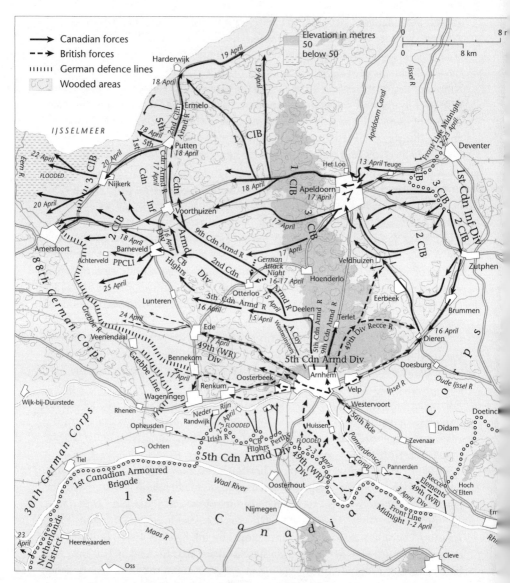

MAP 14 *The western Netherlands, 2-25 April 1945.* Adapted from C.P. Stacey, *The Victory Campaign: The Operations in North-West Europe, 1944-1945* (Ottawa: Queen's Printer, 1960), map 13.

did, however, expect to encounter "a fair number" of self-propelled guns, although these were concentrated mostly in isolated strongpoints, most notably at Deelen and Terlet. No continuous line of defences existed forward of the Grebbe Line. Given 5 CAD's advantage in firepower and manoeuvrability, the situation begged a rapid armoured sweep towards the Grebbe Line.

That was exactly what Hoffmeister planned. At a noon orders group on 14 April he gathered the commander of his armoured brigade and key staff in his map trailer to outline his four-phase plan for Operation CLEANSER.[12] First, 5 CAD would seize the high ground north of Arnhem and capture the enemy strongpoints at Deelen and Terlet. Grabbing this vital ground quickly was crucial. Not only would it protect the right flank of the division advance as it took a hard left turn and headed towards Barneveld and Amersfoort, it would effectively stuff any attempt to fling 1/858 Grenadier Battalion or the 346 Engineer Battalion at the Canadian breakout. With the main enemy counterattack routes blocked, Hoffmeister planned a series of successive armoured thrusts – to Otterloo in the second phase, to Barneveld where the Apeldoorn-Amersfoort road would be cut in the third phase, and then, finally, to Nijkerk and Harderwijk on the Ijsselmeer in the last. Surprise and speed were the keys to clearing the enemy forward of the Grebbe Line. During the first phase, there would be no prepared fire plan to tip-off the enemy as to where and when the main attack was coming – much like the attack at Montecchio in the Gothic Line. But that initial surprise had to be followed by rapid action to take advantage of the enemy's stunned state and nullify any local counterattacks. Never one to leapfrog brigades unnecessarily – that was too slow – Hoffmeister intended to let his armoured brigade handle the entire advance: "If the situation permits all phases will be carried out by 5 Cdn Armd Bde Gp." Ian Johnston's 11 CIB would be "prepared to take over from the armour at any stage." But the division commander clearly preferred for the infantry to mop up pockets of enemy that the armour had bypassed, much as he had intended in the advance on Frosinone in the Liri Valley eleven months earlier, only this time the ground was more conducive to such a course of action.

This was a welcome change for Hoffmeister's armoured brigade commander, Brigadier Ian Cumberland. Like Ian Johnston, Cumberland was a Royal Military College graduate who had served in the pre-war militia, eventually rising to command his regiment, the Governor General's Horse Guards (GGHG) in June 1942. Although he had led his regiment through the Liri Valley and had commanded 5 CAB for nearly a year, Cumberland had encountered few opportunities for armoured manoeuvre. At the Gothic Line, he had mostly watched as his armoured regiments were fed forward for Johnston's fight. Rivers had restricted armoured movement on the Lombard Plain. For eighteen days in October 1944, Cumberland had commanded an independent task force – Cumberland Force – composed of the GGHG, the 27th Lancers, the Royal Canadian Dragoons, and his own British Columbia Dragoons.[13] But during the task force's short life, the first three units had fought as infantry; and flooding, mines, and blown bridges had kept the BCD on the roads, relegated very much to a direct-fire support role for the advancing infantry. Only in the Valli di Comacchio did he have opportunity to fight his armoured brigade as a complete formation, and even that had been limited in its scope for manoeuvre.

Cumberland seized the chance to let his tanks move and shoot freely. Based on the direction he received from Hoffmeister, he carved his mission into six distinct phases, which he outlined at an orders group less than two hours after attending the conference with Hoffmeister.[14] The phases of the advance were essentially the same as Hoffmeister's, the only difference being that Cumberland considered the cutting of the Apeldoorn-Amersfoort road and the capture of Nijkerk as distinct stages. Grasping the importance of speed and momentum, Cumberland determined that as long as his tanks could keep moving forward, they would. After the first-phase capture of Deelen and Terlet to seal off the right flank, any enemy strongpoints encountered en route to the sea, such as the one anticipated at Barneveld, would be bypassed by the armour and left for the units of 11 CIB to mop up. To help deal with minor delaying actions and obstacles that might retard the advance, his two lead armoured regiments – the BCD and the 8th New Brunswick Hussars (8 NBH) – each would have a company of motorized infantry from the Westminster Regiment, a troop of "badger" flame-throwers, and a troop of flail tanks.[15] In reserve, Cumberland kept the Strathconas and the remaining company of Westminsters, which he believed would pass through the lead regiments to capture Otterloo in the second phase. Although he only outlined details for the first two phases at the 14 April orders group, Cumberland had definitely thought through the conduct of the entire advance, which he calculated would take four days to complete.

The Arnhem breakout that started at 06:30 a.m. on 15 April unfolded as both Hoffmeister and Cumberland had anticipated, save, as ever, for a few unforecast events. Despite extensive patrolling on the night of 14-15 April and the forward deployment of the attached Westminster companies to clear the woods of suspected enemy, the BCD ran into resistance from German tank-hunting teams in the wooded area just north of Arnhem. On the left flank, much the same happened with the Hussars. Both battle groups made slow progress, engaging the enemy with flame-throwers, machine guns, tanks, and artillery. After some tedious work, they skirted the defiles, broke out of the woods, and dashed towards their initial objectives and Deelen and Terlet, which they secured shortly after 11:00 a.m.[16] The enemy that had been bypassed was left first to "A" Company of the Westminsters; then, when the woods north of Arnhem proved far too large for a company to clear, Hoffmeister ordered Johnston to send one of his battalions to handle the task. These actions, behind the lead units, allowed the front end of the division to advance with maximum possible speed – and with the desired effect. They shocked the German defenders. The commander of the 858 Grenadier Regiment, whose headquarters the Hussars and Westminsters overran at Deelen, admitted "to having been completely taken by surprise, both as to the direction of [the] attack and its str[ength]."[17] This was the time for fast follow-up action. With the right flank secure and the enemy caught off guard, the opportunity existed for a quick advance towards Otterloo and Barneveld, before the enemy could regroup or muster their meagre reserves for a counterattack.

By this point of the war, Hoffmeister's division was experienced enough, flexible enough, and skilled enough to do just that. Within an hour of the capture of the initial objectives near Terlet and Deelen, the Hussars were advancing on Lunteren as the Strathconas rumbled towards Otterloo along the northern axis. Grouping and regrouping to meet changes in the tactical situation was not a problem for the seasoned soldiers of 5 CAB. The Hussars left one platoon of Westminsters and a troop of tanks at Deelen until 11 CIB could take over the blocking task. When the Strathconas could not take "A" Company with them for the advance as originally planned (that company was still engaged in woods clearing), "C" Company "switched horses" and joined the Strathconas just east of Otterloo in the early evening.[18] By last light on 15 April, the Strathconas were on the outskirts of Otterloo, while the Hussars, having advanced as far to the west, were only two miles south. As those two regiments firmed up their positions and gave orders to break through the most recent line of enemy opposition, the Cape Breton Highlanders were relieving the BCD at Terlet, and the Perth Regiment was taking control of Deelen. The division had done remarkably well. In twelve hours, Hoffmeister's troops had achieved all of their first phase objectives, captured an estimated 250 prisoners, and were poised to capture Otterloo.[19] And they did it while sustaining relatively light casualties – six killed and nineteen wounded.[20]

Hoffmeister, as was his custom, monitored matters from positions not far behind the fighting troops. As the lead regiments of 5 CAB had forced their way out of Arnhem, he had positioned himself with Cumberland's brigade headquarters. From that location, he had travelled to Johnston's headquarters, undoubtedly to discuss the upcoming woods-clearing tasks north of Arnhem, a chore that had to be completed before non-armoured vehicles could move forward. By 10:30 a.m. that same morning, he had assembled with Johnston and his artillery advisor at a "tactical headquarters"[21] in Arnhem. Shortly after the Division Main Headquarters had joined them at that location, he received the commander of 49th WR Division to coordinate operations, traffic control, and terrain management with the flanking British formation. Late that afternoon, the corps commander dropped by to discuss the next day's operations.

Those operations started just before first light on 16 April with the Strathcona assault on Otterloo. With the tanks of the lead squadron traversing their coaxial machine guns and firing them liberally, the regiment destroyed two tanks, knocked out several anti-tank guns, and took thirty-one prisoners as the regiment barged its way into, then out of, the town.[22] Shortly after the action, and as the squadrons paused 2,100 yards west of Otterloo to top up on ammunition before resuming the advance, Hoffmeister came forward to visit the regiment and discuss the situation with the lead squadron commander, whose own tank was the only vehicle casualty during the push through Otterloo.[23] On hearing of the roadblocks and sparse enemy presence, Hoffmeister undoubtedly determined that the enemy had only intended to delay at Otterloo, and resolved to press rapidly forward to Barneveld and Lunteren before the enemy could properly regroup. At 9:00 a.m., he met with Cumberland to arrange for that thrust.

Again, Hoffmeister and his armoured brigade commander did everything to avoid the slow process of leapfrogging depth formations or units. To free the Strathconas and their supporting company of Westminsters so that they could quickly resume the advance to Barneveld, Cumberland called forward a squadron of BCD from the area of Terlet and assigned it the job of guarding Otterloo until Hoffmeister could arrange for 11 CIB to send the Irish forward; this happened before noon.[24] Hoffmeister also tasked Johnston to send a battalion to occupy Barneveld once it fell to the tanks. Johnston, in turn, gave that mission to the Cape Bretons and their attached squadron of tanks from the GGHG. The Perths and their supporting tank squadron would relieve the Hussars after their fight for the high ground 1,000 yards northeast of Lunteren, a battle that was raging by midmorning. Finally, anticipating that the advance would proceed rapidly during the course of the day, Hoffmeister ordered his own main headquarters to set up in Otterloo.

With those actions put in motion, the advance continued with the Strathconas driving towards Barneveld, the BCD towards Voorthuizen. Reaching their objective first, the Strathconas advanced to within 1,500 yards of Barneveld and found the town heavily defended. On hearing of this, Cumberland immediately ordered the regiment to bypass the built-up area to the north. Having anticipated the order, the Strathcona commanding officer, Lieutenant-Colonel J.M. McAvity had already initiated such action by sending a reconnaissance troop, a Westminster scout platoon, and "B" Squadron to find a bypass and a way to cut the Voorthuizen-Amersfoort road. While that was happening, the remainder of the Westminster company and a squadron of tanks were picketing the town from the east. Hoffmeister, who at this time was at Cumberland's brigade headquarters, relieved Cumberland of the burden of taking Barneveld so that he could continue his armoured thrust to the sea. At 3:15 p.m., he sent a short, sharp bit of direction to his infantry brigade commander: "11 CIB to capture TINKER [Barneveld]."[25] Johnston, who shortly thereafter met with Hoffmeister at the Division Main Headquarters in Otterloo, ordered the Cape Bretons, already tasked with occupying Barneveld, to capture the town with the support of a GGHG tank squadron and the Strathcona/ Westminster combat team then picketing the objective. As it turned out, the Cape Bretons did not need all that extra support; when their lead troops probed into the town at 11:00 p.m., they found it abandoned by the enemy, who, it was later learned, had withdrawn only hours earlier.

Meanwhile, the BCD, without infantry support, encircled Voorthuizen to subdue German resistance in the town and cut the Voorthuizen-Amersfoort road. This was a critical task, as the road provided a major escape route for elements of 6 German Parachute Division, currently attempting to disengage from their battle with 1 CID near Apeldoorn. Dutch civilians provided information on the German defences in and around the town, but resistance was haphazard and disorganized. The 1st Canadian Corps's assaults, coming as they did from two directions, had caused a great deal of confusion and some interesting problems for the Dragoons:

> Prisoners began to give themselves up in ever increasing numbers and it soon became apparent that the BCDs were some miles behind the German main position, which was facing the other Canadian forces around Apeldoorn ...
>
> It would happen that some prisoners would surrender to one of the tanks and the tank crews would have to dismount ... to search them for concealed weapons. Then, as the BCDs had not been joined by the infantry, the prisoners would be sent back to brigade escorted by one of the smaller recce (scout) tanks. While some Germans were giving themselves up other Germans would be firing mortars and grenades at any groups they saw regardless as to whether or not the groups contained their own countrymen.[26]

Without infantry, and with darkness descending on the disorderly battlefield, the Dragoons commanding officer, Lieutenant-Colonel Harry Angle, opted to leave the enemy in the town and position his squadrons in tight protective clusters east and northeast of the town to sever the main road.

The 1st Canadian Corps was strangling the enemy in the Apeldoorn-Amersfoort area. With 1 CID across the Apeldoorn Canal and advancing westward, Hoffmeister's division was cutting a northward swath that would block any withdrawal to the protection of the Grebbe Line. At last light on 16 April, Hoffmeister had the Dragoons at Voorthuizen, the Strathconas one and a quarter miles to their southeast, the Cape Bretons clearing Barneveld, and the Hussar/Perth battle group destroying the last remnants of Dutch SS troops in Lunteren. To close the trap, Hoffmeister had only to reach the sea and, at 10:10 p.m. that night he made clear how he intended to do it: first, he would clear Voorthuizen; next he would take Nijkerk; then, with Nijkerk in hand, he would drive to the sea.

But the enemy, sensing the desperation of the situation, turned to desperate acts. The first of these last-ditch attempts to reach the Grebbe Line fell on the BCD straddling the main road northeast of Voorthuizen. At thirty minutes past midnight, fifty enemy infantry moved through the mist to attack "B" Squadron with small arms and light mortars, only to be repulsed by 2:30 a.m.[27] Three hours later, a larger group, perhaps 150-200 "young boys between the ages of 13 and 16," tried again and failed. One troop leader recalled the losses he inflicted on the second group of enemy trying to fight its way back to the Grebbe Line defences: "I called for a flame thrower ... which allowed us to flush the hysterical German youths out of their positions. I shall never forget the awful picture of them running back up the ditches and roadways with their clothes and bodies covered in burning fuel. Many of them were killed and a good number were taken prisoner."[28]

At the same time, a force of "between five and six hundred second rate troops," the remnants of 361 Volksgrenadier Division and 858 Grenadier Regiment, attempted a similar action at Otterloo.[29] That took them right through Hoffmeister's headquarters, as the division commander recalled: "They were swarming all around the place ... They were in on our sentries and outposts before they realized it and it was quite a night, a highly confusing night. People were shooting in all directions and I think it was the one and only time in the war when all the clerks and batmen and so on around divisional headquarters had an opportunity to fire a shot in anger.[30]

Luckily for the division headquarters, the Irish Regiment and the 17th Field Regiment, both located nearby, bore the brunt of the attack. Again, flame-throwers proved useful in breaking up the assault, as did the direct fire of the 17th Field Regiment's guns. Battery Sergeant-Major Gordie Bannerman recalled that the fighting "got very close quarters. They [the Germans] crawled up to the slit trenches and some of our fellows were shooting them at two-foot range."[31] By daybreak on 17 April, the attacks had dissipated, the enemy leaving behind some 200 dead and 104 prisoners.[32] Some of the surviving enemy straggled westward towards Barneveld, potentially cutting road communications between Hoffmeister's headquarters and the units of his two brigades. He placed the Hussars under command of 11 CIB and tasked the brigade with providing a tank squadron and a company of Westminsters "to back-track and clear the OTTERLOO-BARNEVELD r[oa]d again."[33] As it turned out, the Hussar squadron found little evidence of enemy on the route and, by noon, Hoffmeister released them to join the remainder of their regiment for the final phase of Operation CLEANSER.

The Battle of Otterloo had been a close call for the division commander and his headquarters, and Hoffmeister was well aware of who had saved them. At 8:45 a.m., he visited the Irish Regiment to congratulate the commanding officer, Lieutenant-Colonel H.C. Payne, on his regiment's role in repelling the enemy attack. He spoke of the soldiers' determination and bravery under fire, but his visit was an expression of gratitude as much as anything else. And Hoffmeister did not restrict himself to conversations with senior commanders. As was his habit, he spent some time talking to the troops. From the Irish battalion headquarters, he made his way to the site where the 17th Field Regiment had repulsed the attacking Germans by levelling their gun barrels and firing at close range, "over open sights." At the 76th Battery location, Hoffmeister met "with the men [and] reviewed the enemy method of attack."[34] It never hurt to let the troops brag about what they had done, especially when they had definitely earned the right to do so. On hearing that one lieutenant, Alex Ross, had three times made his way from the gun positions, through the swarms of enemy, to get help and ammunition, Hoffmeister asked to speak to Ross. Unfortunately, Ross was unable to make it to Hoffmeister's location before the division commander had to leave, but Ross was later awarded the Military Cross for his actions – something the division commander would have recommended.[35] Gestures such as these left their mark. For Sergeant-Major Gordie Bannerman, who was there when Hoffmeister thanked the 76th Battery gunners, Hoffmeister's actions only reinforced the soldiers' opinion that their division commander was "a soldier's General ... truly the finest general in the Canadian Army. Too bad there were not more like him."[36] Hoffmeister understood what he was doing on the morning of 17 April. He knew that these personal contacts were worth the time because the human factor made a difference in battle, particularly when the unexpected happened as it did at Otterloo. At a time when commanders had very little control of a chaotic battle, the soldiers rose to the occasion, overcame their fears, banded together in small groups, and routed their attackers. It was decisive.

With the tactical situation stabilized, Hoffmeister moved his headquarters near 5 CAB's in Barneveld, where he met with Cumberland and proceeded to discuss how they would capture the last few objectives of Operation CLEANSER. The method did not change. Once again the armour would lead with two major thrusts: one on Nijkerk, one on Harderwijk. The aim was to cut the Putten-Nijkerk road, sever the last enemy escape route, and close the trap. The infantry brigade, with the Horse Guards in support, would follow along to mop up any bypassed enemy concentrations.

After a delay caused by the events at Otterloo, Cumberland hurled his tanks against increasingly frantic enemy resistance. He moved with Hussars on the right, sending them around Voorthuizen to the east, and the Strathconas on the left aiming towards Nijkerk. The Germans, realizing the importance of the Putten-Nijkerk road and the small port of Harderwijk to their withdrawal effort, mustered their remaining guns to form an anti-tank screen in front of 5 CAD. Frenetic though the enemy's actions may have been, a hail of well-aimed anti-tank fire stopped the Strathconas on the left. But, on the right, 3,500 yards past Voorthuizen, the Hussars used artillery and tank fire to blast their way past six anti-tank guns and 150 infantry, and to penetrate the anti-tank screen.[37]

Reinforcing the spectacular Hussar successes, Cumberland ordered the Strathconas to disengage from their fight on the left so that they could follow quickly on the heels of the Hussar breakthrough. McAvity's Strathconas chased after the Hussars until the New Brunswick regiment ran into an anti-tank ambush 1,500 yards short of Putten. With six tanks knocked out and daylight fast disappearing the Hussar commanding officer, Lieutenant-Colonel J.W. Eaton, called off the assault on Putten and consolidated his tanks and his company of the Westminsters south of Putten. Although, he had not yet reduced Putten, Eaton knew that it had been a good day. For a cost of fourteen tanks and only one dead and none seriously wounded, his regiment had advanced five miles through a series of anti-tank defences, killed or wounded 200 Germans, and destroyed fourteen anti-tank and five anti-aircraft guns.[38] Like the other units of 5 CAD, Eaton's was an experienced and proficient one. The next morning, his Hussars skirted Putten to the west and, with the help of "C" Company of the Westminsters, cut the Putten-Nijkerk road, and then drove to the sea directly west of Putten.

Hoffmeister's division had only a few tasks to complete as Foster's infantry division continued its westward advance to the Grebbe Line, sweeping aside all opposition east of the Eem River. While the Hussars were slicing the Putten-Nijkerk road, the Strathconas closed on the town of Harderwijk, having bypassed the town of Ermelo, which they left for the BCD and the Perths to clear. With the Strathconas surrounding Harderwijk and retreating troop ships being engaged by tank and anti-tank fire, the remaining Germans surrendered. Shortly after 6:00 p.m., the Strathconas accepted the surrender of the rag-tag enemy garrison. That marked the end of Operation CLEANSER.

In bursting out of the Arnhem bridgehead and slashing to the Ijsselmeer, Hoffmeister's division scored a tremendous tactical success. By its rapid action, the formation had thoroughly vanquished the enemy forward of the Grebbe Line, netting 34 German officers and 1,755 troops as prisoners of war in the process.[39] It helped that the division, after a year of combat experience, was a finely tuned fighting formation at all levels. Italy had provided a solid mass of seasoned officers, non-commissioned officers, and soldiers who were capable of absorbing and mentoring newly arrived reinforcements and still fighting like a veteran formation. The ability of the Westminster companies to react as they did to changes in the tactical situation, to "switch horses" to another armoured regiment, and still do a superb job is but one example of that level of experience. At the formation level, staffs and commanders knew their business too. Brigade and division staffs had developed into efficient machines, capable of implementing their commanders' plans without difficulty. In Western Holland, guns were never wanting for ammunition, and there were none of the traffic foul-ups of the Liri Valley Campaign. As an armoured brigade commander with an opportunity for armoured manoeuvre, Cumberland showed that he could move tanks and their administrative tails as well as anyone. And Johnston followed up with all the efficiency and foresight that had characterized his earlier battles. There were no Eric Snows here.

All of this enabled the man at the top, Hoffmeister, to achieve his objectives quickly and with minimal casualties to his own troops.[40] He ran the operation as he normally had done: he developed a simple plan, he developed it for speed, he devolved responsibility to an adroit subordinate – Cumberland in this case – for the advance, and he supervised things from positions well forward, anticipating requirements and providing support where and when it was needed. Without a good staff, he was likely to have been more headquarters bound – having to guide the monitoring and controlling of current operations. Without good commanders, he would probably have planned a more deliberate operation: one in which control and initiative were exercised at the division level, one conducted in set stages with formations leapfrogging over each other in bounds. But that did not have to happen. Hoffmeister was efficient and quick because the people under him were efficient and quick. Late on 18 April, he received a letter of congratulations from the army commander: "Congratulations on the very important success which attended the recent op[erations]s of 5 Cdn Armd Div. The determination with which they were conducted and carried out were fully in keeping with the fine and long est[ablished] tradition of your com[mman]d."[41]

AN AWARD CAME LATER. With Hoffmeister already in possession of three Distinguished Service Orders and admitted as a Commander into the Order of the British Empire, his superiors decided that the performance of the division commander was worthy of admission as a Companion into the Most Honourable Order of Bath: "For outstanding and inspiring leadership, as a result of which the 5th Canadian Armoured Division was, on 14 April 1945, able to break out of the Arnhem bridgehead and thrust to the Zuider Zee [Ijsselmeer] to cut off the enemy."[42]

Hoffmeister had little time to contemplate his success in Operation CLEANSER. Three days after the fall of Harderwijk, his division left the 1st Canadian Corps to join Lieutenant-General Guy Simonds's 2nd Canadian Corps, then in the process of reducing German resistance in the northeastern part of Germany and a strip of northwestern Germany between the Ems and Weser rivers. The first of three "formal" conferences with Simonds concerning the clearing of the Ems Estuary took place at noon on 20 April.[43] At that time, the corps commander handed Hoffmeister the independent task of clearing the remaining enemy between the Ijsselmeer and the Dutch-German border, the main focus being the German garrisons and gun batteries in and around Delfzijl, a secondary port that planners believed was critical to bringing relief supplies to the desperate Dutch population. But Simonds also wanted to coordinate 5 CAD's actions with Major-General R.H. Keefler's 3 CID assault on Emden, some seven miles east of Delfzijl on the other side of the estuary. While 3 CID was attacking Emden, 5 CAD was to press the enemy in the Delfzijl Pocket and prevent their withdrawal to the east. Only after the fall of Emden (from which German guns could reach the 5 CAD objectives) was the final assault on Delfzijl to take place.

These planning parameters logically pushed Hoffmeister towards a two-phased operation: first a reduction of the perimeter defences around Delfzijl, then an attack to capture the port. At first, perhaps still flushed with the recent successes of his armoured brigade, Hoffmeister intended to give the task to a "beefed up" 5 CAB, and he accordingly conducted the relief of 3 CID units to do so. Cumberland's armoured brigade, with the Perths and the Irish Regiment under command, took control of the sector south and west of Delfzijl, while Johnston's infantry brigade took over Friesland, which bordered on the North Sea and the Ijsselmeer, to the far west. However, it soon became clear to Hoffmeister, from air photographs and intelligence reports, that the ground conditions in the Delfzijl area dictated infantry-intensive operations: "The ground was extremely flat with very little cover, small villages and towns dispersed over the area. A complicated network of ditches and canals made cross-country movement impossible. The weather was wet and the whole area was subject to flooding, which meant all vehicles were confined to roads."[44] In those conditions, tanks were not going to move anywhere fast, so Hoffmeister decided to give the chore to his infantry brigade, which took control of the Delfzijl sector on the morning of 25 April.

Hoffmeister's stalwart brigadier, Ian Johnston kept the same basic two-phased plan – reducing the perimeter defences, and then assaulting Delfzijl (see Map 15). Because the flooded Ems Canal split the brigade's 16,000-yard frontage, Johnston decided to close in on Delfzijl from two directions. On the right, the Westminsters and a troop of Hussars would swing north and roll up the enemy east of the north-south canal, while the Irish Regiment and a troop of Hussars were to burst out of Wagenborgen to flush the enemy from Oterdum, Heveskes, Weiwerd, and Farmsum. On the other side of the flooded area, Johnston wanted the Perth Regiment, supported by a full squadron of Hussar tanks, to push through Krewerd, Holwierde, and Nansum from the northwest. At the same time, the BCD, in the dismounted role, would hold the enemy at Marsum from a position in Appingedam. The Cape Breton Highlanders and a squadron of Hussar tanks would complete the second-phase assault on Delfzijl. The nature of the terrain dictated that significant indirect fire support, smoke in particular, would be crucial to helping the infantry cross the open ground. However, since the division's mission was a secondary priority in the corps, there were no extra artillery units to subdue the German anti-tank guns and machine guns. Thus, 5 CAD's supporting artillery had to be split, with 17th Field Regiment supporting the Westminsters and Irish, and the 8th Field Regiment (self-propelled) providing fire for the Perths, Dragoons, and Cape Bretons. The openness of the terrain also dictated that the majority of the assaults be conducted at night, which they were.

Operations proceeded as planned.[45] Starting on 26 April, the Westminsters fought their way through some stubborn enemy resistance to the estuary, completely clearing their area of enemy and capturing over 700 prisoners by 1 May.[46] This helped the Irish Regiment on their left, who were advancing with three companies up on Farmsum.[47] Mines, obstacles, and pockets of enemy delaying actions slowed the advance a little bit, but the Irish slogged their way to Oterdum and Heveskes by 30 April. Meanwhile, on the other side of the pocket, the noose was tightening around the remaining German defenders. After some of the toughest fighting of the entire operation, the Perths captured Krewerd, Holwierde and Nansum, all by 29 April.[48]

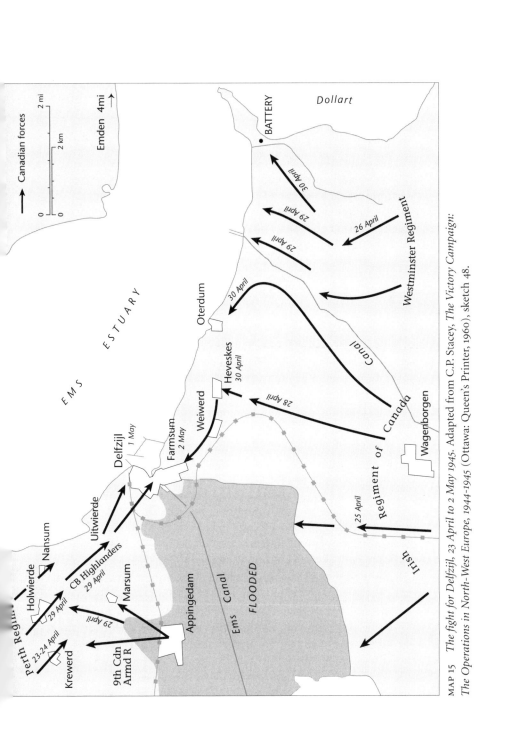

MAP 15   *The fight for Delfzijl, 23 April to 2 May 1945. Adapted from C.P. Stacey,* The Victory Campaign: The Operations in North-West Europe, 1944-1945 *(Ottawa: Queen's Printer, 1960), sketch 48.*

Six days of attacks had cost the battalion seventy-eight casualties, but the actions set the stage for the final act – the Cape Breton assault on Delfzijl. The construction of a bridge at Holwierde, a piece of work critical to bringing forward supporting tanks, delayed the operation by a day, as did the need for the battalion to push a few enemy stragglers out of Uitwierde.[49] The BCD helped by conducting a dismounted daylight attack on Marsum, which they occupied against light resistance on 29 April.[50] Finally stepping off at 10:00 p.m. on 30 April, the Cape Bretons overcame wire obstacles, mines, and the bunker-protected machine guns that covered them. They managed to break into Delfzijl, but it was not an easy advance by any means. The fighting was intense. However, by the morning of 1 May, the enemy was in full withdrawal, attempting to evacuate the Delfzijl garrison by sea. The Irish Regiment assault on Farmsum stopped that harried retreat, bagging another 38 German officers and over 1,300 other ranks.[51] During the battle for Delfzijl, 5 CAD nabbed 4,143 prisoners of war. Just as important to the relief effort, Johnston's brigade captured the port facility intact. It was fitting that the fight for Delfzijl, the final action of Hoffmeister's division in the Second World War, was a hugely successful one.

A historian, looking back on the operation with the benefit of hindsight and in the comfort of his own study, might be inclined to say that the operation "went like clockwork." The casualties for 11 CIB were relatively light – 62 killed and 168 wounded in ten days of fighting. But such simple calculations mean little to the soldiers who fought the actions. One Cape Breton subaltern, Lieutenant Reg Roy, a veteran of the Italian Campaign who later became a noted military historian, recorded his impressions of his company's final "easy" advance on Delfzijl, which started at 1:00 a.m. on 1 May: "No sooner on the road than over come the flares and they had us cold ... Advanced along the dyke bank, contacted enemy with bang ... Were pinned down by snipers and that cursed SP gun ... My God, but it was terrible to see our fellows cut up so ... I hope I shall never see another battle like it. It was murder ... This has been the bitterest battle I've been in."[52]

Hoffmeister, who appreciated the difficulty of every combat situation to those closest to the fighting, took two full hours to visit the soldiers of the Cape Breton Highlanders on 2 May "and congratulated all ranks upon the determination and courage shown during the attack."[53] The soldiers might have regarded the visit with cynicism; more often than not, they considered general officers to be creatures of comfort, fond of the safety of their caravans far behind the fighting. But Hoffmeister's reputation for bravery was well known, and the Cape Bretons accepted his words of congratulations as an expression of their commander's gratitude.[54]

In fact, Hoffmeister continued to thank his troops even after the formal end to the fighting on 8 May. On 23 May, he assembled the entire division, every man and every vehicle, on an airfield near Groningen.[55] Exercise FINALE included an inspection by the army commander and a full-scale roll past, tracked vehicles and all. Hoffmeister wanted the soldiers to see how the sum of all these parts added up to something big: "The men were able to see for the first time what a whole armoured division looked like concentrated in one spot. They were able to move around in their own time before and after the inspection, just to marvel at what they'd seen, and take pictures with their own cameras and so on. They could take back to Canada an impression of this great division of which they were a part."[56]

A little over a week later, when Hoffmeister realized he would soon be taking leave of his men, he spent "mornings and afternoons ... visiting all units of the division in order to bid them goodbye and thank each one for its support, cooperation and performance during the very active period of his command."[57] His words were well received. The division war diarist captured a commonly held impression of Hoffmeister's farewell addresses: "one can easily realize the qualities of the man under whom so many thousand have been pleased to serve.[58] His gratitude duly expressed, Hoffmeister left his soldiers in the able hands of Ian Johnston on 5 June 1945.

When Hoffmeister departed Northwest Europe, he left not for a position in the HR MacMillan Export Company as he had planned, but for command of the Canadian Army Pacific Force – a new infantry division that Canada was raising to fight alongside Americans in the Pacific. Hoffmeister had already been in contact with MacMillan, who had reserved the position of company superintendent for Hoffmeister. Through his political contacts, Hoffmeister's old mentor lobbied for the division commander's expeditious return to civilian life, but the army commander had other plans.[59] Crerar had to appoint a commander for the new force, and he had recommended both Foulkes and Simonds, should the assignment demand a lieutenant-general, and Hoffmeister if a major-general would do. National Defence Headquarters wanted a major-general and had balked at the idea of either Simonds or Foulkes taking a reduction in rank, so Crerar turned to Hoffmeister.[60] Like many of the other turns in Hoffmeister's career, this was not something the thirty-eight-year-old Vancouverite wanted. As he explained to Crerar, he did not understand the logic of his selection: "there are many other officers in the Canadian Army who would give their right arms for this privilege, and since I've no intention of staying in the army then why not offer it to one of them and let me get back to civvy street."[61] But Crerar pushed his point on 24 May, eventually eliciting reluctant agreement from Hoffmeister, but Hoffmeister got something in return – his choice of officers for command and staff appointments.[62]

The following day, Hoffmeister interviewed a few command prospects.[63] At lunch, he met with Brigadier J.A. Rockingham, an extremely tough officer who had distinguished himself in battle with the Royal Hamilton Light Infantry and as commander of 9 CIB. That evening, he hosted two familiar and reliable subordinates – Brigadier "Budge" Bell-Irving and Lieutenant-Colonel Syd Thomson. In all, Hoffmeister took a week to make queries and conduct interviews before meeting again with Crerar on 31 May. Hoffmeister remembered that the army commander "balked at two or three of them," but, after some discussion, the two men eventually agreed on the officer slate.[64] Predictably, he pulled in as many of his most dependable subordinates as he could gather.[65] For his division staff, Lieutenant-Colonel Dick agreed to be chief of staff, while Brigadier H.A. Sparling, Acting Brigadier Wrinch, and Lieutenant-Colonel Drury agreed to assume their old divisional responsibilities for artillery, signals, and logistics, respectively.[66] For commanders, Hoffmeister picked a combination of those he knew were good and those whose reputations were good. Des Smith, whom he had known as the commander of 5 CAB in the Liri Valley, agreed to leave 1 CIB to take up an appointment as a regimental commander in the Pacific Force. John Rockingham and Paul Bernatchez, both experienced brigade commanders who Hoffmeister had heard could fight their formations with verve and ability, filled the other two regimental command positions. His battalion commanders included two of his old favourites: Syd Thomson, one of his old Seaforth protégés who had just finished commanding the Black Watch, and W.W. Reid, who had led the Perths with such élan at the Gothic Line. Also on the commanding officer's list were J.R. "Jim" Stone, an extremely brave officer who had risen from the rank of private in 1939 to command the Loyal Edmonton Regiment in September 1944, and J.A. Dextraze, who was destined to become Chief of Defence Staff in the 1970s.[67] It was a definite A-list team, tried and skilled, that Hoffmeister brought back to Canada in June 1945.

Not long after Hoffmeister and his key staff and commanders landed in Ottawa on 13 June, the hard work of cobbling together his new division's war establishment began. The first order of business was a pleasant one, however; wives and families of the returning soldiers greeted their kin at the airport. Margot and Donalda Hoffmeister were there, and Hoffmeister delighted in seeing his daughter who had grown so much since he last saw her during his 1942 staff course in Kingston. Donalda was happy to see her husband, but understandably upset at the same time. After enduring his absence through nearly six years of war, news that Hoffmeister would be leaving the war in Europe to fight the Japanese was "just the end."[68] In spite of that, she wore a brave face, endured a few press photographs and questions, and then retired with her husband and daughter to the Chateau Laurier for some long-awaited private family time.

Raising a force to fight with the Americans was not so simple for soldiers who had grown up under British Army tutelage. Planning began in earnest the next day, with Hoffmeister attending briefings by National Defence Headquarters staff in the morning and a meeting with Prime Minister William Lyon Mackenzie King and the Minister of National Defence.[69] The 6th Canadian Infantry Division (6 CID), as the Pacific Force was now designated, was to be organized along American lines, equipped with American weapons, and fought with American doctrine and procedures. National Defence planners had already worked out a three-month training package to ready the force for battle in the Pacific theatre – the first month to train on US weapons, the second to do collective training to regimental level, and the final month for divisional training and embarkation.[70] As soon as possible, 200 officers and 1,200 non-commissioned officers would proceed to the United States "to be prepared as instructional cadre, and so be ready to receive units upon concentration in the US."[71] In the initial meeting, Hoffmeister accepted most of what had already been done, although he did insist on a few things. First, he suggested that every effort be made to man the instructional cadre with "proven instruction ability and battle experience," repatriating suitable volunteers from Europe by air if need be. Perhaps recalling his own admiration for British staff college instructors with North African experience, he knew that the soldiers would not only get better training with NCOs and officers who had been in action, they would be more comfortable and confident too. Second, he made two suggestions for the sake of morale. He wanted the units to have affiliations with established regiments. Thus, the nine infantry units came to be designated as the second or third battalions of units in 1 CID.[72] And if the division was to be the 6th, it should have some sort of badges or insignia that were "as distinctive as possible." Soldiers enjoyed being distinct, something that was never bad for morale. There were also liaison visits to the United States to meet with US Army officers and pin down what had to be done to prepare the Canadian division for war against the Japanese. These included a one-on-one conference with Army Chief of Staff General George Marshall.[73]

Preparations continued in accordance with the plan and the arrangements that had been put in place, but problems began to surface before the end of summer. Hoffmeister established his headquarters in Brockville, Ontario, dispatched a cadre of instructors to Kentucky, and sent concentrated fighting units to Canadian bases like Shilo, Manitoba, and Debert, Nova Scotia, but the thorny issue of manpower shortages eventually revealed themselves: "We had all the officers we needed at that time but less than half the other ranks."[74] He met weekly with the Prime Minister to discuss the potentially grave issue. Hoffmeister's concern was essentially military: he needed soldiers to fill out his war establishment *and* replacements for the casualties that were sure to follow any invasion of the Japanese home islands. King's concern was political: in November 1944, he had been forced to send 16,000 men who had been conscripted for home service to the war in Europe.[75] Although less than three thousand of that total actually saw active service with the First Canadian Army, the decision was wildly unpopular in French-speaking Canada and rural Ontario, and King, ever the wily politician, wanted to avoid having to conscript another draft for overseas service. Fortunately for both men, the dropping of atomic bombs on Hiroshima and Nagasaki precipitated Japanese surrender and negated any requirement for an invasion of the home islands. The Canadian Army Pacific Force was disbanded in September, the same month that Hoffmeister took his release and returned to his family and the lumber business in Vancouver. He would fight no more battles.

THE 5TH CANADIAN ARMOURED DIVISION's two major battles in Holland capped Hoffmeister's period of division command. What can be said of those two actions in relation to his other divisional fights? Paradoxically, probably his greatest management attribute was that he managed very little. His had always been a very subordinate-dependent manner of command. Once he had completed his battle estimate and assigned the tasks, he let his subordinates get on with their portion of the plan.

He still visited his subordinates daily, though, to keep abreast of the situation, anticipate requirements, and ensure his brigadiers had what they needed for their tasks. During the battle of the Delfzijl Pocket, he dropped into Johnston's headquarters every morning, just after Johnston had completed his own morning conference. He did much the same with Cumberland during the Arnhem breakout. Mornings and afternoons, he divided his time between visits to forward units or supporting arms, conferences with key staff at his own headquarters, and, if need be, visits back to higher headquarters. In this way, away from the sterile environment of his caravan, Hoffmeister maintained a very good feel for the battle. Then, every evening, after Hoffmeister had reviewed current operations and considered what would take place in the days ahead, he communicated his intentions for future actions. It was never more than a few simple lines. The direction he gave to subordinate, higher, and flanking formations at 10:10 p.m. on 16 April was typical: "INTENTION. ONE. capture BARNEVELD [Map Grid] 5395. TWO. capture NIJKERK 4606. THREE. exploit to ZUIDER ZEE [Ijsselmeer] area 4406."[76] The next morning he closed the loop with a visit to the brigadier principally responsible for completing those tasks to see how it was to be done and give guidance if guidance was needed. By this stage in the war, Hoffmeister's battle routine had a definite rhythm, something that it definitely did not have in the Liri Valley Campaign, but, as Ian Johnston remembered, it was still Eighth-Army-style informal: "He would say I would like you to do this, I would say maybe that. Certainly I was always doing what he told me to do. He would make the decisions and I would just be carrying them out."[77]

This approach stood in marked contrast to the one employed by Hoffmeister's immediate boss during the battle for the Delfzijl Pocket, Guy Simonds. Although Simonds had gained his first battle experience with the Eighth Army, Hoffmeister did not enjoy working for him. He found Simonds rigid, fond of calling commanders back for direction, less likely to delegate responsibility to subordinate commanders, and abrupt: "I was summoned to his headquarters from time to time to report, or to be given my orders for an operation, and it was all done very formally and that was it."[78] In the period 20 April-2 May, Hoffmeister went back three times for conferences with Simonds.[79] Hoffmeister, on the other hand, took a more informal and consensual approach to orders, rarely called subordinate commanders back to give direction, and gave his brigadiers tremendous freedom in determining how best to accomplish their tasks. From the time his division joined

Simonds's corps to the time that the German garrison at Delfzijl surrendered, Hoffmeister held two conferences forward with the formations 5 CAD was relieving, seven at 11 CIB while it was doing most of the fighting, and only one at his own division headquarters.[80] Given such drastically different approaches, it should come as no surprise that personal relations between Hoffmeister and Simonds were not good. To some, such as Hoffmeister's aide-de-camp, it was painfully apparent: "When General Simonds and General Hoffmeister were together ... it was quite unpleasant."[81] Unpleasant though it may have been, Hoffmeister adjusted to the new command environment, but his relations with his own staff and subordinates remained unchanged.

Hoffmeister could keep that longstanding modus operandi because he had top-notch subordinates. His principal staff officers, while they had experienced a very rough introduction to battle in the Liri Valley, were all very competent. Sparling, Christian, and Wrinch all went on to higher appointments in 1st Canadian Corps, while Drury and Dick (who was handpicked as Hoffmeister's GSO I in September 1944) stayed with their commander until the end of the war. Of his brigadiers, only Snow can be said to have been below par. Cumberland commanded his armoured brigade capably, as did his predecessor, Des Smith. Until its disbandment when 1st Canadian Corps moved to Northwest Europe, J.S.H. Lind also led his green, ad hoc brigade with skill and alacrity. The best of the lot, however, was Johnston. An exceptional brigadier, Johnston was the one on whom his boss leaned most often. Indeed, the breaking of the Gothic Line, the Valli di Comacchio, and Delfzijl were every bit as much his victories as they were Hoffmeister's. For a division commander, having subordinates capable of fighting their own battles meant that you could fight yours.

The importance of solid subordinate performance was nothing new to Hoffmeister. His understanding of it dated at least as far back as 1935, when his reputation had hung on the ability of small mill owners to make up for the output of lost suppliers in the Seaboard lumber crisis. Hoffmeister thought hard how to make subordinates perform to their potential, how to make them *want* to perform to their potential. That was why he brought them in so closely in the planning process. That was why he consulted them and accepted their advice. Once, when Hoffmeister complained "he was being held up by [the] failure of ... [a] crossing [site]," his CRE explained that the infantry "had to be prepared to push on at least 3,000 yards in order to force enemy mortars to move back," and that, when tanks reached a minefield, "the present drill of screaming for engineers is not on." Hoffmeister allowed Christian his retort about the employment of scarce resources "and promised to discuss this with his brigadiers."[82] When things got hectic, keeping the family peace was also important.

In spite of the occasional disagreement, Hoffmeister got on well with his staff and subordinate commanders. The more they worked together, the more they understood each other, the better they functioned. It helped that all of them had gained their combat experience in the Eighth Army. They may have received their staff training elsewhere, but they had all learned the business of battle by doing it, some as early as the invasion of Sicily, and some a little later.[83] They had grown accustomed to the easy-going professionalism of the Eighth Army, something that continued long after Montgomery's departure, with both Leese and Sir Richard McCreery. Face-to-face, informal, forward, and fast: that was the way Hoffmeister preferred to operate; that was what he learned from commanders, mostly British, in the Eighth Army.[84] As Ian Johnston remembered, "There were not many formal 'O' [orders] Groups ... [Most often] there was just him giving orders to me."[85] Commanders and staffs in 5 CAD continued in this tradition, even after joining the more formal and paper-driven First Canadian Army in Northwest Europe. They liked it the Eighth Army way.

Getting the most out of soldiers was also crucial, though not always easy. A divisional commander's opportunities to make his mark on the rank and file were rare, but Hoffmeister did it better than most. He visited them, spoke with them, and shared some of their risks under fire. His forays forward impressed those who witnessed them. Less direct, but just as important, he made sure that his soldiers had good leaders, officers, and non-commissioned officers who could train them for battle and then lead them through it when that awful time came. He cared too much to tolerate anything less.

11
Hoffmeister and Command

He was our general – the soldiers' general.[1]

SERGEANT RON HURLEY, THE WESTMINSTER REGIMENT

Returning to his beloved Vancouver in September 1945, Hoffmeister happily resumed his pre-war duties as husband, father, and businessman. Donalda and Margot delighted in having him back in their Belmont Avenue home. It had been an awfully long war for both of them. A second child, Rod, was added to the family before very long, and the four of them settled into a new, more stable routine. Hoffmeister also picked up pretty much where he left off at H.R. MacMillan Export Company. In the autumn of 1945, he accepted a position as general manager of Canadian White Pine and proceeded to climb the corporate ladder, something he believed his wartime experience and training made easier. He became president of the newly merged MacMillan Bloedel Limited in 1951, and he succeeded his mentor, H.R. MacMillan, as chairman in 1956. In 1957, he resigned from his chairmanship and accepted a post as the Agent General for British Columbia in London, England, shortly thereafter. He held that position in the United Kingdom until 1961, when he returned to Vancouver to act as president of a lumber-industry association. Through it all, he remained active in numerous charities and kept up an impressive level of physical fitness, skiing until he was eighty years old. Bert Hoffmeister died in December 1999 at the age of ninety-two.

WHY DID HOFFMEISTER SUCCEED in battle where others did not? Was he a natural commander? Or was it something he just learned better than most? Analysis of his development as a military commander, based on an acknowledgement of the technical and human dimensions of command, suggests that it was both. The technical skills, those needed to manage men and resources in battle, he learned during his service overseas – through study, training, and, ultimately, combat. This took years. The ability to tap into human potential, on the other hand, was a skill he possessed from a very early age. His understanding of human nature, combined with his strong personality and his sensitive disposition, helped him "read" his subordinates and prescribe the right actions to draw on their potential.

The technical tools of generalship did not come as easily, although he did have solid building blocks before 1939. An inbred competitiveness, honed by sports and exposure to entrepreneurial relatives, made him want to win, a hunger that he carried from the rowing basin to the boardroom to the battlefield. The corollary, of course, was that Hoffmeister found personal failure unacceptable. This made him extremely hard on himself, and at times it caused problems. Most often, however, his characteristic conscientiousness allowed him to digest lessons, learn what had to be learned, and then do what had to be done – successfully. His mother had encouraged such a disciplined approach to personal development, and it was something that he exhibited as a cadet drill instructor, as an office boy learning the lumber business, and as a company commander foraging for his own orders formats.

His experience under the tutelage of H.R. MacMillan in the mid-to-late 1930s served him well. He learned how organizations operated, starting with the people running them. In MacMillan Export, Hoffmeister studied an organization in which the man at the top effectively delegated responsibility such that he was able to devote his attention to "big picture" issues and look into the future. Hoffmeister took note of how effectively MacMillan imparted his vision to subordinates and "energized" them for their tasks. He watched as the company president used a variety of advisors to help him formulate plans, issue direction, and then monitor operations. And, in his own areas of responsibility, he had plenty of practice designing solutions for complex issues. All of this disposed him well to embracing the lessons of the commander-staff relationship, whether at staff college or in the field.

But it would be folly to suggest that Hoffmeister could have walked out of the offices of MacMillan Export to command a division, a brigade, a battalion, or even a rifle company. Some principles of sound management and good leadership may have been portable, but the technical skills were not. The nervous crisis that led to his breakdown in 1941 clearly indicated that neither his business experience nor his pre-war training in the Non-Permanent Active Militia were enough. Only through a long period of training and experience did he acquire the technical skills of a military officer. At first, the Canadian Army, unprepared as it was for war, could not provide the skill training he needed. But later, as the army got better, so did Hoffmeister. In the ten months that Montgomery had 1st Canadian Corps in his Southeastern Army, the Canadians improved markedly. "Monty" excised them of ineffective commanders and taught them *how* to train. Consequently, the army to which Hoffmeister returned after staff training in October 1942 was much sharper than the one he left seven months earlier, and immeasurably more efficient than the one that had floundered so badly during its first year in England. By 1943, officers trained as officers, troops trained as troops, and collective training tested teams – all of it progressive, all of it systematic, all of it with purpose. Like everyone else in the Canadian army, Hoffmeister profited from improvements; he just assimilated the lessons better than most.

Impending operational tasks also focused training. As an example, the combined-arms training at Inverary during the first half of 1943 prepared the 1st Canadian

Division (1 CID) for the amphibious invasion of Sicily. Prior to mock beach landings onto objectives designed to look like the beaches at Pachino, commanders planned their assaults while staffs worked on the movement and landing plans to get them there. For Hoffmeister, those exercises provided excellent opportunities to put planning into practice and to determine what arrangements worked best for controlling battalion battles. Only combat could have taught him more.

And it did. Take, for example, how Hoffmeister adjusted his method of command and control as he rose up the chain of command. The confusion he experienced during the initial landings at Pachino convinced him that he needed to be further forward in order to get a proper read of the battle, not *just behind* the lead elements, but *with* them. In subsequent battalion battles, being forward helped him make quicker decisions. Waiting for the information to filter back, particularly when communications were unreliable, was a sure-fire way to slow the tempo of the battle. Three months later, as brigade commander, he operated much the same way, staying well forward, directing the battle himself and paying little attention to administrative matters. This proved adequate for the direction of an infantry brigade, because the "logistic tail" for three battalions of foot soldiers and a few supporting arms was not all that extensive. But an armoured division was a different story. In the hilly Italian terrain, tanks and the trucks that supplied them needed routes – good routes – to move forward and keep the fighters fighting. To get forces where the commander wanted them, when he wanted them, his staff needed time to bid for routes and waiting areas from higher headquarters. In the Liri Valley, Hoffmeister's habit of being far forward meant that he was often out of communications with his main divisional headquarters, which, consequently, could not make the necessary arrangements early enough. Making matters worse, Snow's painfully slow advance preoccupied Hoffmeister to the point where he was unable to anticipate requirements soon enough anyway. By August 1944, Hoffmeister corrected the problem, settling on a workable compromise that balanced his desire to be forward with the need to keep the staff apprised of what was coming next. On the recommendation of Eighth Army staff officers, 5th Canadian Armoured Division (5 CAD) reorganized its headquarters based on a "chief of staff" system – one in which the main headquarters, under the GSO I, had greater responsibility for monitoring and coordinating the battle. The hub of battle direction and control was no longer Hoffmeister's tactical headquarters, but the main headquarters, which acted in accordance with Hoffmeister's intentions. Hoffmeister still went forward, but he always made sure that he had a sound link with his main headquarters, and he usually returned during hours of darkness. Other changes, such as the creation of a large traffic control organization with enough personnel and communications infrastructure to respond quickly to changes, also helped.

With experience, Hoffmeister eventually gained enough confidence to step out of the British/Canadian doctrinal template for offensive action. In November 1943, he advocated the use of all available firepower – air attack, followed by artillery, followed by mortars and machine guns, followed by infantry assault – to save lives. Later, at the Gothic Line, he went for a silent night attack. This way, if the enemy were unprepared, there would be no barrage to give warning of impending attack or time to occupy the trenches. The doctrinal departure was not huge. Hoffmeister simply modified a simple set-piece attack plan by holding back the barrage and sending patrols forward to seize key terrain. His exploitation of the initial break-in occurred because he anticipated future requirements and moved units such that they could enter the battle without delay, which they did. It was really just bread-and-butter tactics with a few changes based on experience. At the Gully in December 1943, Hoffmeister had learned that it took more than firepower to dislodge a dug-in enemy from a reverse-slope position. Sometimes – not always – surprise, manoeuvre, and stealth forged better foundations for an attack. The slow, safe, set-piece method, while suitable in some instances, often failed to exploit initial success. Hoffmeister was not alone in modifying the doctrinal template. After the battles of the Moro and the Liri Valley, almost everyone in the Eighth Army realized the dangers of not pursuing retreating Germans quickly enough – they lived to fight another day. Thus, the gate-crashing that commanders from Leese down hoped to effect at the Gothic Line was still related to saving lives, only experience had tempered the method.

Still, although Hoffmeister grew to rely less on any specific method or doctrine, he did have a few tactical tendencies worth noting. First, even when he had three brigades under his command, he never attacked two-up. The reason for this was simple: he liked flexibility – the flexibility to blast his way through enemy defences on a narrow front if need be, and the flexibility to reinforce success with follow-on forces, wherever and whenever a breakthrough may have occurred. At the Gothic Line, when the Cape Bretons failed to gate-crash past Point 120, he attempted to fire them onto the objective with every bit of firepower he had. This did not dislodge the enemy from the reverse slope, success only coming when the Irish outflanked Point 120 from the north. However, it did, as Hoffmeister later commented, keep the Germans on the position "occupied" and convinced that the main attack would come from the front. That set the conditions for the success of the Irish flanking. The point is that he and Johnston had three options, all of which they employed as the situation changed – gate-crashing with a silent attack, assaulting behind a heavy barrage, and outflanking the position from the rear. With that many options, they not only took advantage of opportunities, they created them. Hoffmeister had learned this lesson hard, but well. As a brigade commander at the Moro River, when all three of his battalions had been engaged at once, he had not left himself many options. Even if a breakthrough had occurred, he would not have been able to take advantage of it quickly. Nine months later, at the Foglia River, things were different.

This leads to Hoffmeister's second prominent tendency as a division commander; his desire for speed. Consideration of the need to maintain a high tempo of operations affected how he moved and grouped his forces. At the Gothic Line, he moved the regiments of his armoured brigades forward and across the Foglia as soon as he learned that the Perths had reached their objectives. In doing so, he made sure the tanks were close enough to enter the battle quickly, thereby maintaining the momentum of his attack and ensuring that the enemy had little time to recover. But he did not pass 5 CAB through 11 CIB, something that would definitely have slowed the advance. Instead, he adjusted his plan and fed 5 CAB regiments into 11 CIB and let Johnston continue the fight. This decision was every bit as important as the one to have follow-on forces forward and ready to enter the fray. Johnston did the same when, immediately after they captured Points 111 and 115, he sent the Perths to Point 204 (with the British Columbia Dragoons), instead of using a unit that was out of contact with the enemy and unfamiliar with the tactical situation.

Hoffmeister often "stacked" his lead brigade to avoid – or at least postpone – the complications inherent with passing one formation through another. To break out from the Hitler Line, 5 CAB had, in addition to its three armoured regiments and motorized infantry battalion, an extra manoeuvre unit, the Irish Regiment of Canada. To clear enemy from the Delfzijl Pocket in May 1945, Hoffmeister placed under Johnston's command the British Columbia Dragoons, two squadrons of New Brunswick Hussars, two anti-tank batteries, a machine-gun company, and a light anti-aircraft battery. Also to maintain momentum, when the situation permitted, he bypassed enemy pockets with his lead brigade, leaving follow-on forces to mop-up. Again, this negated the time-consuming task of passing one brigade through another. It worked extremely well when 5 CAB dashed across the undulating ground north of the Arnhem bridgehead in April 1945 and 11 CIB cleaned up in its wake; it worked less well when 12 CIB had led across the rain-soaked, river-crossed, and highly contested ground beyond the Marecchia River in September the previous year.

Hoffmeister's genuine desire to save lives, not surprisingly, went over well with subordinates. It was part of his character. The man who would have become a physician, who later immersed himself in charity work, and who was active in finding work for veterans after the war, liked people and cared for their well-being, and his soldiers knew it. Failure could be devastating to morale, so, like Montgomery, Hoffmeister tried to give them successes. He prepared meticulously for battles. He rarely assigned tasks that were beyond the capabilities of his people, or which they had not trained to do. And because he kept things simple, he did not confuse them. In short, his subordinates trusted that he had their welfare at heart, and that, in turn, made them want to work for him.

Yet, paradoxically, Hoffmeister's concern for soldiers was also an Achilles heel. In 1941, when exacerbated by his own lack of preparedness, it overtook him and led to a nervous crisis that nearly ended his military career. For this reason, he later curtailed his visits with wounded soldiers in hospitals; it caused him too much anxiety and affected his objectivity. It was something he had to keep in check.

Soldier and staff officer alike were impressed by Hoffmeister's tremendous physical courage. He shared their risks. Unlike in business, where the assumption of risk – mainly financial – was most heavily borne by those at the top, Hoffmeister understood that, in combat, the perils are most acute for those at the lower echelons. As he once stated, battle consequences were measured in lives, not dollars.[2] The ability of the commander to influence the common soldier, to elicit the best possible performance, and to implement his plans, was, and still is, directly and profoundly influenced by a willingness to share in that risk. Hoffmeister's propensity for placing himself in harm's way affected those who witnessed his appearance at decisive and dangerous points on the battlefield. It also had an impact on those who learned of his reputation by word of mouth. Either way, the effect was the same; in one subordinate's analogy, Hoffmeister's reputation as a "soldier's officer" convinced his subordinates that he was piloting the airplane in which they all had a stake.

Hoffmeister's ability to motivate subordinates, his mastery of the human factors of command, was undoubtedly his greatest strength. Here too, he benefited from improvements in army training and preparation. Not only had better training and combat experience made Hoffmeister a more able commander, it gave him better subordinates as well. Just as he was completely unprepared to enter combat in 1939-1940, so were the people who worked for him. Without the benefit of the training, individual and collective, that the Canadians received throughout 1942 and 1943, no soldier or non-commissioned officer would have been ready for the battles of Sicily or the Italian mainland. Similarly, without an adequate number of staff-trained officers to assist Canada's brigade, division, and corps commanders, the Canadians would have been a very poor lot indeed. There were shortfalls in much of the training to be sure, but by the time of the Italian Campaign, Hoffmeister had adequate human resources at his disposal. Those human resources simply were not there in 1940, 1941, or even 1942.

Hoffmeister's ability to use those soldiers and staff officers effectively was the key to his command success. While some commanders could move the chess pieces of battle with competence and aplomb, Hoffmeister was a master at getting the pieces to move themselves. Consulting subordinate commanders, sharing the risks of soldiers, keeping them informed, demonstrating personal commitment and competence; these all had the effect of bringing people on board, of making them *want* to work for their commander. Hoffmeister strove for that. In a way, it was also an insurance policy. Should he have stumbled, or erred, or missed something in the planning, someone else would have picked up on it. But that had always been his way: better to have all the cogs in the machine operating at maximum efficiency, not just the one at the top.

Notes

1 CID	1st Canadian Infantry Division
2 CIB	2 Canadian Infantry Brigade
ASHC	Archives of the Seaforth Highlanders of Canada
BCA	British Columbia Archives
BCD	British Columbia Dragoons
BLM	Papers of Field-Marshal the Viscount Montgomery of Alamein
DHH	Directorate of History and Heritage (National Defence Headquarters, Ottawa)
IWM	Imperial War Museum
JACP	John Arthur Clark Papers
LER	Loyal Edmonton Regiment
LHCMA	Liddell Hart Centre for Military Archives, King's College, London
MBLC	MacMillan Bloedel Limited Collection
NAC	National Archives of Canada
PDMIA	Personal Diaries, Memoirs, Interviews, Accounts of Battle
RMC	Royal Military College of Canada
SHC	Seaforth Highlanders of Canada
UBCSC	University of British Columbia Special Collections
WD	War Diary

Chapter 1: Looking at Command

1 Field-Marshal the Viscount Montgomery of Alamein, K.G., *The Path to Leadership* (London: Fontana Books, 1963), 20.

2 Only Chris Vokes, whose uninterrupted combat commands started with the 2nd Canadian Infantry Brigade (2 CIB) in July 1943, continued with the 1st Canadian Infantry Division (1 CID), and ended with command of the 4th Canadian Armoured Division (4 CAD) in May 1945, could match Hoffmeister's period of fighting.

3 Hoffmeister commanded the Seaforth Highlanders of Canada for the landing in Sicily (July 1943), during the battles at Valguarnera and Leonforte (July 1943), Agira (July 1943), the Salso River valley (August 1943), as well as the landing in Italy (September 1943) and the advance through Southern Italy (September 1943). He commanded the 2nd Canadian Infantry Brigade throughout the advance to the Biferno (October 1943) and for the battles for the Moro (December 1943), the Gully (December 1943), and Ortona (December 1943). As a division commander, Hoffmeister led the 5th Canadian Armoured Division in the actions of the Liri Valley (May 1944), the Gothic Line (August-September 1944), Coriano Ridge (September 1944), the Marchecchia breakout (September 1944), the Lamone Crossing (December 1944), the Valli di Comacchio (January 1945), Arnhem (April 1945), and Delfzijl (May 1945).

4 Hoffmeister's accomplishments were rare in the Canadian Army, unheard of in the British Army. Only three officers from Britain's Territorial Army, the equivalent of Canada's Non-Permanent Active Militia, were ever appointed to divisional command. All of them were relieved before they had the chance to lead their divisions in combat. See David French,

"Colonel Blimp and the British Army: Divisional Commanders in the War against Germany, 1939-1945," *English Historical Review* 111 (1996): 1187.

5 On the Canadian participation in the Italian Campaign, the best overall source is still Lieutenant-Colonel G.W.L. Nicholson, *The Canadians in Italy, 1943-1945* (Ottawa: Queen's Printer, 1966). For a doctrinal look at Canadian operations, see Michael Pearson Cessford, "Hard in the Attack: The Canadian Army in Sicily and Italy, July 1943-June 1944 (PhD diss., Carleton University, 1996).

6 See Marchk Zuehlke, *Ortona: Canada's Epic World War II Battle* (Toronto: Stoddart, 1999).

7 On the 5th Canadian Armoured Division at the Gothic Line, see Marchk Zuehlke, *The Gothic Line: Canada's Month of Hell in World War II Italy* (Toronto: Douglas and McIntyre, 2003).

8 For a lucid discussion of the historical antecedents to the militia myth and its remarkable longevity, see J.L. Granatstein, *Canada's Army: Waging War and Keeping the Peace* (Toronto: University of Toronto Press, 2002), 3-23.

9 Marchtin Van Crevald, *Command in War* (Cambridge, MA: Harvard University Press, 1985), 1-16.

10 Ross Pigeau and Carol McCann, "What is a Commander?" in *Generalship and the Art of the Admiral: Perspectives on Canadian Senior Military Leadership*, ed. Bernd Horn and Stephen J. Harris (St. Catharines, ON: Vanwell, 2001), 79-104. Lieutenant-Colonel Peter Bradley, "Distinguishing the Concepts of Command, Leadership and Management," *Generalship and the Art of the Admiral*, 105-20.

11 Marchtin Blumenson and James L. Stokesbury, *Masters of the Art of Command* (Boston: Houghton Mifflin, 1975) 1. A common sense and anecdotal work on what makes a good commander is Major General Aubrey S. "Red" Newman's *What Are Generals Made Of?* (Novato, CA: Presidio Press, 1987).

12 Montgomery, *The Path to Leadership*, 15, 16.

13 Field-Marshal Sir William Slim, *Defeat into Victory* (London: Cassel, 1956), 182.

14 See C.P. Stacey, *A Date with History* (Ottawa: Deneau, 1983), 229. See also John A. English, *The Canadian Army and the Normandy Campaign: A Study of Failure in High Command* (New York: Praeger, 1991), 2.

15 Sergeant Denis Meade, MM, interview with the author, 5 December 2000, Vancouver, BC (hereafter Meade interview).

16 Will R. Bird, *Ghosts Have Warm Hands: A Memoir of the Great War, 1916-1919* (Nepean, ON: CEF Books, 1997), 144. Bird's actual account of the encounter is found on pages 14-15.

17 Michael Howard, "Leadership in the British Army in the Second World War: Some Personal Observations," in *Leadership & Command: The Anglo-American Military Experience since 1861*, ed. G.D. Sheffield (London: Brassey's, 1997), 118.

18 W.H.A. Groom, *Poor Bloody Infantry: A Memoir of the First World War* (London: William Kimber, 1976), 25.

19 Montgomery, *The Path to Leadership*, 24.

20 John Swettenham, *McNaughton*, three vols. (Toronto: Ryerson Press, 1969); Paul Dickson, "The Limits of Professionalism: General H.D.G. Crerar and the Canadian Army, 1914-1944." (PhD diss., Guelph University, 1993); and Dominick Graham, *The Price of Command: A Biography of General Guy Simonds* (Toronto: Stoddart, 1993).

21 J.L. Granatstein's *The Generals: The Canadian Army's Senior Commanders in the Second World War* (Toronto: Stoddart, 1993) is a survey of selected senior Canadian commanders of the Second World War with particular emphasis on A.G.L. McNaughton, H.D.G. Crerar, G.G. Simonds, E.L.M. Burns, A.B. Matthews, B.M. Hoffmeister, M.A. Pope, and K. Stuart. See also Bernd Horn and Stephen Harris, eds., *Warrior Chiefs: Perspectives on Senior Canadian Military Leaders* (Toronto: Dundurn, 2001).

22 Daniel Byers has written a battle study that deals with Hoffmeister's handling of a specific 5th Canadian Armoured Division action. "Operation 'Canada': 5th Canadian Armoured Division's Attack on Delfzijl, 23 April to 2 May 1945." *Canadian Military History* 7, 3 (1998): 35-46.

23 Granatstein, *The Generals*, 3.

24 Ibid., 189-202.

Chapter 2: A Young Man before the War

1 Dot Moore, interview with the author, Vancouver, 8 December 2000 (hereafter Dot Moore interview). Dot Moore was a childhood friend of Hoffmeister and a girlfriend in adolescence.

2 See Patricia E. Roy, *Vancouver: An Illustrated History* (Toronto: James Lorimer, 1980), 51, and Norbert McDonald, "A Critical Growth Cycle for Vancouver, 1886-1914." *BC Studies* (Spring 1973): 26-42.

3 Roy, *Vancouver*, 168.

4 In 1911, the percentage of Vancouver's foreign-born population was 56.2 percent. Immigrants from England, Scotland, Wales, and Ireland accounted for 31.4 percent of the population. Roy, *Vancouver*, 169.

5 Canadian-born Vancouverites represented 43.8 percent of the population in 1911. Of those, more than one-third (37.8 percent) came from Ontario. Roy, *Vancouver*, 169.

6 City of Vancouver Archives, Microfiche # AM0054.013.02295, Memo of Conversation with Mr. R. Hoffmeister, 6 October 1944.

7 City of Vancouver Archives, Microfiche # AM0054.013.02295, Memo of Conversation with Mr. and Mrs. Reinhardt Hoffmeister, 28 September 1944.

8 University of British Columbia Special Collections (hereafter UBCSC), MacMillan Bloedel Limited Collection (hereafter MBLC), box 131, file 36, B.M. Hoffmeister, interview with Don Mackay, 15 May 1980 (hereafter Mackay-Hoffmeister interview), 1.

9 Donalda Hoffmeister, interview with the author, West Vancouver, 11 December 2000 (hereafter Donalda Hoffmeister interview). Donalda Hoffmeister is the widow of B.M. Hoffmeister. See also Dot Moore interview.

10 The home still stands at 2150 West First Avenue in Vancouver. See Major-General B.M. Hoffmeister Collection (hereafter Hoffmeister Collection), "Oath of Allegiance" (15 March 1934).

11 Roy, *Vancouver*, 67. See also ibid., map of Vancouver neighbourhoods, 120.

12 Dot Moore interview; Donalda Hoffmeister interview.

13 Roy, *Vancouver*, 60, 61.

14 Ibid., Table VIII, 169.

15 Rod Hoffmeister, interview with the author, 11 December 2000 (hereafter Rod Hoffmeister interview). Rod Hoffmeister is the son of B.M. Hoffmeister. Most of the Seaforth Highlanders who served under Hoffmeister still refer to Lieutenant-Colonel "Hoffmaster." See Colonel David Fairweather, interview with the author, 7 December 2000 (hereafter Fairweather interview, 7 December 2000), and Billy Worton, interview with the author, 8 December 2000 (hereafter Worton interview).

16 Dot Moore interview; Donalda Hoffmeister interview; Margot Ketcham (née Hoffmeister), interview with the author, 6 December 2000 (hereafter Margot Ketcham interview). Margot Ketcham is the daughter of B.M. Hoffmeister.

17 Major-General B.M. Hoffmeister Scrapbooks (hereafter Hoffmeister Scrapbooks).

18 Hoffmeister Scrapbooks, "A Mother's Prayer."

19 The Hoffmeister Scrapbooks are replete with evidence of Hoffmeister's involvement with a number of charities and trusts. The Nature Trust, The Children's Hospital of Vancouver,

and Save the Children Fund are just a few of the organizations with which Hoffmeister had a lengthy association.

20 Rod Hoffmeister interview.

21 Sergeant Denis Meade, MM, interview with the author, 5 December 2000 (hereafter Meade interview). Meade was one of Hoffmeister's radio operators during the Sicilian Campaign.

22 The Hoffmeister Scrapbooks are largely a collection of saved items that document his achievements.

23 Military records show that in March 1934 Hoffmeister measured 5 feet, 11½ inches in height and weighed 174 pounds. Hoffmeister Collection, Certificate of Medical Examination, 15 March 1934.

24 During the early 1930s, Vancouver Rowing Club teams enjoyed considerable success against competitors from British Columbia and Washington State. Hoffmeister Scrapbooks.

25 UBCSC, MBLC, box 131, file 36, Mackay-Hoffmeister interview, 1-2.

26 Ken Drushka, *HR: A Biography of H.R. MacMillan* (Madeira Park, BC: Harbour Publishing, 1995), 151.

27 UBCSC, MBLC, box 131, file 36, Mackay-Hoffmeister interview, 4.

28 Ibid., 6.

29 On the Seaboard crisis, see Drushka, *HR*, 140-43, 170-74; and Donald Mackay, *Empire of Wood: The MacMillan Bloedel Story* (Vancouver: Douglas and McIntyre, 1982), 119-37.

30 UBCSC, MBLC, box 131, file 36, Mackay-Hoffmeister interview, 7. See also Mackay, *Empire of Wood*, 125-26.

31 Ralph M. Shaw, interview with the author, 10 December 2000 (hereafter Shaw interview). Shaw started in the document department at the H.R. MacMillan Export Company in the 1920s, and later became president and vice chairman of MacMillan Bloedel Limited.

32 Shaw interview.

33 Royal Military College of Canada (hereafter RMC), William J. McAndrew Collection (hereafter McAndrew Collection), "Notes of interview with BGen Bell-Irving, 23 May 1980"; National Defence Headquarters (Ottawa), Directorate of History and Heritage (hereafter DHH), "Notes on interview with Brig. H.P. Bell-Irving by J.L. Granatstein, 4 March 1992" (hereafter Granatstein-Bell-Irving interview).

34 Ralph M. Shaw, quoted in Mackay, *Empire of Wood*, 125.

35 RMC, McAndrew Collection, General B.M. Hoffmeister, interview with W. McAndrew and B. Greenhous, 1980 (hereafter McAndrew/Greenhous-Hoffmeister interview), 32.

36 RMC, McAndrew Collection, McAndrew/Greenhous-Hoffmeister interview, 33.

37 War Office (UK), *Operations, Military Training Pamphlet no. 23: Part III – Appreciations, Orders, Intercommunications and Movements, 1939* (Ottawa: King's Printer, 1941), 2-3.

38 War Office (UK), *Field Service Regulations*, vol. 2, *Operations – General* (Ottawa: King's Printer, 1939), 23.

39 Cited in Mackay, *Empire of Wood*, 115, and UBCSC, H.R. MacMillan Personal Papers (hereafter MacMillan Papers), box 27, file 14, Letter from MacMillan to R.H. McMaster, 17 April 1943. I am grateful to Mary McRoberts for this reference.

40 The organizational division of responsibilities as presented in Figure 2-1 is based on Mackay, *Empire of Wood*, 109.

41 UBCSC, MBLC, box 131, file 27, Harold Dagg, interview with Donald Mackay. I am grateful to Mary McRoberts for this reference.

42 H.R. MacMillan, cited in Mackay, *Empire of Wood*, 109.

43 UBCSC, MBLC, box 131, file 36, Mackay-Hoffmeister interview, 5.

44 RMC, McAndrew Collection, McAndrew/Greenhous-Hoffmeister interview, 32-33. See also Mackay-Hoffmeister interview, 5.

45 On Hoffmeister's immediate family, see Donalda Hoffmeister interview.

46 Ibid.
47 Ibid. See also Margot Ketcham interview.
48 McAndrew Collection, McAndrew/Greenhous-Hoffmeister interview, 2.
49 Ken MacLeod Collection (Langley, BC). Bert Hoffmeister, interview with George Campbell, videotape, 1993 (hereafter Campbell-Hoffmeister interview).
50 RMC, McAndrew Collection, McAndrew/Greenhous-Hoffmeister interview, 2.
51 RMC, McAndrew Collection, McAndrew/Greenhous-Hoffmeister interview, 2. See also MacLeod Collection, Campbell-Hoffmeister interview.
52 Hoffmeister Collection, "Statement of Service Qualifications," Maj-General B.M. Hoffmeister, dated 25 February 1946.
53 RMC, McAndrew Collection, McAndrew/Greenhous-Hoffmeister interview, 6.
54 For a discussion of the Seaforth Highlanders during the interwar years, see Reginald H. Roy, *The Seaforth Highlanders of Canada, 1919-1965* (Vancouver: Evergreen Press, 1969), 1-39.
55 British Columbia Archives (hereafter BCA), MS 0815, John Arthur Clark Papers (hereafter JACP), box 9, files 2-7; and Roy, *Seaforth Highlanders of Canada*, 34.
56 BCA, MS 0815, JACP, box 1, file 4, J.A. Clark, letter to W.L.M. King, 14 April 1938; Letter King to Clark, 12 April 1938; and Letter Clark to R.B. Bennett, 21 April 1938.
57 Genealogical information can be found at the City of Vancouver Archives. On the Merritt family, see City of Vancouver Archives, microfiche 03191. For the Bell-Irvings and Forins, see microfiches 000261 and 01546 respectively.
58 BCA, MS 0815, JACP, box 1, file 2, Seaforth Highlanders of Canada – Memorandum re Finances, dated 24th July 1934. See also DHH, Granatstein-Bell-Irving interview.
59 On the obsolete equipment and the limited training it afforded, see Roy, *Seaforth Highlanders of Canada*, 23-25.
60 Roy, *Seaforth Highlanders of Canada*, 27-28. Hoffmeister remembered the ship on which he was embarked as being "barely seaworthy." See MacLeod Collection, Campbell-Hoffmeister interview.
61 For an informed discussion of the inadequacies of Canadian interwar training, see John A. English, *The Canadian Army and the Normandy Campaign: A Study of Failure in High Command* (New York: Praeger, 1991), 39-62. On the dismal results of the 1928 Permanent Force concentration, see Stephen J. Harris, *Canadian Brass: The Making of a Professional Army, 1860-1939* (Toronto: University of Toronto Press, 1988), 196-98.
62 RMC, McAndrew Collection, McAndrew/Greenhous-Hoffmeister interview, 3, 15, 25.
63 MacLeod Collection, Campbell-Hoffmeister interview.
64 Regimental strength numbers are from the Seaforth War Diary for September 1939. National Archives of Canada (hereafter NAC), Record Group (hereafter RG) 24, vol. 15253, War Diary (hereafter WD), Seaforth Highlanders of Canada (hereafter SHC), September 1939.
65 Hoffmeister actually enlisted in the Canadian Active Service Force on 9 September 1939. Hoffmeister Collection, Record of Service of Bertram Meryl Hoffmeister.
66 On the frenzied preparations of the Seaforth Highlanders for overseas deployment, see Roy, *Seaforth Highlanders of Canada*, 42-69.
67 NAC, RG 24, vol. 15253, WD SHC, 21 September 1939.
68 Ibid., 9 September 1939, 16 November 1939.
69 On pre-deployment training, see ibid., October-December 1939.
70 *Vancouver Sun*, 15 December 1939, 1. Cited in Roy, *Seaforth Highlanders of Canada*, 61.

Chapter 3: The Years of Company Command and Personal Turmoil
1 Royal Military College of Canada (hereafter RMC), William J. McAndrew Collection (hereafter McAndrew Collection), General B.M. Hoffmeister, interview with W. McAndrew and B. Greenhous, 1980 (hereafter McAndrew/Greenhous-Hoffmeister interview), 12-13.

2 Hoffmeister was promoted to the rank of major on 24 October 1939. The promotion was retroactive to 2 September 1939. National Archives of Canada (hereafter NAC), Record Group (hereafter RG) 24, vol. 15253, War Diary (hereafter WD), Seaforth Highlanders of Canada (hereafter SHC), October 1939, Appendix 1, Battalion Order no. 38, 25 October 1939.

3 RMC, McAndrew Collection, McAndrew/Greenhous-Hoffmeister interview, 11. See also J.L. Granatstein, *The Generals: The Canadian Army's Senior Commanders in the Second World War* (Toronto: Stoddart, 1993), 190-91.

4 RMC, McAndrew Collection, McAndrew/Greenhous-Hoffmeister interview, 10.

5 NAC, RG 24, vol. 13,721, WD 1 CID, December 1939, 1 Canadian Division Training Instruction no. 1, 26 December 1939. See also ibid., vol. 15,253, WD SHC, 8 January 1940.

6 Ibid., vol. 15,253, WD SHC, January 1940.

7 A 1940 military training pamphlet notes that "training of officers" was but one of six categories of individual training within an infantry battalion. War Office (UK), *The Training of an Infantry Battalion, Military Training Pamphlet no. 37 – 1940* (Ottawa: King's Printer, 1940), 5. Obviously, this doctrine was neither widely read nor followed in 1940.

8 NAC, RG 24, vol. 15,253, WD SHC. See entries for 10, 12, 15, and 30 January 1940.

9 War Office (UK), *The Training of an Infantry Battalion*, 10.

10 NAC, RG 24, vol. 15,253, WD SHC, March 1940. See also Reginald H. Roy, *The Seaforth Highlanders of Canada, 1919-1965* (Vancouver: Evergreen Press, 1969), 72-73.

11 For discussion of the shortfalls of the Militia Staff Course, see John A. English, *The Canadian Army and the Normandy Campaign: A Study of Failure in High Command* (New York: Praeger, 1991), 98.

12 RMC, McAndrew Collection, McAndrew/Greenhous-Hoffmeister interview, 11, 23; and Ken MacLeod Collection, Langley, BC (hereafter MacLeod Collection), Bert Hoffmeister, interview with George Campbell, videotape, c. 1993 (hereafter Campbell-Hoffmeister interview).

13 RMC, McAndrew Collection, McAndrew/Greenhous-Hoffmeister interview, 12-13.

14 NAC, RG 24, vol. 15,253, WD SHC, Appendix 17. Report of Umpire, 11 May 1940. The report is also cited in Roy, *Seaforth Highlanders of Canada*, 83-84.

15 Hoffmeister recalled that his plan for the exercise was to "make like cowboys and Indians." RMC, McAndrew Collection, McAndrew/Greenhous-Hoffmeister interview, 13.

16 A cloth model exercise (CMX) is a training activity in which a table-top terrain replica is used to plan or discuss tactical problems.

17 English, *Canadian Army and the Normandy Campaign*, 76-77.

18 Colonel C.P. Stacey, *Six Years of War: The Army in Canada, Britain and the Pacific* (Ottawa: Queen's Printer, 1966), 232. NAC, RG 24, vol. 13,721, WD 1 CID, December 1939, 1 Canadian Division Training Instruction no. 1, 26 December 1939.

19 NAC, RG 24, vol. 15,253, WD SHC, March 1940, Training Syllabus for Week ending 23 March 1940.

20 NAC, RG 24, vol. 15,253, WD SHC, Inspection Report on Seaforth Highlanders of Canada, 21 March 1940 (dated 9 April 1940).

21 NAC, MG 30, E 157, General H.D.G. Crerar Papers (hereafter Crerar Papers), vol. 2, Lieutenant-General B.L. Montgomery, "Some General Notes on What to Look for When Visiting a Unit." The document also appears as an appendix in English, *Canadian Army and the Normandy Campaign*, 315-19.

22 NAC, RG 24, vol. 15,253, WD SHC, 19 April 1940; and Archives of the Seaforth Highlanders of Canada (hereafter ASHC), box 998.135.118, Personal Diaries, Memoirs, Interviews, Accounts of Battle (hereafter PDMIA), Brig. Stevenson, interview, 25 August 1961.

23 The strength of the Army more than doubled again, to 177,810 in December 1940. Granatstein, *The Generals*, 259; and Stacey, *Six Years of War*, 115, and Table 1 in Appendix A, 522-23.

24 For an example of the trench-warfare mindset, see the direction given by McNaughton's 1st Canadian Division Headquarters, NAC, RG 24, vol. 13,722, WD 1 CID, April 1940, 1 Canadian Division Training Instruction no. 3, 27 April 1940.

25 ASHC, PDMIA, Narrative of J.D. Pierce (hereafter Pierce Narrative). At first an NCO, Pierce later received his commission as an officer and served with the Seaforths during the Italian Campaign. See also Roy, *Seaforth Highlanders of Canada,* 81; Stacey, *Six Years of War,* 233; and English, *Canadian Army and the Normandy Campaign,* 76-77.

26 RMC, McAndrew Collection, McAndrew/Greenhous-Hoffmeister interview, 14.

27 NAC, RG 24, vol. 13,722, WD 1 CID, April 1940, 1 Canadian Division Training Instruction no. 3, 27 April 1940. See also English, *Canadian Army and the Normandy Campaign,* 76-77.

28 David Fraser, *And We Shall Shock Them: The British Army in the Second World War* (London: Hodder and Stoughton, 1983), especially 3-80, 392-97.

29 David French, *Raising Churchill's Army: The British Army and the War against Germany, 1919-1945* (Oxford: Oxford University Press, 2000), 192-211.

30 This is the crux of Michael Cessford's thesis. Michael Pearson Cessford, "Hard in the Attack: The Canadian Army in Sicily and Italy, July 1943-June 1944" (PhD diss., Carleton University, 1996).

31 Stacey, *Six Years of War,* 257-63.

32 NAC, RG 24, vol. 15,253, WD SHC, 2 Cdn Inf Bde [2 CIB] Instruction. G.B. 1, 10 May 1940.

33 Ibid., vol. 15253, WD SHC, 20-25 May 1940.

34 The best discussion of Canadian "bite-and hold" tactics during the First World War is Shane B. Schreiber's *The Shock Army of the British Empire: The Canadian Corps in the Last 100 Days of the Great War* (Westport, CT: Praeger, 1997).

35 NAC, RG 24, vol. 15,254, WD SHC, June 1940, Minutes of Conference at 1100 hrs on 20 June 1940 held at Pinewood, Farnborough, 23 June 1940.

36 The Seaforths moved to their new location on 23 June. NAC, RG 24, vol. 15,254, WD SHC, June 1940, 2 Cdn Inf Bde [2 CIB] O.O. [Operation Order] no. 5, dated 23 June 1940.

37 Ibid., vol. 15,254, WD SHC, Minutes of Conference at 1100 hrs on 20 June 1940 held at Pinewood, Farnborough, 23 June 1940.

38 For a discussion of the adverse short-term impact of the fall of France on the training of Canadian forces, see Cessford, "Hard in the Attack," 123-26.

39 For examples of the litany of tasks the Seaforths performed in 1940-41 see NAC, RG 24, vol. 15,254, WD SHC, July 1940 – January 1941; and NAC, RG 24, vol. 14,072, WD 2 CIB, November 1941. 2 Cdn Inf Bde [2 CIB] O.O. [Operations Order] no. 1, 18 November 1941.

40 Prime Minister William Lyon Mackenzie King announced the intended creation of a Canadian Corps to the House of Commons on 20 May 1940, but the corps that McNaughton was actually promoted to command in July 1940 was 7th British Corps. Formed as an emergency response to the invasion threat, 7th Corps became 1st Canadian Corps on 25 December 1940. The name of the corps notwithstanding, McNaughton still had the complicated problems of creating a corps headquarters, establishing an administrative relationship for non-Canadian ancillary troops, and, eventually, integrating the 2nd Canadian Infantry Division into the new order of battle. See Stacey, *Six Years of War,* 72-87.

41 Of the four exercises conducted under the direction of Pearkes' replacement as commander of 2 CIB, Brigadier A.E. Potts, one (30 July) was a demonstration. The other half-day schemes took place on 1 August, 28 August (interrupted by air raids), and 1 October. NAC, RG 24, vol. 15,254, WD SHC, July-December 1940. See also ibid., 2 Cdn Inf Bde and 1 Army Tk Bde Exercise, 29 September 1940.

42 Sergeant Denis Meade spoke of how soldiers genuinely "liked" Hoffmeister and wanted to "put out for him." Sergeant Denis Meade, MM, interview with the author, 5 December 2000, Vancouver, BC (hereafter Meade interview).

43 On the lack of heat and adequate accommodations, see ASHC, PDMIA, Brig. [J.B.] Stevenson, interview, 25 August 1961.

44 The Seaforth War Diary shows that the influenza epidemic peaked on 20 January 1940 when 267 of the unit's soldiers went to hospital. NAC, RG 24, vol. 15,253, WD SHC, January 1940.

45 Colonel David Fairweather, letter to the author, 5 January 2001.

46 NAC, RG 24, vol. 13,733, WD 1 CID, December 1939, Instructions For Incoming Units 14 December 1939; and ibid., Post Mobilization Billeting Scheme (Aldershot Command Undated), March 1940, Progress Report: Period March 24th to March 30th, 1940.

47 RMC, McAndrew Collection, McAndrew/Greenhous-Hoffmeister interview, 11.

48 Colonel S.W. Thomson, telephone interview with the author, 10 December 2000. See also McAndrew/Greenhous-Hoffmeister interview, 81-82.

49 MacLeod Collection, Campbell-Hoffmeister interview.

50 The method for conducting an appreciation of a tactical problem prescribed consideration of the matter in the following "logical sequence": (a) the object to be attained, (b) the factors to be considered (relative strengths of friendly and enemy, ground, time and space, weather, communications, etc.), (c) courses open to both enemy and friendly, and (d) the plan. War Office (UK), *Field Service Pocket Book: Part I – Pamphlet no. 4, Appreciations, Orders, Messages, and Intercommunication* (United Kingdom: The War Office, 1943).

51 These rough approximations for the execution of hasty attacks were confirmed with Colonel David Fairweather. Colonel David Fairweather, telephone interview with the author, 20 February 2001. Colonel Fairweather was a rifle platoon commander with the Seaforths during the Italian Campaign.

52 MacLeod Collection, Campbell-Hoffmeister interview.

53 Directorate of History and Heritage (hereafter DHH), J.L. Granatstein, *The Generals* interviews, "Notes on interview between J.L. Granatstein and Bert Hoffmeister, 2 March 1992" (hereafter Granatstein-Hoffmeister interview). Granatstein also refers to the incident in *The Generals*, 191-92.

54 McGill University, William Osler Library, Colin Russell Papers, Folio, box 4, Access no. 325, Discharges and Disposal, Major H.H. Hyland (1 January 1941 to 31 March 1941). Unit records also show that Hoffmeister was struck off unit strength on 11 January. NAC, RG 24, vol. 15,254, WD SHC, January 1941, Nominal Role of Officers 17 January 1941. Personnel records indicate admission to No. 1 Neurological Hospital at Basingstoke on 13 January. Major-General B.M. Hoffmeister Collection, Service and Casualty Form (n.d).

55 *Stedman's Medical Dictionary,* 24th Edition (Baltimore: Williams and Wilkins, 1982). I am grateful to Dr. J. Scott Delaney, MD, for this reference. See also Terry Copp, "Stress Casualties and the Role of the Commander," in *Generalship and the Art of the Admiral: Perspectives on Canadian Senior Military Leadership,* ed. Bernd Horn and Stephen Harris (St. Catharines, ON: Vanwell, 2001), 319-20.

56 Copp, "Stress Casualties," 319. See also Terry Copp and William J. McAndrew, *Battle Exhaustion: Soldiers and Psychiatrists in the Canadian Army, 1939-1945* (Montreal: McGill-Queen's, 1990), 19.

57 DHH, Granatstein-Hoffmeister interview.

58 Hoffmeister returned to Number 1 Neurological Hospital on 21 February. He was released three days later. Hoffmeister Collection, Record of Service: Bertram Meryl Hoffmeister.

59 This information comes from an interview of Dr. R.J. Richardson by T. Copp, December 1982. Cited in Copp, "Stress Casualties," 319-20.

60 During his period of hospitalization, Hoffmeister's name appeared consistently under the section "Description of Officers Whose Return is Particularly Desired" on the weekly "Return of Officers" form. Because the commanding officer and the adjutant signed the forms,

those two officers were aware of Hoffmeister's hospitalization at the neurological hospital. Beyond that, it is not clear that anyone else knew. NAC, RG 24, vol. 15,254, WD SHC, January 1941, Return of Officers (17 January, 24 January, 31 January).

61 Force-against-force exercises pit a designated enemy group against the exercising unit or formation. Such exercises brought more realism to the training.

62 English, *Canadian Army and the Normandy Campaign*, 79-80. See also Cessford, "Hard in the Attack", 124-25; and Stacey, *Six Years of War*, 238.

63 NAC, RG 24, vol. 15,254, WD SHC, 4-11 April 1941. The Seaforths also used scouts effectively during a bridging exercise on 22 April; ibid., 22 April 1941.

64 See French, *Raising Churchill's Army*, 184-211.

65 Timothy Harrison Place believes that battle drill, because minor infantry tactics were ultimately overshadowed by the doctrinal reliance on artillery-based attacks, failed to live up to its promise. See Timothy Harrison Place, *Military Training in the British Army, 1940-1944: From Dunkirk to D-Day* (London: Frank Cass, 2000), 40-79.

66 WATERLOO, a counter-invasion exercise, was the first set of manoeuvres that 1st Canadian Corps completed under Lieutenant-General McNaughton's command. British umpires criticized McNaughton's headquarters for being too ponderous and too inclined to produce long-winded written orders and for having too many conferences. English, *Canadian Army and the Normandy Campaign*, 80. NAC, RG 24, vol. 15,254, WD SHC, June 1941, Appendix 12, Lessons – S.E. Command Exercise WATERLOO, 1 CD/CS 4-5-8, dated 21 June 1941.

67 NAC, RG 24, vol. 15,254, WD SHC, 1-7 May 1941.

68 From 26 to 31 May, Hoffmeister attended an Officer's Driving and Maintenance Course at the Driving and Maintenance Wing of the Canadian Training School at Bordon, Hants. Hoffmeister Collection, Record of Service, B.M. Hoffmeister.

69 NAC, RG 24, vol. 15,254, WD SHC, 24-25 July 1941.

70 The exercises were BEAGLE (12-14 March), RENOWN (19 March), HARE (9-11 April), BULLDOG (20-25 June), SOCKEYE (23-24 June), ROFT (13-16 August), REDEX (24-25 September), BUMPER (26 September-4 October), and PLUNGER (28 October). NAC, RG 24, vol. 15,254, WD SHC, March-November 1941. Reflecting the operational requirements to destroy enemy incursions *and* defend vital points and coastlines, the exercises were about evenly split between offensive and defensive operations. Used primarily to teach the process for tactical appreciations, TEWTs are conducted outdoors. They are usually conducted using a piece of terrain on which the officer plans operations based on a given scenario.

71 NAC, RG 24, vol. 14,072, WD 2 CIB, December 1941.

72 RMC, McAndrew Collection, McAndrew/Greenhous-Hoffmeister interview, 24.

73 NAC, RG 24, vol. 14,072, WD 2 CIB, 2 December, 8 December, 13-15 January 1941.

74 Ibid., 30 January 1942.

75 The brigade major was the brigade commander's primary staff planner for operations. He was also the coordinator of the other staff functions of personnel, intelligence, and logistics. The 2 CIB War Diary noted Hoffmeister's conduct of the reconnaissance on 27 January. Regarding the activities of Brigadier Potts for the same day, however, it only made mention of his daily conference at 0830 in the morning. NAC, RG 24, vol. 14,072, WD 2 CIB, 27 January 1942. Author's emphasis.

76 RMC, McAndrew Collection, McAndrew/Greenhous-Hoffmeister interview, 24-25; DHH, Granatstein-Hoffmeister interview.

77 NAC, MG 30 E 157, Crerar Papers, vol. 2, B.L. Montgomery Notes on Inf Bdes [Infantry Brigades] of Canadian Corps, 3 February 1942-4 March 1942.

78 The "G" stood for "general," meaning the primary coordinator of all the staff functions. A "staff learner" was an understudy to an officer holding a key staff appointment. Hoffmeister

assumed the appointment as understudy to the brigade major in February 1942. NAC, RG 24, vol. 14,072, WD 2 CIB, February 1942, Return of Officers dated 6 February 1942.

79 MacLeod Collection, Campbell-Hoffmeister interview. Hoffmeister also described Major "Knobby" Clark as an "old dyed-in-the-wool" PF [Permanent Force] who was "overweight" and "drank too much." RMC, McAndrew Collection, McAndrew/Greenhous-Hoffmeister interview, 25-26. It was Knobby Clark who first brought Hoffmeister's talents to Vokes's attention. Major-General Chris Vokes with John P. Maclean, *My Story* (Ottawa: Gallery Books, 1985), 76-77.

80 Montgomery commanded the Third Division in Brooke's corps during the retreat from Dunkirk.

81 Field-Marshal the Viscount Montgomery of Alamein, *Memoirs* (London: Collins, 1958), 74.

82 RMC, McAndrew Collection, McAndrew/Greenhous-Hoffmeister interview, 21.

83 Ibid. Montgomery's zeal for getting rid of "dead wood" was not restricted to Canadian units and formations. While he was the commander of Fifth British Corps, he was equally ruthless with ineffective British commanders. Montgomery, *Memoirs,* 70-73. As an example, after inspecting the 4th Division, he ordered the immediate removal of the commander royal artillery (CRA), two field [artillery] regiment commanders, the commander royal army service corps (CRASC), and the general staff officer second class (GSO II). On the last, Montgomery wrote bluntly: "I know him well and have seen him in the stress of battle; he lacks guts." Imperial War Museum (hereafter IWM), Papers of Field-Marshal the Viscount Montgomery of Alamein, BLM 25/30 (n.d.).

84 NAC, RG 24, vol. 14,072, WD 2 CIB, 28 February 1942. For Montgomery's explanation of his own "doctrine of command" see Montgomery's "My Doctrine of Command," in *Memoirs,* 80-90; and "Military Command – Some Reflections," in *The Path to Leadership* (London: Fontana, 1963), 18-24.

85 For Montgomery's assessments of Canadian commanders, as well as his guidance on training leaders, see English, *Canadian Army and the Normandy Campaign,* 125-42.

86 NAC, RG 24, vol. 14,072, WD 2 CIB, 9 December 1941.

87 RMC, McAndrew Collection, McAndrew/Greenhous-Hoffmeister interview, 21.

88 ASHC, PDMIA, Diary of W.H. Melhuish, Notes on Brig. Hoffmeister Lecture, November 1943.

89 Donalda Hoffmeister interview; MacLeod Collection, Campbell-Hoffmeister interview; and RMC, McAndrew Collection, McAndrew/Greenhous-Hoffmeister interview, 29.

90 This information is actually based on the course outline for the sixth serial of the Canadian War Staff Course, 6 February-28 May 1943. The curriculum varied only slightly during the war. John A. MacDonald, "In Search of Veritable: Training the Canadian Army Staff Officer, 1899-1945" (M.A. thesis, Royal Military College of Canada, 1992), 299-305. See also the syllabus for the course that immediately preceded the one Hoffmeister attended: NAC, RG 24, vol. 16,871, WD RMC, April 1942, CANADIAN JUNIOR WAR STAFF COURSE NO. 3 (December 1941).

91 Sometimes called "map wars," CPXs are exercises in which headquarters staffs practise the planning, coordination, and control of operations, based on a scripted scenario.

92 The term "combined" refers to interservice cooperation. Later the Allies would adopt the term "joint" for interservice operations and use "combined" for international operations.

93 See War Office (UK), *Operations, Military Training Pamphlet no. 23, Part III – Appreciations, Orders, Intercommunications and Movements, 1939* (Ottawa: King's Printer, 1941), 1-4.

94 On battle procedure, see War Office (UK), *Infantry Training: Training and War, 1937* (Ottawa: King's Printer, 1941), 55-57.

95 For a critical opinion on the quality of the Canadian staff training and the directing staff, see English, *Canadian Army and the Normandy Campaign,* 100-2.

96 RMC, McAndrew Collection, McAndrew/Greenhous-Hoffmeister interview, 32-33.
97 University of British Columbia Special Collections (hereafter UBCSC), H.R. MacMillan Personal Papers (hereafter MacMillan Papers), box 8, file 4, Hoffmeister to MacMillan, 29 November 1943.
98 RMC, McAndrew Collection, McAndrew/Greenhous-Hoffmeister interview, 28.
99 Ibid., 27.
100 Ibid., 27-28. See also DHH, Granatstein-Hoffmeister interview.
101 Major-General B.M. Hoffmeister Scrapbooks, Canadian Junior War Staff Course 4 Final Report on Student B.M. Hoffmeister, dated 22 August 1942.
102 MacLeod Collection, Campbell-Hoffmeister interview; DHH, Granatstein-Hoffmeister interview; RMC, McAndrew Collection, McAndrew/Greenhous-Hoffmeister interview, 30.

Chapter 4: Battalion Command, Training for War

1 War Office (UK), *The Training of an Infantry Battalion: Military Training Pamphlet no. 37 – 1940* (Ottawa: King's Printer, 1940), 12.
2 *See John A. English, The Canadian Army and the Normandy Campaign: A Study of Failure in High Command* (New York: Praeger, 1991), 125-42; and J.L. Granatstein, *Canada's Army: Waging War and Keeping the Peace* (Toronto: University of Toronto Press, 2002), 202-5. For a negative opinion of Montgomery's influence on doctrine and training in the British Army, see Timothy Harrison Place, *Military Training in the British Army, 1940-1944: From Dunkirk to D-Day* (London: Frank Cass, 2000), especially 147-52, 168-75.
3 McNaughton suffered a physical breakdown that resulted in his handing temporary command of the corps to George Pearkes on 17 November 1941. Pearkes, in turn, relinquished acting command of the corps to Major-General H.D.G. Crerar in December 1941. On promotion to lieutenant-general in April 1942, Crerar assumed permanent command of the corps.
4 National Archives of Canada (hereafter NAC), MG 30, E 133, A.G.L. McNaughton Papers (hereafter McNaughton Papers), vol. 238, Canadian Corps Exercise HARE, dated 28 March 1941.
5 NAC, Record Group (hereafter RG) 24, vol. 13,725, War Diary (WD), 1st Canadian Infantry Division (hereafter 1 CID), March 1943, Appendix C to 1 CDN DIV [1 CID] Exercise "PAST," dated 23 March 1943.
6 Ibid., Appendix D.
7 NAC, MG 30, E 157, General H.D.G. Crerar Papers (hereafter Crerar Papers), vol. 2, Notes on Inf [Infantry] Bdes [Brigades] of Canadian Corps, 3-2-42. See also ibid., "Points for Crerar."
8 NAC, MG 30, E 157, Crerar Papers, vol. 2, Notes on Inf Bdes of Canadian Corps, 3-2-42.
9 A skeleton-force exercise is a field training exercise in which all levels of headquarters go to the field, but only the bare minimum of troops participate. For example, a brigade skeleton-force exercise might only include a brigade headquarters, and the headquarters of all the infantry, armour, and artillery units, but only one vehicle for each company, squadron, or battery.
10 English, *Canadian Army and the Normandy Campaign,* 128. Montgomery's idea for a corps "study week" to foster a common understanding of tactical doctrine among officers under his command was not a new one. As the commander of 12 Corps (May-November 1941), he had planned one for 15-20 December 1941, but he left to command Southeastern Army before it took place. Liddell Hart Centre for Military Archives, King's College, London (hereafter LHCMA), Allfrey Papers, 1/7, 12 Corps Study Week for Commanders – 15 to 20 December 1941, Note by Corps Commander, dated 11 November 1941.

11 NAC, MG 30, E 157, Crerar Papers, vol. 2, Letter Montgomery to Crerar, 3 March 1942. See also Montgomery's comments on being "well satisfied with the [1st Canadian] Corps" after Exercise TIGER; and ibid., Letter Montgomery to Crerar, 30-5-42.

12 C.P. Stacey, *Six Years of War: The Army in Canada, Britain and the Pacific* (Ottawa: Queen's Printer, 1966), 243-45.

13 NAC, MG 30, E 157, Crerar Papers, vol. 2, Montgomery, "Points for Crerar" (undated).

14 Ibid., Beaver III Notes on Commanders, 25 April 1942. Cited in English, *Canadian Army and the Normandy Campaign,* 136.

15 NAC, MG 30, E 157, Crerar Papers, vol. 2, Beaver III Notes on Commanders, 25 April 1942. Cited in English, *Canadian Army and the Normandy Campaign,* 135.

16 NAC, MG 30, E 157, Crerar Papers, vol. 2, Beaver III Notes on Commanders, 25 April 1942.

17 The GSO I, usually a lieutenant-colonel, was the primary staff coordinator in a division headquarters.

18 Richard S. Malone, *A Portrait of War* (Don Mills, ON: Totem Press, 1983), 152. Malone was Vokes's brigade major in 2 CIB. For positive subordinate testimony on Vokes, see also Mark Zuehlke, *Ortona: Canada's Epic World War II Battle* (Toronto: Stoddart, 1999), 18-20. A highly critical assessment of Vokes's generalship was Brereton Greenhous's article, "Would It Not Have Been Better to Bypass Ortona Completely ...?" *Canadian Defence Quarterly* (April 1989): 51-55. Describing Vokes as a "good plain cook," Montgomery's assessment was somewhere in the middle. NAC, MG 30, E 157, Crerar Papers, vol. 2, Montgomery to Crerar, 21-12-43. It was Hoffmeister's opinion that Vokes's strength lay in troop training. Royal Military College of Canada (hereafter RMC), William J. McAndrew Collection, General B.M. Hoffmeister, interview with W. McAndrew and B. Greenhous, 1980 (hereafter McAndrew/Greenhous-Hoffmeister interview), 37.

19 As an example, during a December 1942 exercise, Vokes made one Seaforth company repeat a combined infantry-tank attack because he thought the results of the first run-through poor. Archives of the Seaforth Highlanders of Canada (hereafter ASHC), box 998.135.118, Personal Diaries, Memoirs, Interviews, Accounts of Battle (hereafter PDMIA), Narrative of J.D. Pierce (hereafter Pierce Narrative), Ch. 4, 47.

20 ASHC, PDMIA, "Interview by Dr. R.L. McDougall with Major-General B.M. Hoffmeister on Certain Aspects of the Sicilian Campaign – July 25, 1960" (hereafter McDougall-Hoffmeister interview).

21 RMC, McAndrew Collection, McAndrew/Greenhous-Hoffmeister interview, 35. Forin was the Vancouver Rowing Club team coach during the 1935 season. Major-General B.M. Hoffmeister Scrapbooks.

22 RMC, McAndrew Collection, McAndrew/Greenhous-Hoffmeister interview, 36. On Exercise BINGO, see NAC, RG 24, vol. 15,255, WD Seaforth Highlanders of Canada (hereafter SHC), 13-14 October 1942; and ASHC, PDIMA, Pierce Narrative, Ch. 3.

23 Brigadier Vokes later indicated that the problems within the Seaforths were "part of a larger problem" within the 1st Canadian Division. There was "a lack of trained officers and NCOs capable of properly training the men under their command." RMC, McAndrew Collection, Major-General Vokes, interview with W.J. McAndrew, transcript, June 1980 (hereafter McAndrew-Vokes interview).

24 RMC, McAndrew Collection, Lt. Col. S.W. Thomson, interview with W.J. McAndrew, transcript, 6 April 1980 (hereafter McAndrew-Thomson interview), 2.

25 ASHC, PDMIA, Diary of Captain B.G. Parker (hereafter Parker Diary), 16 February 1943. Parker was a rifle company second in command who noted how one unfortunate officer received "quite a blast" for "non-cooperation & lousy turn out!" On the posting of officers and NCOs, see ASHC, PDMIA, Pierce Narrative, Ch. 5, 4-6.

26 Until he was wounded during the invasion of Sicily, Thomson commanded "A" Company. In December 1943, he commanded the Seaforths as part of Hoffmeister's 2 CIB during the Battle of Ortona.

27 ASHC, PDMIA, Private F.C. Wood, interview with Dr. R. Roy, transcript, 1967.

28 RMC, McAndrew Collection, McAndrew-Thomson interview, 1. Author's emphasis.

29 Thomson remarked on Hoffmeister's leadership, "you just wanted to follow, you wanted to satisfy him." RMC, McAndrew Collection, McAndrew-Thomson interview, 5.

30 Colonel David Fairweather, interview with the author, Vancouver, 7 December 2000 (hereafter Fairweather interview, 7 December 2000). On 12 December 1942, one Seaforth officer noted the pace of unit activity in his diary: "we're kept on the hop these days." Parker Diary, 12 December 1942.

31 Sergeant Denis Meade, MM, interview with the author, 5 December 2000 (hereafter Meade interview); and Fairweather interview, 7 December 2000.

32 Al Worrington, a mortar platoon sergeant with the Seaforth Highlanders during the Italian Campaign, described Hoffmeister as an "other ranks general." Al Worrington, interview with the author, 8 December 2000.

33 Pierce Narrative, Ch. 3, 40.

34 NAC, RG 24, vol. 15,254, WD SHC, 1 February 1943; and ASHC, PDMIA, Pierce Narrative, Ch. 5, 5. Colonel Fairweather also discussed Hoffmeister's decision to replace the RSM. Fairweather interview, 7 December 2000.

35 NAC, RG 24, vol. 15,254, WD SHC, March 1943, Appendix 14. 1 Cdn Div Umpire's Report, Inspection – Seaforth of C, 20 March 1943. See also NAC, RG 24, vol. 13,725, WD 1 CID, Inspection Programme – Seaforth Highlanders of Canada, dated 16 March 1943.

36 NAC, RG 24, vol. 15,255, WD SHC, 7 April 1943; and Reginald H. Roy, *The Seaforth Highlanders of Canada, 1919-1965* (Vancouver: Evergreen Press, 1969), 205.

37 The war establishment change was temporary. It only lasted until April 1943, at which time battalions reverted back to the four-company order of battle. See Roy, *Seaforth Highlanders of Canada*, 135; and ASHC, PDMIA, Pierce Narrative, Ch. 5, 4-5.

38 NAC, RG 24, vol. 15,254, WD SHC, 1 February 1943.

39 ASHC, PDMIA, Pierce Narrative, Ch. 5, 5.

40 NAC, MG 30, E 133, A.G.L. McNaughton Papers (hereafter McNaughton Papers), vol. 157, First Cdn Army Trg [Training] Directive no. 1, 30 October 1942.

41 NAC, RG 24, vol. 15,255, WD SHC, October-December 1942, Training Report for Week Ending 7 November 1942. NAC, RG 24, vol. 14,072, WD 2 CIB, October-November 1942, Training Report Ending 17 October 1942. Int [Intelligence] Training Scouts and Snipers, Report on 3-Day Training Period 7-9 October 1942.

42 NAC, RG 24, vol. 15,255, WD SHC, December 1942, EXERCISE "NINA" – General Instructions, 28 December 1942.

43 ASHC, PDMIA, Pierce Narrative, Ch. 4, 45-46.

44 War Office (UK), *Infantry Training, 1937 Supplement: Tactical Notes for Platoon Commanders – 1941* (Ottawa: King's Printer, 1941), 2.

45 For a critical appraisal of battle drill and its impact, see English, *Canadian Army and the Normandy Campaign,* 107-23; and Dominick Graham, "Observations on the Dialectics of British Tactics, 1904-1945," in *Men, Machines and War,* ed. R. Haycock and K. Neilson (Waterloo, ON: Wilfrid Laurier University Press, 1984), 69.

46 NAC, RG 24, vol. 15,255, WD SHC, December 1942, Appendix A, 2 Cdn Inf Bde Instruction, 25 December [sic] 1942. Obviously the drafter of the instruction dated it incorrectly.

47 Ibid. The following statement from the instruction is worth noting: "As the action develops, the Inf may find that they cannot adv [advance] unassisted. Tks [tanks] are to be

advised by wireless. Tks [Tanks] being, say 300/400 yds [yards] away, then assisted by fire or flank attack."

48 ASHC, PDMIA, Pierce Narrative, Ch. 4, 47.

49 To ensure survivability of units as fighting forces, landing craft were also tactically "cross-loaded" to ensure that the loss of a particular craft did not eliminate the entire leadership of a given organization. A commanding officer, for example, would never travel in the same landing craft as his second in command.

50 NAC, RG 24, vol. 15,255, WD SHC, February 1943, Appendix 5, O.O. [Operations Order] no. 1, 18 February 1943.

51 Ibid., 19 February 1943.

52 NAC, RG 24, vol. 14,072, 2 CIB WD, February 1943, Instructions for Exercise EAGLE II, dated 21 February 1943.

53 NAC, RG 24, vol. 15,255, WD SHC, February 1943, Appendix 11, O.O. no. 1. 24 February 1943.

54 Ibid., 24 February 1943.

55 Ibid., February 1943, Appendices 16-18, O.O. no. 3, 26 February 1943.

56 Ibid., 28 February-1 March 1943.

57 Ibid., 1 March 1943.

58 RMC, McAndrew Collection, McAndrew/Greenhous-Hoffmeister interview, 36.

59 ASHC, PDMIA, J.O. Moxon, interview with Dr. R.L. McDougall, transcript, 22 July 1960.

60 NAC, RG 24, vol. 15,255, WD SHC, 22-23 April 1943; NAC, RG 24, vol. 13,725, WD 1 CID, March 1943, 1 Cdn Div Trg Instr no. 3, dated 22 March 1943; and ibid., 1 Cdn Div Exercise "Past," dated 25 March 1943.

61 NAC, RG 24, vol. 14,073, WD 2 CIB, April 1943, 2nd Cdn Inf Bde Trg Instr no. 5, dated 16 April 1943.

62 Ibid. These exercises did not take place due to preparations for the invasion of Sicily.

63 Ibid.; and NAC, RG 24, vol. 15,255, WD SHC, 22 April 1943.

64 NAC, RG 24, vol. 14,073, WD 2 CIB, 2nd Cdn Inf Bde Trg Instr no. 3, 23 March 1943. Hoffmeister was the acting brigade commander for the exercise.

65 Roy, *Seaforth Highlanders of Canada*, 144.

66 The "zeroing" of a weapon refers to the process of adjusting the sights so that the firer can hit the target at a given point of aim.

67 NAC, RG 24, vol. 15,255, WD SHC, May 1943, Appendix 8, O.O. no. 1, 12 May 1943; and NAC, RG 24, vol. 14,073, WD 2 CIB, 13 May 1943.

68 Here there are discrepancies in the War Diaries of the Seaforths and 2 CIB. The Seaforth War Diary makes no mention of the "mix up in the assault craft that were landing the Seaforths" that appears in the 2 CIB entry for 15 May. The Seaforth war diarist does, however, note, "communication with bde by #22 set [radio] was unsatisfactory." Whether or not the two incidents are related is unclear, but it does appear that Hoffmeister and Vokes came to some resolution on the communication problem. For Exercise WETSHOD (21-22 May), Vokes sent a signals detachment from his headquarters to the Seaforths. NAC, RG 24, vol. 14,073, WD 2 CIB, 15 May 1943; NAC, RG 24, vol. 15,255, WD SHC, May 1943, Appendix 11, O.O. no. 2, 17 May 1943.

69 RMC, McAndrew Collection, Hoffmeister, "Notes Re History of Seaforth Highlanders of Canada," 8; ASHC, PDMIA, Pierce Narrative, Ch. 5, 30; NAC, RG 24, vol. 15,255, WD SHC, 22 May 1943; and NAC, RG 24, vol. 14,073, WD 2 CIB, 21 May 1943.

70 RMC, McAndrew Collection, McAndrew/Greenhous-Hoffmeister interview, 40. In "Notes Re History of Seaforth Highlanders of Canada," Hoffmeister has confused the title of the WETSHOD exercise with STYMIE I, 4-5.

71 RMC, McAndrew Collection, McAndrew/Greenhous-Hoffmeister interview, 40; Jock Gibson, interview with the author, Langley, BC, 9 December 2000 (hereafter Jock Gibson interview); and NAC, RG 24, vol. 15,256, WD SHC, 2 July 1943.

72 The planning for Operation HUSKY was well documented. See, for example, NAC, MG 30 E 133, McNaughton Papers, vol. 136, Operation Husky files; and NAC, RG 24, vol. 13,725, WD 1 CID, April-May 1943; ibid., Operation "Husky" no. 1 Security in the Planning Stages, 25 April 1943; ibid., Appreciation By Commander 1 Canadian Division, 27 April 1943; and ibid., Minutes of Staff Conference, 28 April 1943. Quotation from Malone, *Portrait of War*, 135.

73 NAC, RG 24, vol. 14,073, WD 2 CIB, June-July 1943, Outline for STYMIE and ROCKET Exercises 9 June 1943; and ibid., 2 Canadian Infantry Brigade Operation Order no. 1 Operation HUSKY, 15 June 1942. The date on Appendix D to both of these documents is 26 May 1943.

74 ASHC, PDMIA, Pierce Narrative, Ch. 5, 37.

75 A tactical headquarters (commonly called a "tac") was a small, mobile command-and-control element, separate from the more cumbersome main headquarters, which the commander used as he moved about the battlefield to evaluate the situation for himself. Hoffmeister kept his battalion tac very small. It consisted of his intelligence officer, the adjutant, the artillery FOO, and himself. RMC, McAndrew Collection, McAndrew/Greenhous-Hoffmeister interview, 48.

76 Ibid., 37.

77 NAC, RG 24, vol. 15,256, WD SHC, 29 June 1943.

78 Ibid.

79 Ibid., 2 July 1943.

80 Hoffmeister's written order for HUSKY was twenty-five pages long, including appendices – five pages for the main order, four pages for the landing table, four pages of administrative instructions, one page on procedures to be followed on becoming a prisoner of war, two pages of recognition signals, three pages of codes, four pages for an intelligence summary of the beach landing sites, and two pages on the German order of battle in Sicily. With the exception of the landing table (which was essentially the same as that used on STYMIE) all of the annexes originated at 1 CID headquarters. NAC, RG 24, vol. 15,256, WD SHC, July 1943, Appendix 12, Operation "HUSKY" – Seaforth Highlanders of Canada O.O. no. 1, dated 2 July 1943. For 2 CIB orders, see NAC, RG 24, vol. 14,073, WD 2 CIB, June 1943, 2 CANADIAN INFANTRY BRIGADE OPERATION ORDER no. 1. OPERATION HUSKY, 15 June 1943. For 1 CID, see NAC, RG 24, vol. 13,726, WD 1 CID, 1 Canadian Division Operation Order No, dated 7 June 1943.

81 RMC, McAndrew Collection, Hoffmeister, "Notes Re History of the Seaforth Highlanders of Canada," 7.

82 Ibid., 7. Accounts of Hoffmeister's briefings aboard *Circassia* appear in several other sources. See, for example, Charles Monroe Johnson, *Action with the Seaforths* (New York: Vintage Press, 1954), 137; and ASHC, PDMIA, Parker Diary, 2 July 1943.

83 War Office (UK), *Operations, Military Training Pamphlet no. 23, Part III – Appreciations, Orders, Intercommunications and Movements – 1939* (Ottawa: King's Printer, 1941), 6.

84 See War Office (UK), *Field Service Pocket Book: Part I – Pamphlet no. 4, Appreciations, Orders, Messages and Intercommunication* (United Kingdom: The War Office, 1943), Appendix 3.

85 RMC, McAndrew Collection, McAndrew/Greenhous-Hoffmeister interview, 43.

86 NAC, RG 24, vol. 15,256, WD SHC, 6 July 1943.

87 Meade interview.

88   Denis Meade, email to author, 3 January 2001.
89   Jock Gibson interview.

Chapter 5: Battalion Command, The Battlefield Test

1   Cited in William J. McAndrew, "Canadian Officership: An Overview," in *Generalship and the Art of the Admiral: Perspectives on Canadian Senior Military Leadership*, ed. Bernd Horn and Stephen Harris (St. Catharines, ON: Vanwell, 2001), 37.

2   For an article based on this chapter, see Douglas E. Delaney, "Hoffmeister in His Proving Ground: Sicily, July-August 1943." *Canadian Military History* 12, 3 (2003): 19-34.

3   On the wider aspects of the invasion plan, see Lieutenant-Colonel G.W.L. Nicholson, *The Canadians in Italy, 1943-1945* (Ottawa: Queen's Printer, 1966), 19-20; and Brigadier C.J.C. Molony, *The Mediterranean and the Middle East*, vol. 5 (London, Her Majesty's Stationery Office, 1973), 1-34.

4   For the 30 Corps plan and an account of the Sicilian Campaign, see Corps Commander Oliver Leese's summary. National Archives of Canada (hereafter NAC), Record Group (hereafter RG) 24, vol. 10,775, file 223B30.016 (D1), 30 Corps Operations in the Battle for Sicily – July and August 1943. From the initial planning in April 1943 to the final operation order, the 1 CID planning for Operation HUSKY is very well documented in NAC, RG 24, vols. 13,725-13,726. In particular, see NAC, RG 24, vol. 13,725, War Diary (hereafter WD), 1st Canadian Infantry Division (hereafter 1 CID), Appreciation by Comd [commander] 1 Cdn Div at Norfolk House 27 April 1943; and ibid., vol. 13,726, 1 Canadian Division Operation Order no. 1, 7 June 1943.

5   Simonds replaced Major-General H.L.N. Salmon, who was killed in a plane crash on 29 April 1943. After five days of initial planning at Norfolk House in London, Salmon and several other high-ranking Canadian and British officers were en route to an Operation HUSKY planning conference in Cairo when their plane went down.

6   NAC, RG 24, vol. 14,073, WD, 2nd Canadian Infantry Brigade (2 CIB), 2 Canadian Infantry Brigade, Operation Order no. 1, Operation "Husky", 15 June 1943.

7   NAC, RG 24, vol. 15,256, WD, Seaforth Highlanders of Canada (hereafter SHC), July 1943, Appendix 12. Operation "HUSKY," Seaforth Highlanders of Canada O.O. [Operations Order] no. 1, 2 July 1943. On the British and Canadian doctrinal predilection for firepower and centralized control at the expense of manoeuvres, see William J. McAndrew, "Fire or Movement? Canadian Tactical Doctrine, Sicily – 1943," *Military Affairs* (July 1987): 140-45; and Michael Pearson Cessford, "Hard in the Attack: The Canadian Army in Sicily and Italy, July 1943-June 1944 (PhD diss., Carleton University, 1996), 422-32.

8   A firm base is a piece of terrain that is held by friendly forces and can be used to provide fire support to other manoeuvring elements. In the case of a battalion, a firm base was usually held by one of its companies.

9   War diary information differs on the landings of the forward companies. While the Seaforth War Diary entry for 10 July 1943 indicates that "A" and "C" Companies landed "too far off to the right" because the "Naval personnel in charge of the LCAs [Landing Craft Assaults] were a little out in their bearings," the "C" Company War Diary indicates that they were "slightly off the mark ... to the left." In any event, the error did not cause a serious problem with the first wave. NAC, RG 24, vol. 15,256, WD SHC, 10 July 1943; and ibid., Appendix 27.

10 Archives of the Seaforth Highlanders of Canada (hereafter ASHC), Personal Diaries, Memoirs, Interviews, Accounts of Battle (hereafter PDMIA), Major General B.M. Hoffmeister, interview with Dr. R.H. Roy, transcript, February 1967 (hereafter Roy-Hoffmeister interview).

11 ASHC, PDMIA, Roy-Hoffmeister interview. See also Royal Military College of Canada (hereafter RMC), William J. McAndrew Collection (hereafter McAndrew Collection). B.M. Hoffmeister, "Notes Re History of Seaforth Highlanders of Canada," 11.

12 Crossing unit boundaries at night always brought with it the possibility of friendly-on-friendly fire and fratricide.

13 In all of the combined exercises of 1943, Hoffmeister's tactical headquarters travelled immediately behind the first wave, but not with it. See the written orders for Exercises EAGLE and WETSHOD. NAC, RG 24, vol. 15,255, WD SHC, February 1943, Appendices 5, 11, 16; and ibid., May 1943, Appendices 8, 11.

14 NAC, RG 24, vol. 15,256, WD SHC, 10-16 July 1943. A shuttle service, using limited battalion transportation assets and the carrier platoon was used for some of the moves.

15 ASHC, PDMIA, Diary of Major Durnford (hereafter Durnford Diary), 35.

16 There were delays in bringing the fire of battalion mortars (packed on uncooperative mules) to bear on the enemy positions. See Reginald H. Roy, *The Seaforth Highlanders of Canada, 1919-1965* (Vancouver: Evergreen Press, 1969), 174-75.

17 This process firing on the enemy to nullify the effects of his weapons was often referred to as "winning the firefight."

18 ASHC, PDMIA, Major-General B.M. Hoffmeister, interview with Robert L. McDougall (hereafter McDougall-Hoffmeister interview), 6.

19 Sergeant Denis Meade, MM, interview with the author, 5 December 2000 (hereafter Meade interview).

20 RMC, McAndrew Collection, Col S.W. Thomson, interview with William J. McAndrew, Sydney, BC, 6 April 1980 (hereafter McAndrew-Thomson interview), 2.

21 ASHC, PDMIA, McDougall-Hoffmeister interview, 7.

22 While a 2 CIB document mentions that the shells were "believed to be enemy," the weight of evidence suggests otherwise. See NAC, RG 24, vol. 14,074, WD 2 CIB, July 1943, THE BATTLE OF LEONFORTE, dated July 1943. For accounts that state the shells were fired from friendly guns, see RMC, McAndrew Collection, B.M. Hoffmeister, "Notes re History of the Seaforth Highlanders of Canada"; ASHC, PDMIA, McDougall-Hoffmeister interview, 16; ASHC, PDMIA, Durnford Diary, 41, 52; ASHC, PDMIA, Correspondence of Major J.D. Forin to his family – World War II, 1943-1944 (hereafter Forin Letters), Letter 23 July 1943.

23 ASHC, PDMIA, Durnford Diary, 52-53. Douglas Strain had also worked with Hoffmeister at H.R. MacMillan Export Co. See RMC, McAndrew Collection, General B.M. Hoffmeister, interview with W. McAndrew and B. Greenhous, 1980 (hereafter McAndrew/Greenhous-Hoffmeister interview), 59-60.

24 ASHC, PDMIA, Durnford Diary, 53.

25 RMC, McAndrew Collection, McAndrew/Greenhous-Hoffmeister interview, 60.

26 Army Commander's Meeting, 21 July 1943, Appendix B to War Diary, General Staff, Headquarters 30th Corps. Cited in Nicholson, *Canadians in Italy,* 118. The town of Adrano appears in most contemporary documents as Aderno.

27 For critical appraisals of Simonds's direction of the Battle of Nissoria, see McAndrew, "Fire or Movement?"; and Cessford, "Hard in the Attack," 173-79.

28 NAC, RG 24, vol. 10,775, Account of the Battle for Agira As Written by Brig. C. Vokes, Comd 2 Cdn Inf Bde, on 29 July 1943; and ASHC, PDMIA, Account by Lt-Col B.M. Hoffmeister, OC Seaforth of C On the part that his bn [battalion] played in the Capture of AGIRA, 31 July 1943 (hereafter Hoffmeister Account, 31 July 1943).

29 Commanders issued "Warning Orders" to commence preparations for upcoming operations. Typically, the information provided in a warning order contained an outline of

enemy and friendly situations, a probable mission, and outline timings. Warning orders were (and still are) part of a process of preparation known in the military lexicon as "battle procedure."

30 NAC, RG 24, vol. 15,256, WD SHC, 26 July 1943. An assembly area was a location in which a unit or formation waited in preparation to cross the start line for an operation.

31 The Seaforth War Diary indicates that Hoffmeister went to brigade headquarters for a 3:00 p.m. "conference" – undoubtedly for a quick situation update. NAC, RG 24, vol. 15,256, WD SHC, 26 July 1943. See also ibid., vol. 14,074, WD 2 CIB, 26 July 1943.

32 NAC, RG 24, vol. 15,256, WD SHC, 26 July 1943.

33 Ibid.

34 The 2 CIB Intelligence Log shows that the PPCLI reported having two companies on "Lion" at 8:55 p.m. and one company "within 300 yds of 'Tiger'" at 10:10 p.m. Obviously, this was not the case. NAC, RG 24, vol. 14,074, WD 2 CIB, Intelligence Log, July 1943.

35 The term "formation" in this instance refers to the tactical deployment of the companies for the advance: two forward and two back.

36 ASHC, PDMIA, Major H.P. Bell-Irving, Account of "A" Company, Seaforth Highlanders of Canada – Attack on Agira, 26-28 July 1943 (hereafter Bell-Irving Agira Account).

37 ASHC, PDMIA, Bell-Irving Agira Account.

38 ASHC, PDMIA, Bell-Irving Agira Account.

39 NAC, MG 30, A.G.L. McNaughton Papers (hereafter McNaughton Papers), vol. 156, THE Cooperation of Tanks with Infantry Divisions in Offensive Operations (21st Army Group). The document was circulated army-wide under cover of Trg Cooperation of Tks with Inf Divs in Offensive Ops, HQ First Canadian Army, 25 November 1943.

40 NAC, RG 24, vol. 14,074, WD 2 CIB, Intelligence Log, July 1943. See also ibid., vol. 15,256, WD SHC, 27 July 1943.

41 A bomb line was a control measure designed to prevent fratricide during air attacks. Simply put, once a bomb line was established, aircraft could attack forward of it, but not behind it, due to the proximity of friendly ground troops.

42 NAC, RG 24, vol. 14,074, WD 2 CIB, Intelligence Log, July 1943.

43 An orders group (usually called an "O" Group) was a conference at which a commander conveyed direction to subordinates.

44 NAC, RG 24, vol. 15,256, WD SHC, 27 July 1943. A "start line" was the line that troops crossed at the commencement of an advance or attack. It was usually an easily distinguishable linear feature – a road, a river, a ditch – that all participating troops can recognize.

45 Ibid. Agira was bombed and enemy positions on "Grizzly" strafed in air attacks at midday.

46 ASHC, PDMIA, Hoffmeister Account, 31 July 1943.

47 Ibid. There were also an unknown number of wounded who escaped.

48 NAC, RG 24, vol. 15,256, WD SHC, 27 July 1943.

49 ASHC, PDMIA, Bell-Irving Agira Account. The War Diary also noted that Hoffmeister personally gave targets to the FOOs. NAC, RG 24, vol. 15,256, WD SHC, 28 July 1943. See also Hoffmeister Account, 31 July 1943 on the devastating effect of concentrated 3-inch mortar fire.

50 Major-General B.M. Hoffmeister Scrapbooks, Distinguished Service Order Citation, Lieutenant-Colonel B.M. Hoffmeister.

51 NAC, RG 24, vol. 14,074, WD 2 CIB, August 1943, Appendix 11, Letter Simonds to Vokes, 4 August 1943. See also NAC, RG 24, vol. 14,074, WD 2 CIB, August 1943, Appendix 8, THE Battle for Aderno; and ibid., vol. 13,726, WD 1 CID, 4 August 1943.

52 ASHC, PDMIA, McDougall-Hoffmeister interview.

53 On the communications arrangements, see ASHC, PDMIA, McDougall-Hoffmeister interview; and RMC, McAndrew Collection, McAndrew/Greenhous-Hoffmeister interview, 52-53.

54 On the Salso River action, see Nicholson, *Canadians in Italy,* 160-61; and ASHC, PDMIA, Account by Lt-Col B.M. Hoffmeister, OC [Officer Commanding] Seaforth of C[anada] given on 19 August 1943 (hereafter Hoffmeister Account, 19 August 1943).

55 Roy, *Seaforth Highlanders of Canada,* 193-202.

56 NAC, RG 24, vol. 15,256, WD SHC, 5 August 1943.

57 ASHC, PDMIA, Hoffmeister Account, 19 August 1943.

58 RMC, McAndrew Collection, McAndrew/Greenhous-Hoffmeister interview, 52-53. See also NAC, RG 24, vol. 14,073, WD 2 CIB, 2 Cdn Inf Bde Training Instruction [dated incorrectly as 25 December 1942. The training actually took place 1-9 December 1942].

59 In this, Hoffmeister undoubtedly learned from Vokes. He liked Vokes's manner of giving direction: "I was given my objectives and how I got there was strictly my own business." ASHC, PDMIA, Roy-Hoffmeister interview.

60 ASHC, PDMIA, Bell-Irving Agira Account.

61 In his account of the battle, Hoffmeister duly recognized the "magnificent show put on by 'A' coy [company] under the comd [command] of Major Bell-Irving." ASHC, PDMIA, Hoffmeister Account, 31 July 1943.

62 For psychological analyses on why soldiers fight, see Wm. Darryl Hendersen, *Cohesion: The Human Element in Combat* (Washington: National Defence University Press, 1985); Elmar Dinter, *Hero or Coward? Pressures Facing the Soldier in Battle* (London: Frank Cass, 1985); and Ben Shalit, *The Psychology of Conflict and Combat* (New York: Praeger, 1988).

63 Denis Meade, letter to the author, 16 September 2001.

64 Meade interview, 5 December 2000.

Chapter 6: Brigade Command

1 C.A. Rivers, letter to R.H. Roy. Cited in Reginald H. Roy, *The Seaforth Highlanders of Canada, 1919-1965* (Vancouver: Evergreen Press, 1969), 201-2.

2 Royal Military College of Canada (hereafter RMC), William J. McAndrew Collection (hereafter McAndrew Collection), General B.M. Hoffmeister, interview with W. McAndrew and B. Greenhous, 1980 (hereafter McAndrew/Greenhous-Hoffmeister interview), 63; and National Archives of Canada (hereafter NAC), Record Group (hereafter RG) 24, vol. 14,074, War Diary (hereafter WD), 2 Canadian Infantry Brigade (hereafter 2 CIB), 29 September 1943.

3 NAC, RG 24, vol. 15,256, WD Seaforth Highlanders of Canada (hereafter SHC), 29 September 1943; and Archives of the Seaforth Highlanders of Canada (hereafter ASHC), Personal Diaries, Memoirs, Interviews, Accounts of Battle (hereafter PDMIA), Correspondence of Major J.D. Forin to his family – World War II, 1943-1944, Letter 1 October 1943.

4 On the planning and conduct of the assaults on the Italian mainland, see Brigadier C.J.C. Molony, *The Mediterranean and the Middle East,* vol. 5 (London: Her Majesty's Stationary Office, 1973), 219-87; and Shelford Bidwell and Dominick Graham, *Tug of War: The Battle for Italy 1943-1945* (London: Hodder and Stoughton, 1986), 1-100. For a Canadian perspective, see Lieutenant-Colonel G.W.L. Nicholson, *The Canadians in Italy, 1943-1945* (Ottawa: Queen's Printer, 1966), 186-212.

5 The 1 CID plan for Operation BAYTOWN is found at NAC, RG 24, vol. 13,726, WD 1 CID, August 1943, Appendix 32, "BAYTOWN," 1 CANADIAN DIVISION OPERATION ORDER no. 1, 28 August 1943. For the intended plan of operations beyond the Reggio bridgehead, see NAC, RG 24, vol. 13,726, WD 1 CID, September 1943, Appendix 1, 1 CANADIAN DIVISION Outline Plan of Operations Following the capture of REGGIO bridgehead, 1 September 1943.

6 Appendix Z to War Diary, General Staff Headquarters, Eighth Army, 4 October 1943. Cited in Molony, *The Mediterranean and the Middle East,* vol. 5, 347. See also Field-Marshal the Viscount Montgomery of Alamein, *Memoirs* (London: Collins, 1958), 198-200 and also 433-42.

7 Nigel Hamilton, *Monty: Master of the Battlefield, 1942-1944* (London: Hamish Hamilton, 1983), 438.

8 Telegraph, O.K.W./W.F.St./Op. no. 662409/43, 4 October, *Fuehrer Directives*. Cited in Nicholson, *Canadians in Italy*, 266 (author's emphasis).

9 The mortars and machine guns came from the Saskatoon Light Infantry, a divisional unit. Unlike the artillery battery, the reconnaissance squadron, the anti-tank platoon, or even tanks, these elements were regularly assigned to the brigades.

10 NAC, RG 24, vol. 13,727, WD 1 CID, 1-3 October 1943; and NAC, RG 24, vol. 14,074, WD 2 CIB, 3 October 1943.

11 RMC, McAndrew Collection, McAndrew/Greenhous-Hoffmeister interview, 63.

12 Major-General B.M. Hoffmeister Scrapbooks (hereafter Hoffmeister Scrapbooks).

13 ASHC, PDMIA, Major-General Hoffmeister, interview with R.H. Roy, February 1967 (hereafter Roy-Hoffmeister interview).

14 RMC, McAndrew Collection, McAndrew/Greenhous-Hoffmeister interview, 64.

15 ASHC, PDMIA, Account Given By Brigadier B.M. Hoffmeister, DSO, Commander 2 CIB, Given to Captain Hughes, 16 November 1943 in the Campobasso area (hereafter Hoffmeister Account, 16 November 1943).

16 On the formation of Scout and Sniper Platoons, see NAC, RG 24, WD 2 CIB, 11 November 1943; and C. Sydney Frost, *Once a Patricia: Memoirs of a Junior Infantry Officer in World War II* (St. Catharines, ON: Vanwell, 1988), 128-30.

17 RMC, McAndrew Collection, McAndrew/Greenhous-Hoffmeister interview, 65-66. The 2 CIB Intelligence Log and War Diary entries for 6 October 1943 are consistent with this account. They cite fifteen casualties "killed or missing" and four vehicles destroyed. NAC, RG 24, vol. 14,074, WD 2 CIB, October 1943, Appendix 1, Intelligence Log.

18 See, for example, employment of "B" Squadron, Princess Louise Dragoon Guards, to the southern flank, 6-10 October and 12 October. NAC, RG 24, vol. 14,074, WD 2 CIB, Intelligence Log, 6-12 October.

19 The practice of conveying direction verbally left few written orders. However, the 2 CIB Intelligence Log for October 1943 is an excellent source for chronicling Hoffmeister's decisions and methods. On sending infantry patrols in advance of attacks, see the Intelligence Log entries for the attacks on the Decorata crossroads (7-8 October), Riccia (9-10 October), Mount Saraceno (10 October), San Croce (10-12 October), Point 1000/La Rocca (13-14 October), and Cercepiccola (13-14 October). NAC, RG 24, vol. 14,074, WD 2 CIB WD, Appendix 1, Intelligence Log, October 1943.

20 NAC, RG 24, vol. 15,156, WD PPCLI, 9 October 1943.

21 Ibid., vol. 14,074, WD 2 CIB, 13 October 1943.

22 Ibid., Appendix 1, Intelligence Log 9 October 1943 (0825 hrs).

23 NAC, RG 24, vol. 14,074, WD 2 CIB, 12 October 1943, Appendix 1, Intelligence Log, entries for 2020 hrs 11 October 1943 and 1207 hrs 12 October 1943. See also the "Tac R [Reconnaissance]" request for the west bank of the Biferno, ibid., 0845 hrs 20 October.

24 NAC, RG 24, vol. 14,074, WD 2 CIB, Appendix 1, Intelligence Log October 1943, entry 1835 hrs 3 October 1943.

25 ASHC, PDMIA, Hoffmeister Account, 16 November 1943.

26 NAC, RG 24, vol. 15,114, WD Loyal Edmonton Regiment (hereafter LER), 5 October 1943. The 2 CIB Intelligence Log notes that Hoffmeister had gone forward to "tee up the attack" on 5 October. NAC, RG 24, vol. 14,074, WD 2 CIB, Appendix 1, Intelligence Log, 5 October 1943 (1150 hrs). The Edmonton Regiment action is recounted briefly in the regimental history by G.R. Stevens, *A City Goes to War: A History of the Loyal Edmonton Regiment* (Brampton, ON: Charters, 1964), 256-57.

27 NAC, RG 24, vol. 15,256, WD SHC, 6 October 1943. See also Roy, *Seaforth Highlanders of Canada*, 218-20.

28 There were, however, problems with the coordination of air-ground attacks. On 10 October, the DAF mistakenly dropped bombs on Cercepiccola instead of the intended target, Cercemaggiore. NAC, RG 24, vol. 14,074, WD 2 CIB WD, 9-10 October 1943.

29 NAC, RG 24, vol. 14,074, WD 2 CIB, 17 October 1943, 18 October 1943. On the enemy gun positions in Boiano, Colle d'Anchise, and Spinete, see the 2 CIB Intelligence Log entries for 2000 hrs 17 October 1943, 0720 hrs 18 October 1943, and 1415 hrs 19 October 1943. Ibid., Appendix 1.

30 War Office (UK), *Operations, Military Training Pamphlet no. 23, Part I – General Principles, Fighting Troops and Their Characteristics – 1942* (Ottawa: His Majesty's Stationary Office, 1942), 4 (emphasis in original). The other tactical principles were *concentration* (of will-power and firepower), *surprise, security* (protecting vital points and lines of communication), *cooperation* (between levels of command and the fighting arms), and *mobility*.

31 For critical analyses of this fighting doctrine, see Michael Pearson Cessford, "Hard in the Attack: The Canadian Army in Sicily and Italy, July 1943-June 1944" (PhD diss., Carleton University, 1996), 422-29; and William McAndrew, "Operational Art and the Canadian Army's Way of War," in *The Operational Art: Developments in the Theories of War*, ed. B.J.C. McKercher and Michael A. Hennessy (Westport, CT: Praeger, 1996), 87-102.

32 NAC, RG 24, vol. 14,074, WD 2 CIB, 8 October 1943.

33 Ibid., 9 October 1943; and RMC, McAndrew Collection, McAndrew/Greenhous-Hoffmeister interview, 56.

34 On 5 October, for example, the brigade major went "fwd to recce [reconnoitre] demolitions [destroyed bridges] and take messages at OP [Observation posts] for the Comd Post [Brigade Headquarters]." NAC, RG 24, vol. 14,074, WD 2 CIB, Intelligence Log, entry 0710 hrs 5 October 1943.

35 RMC, McAndrew Collection, McAndrew/Greenhous-Hoffmeister interview, 66.

36 NAC, RG 24, vol. 14,074, WD 2 CIB, 14 October 1943. Hoffmeister related the story with some humour in an interview. RMC, McAndrew Collection, McAndrew/Greenhous-Hoffmeister interview, 54-55.

37 NAC, RG 24, vol. 14,074, WD 2 CIB, 13 October 1943.

38 Ibid., 14 October 1943.

39 During the second week of October 1943, the Edmonton Regiment received royal assent to the designation "Loyal"; hence the name change to Loyal Edmonton Regiment.

40 NAC, RG 24, vol. 14,074, WD 2 CIB, 20 October 1943.

41 Ibid., Intelligence Log, entries 20-22 October; NAC, RG 24 vol. 15,156, WD PPCLI, 20-22 October 1943; vol. 15,114, WD LER, 20-22 October 1943; and vol. 15,256, WD SHC, 20-22 October 1943.

42 NAC, RG 24, vol. 14,074, WD 2 CIB, 21 October 1943. After attending Simonds's orders at 11:00 a.m. on 22 October, Hoffmeister confirmed his plan at a second orders group at 2:00 p.m. that same day.

43 NAC, RG 24, vol. 15,114, WD LER, 22-24 October 1943.

44 NAC, RG 24, vol. 14,074, WD 2 CIB, Intelligence Log, 23 October 1943.

45 NAC, RG 24, vol. 15,156, WD PPCLI, 22-24 October 1943. It is interesting to note that the PPCLI Commanding Officer, Lieutenant-Colonel C.B. Ware, held his orders group at one of his forward company locations "where there was the best possible view of the ground over which we will be going."

46 NAC, RG 24, vol. 15,156, WD PPCLI, 24 October 1943. On the PPCLI action at the Biferno, see G.R. Stevens, *Princess Patricia's Canadian Light Infantry, 1919-1957*, vol. 3 (Montreal:

Southam Printing, 1960), 114-16. On the reconnaissance that preceded the attack, see the memoir account of the PPCLI scout platoon commander, Sydney Frost, *Once a Patricia*, 168-74.

47   National Defence Headquarters (Ottawa), Directorate of History and Heritage (DHH), "Notes on interview between J.L. Granatstein and Bert Hoffmeister, 2 March 1992" (hereafter Granatstein-Hoffmeister interview).

48   Hoffmeister's promotion to the rank of acting brigadier came the same day that his assignment as commander of 2 CIB was made permanent. However, promotion to substantive rank lagged substantially behind his appointments. His promotion to substantive brigadier did not occur until 20 March 1944, at which time he was also appointed Acting Major-General in command of the 5th Canadian Armoured Division. Substantive promotion to Major-General did not come until 20 March 1945, fourteen months after his assumption of divisional command. Hoffmeister Collection, Statement of Service and Qualifications, 25 February 1946. See also NAC, MG 30, E 157, General H.D.G. Crerar Papers (hereafter Crerar Papers), vol. 5, Cipher Message CANMILITRAY to 15 ARMY GROUP REAR, 20 October 1943; ibid., Message from Crerar to Stuart, 030915 [March 1944].

49   There is no record of direction from 1 CID, and 1 CIB did not conduct anything analogous to Hoffmeister's centralized program for staff and sub-unit commanders. (3 CIB was occupied with an independent brigade group task in support of 13 Corps operations 16-30 November.) On 1 CIB activities in this period, see the memoir of its brigade commander: Howard S. Graham, *Citizen and Soldier* (Toronto: McClelland and Stewart, 1987), 188-90; and NAC, RG 24, vol. 14,076, WD 1 CIB, November 1943. On 3 CIB's feint attack to close up to the Sangro River, see Nicholson, *Canadians in Italy*, 277-82; and NAC, RG 24, vol. 14,161, WD 3 CIB, 8-30 November 1943.

50   NAC, RG 24, vol. 14,074, WD 2 CIB, 4 November 1943.

51   NAC, RG 24, vol. 14,074, WD 2 CIB, November 1943, Appendix 13, Timetable 2 Cdn Inf Bde L.O. [liaison officer] Trg Period, 3 November 1943.

52   NAC, MG 30 157, Crerar Papers, vol. 2, [Montgomery], Some General Notes on What to Look For When Visiting a Unit.

53   ASHC, PDMIA, Diary of Capt W.H. Melhuish, Brig Hoffmeister lecture.

54   Ibid., The Advance (Brig. Hoff).

55   Ibid., Attack.

56   NAC, RG 24, vol. 14,074, WD 2 CIB, November 1943, Appendix 21, Timetable 2 Cdn Inf Bde – Coy Comd's Gen Knowledge Course, 14 November 1943.

57   Cessford, "Hard in the Attack," 213.

58   Cessford argues that by the beginning of December, Montgomery should have realized the futility of the offensive and called it off "to preserve manpower the Eighth Army could not afford to lose." Cessford, "Hard in the Attack," 213-15, 251-52. In retrospect, Montgomery's Chief of Staff, Major-General Francis de Guingand also believed the plan to advance rapidly on Pescara was overly optimistic. See Sir Francis De Guingand, *Operation Victory* (London: Hodder and Stoughton, 1947), 330.

59   Montgomery to General Sir Alan Brooke, 18 November 1943. Cited in Hamilton, *Monty: Master of the Battlefield*, 446.

60   Montgomery of Alamein, *Memoirs*, 197.

61   De Guingand, *Operation Victory*, 330.

62   Liddell Hart Centre for Military Archives, King's College, London (hereafter LHCMA), Papers Field-Marshal Lord Alanbrooke (14/21), Montgomery to Brooke (undated). Cited in Hamilton, *Monty: Master of the Battlefield*, 451.

63   Imperial War Museum (hereafter IWM), Papers of Field-Marshal the Viscount Montgomery of Alamein, BLM 50/13, Montgomery to Dempsey, 4.12.43.

64 ASHC, PDMIA, Major-General C. Vokes, Narrative: Crossing MORO R [River] and subsequent operations including capture of ORTONA (hereafter Vokes Moro Narrative), 14 May 1944.

65 Due to a map typographical error, most contemporary documents refer to "Roatti."

66 ASHC, PDMIA, Vokes Moro Narrative. Because 1 CIB did not take over its sector on the Moro until 5 December, the reconnaissance on the coast road was actually conducted by the outgoing units of 38 Infantry Brigade.

67 Ibid. Vokes's intention was confirmed in notes from Hoffmeister's orders on 5 December. NAC, RG 24, vol. 14,074, WD 2 CIB, Appendix 15, NOTES ON BRIGADE "O" GP 1445 hrs 5 December 1943.

68 NAC, RG 24, vol. 10,982, Account by Capt W.S. Dewar, I.O. [Intelligence Officer] 2 CIB, given to Capt Hughes at Punta di Acquebella on 12 January 1944 (hereafter Dewar Account). See also ASHC, box – Professor Roy's Manuscript (hereafter PRM), Letter C. Vokes to R.H. Roy, 4 July 1967.

69 NAC, RG 24, vol. 10,982, Dewar Account. See also NAC, RG 24, vol. 14,074, 2 CIB WD, Appendix 15, NOTES ON BRIGADE "O" GP 1445 hrs 5 December 1943.

70 ASHC, PDMIA, Lieut-Col C.B. Ware, THE CROSSING OF THE MORO AND THE CAPTURE OF VILLA ROATTI (hereafter Ware account). Also on the fight for Villa Rogatti, see Nicholson, *Canadians in Italy,* 292-97; and Stevens, *Princess Patricia's Canadian Light Infantry,* 124-29.

71 The systematic penetration of Rogatti defences and the "mopping up" are described in NAC, RG 24, vol. 15,156, WD PPCLI, 6 December 1943; and ASHC, PDMIA, Ware Account.

72 ASHC, PDMIA, Lt-Col. J.D. Forin, Baranello to San Leonardo. On the Seaforth crossing of the Moro, see Roy, *Seaforth Highlanders of Canada,* 235-72.

73 ASHC, PDMIA, Forin, Baranello to San Leonardo.

74 NAC, RG 24, vol. 10,982, Dewar Account.

75 Ibid.; and ASHC, PDMIA, Forin, Baranello to San Leonardo.

76 ASHC, PRM, Vokes to Roy, 4 July 1967. The letter is also quoted in Roy, *Seaforth Highlanders of Canada,* 241.

77 When engineers from the 8th Indian Division erected a bridge at the same site only a few days later, they mockingly nicknamed the structure "Impossible" Bridge.

78 LHCMA, Papers of Lieutenant-General Sir Charles Allfrey (hereafter Allfrey Papers), 4/1, Diaries 6-7 December 1943.

79 NAC, RG 24, vol. 14,074, WD 2 CIB, Appendix 18, NOTES ON BRIGADE "O" GROUP, 0830 hrs 8 December 1943.

80 Ibid.

81 NAC, RG 24, vol. 14,074, WD 2 CIB, Intelligence Log, entry for 1315 hrs 8 December 1943.

82 The engineers of 3 Field Engineer Company completed this task at 0600 hrs 9 December. NAC, RG 24, vol. 14,074, WD 2 CIB, Intelligence Log, entry for 0505 hrs 9 December 1943.

83 ASHC, PDMIA, Forin, Baranello to San Leonardo.

84 Ibid.

85 NAC, RG 24, vol. 14,074, WD 2 CIB, Intelligence Log, entries for 1007 hrs 9 December 1943, and 0200 hrs 10 December; and NAC, RG 24, vol. 15,114, WD LER, 9 December 1943.

86 NAC, RG 24, vol. 14,074, 2 CIB WD, Intelligence Log, entry for 1000 hrs 10 December 1943.

87 Mark Zuehlke, *Ortona: Canada's Epic World War II Battle* (Toronto: Stoddart, 1999), 167-69.

88 Cessford expands on this point in "Hard in the Attack," 233-40.

89 NAC, RG 24, vol. 10,776, 5 Corps Intelligence Summaries, file 224B5.023 (D1), 5 Corps Intelligence Summary no. 248 (for period ending 2300 hrs 10 December 1943).

90 Cessford, "Hard in the Attack," 254-56.

91 NAC, RG 24, vol. 14,074, WD 2 CIB, 14 December 1943; ibid., vol. 10,776, file 224B5.O23 (D1), 5 Corps Intelligence Summaries, 5 Corps Intelligence Summary no. 248 (for period ending 2300 hrs 10 December 1943); and ibid., 5 Corps Intelligence Summary no. 261 (for the period ending 2300 hrs 23 December 1943).

92 NAC, RG 24, vol. 10,776, 5 Corps Intelligence Summaries; and Cessford, "Hard in the Attack," 227.

93 NAC, RG 24, vol. 15,156, PPCLI WD, 15 December 1943.

94 LHCMA, Allfrey Papers, 4/1, Diaries, 18 December 1943. By the time the RCR took "Cider," two-thirds of the battalion's soldiers were casualties.

95 RMC, McAndrew Collection, Hoffmeister/Greenhous-McAndrew interview, 68.

96 Brereton Greenhous, "Would It Not Have Been Better to Bypass Ortona Completely ...?" *Canadian Defence Quarterly* (April 1989): 51-55. For more criticism of Vokes's generalship, see Cessford, "Hard in the Attack," 256-58; and Zuehlke, *Ortona*, 377-80.

97 RMC, McAndrew Collection, Lt Col S.W. Thomson, interview with William J. McAndrew, Sydney, BC, 6 April 1980 (hereafter McAndrew-Thomson interview).

98 NAC, RG 24, vol. 14,074, WD 2 CIB, Intelligence Log, entry for 1745 hrs 24 December 1943.

99 NAC, RG 24, vol. 10,776, file 224B5.O23 (D1), Intelligence Summaries 5 (British) Corps, 5 Corps Intelligence Summary, no. 256 (for period ending 2300 hrs 18 December 1943).

100 NAC, RG 24, vol. 14,074, WD 2 CIB, 23 December 1943. The 2 CIB War Diary refers to the efforts of 1 CIB to advance from the area east of Casa Berardi towards Villa Grande, San Nicola, and San Tommaso.

101 For the barrage plan on 20 December, see NAC, RG 24, vol. 14,074, WD 2 CIB, Appendix 23, Barrage Trace, 20 December 1943. On the part played by the Loyal Edmonton Regiment during the battle of Ortona, see Shaun R.G. Brown, "'The Rock of Accomplishment': The Loyal Edmonton Regiment at Ortona," *Canadian Military History* 2, 2 (1993): 11-22.

102 The description of the view from Hoffmeister's tactical headquarters was Allfrey's. LHCMA, Allfrey Papers, 4/1, Diaries, 20 December 1943.

103 NAC, RG 24, vol. 14,074, 2 CIB WD, Intelligence Log, entries for 1411 hrs, 1415 hrs 20 December 1943.

104 The main brigade headquarters later moved to the location vacated by the tactical headquarters.

105 NAC, RG 24, vol. 10,982, Dewar Account.

106 Extracts from Brigadier S.W. Thomson, interview with Robert L. McDougall, Victoria, BC, 15 July 1960. Reprinted in Robert L. McDougall, *A Narrative of War: From the Beaches of Sicily to the Hitler Line with the Seaforth Highlanders of Canada, 1943-1944* (Ottawa: Golden Dog Press, 1996), 156.

107 LHCMA, Allfrey Papers, 4/8, ORTONA, Report by H.Q. 1 CDN INF DIV, 16 February 1944, 2-3.

108 Ibid., 5.

109 NAC, RG 24, vol. 10,982, Dewar Account.

110 NAC, RG 24, vol. 14,074, WD 2 CIB, Reports of "Approximate Fighting Strength," 20-29 December 1943.

111 Ibid., 5-19 December 1943.

112 MacLeod Collection, MacLeod interviews, vol. 6., Private Jimmy "Tubby" Keith, interview, undated. Keith was Hoffmeister's dispatch rider in the Seaforth Highlanders of Canada.

113 MacLeod Collection, MacLeod interviews, vol. 6, Jock Gibson, interview, undated.

114 Jock Gibson, interview with the author, Langley, BC, 9 December 2000.

115 The incident is recounted in Zuehlke, *Ortona*, 300-2.

116 RMC, McAndrew Collection, Col. S.W. Thompson, interview with William McAndrew, Sydney, BC, 6 April 1980.

117 The details of the visit, based on an interview with Hoffmeister, are recounted in Zuehlke, *Ortona,* 290-91.
118 Hoffmeister, quoted in ibid.
119 NAC, RG 24, WD 2 CIB, Intelligence Log December 1943. For reports on the enemy situation, see entries 1925 hrs 20 December 1943, 1425 hrs 23 December 1943, 2300 hrs 27 December 1943. On 1 CIB actions, see the entry for 1050 hrs 24 December 1943. On restricting the movement of civilians, see the entry 0950 hrs 21 December 1943.
120 NAC, RG 24, vol. 14,074, WD 2 CIB, Intelligence Log, entry for 1450 hrs 22 December 1943.
121 RMC, McAndrew Collection, McAndrew/Greenhous-Hoffmeister interview, 70.
122 NAC, RG 24, vol. 14,074, WD 2 CIB, Intelligence Log, entries 0800 hrs and 0940 hrs 28 December 1943. See also NAC, RG 24, vol. 10,982, Dewar Account.
123 ASHC, PDMIA, Vokes Moro Account. See also LHCMA, Allfrey Papers, 4/2, 27 and 28 December 1943.
124 Nicholson, *Canadians in Italy,* 338.
125 LHCMA, Allfrey Papers, 4/2, 2 January 1944.
126 ASHC, PDMIA, Vokes Moro Account.
127 Hoffmeister Scrapbooks, Citation – Bar to the Distinguished Service Order, Brigadier B.M. Hoffmeister, DSO.
128 Colonel David Fairweather, interview with the author, Vancouver, 7 December 2000.

Chapter 7: Division Command and the Liri Valley

1 Colonel C.P. Stacey, *Six Years of War: The Army in Canada, Britain and the Pacific* (Ottawa: Queen's Printer, 1966), 415.
2 Liddell Hart Centre for Military Archives, King's College, London (hereafter LHCMA), Lieutenant-General Charles Allfrey Papers (hereafter Allfrey Papers), 4/2, 20 January 1944.
3 Of the other two brigade commanders in 1 CID, T.G. Gibson of 3 CIB had roughly the same seniority as Hoffmeister, but his performance as a brigade commander had been abysmal, and D.C. Spry of 1 CIB, although more capable than Gibson, was the junior of the group, having succeeded H.D. Graham only in mid-December 1943. For an extremely critical appraisal of Gibson's generalship, see Michael Pearson Cessford, "Hard in the Attack: The Canadian Army in Sicily and Italy, July 1943-June 1944 (PhD diss., Carleton University, 1996), 235-36, 255.
4 National Archives of Canada (NAC), MG 30, E 157, General H.D.G. Crerar Papers (hereafter Crerar Papers), vol. 5, Crerar to E.L.M. Burns (undated, probably 6 February 1944). The letter also dealt with prospective commanders for 1st and 2nd Canadian Armoured Brigades (CABs).
5 Ibid., Burns to Crerar, 7 February 1944.
6 Ibid., Message, 1 Cdn Corps to CANMILITARY (UK), 03 [March] 0915.
7 Royal Military College of Canada (hereafter RMC), William J. McAndrew Collection (hereafter McAndrew Collection), General B.M. Hoffmeister, interview with B. Greenhous and W. McAndrew, 1980 (hereafter McAndrew/Greenhous-Hoffmeister interview), 78.
8 Ibid.
9 RMC, McAndrew Collection, Major General A.E. Wrinch, interview with William J. McAndrew, Toronto, June 1980 (hereafter McAndrew-Wrinch interview).
10 National Defence Headquarters (Ottawa), Directorate of History and Heritage (DHH), J.L. Granatstein interviews, "Notes on interview with MGen J. Desmond B. Smith, London, UK, 14 September 1991."
11 DHH, Granatstein interviews, "Notes on interview with Gen. S.F. Clark, Victoria, BC, 24 February 1992." The incident was also related in J.L. Granatstein, *The Generals: The Canadian Army's Senior Commanders in the Second World War* (Toronto: Stoddart, 1993), 163.

12 DHH, Granatstein interviews, "Notes on interview with Brig. Jack Christian, Thornhill, ON, 31 May 1991" (hereafter Granatstein-Christian interview).
13 RMC, McAndrew Collection, War Diary Lt Col J.D. Christian, CRE, 23 March 1944.
14 RMC, McAndrew Collection, McAndrew-Wrinch interview.
15 RMC, McAndrew Collection, Mr. Edward Devlin, interview with B. Greenhous, Royal Canadian Military Institute, Toronto, undated (hereafter Greenhous-Devlin interview). Devlin was a lieutenant with 2nd Canadian Armoured Regiment, the Lord Strathcona's Horse (Royal Canadians). Later, in the fall of 1944, he became Hoffmeister's aide de camp (ADC).
16 RMC, McAndrew Collection, McAndrew-Wrinch interview.
17 RMC, McAndrew Collection, Major-General Sparling, interview with William J. McAndrew, June 1980 (hereafter McAndrew-Sparling interview).
18 Ibid., 9.
19 RMC, McAndrew Collection, McAndrew/Greenhous-Hoffmeister interview, 7.
20 Fifth US Army launched offensive operations to break through in the Cassino sector on 17 January, the same day 11 CIB conducted its "limited" attack at the Arielli and Riccio rivers. Also to support Fifth Army, a landing by 6 US Corps behind the Gustav and Hitler Lines, at Anzio, took place five days later, but the much anticipated link-up between the two operations did not occur until May.
21 For solid historical accounts of the Arielli Show, see Lieutenant-Colonel G.W.L. Nicholson, *The Canadians in Italy, 1943-1945* (Ottawa: Queen's Printer, 1966), 362-72; and William J. McAndrew, "Fifth Canadian Armoured Division: Introduction to Battle," *Canadian Military History* 2, 2 (1993): 45-46. See also the memoir account of the 11 CIB commander, George Kitching, *Mud and Green Fields* (St. Catharines, ON: Vanwell, 1993), 170-77. For a soldier's view of the action, see Stanley Scislowski, *Not All of Us Were Brave: Perth Regiment, 11th Infantry Brigade, 5th Canadian Armoured Division* (Toronto: Dundurn, 1997), 112-31.
22 LHCMA, Allfrey Papers, 4/2, Diaries, 14-15 January 1944. The casualty figures are from Nicholson, *Canadians in Italy,* 370-71. For contemporary records of the action, see NAC, Record Group (hereafter RG) 24, vol. 14,158, WD 11 CIB, January 1944, Appendix 4, Intelligence Log, Battle of Arielli – 11 Cdn Inf Bde.
23 Scislowski, *Not All of Us Were Brave,* 122-23.
24 Ibid., 123.
25 RMC, McAndrew Collection, McAndrew/Greenhous-Hoffmeister interview, 79.
26 McAndrew, "Fifth Canadian Armoured Division," 47-50.
27 During the period 9 February 1944 to 7 March 1944, 1st Canadian Corps occupied a position in the line. NAC, RG 24, vol. 13,686, WD "G" Branch H.Q. 1 Cdn Corps (hereafter WD "G" 1 Cdn Corps), February-March 1944; and ibid., vol. 13,796, WD General Staff H.Q. (hereafter "G") 5 CAD, February-March 1944.
28 NAC, RG 24, vol. 13,796, WD "G" 5 CAD, March 1944, Appendix 9, 5 CDN ARM DIV TRG INSTR no. 25, 12 March 1944.
29 Ibid.
30 NAC, RG 24, vol. 14,229, WD British Columbia Dragoons (hereafter BCD), March 1944, 5 Cdn Armd Bde – Exercise with Tps – SLUGGEM SERIES (hereafter SLUGGEM Instruction), (n.d.).
31 The live-fire exercise was called DESMOND. NAC, RG 24, vol. 10,932, file 244C.5 – 039 (D1), 5 Cdn Armd Div – Highlights of Training 2-9 APR.
32 Ibid. See also NAC, RG 24, vol. 14,191, WD Lord Strathcona's Horse (hereafter LdSH) (2 CAR), April 1944; vol. 14,229, WD BCD (9 CAR), April 1944.
33 NAC, RG 24, vol. 14,056, WD "G" 5 CAD, April 1944, Appendix 8, Exercise "THRUSTER" (3 April 1944).

34 NAC, RG 24, vol. 13,796, WD "G" 5 CAD, April 1944, Appendix 8, Exercise "THRUSTER" file, GEN NOTES (n.d.).

35 NAC, RG 24, vol. 14,056, WD 5 CAB, Appendix 10, Brig's Conference at Bde HQ 09 [March at] 1400.

36 For a succinct overview of a provost company's organization and roles, see Andrew L. Ritchie, *Watchdog: A History of the Canadian Provost Corps* (Burlington, ON: Canadian Provost Corps Association, 1995), 29-39.

37 NAC, RG 24, vol. 13,796, WD "G" 5 CAD, April 1944, Appendix 8, THRUSTER file, Umpires Reports (n.d.).

38 Ibid., IR RC LEFT FLANK (n.d).

39 NAC, RG 24, vol. 13,796, WD "G" 5 CAD, April 1944, Appendix 8, THRUSTER file, EXERCISE THRUSTER Confirming Notes – GOC's verbal orders.

40 RMC, McAndrew Collection, McAndrew-Wrinch interview.

41 Scislowski, *Not All of Us Were Brave*, 165.

42 RMC, McAndrew Collection, McAndrew/Greenhous-Hoffmeister interview, 80.

43 See NAC, RG 24, vol. 13,796, WD "G" 5 CAD, March-May 1944.

44 RMC, McAndrew Collection, BGen W.W. Reid, interview with William J. McAndrew, undated.

45 RMC, McAndrew Collection, Letter Stanley Scislowski to Dr. McAndrew, 7 March 1981.

46 RMC, McAndrew Collection, McAndrew/Greenhous-Hoffmeister interview, 81-82.

47 It is difficult to determine the precise date of the encounter, but the Perth Regiment War Diary notes that four officers were "struck off strength" between 3 May and 11 May – two to holding units, two to 11 CIB headquarters. NAC, RG 24, vol. 15,136, WD Perth Regiment, May 1944. The meeting had to have taken place earlier in May. The 5 CAD "G" Staff War Diary, which diligently documents all of the division commanders' visits, inspections, and movements, has a peculiar entry for the morning of 2 May 1944: "The GOC enjoyed a long hike during the course of the morning." NAC, RG 24, vol. 13,796, WD "G" 5 CAD, 2 May 1944.

48 Quoted in Brigadier C.J.C. Molony, *The Mediterranean and the Middle East,* vol. 5 (London: Her Majesty's Stationary Office, 1973), 832.

49 On the planning for the advance on Rome, see Nicholson, *Canadians in Italy,* 387-99; and Molony, *Mediterranean and the Middle East,* 5: 832-46.

50 See the signal instruction for Exercise WILDERNESS, NAC, RG 24, vol. 13,796, WD "G" 5 CAD, April 1944, Signal Instruction Exercise "WILDERNESS", 17 April 1944. See also Nicholson, *Canadians in Italy,* 391-94.

51 NAC, RG 24, vol. 13,686, WD General Staff (hereafter GS) 1 Cdn Corps, May 1944, Appendix 6, 1 Cdn Corps Study Period, dated 5 May 1944.

52 NAC, RG 24, vol. 13,686, WD GS 1 Cdn Corps, May 1944; NAC, RG 24, vol. 13,796, WD "G" 5 CAD, May 1944, Appendix 14, 5 Cdn Armoured Div Study Period.

53 NAC, RG 24, vol. 13,686, WD GS 1 Cdn Corps, 11 May 1944.

54 See C.J.C. Molony, *The Mediterranean and the Middle East,* vol. 6, part 1 (London: Her Majesty's Stationary Office, 1986), 104-9, 115-20.

55 NAC, MG 31, G6, Papers of Lieutenant-General E.L.M. Burns (hereafter Burns Papers), vol. 1, Personal War Diary (hereafter PWD), 19 May 1944.

56 NAC, RG 24, vol. 13,797, WD "G" 5 CAD, June 1944, Appendix 23, 5 Cdn Armd Div Report on Ops 23-31 May and Lessons Learned HITLER Line to Frosinone (hereafter 5 CAD Report 23-31 May 1944). This is an extensive report on operations compiled by Hoffmeister and his staff within a month of the Liri Valley Campaign. The main body of the document is Hoffmeister's synopsis of operations (8 pp.) and lessons learned (6 pp.). Appendices include similar reports by the brigades, units, and supporting arms. Operations orders, if written, have also been included.

57   Ibid., Report on Operations, 14 May to 31 May, 2nd Canadian Armoured Regiment, Lord Strathcona's Horse (Royal Canadians).

58   NAC, RG 24, vol. 13,686, WD GS 1 Cdn Corps, May 1944, Appendix 22, 1 Cdn Corps Operation Instr no. 8, dated 15 May 1944; and Appendix 27, 1 Cdn Corps Operation Instr no. 9, dated 17 May.

59   NAC, RG 24, vol. 13,796, WD "G" 5 CAD, Appendix 60, Notes Taken at "O" GP, 16 May 1944.

60   NAC, MG 31, G6, Burns Papers, vol. 1, PWD, 19 May 1944; and NAC, RG 24, vol. 13,796, "G" 5 CAD, 19 May 1944.

61   NAC, RG 24, vol. 13,796, WD "G" 5 CAD, May 1944, Appendix 60, Notes Taken at "O" GP, 16 May 1944.

62   Cessford discussed the effects that the battles of December 1943 and the subsequent reinforcements had on 1 CID's "sluggish" breakout from the Gustav Line. See "Hard in the Attack," 319, 321-22.

63   NAC, MG 31, G6, Burns Papers, vol. 1, PWD, 19 May 1944; Planning Notes OPERATION "HONKER": Skeleton Appreciation by GOC 1 Cdn Corps. See also NAC, RG 24, vol. 13,796, WD "G" 5 CAD, 20 May 1944.

64   NAC, RG 24, vol. 13,686, WD GS 1 Cdn Corps, May 1944, Appendix 33, 1 Canadian Corps Operation Order no. 1 (22 May 1944). For Burns's memoir account of Operation CHESTERFIELD, see Lt.-Gen. E.L.M. Burns, *General Mud: Memoirs of Two World Wars* (Toronto: Clark, Irwin, 1970), 145-61.

65   Burns, *General Mud*, 146.

66   On the part played by 1 CID in breaking the Hitler Line, see Cessford, "Hard in the Attack," 340-58; and Nicholson, *Canadians in Italy*, 417-26. For a soldier's perspective of the battle, see Mark Zuehlke, *The Liri Valley: Canada's World War II Breakthrough to Rome* (Toronto: Stoddart, 2001), 199-323; and William J. McAndrew, *The Canadians and the Italian Campaign, 1943-1945* (Montreal: Art Global, 1996), 97-101. Quotation from RMC, McAndrew Collection, McAndrew/Greenhous-Hoffmeister interview, 87.

67   NAC, MG 31, G6, Burns Papers, vol. 1, PWD, 19 May 1944; NAC, RG 24, vol. 13,796, WD "G" 5 CAD, 23 May 1944.

68   NAC, RG 24, vol. 13,797, WD "G" 5 CAD, June 1944, Appendix 23, 5 CAD Report 23-31 May 1944. Good secondary accounts of the 5 CAD breakout from the Hitler Line include Nicholson, *Canadians in Italy*, 427-36; and Zuehlke, *The Liri Valley*, 327-421.

69   See also Cessford, "Hard in the Attack," 370-1.

70   NAC, RG 24, vol. 13,797, WD "G" 5 CAD, June 1944, 5 CAD Report 21-31 May 1944, Appendix D, The Crossing of the Melfa and the securing of a bridgehead by 5 Cdn Armd Bde, (hereafter 5 CAB Melfa Report), signed by J.D.B. Smith, 4 June 1944.

71   Ibid. See also Hoffmeister's report in the main body of the document.

72   NAC, RG 24, vol. 13,797, WD "G" 5 CAD, June 1944, 5 CAD Report 23-31 May 1944, Appendix D, 5 CAB Melfa Report. See also the reports by the LdSH, the 8th New Brunswick Hussars, and the BCD, which are attachments to the 5 CAB report. See also the unit War Diary NAC, RG 24, vol. 14,229, WD BCD (9 CAR), 23-31 May 1944.

73   NAC, RG 24, vol. 13,797, WD "G" 5 CAD, June 1944, 5 CAD Report 23-31 May 1944, Appendix 23, 9th Canadian Armoured Regiment (British Columbia Dragoons) Report on Operations – 19 May 1944 to 29 May 1944, dated 7 June 1944 (hereafter BCD Report). See also the regimental history of the British Columbia Dragoons, R.H. Roy, *Sinews of Steel: The History of the British Columbia Dragoons* (Kelowna, BC: British Columbia Dragoons, 1965), 244-53.

74   Cessford is critical of Smith's phased approach to the pursuit, which he believes slowed the advance unnecessarily and permitted the Germans to reinforce defences along the Melfa and beyond. Cessford, "Hard in the Attack," 373-74.

75 NAC, RG 24, vol. 13,797, WD "G" 5 CAD, June 1944, 5 CAD Report 23-31 May 1944, Appendix 23, Report on Operations [LdSH] 14-31 May 1944 (hereafter LdSH Report). See also the unit War Diary, NAC, RG 24, vol. 14,192, WD LdSH (2 CAR), 14-31 May 1944.

76 NAC, RG 24, vol. 13,797, WD "G" 5 CAD, June 1944, 5 CAD Report 23-31 May 1944, LdSH Report. The term "fire and movement" refers to the tactic of one element, be it a single tank or an infantry company, firing to keep the enemy's heads down while another element moves.

77 See the memoir account of the reconnaissance troop leader, Lieutenant Edward J. Perkins, DSO, "Crossing the Melfa River," *Canadian Military History* 2, 2 (1993): 35-42.

78 The Westminster action on the Melfa River is recounted in detail in the regimental history. Major J.E. Oldfield, M.C., *The Westminsters' War Diary: An Unofficial History of the Westminster Regiment (Motor) in World War II* (New Westminster, BC: Mitchell Press, 1964), 74-102.

79 NAC, MG 31, G6, Burns Papers, vol. 1, PWD, 19 May 1944; and NAC, RG 24, vol. 13,796, WD "G" 5 CAD, 24 May 1944.

80 RMC, McAndrew Collection, McAndrew/Greenhous-Hoffmeister interview, 88.

81 NAC, MG 31, G6, Burns Papers, vol. 1, PWD, 19 May 1944; and NAC, RG 24, vol. 13,796, WD "G" 5 CAD, 24 May 1944.

82 NAC, RG 24, vol. 13,796, WD "G" 5 CAD, May 1944, SITREP (dated 25 [May] 1200B).

83 Ibid.

84 NAC, MG 31, G6, Burns Papers, vol. 1, PWD, 19 May 1944; and NAC, RG 24, vol. 13,796, WD "G" 5 CAD, 24 May 1944.

85 Imperial War Museum (hereafter IWM), Papers of General Sir Oliver Leese (hereafter Leese Papers), box 1, Biography Transcript, Chapter 12, 8.

86 NAC, RG 24, vol. 13,686, WD GS 1 Cdn Corps, G LOG, MAY 1944, 24 [May] 0735 hrs. A squadron of the Governor General's Horse Guards (hereafter GGHG) also reported having found a "hastily abandoned German position" southwest of Aquino on 24 May, but there is no evidence that this report reached 1st Canadian Corps or even Eighth Army before 25 May. NAC, RG 24, vol. 14,199, WD GGHG, 24 May 1944.

87 NAC, RG 24, vol. 13,686, WD GS 1 Cdn Corps, May 1944, 1 CDN CORPS INTELLIGENCE SUMMARY no. 63, 25 May 1944.

88 IWM, Leese Papers, box 2, Letters to his Wife, 24 May 1944.

89 Ibid., box 1, Biography Transcript, Chapter 12, 8.

90 NAC, RG 24, vol. 13,686, WD GS 1 Cdn Corps, G LOG, MAY 1944, entry for 25 [May] 1005 [hrs].

91 NAC, RG 24, vol. 13,797, WD "G" 5 CAD, June 1944, Appendix 23, 5 CAD Report 23-31 May 1944. See also 11 Cdn Inf Bde Report on Ops – Battle of the Liri Valley (hereafter 11 CIB Liri Report) in ibid.; and NAC, RG 24, vol. 15,136, WD Perth Regiment, 26 May 1944.

92 NAC, RG 24, vol. 10,982, Brig. T.E. Snow, Report on the Battle of the Liri Valley (hereafter Snow Report).

93 NAC, RG 24, vol. 13,797, WD "G" 5 CAD, June 1944, Appendix 23, 5 CAD Report 23-31 May 1944, 5 Cdn Armd Regt (8 New Brunswick Hussars), Report on Operations from the Hitler Line to Ceccano – 24-31 May 1944 (hereafter 8 NBH Report).

94 Ibid. See also the war diaries of the units involved. NAC, RG 24, vol. 15,047, WD CBH (Cape Breton Highlanders), 25 May; and vol. 14,028, WD 8 NBH, 25 May.

95 NAC, RG 24, vol. 13,797, WD "G" 5 CAD, June 1944, Appendix 23, 5 CAD Report 23-31 May 1944, 8 NBH Report.

96 RMC, McAndrew Collection, Col. Clement Dick, former GSO I, 5 Cdn Armoured Division, interview with William J. McAndrew, 26 May 1980.

97 NAC, MG 31, G6, Burns Papers, vol. 1, PWD, 19 May 1944; and NAC, RG 24, vol. 13,796, "G" 5 CAD, 26-27 May 1944.

98   RMC, McAndrew Collection, McAndrew-Sparling interview.

99   Ibid., McAndrew-Wrinch interview.

100 Montgomery made this point in a 21 Army Group pamphlet entitled *The Armoured Division in Battle*: "The Divisional Commander must be well forward where he can keep in touch with the tactical battle, leaving his GSO I to move forward, and run, the divisional headquarters. Whenever possible the commander should return to his headquarters at night." 21 Army Group, *The Armoured Division in Battle* (Holland: December 1944), 9.

101 NAC, RG 24, vol. 10,982, Snow Report.

102 Scislowski, *Not All of Us Were Brave*, 206-7.

103 Ibid., 208-9.

104 RMC, McAndrew Collection, McAndrew/Greenhous-Hoffmeister interview, 88.

105 NAC, RG 24, vol. 13,797, WD "G" 5 CAD, June 1944, Appendix 23, 5 CAD Report 23-31 May 1944, 11 CIB Liri Report.

106 NAC, RG 24, vol. 10,982, Snow Report.

107 NAC, RG 24, vol. 14,159, WD 11 CIB, "G" Branch Ops Log; NAC, RG 24, vol. 15,047, WD CBH, 27 May 1944.

108 NAC, RG 24, vol. 15,047, WD CBH, 27 May 1944.

109 NAC, RG 24, vol. 13,797, WD "G" 5 CAD, 5 CAD Report, Lessons From Ops 23 to 31 May 1944 (signed by B.M. Hoffmeister, 22 June 1944); RMC, McAndrew Collection, McAndrew-Wrinch interview. See also Cessford, "Hard in the Attack," 385.

110 NAC, RG 24, vol. 13,797, WD "G" 5 CAD, 5 CAD Report 23-31 May 1944, Appendix B, Exercise CHESTERFIELD, 5 CDN ARMD DIV O.O. [Operation Order] no. 1, 28 May 1944.

111 NAC, MG 31, G6, Burns Papers, vol. 1, PWD, 28 May 1944; and NAC, RG 24, vol. 13,797, WD "G" 5 CAD, 5 CAD Report 23-31 May 1944. For cogent criticism of this decision, see Cessford, "Hard in the Attack," 376-78.

112 RMC, McAndrew Collection, Christian Diary, 28 May 1944.

113 NAC, RG 24, vol. 13,686, WD GS 1 Cdn Corps, G LOG, 28 May 1944.

114 Burns, *General Mud*, 159.

115 NAC, RG 24, vol. 10,930, Ops Log 5 Cdn Armd Div, 27 May 1944.

116 NAC, RG 24, vol. 13,686, WD GS 1 Cdn Corps, G LOG, 28 May 1944; NAC, RG 24, vol. 13,797, WD "G" 5 CAD, 5 CAD Report 23-31 May 1944.

117 See the after-action reports of the BCD, the 8 NBH, the LdSH, and the Westminster Regiment. NAC, RG 24, vol. 13,797, WD "G" 5 CAD, 5 CAD Report 23-31 May 1944, Appendix D.

118 The BCD had to cross two rivers – the Fornelli and the Meringo – using scissors bridges. Then, to make matters worse, friendly aircraft dropped bombs on one of their squadrons. NAC, RG 24, vol. 14,229, WD BCD, 29 May 1944.

119 NAC, RG 24, vol. 10,982, Snow Report.

120 NAC, RG 24, vol. 13,797, WD "G" 5 CAD, 5 CAD Report 23-31 May 1944; and NAC, RG 24, vol. 10,982, Snow Report.

121 NAC, RG 24, vol. 10,982, Snow Report.

122 NAC, RG 24, vol. 13,797, WD "G" 5 CAD, 5 CAD Report 23-31 May 1944, Appendix D, LdSH Report.

123 Ibid.

124 RMC, McAndrew Collection, McAndrew/Greenhous-Hoffmeister interview, 142-43.

125 Ibid.

126 Hoffmeister Collection, Citation – Second Bar to the Distinguished Service Order, Major-General B.M. Hoffmeister.

127 NAC, RG 24, vol. 13,796, WD "G" 5 CAD, June 1944, Comd Eighth Army to GOC 5 Cdn Armd Div, 5 June 1944.

128 IWM, Leese Papers, box 4, Letters to MGen J.N. Kennedy, Leese to Kennedy, 8 June 1944.
129 Ibid.
130 Hoffmeister Collection, Leese to Hoffmeister, 8 June 1944.

Chapter 8: The Lessons from Liri
1 Imperial War Museum (hereafter IWM), Papers of General Sir Oliver Leese (hereafter Leese Papers), box 4, Letters to MGen J.N. Kennedy, Leese to Kennedy, 26 May 1944.
2 NAC, MG 30 G6, Papers of Lieutenant-General E.L.M. Burns (hereafter Burns Papers), vol. 1, Personal War Diary (hereafter PWD), 5 June 1944.
3 As the senior staff officer in the corps, the BGS was responsible for the direction and coordination of all staff activities in the corps.
4 NAC, MG 30, E 157, Papers of General H.D.G. Crerar (hereafter Crerar Papers), vol. 7, file 958C.009 (D 183), Burns to Crerar, 7 June 1944.
5 IWM, Leese Papers, box 4, Letters to MGen J.N. Kennedy, Leese to Kennedy, 8 June 1944.
6 NAC, MG 30, E 157, Crerar Papers, vol. 7, file 958C.009 (D 183), Burns to Crerar, 7 June 1944.
7 Ibid.
8 Ibid.
9 Compare IWM, Leese Papers, Leese to Kennedy, 8 June 1944; and Lieutenant-General E.L.M. Burns, *General Mud: Memoirs of Two World Wars* (Toronto: Clarke Irwin, 1970), 162-63.
10 National Archives of Canada (hereafter NAC), Record Group (hereafter RG) 24, vol. 13,796, War Diary (hereafter WD), General Staff Branch Headquarters 5 Canadian Armoured Division (hereafter "G" 5 CAD), 1 June 1944.
11 NAC, RG 24, vol. 13,797, WD "G" 5 CAD, June 1944, Appendix 23, 5 Cdn Armd Div Report on Ops 23-31 May 1944 and Lessons Learned (hereafter 5 CAD Report 23-31 May).
12 Lieutenant-Colonel G.W.L. Nicholson, *The Canadians in Italy, 1943-1945* (Ottawa: Queen's Printer, 1966), 452; and RMC, McAndrew Collection, Major General A.E. Wrinch, interview with William J. McAndrew, Toronto, June 1980 (hereafter McAndrew-Wrinch interview).
13 NAC, RG 24, vol. 13,796, WD "G" 5 CAD, 29 July 1944.
14 NAC, RG 24, vol. 13,796, WD "G" 5 CAD, Appendix 11, 5 CDN Armd Div Sigs Exercise "STOP PRESS," 3 June 1944.
15 NAC, RG 24, vol. 13,797, WD "G" 5 CAD, June 1944, Appendix 11, Exercise "STOP PRESS," 9 June 1944.
16 NAC, MG 30 G6, Burns Papers, PWD, 7 June.
17 NAC, RG 24, vol. 13,687, WD General Staff Branch Headquarters 1 Canadian Corps (hereafter GS 1 Cdn Corps) June 1944, Appendix 30, Notes on Conference Held by GOC 1 Cdn Corps with Comds 1 Cdn Inf Div and 5 Cdn Armd Div, 9 June 1944.
18 Ibid. See also Appendix 38, Trg Conference, 10 June 1944.
19 NAC, RG 24, vol. 13,687, GS 1 Cdn Corps, Appendix 48, Memorandum on Trg Conference Held at 1 Cdn Corps 0900 hrs 16 June 1944 (dated 17 June 1944).
20 Ibid.
21 Ibid.
22 NAC, RG 24, vol. 13,797, WD "G" 5 CAD, June 1944, Appendix 51, 1 Cdn Corps Training Instruction NO 4 – The Pursuit (dated 18 June 1944); and ibid., Appendix 62, Explanatory Notes on 1 Cdn Corps Training Instruction no. 4 "THE PURSUIT" (dated 23 June 1944). The same lessons also appear in the corps's after-action report. NAC, RG 24, vol. 13,687, GS 1 Cdn Corps, July 1944, Appendix 113, The Liri Valley battle and 1 Cdn Corps – 15 May to 4 June 1944 (dated 6 July 1944).
23 NAC, RG 24, vol. 13,687, WD GS 1 Cdn Corps, June 1944, Appendix 51 Training Instruction NO 4 – The Pursuit (dated 18 June 1944).

24 NAC, RG 24, vol. 14,056, WD 5 CAB, July 1944, Appendix 5, 5 Cdn Armd Bde, Study Period – JUL 44 – "THE PURSUIT" (dated 2 July 1944). 5 CAB conducted the study period, but it did so on behalf of 5 CAD. Division staff, 11 CIB officers, and supporting arms representatives all attended.

25 NAC, RG 24, vol. 13,796, WD "G" 5 CAD, July 1944, Appendix 16, Exercise "FRAME-UP" (dated 19 July 1944). See also NAC, RG 24, vol. 14,159, WD 11 CIB, July 1944, Exercise "FRAMEUP" (dated 20 July 1944).

26 See NAC, RG 24, vol. 13,687, WD GS 1 Cdn Corps, June 1944, Exercise "GUESS WHAT" (n.d); and NAC, RG 24, vol. 14,056, WD 5 CAB, July 1944, Appendix 9, LOs' Course (dated 18 July 1944).

27 NAC, RG 24, vol. 13,796, WD "G" 5 CAD, July 1944, Appendix 8, EXERCISE "DYNAMITE" (dated 8 July 1944).

28 NAC, RG 24, vol. 13,687, GS 1 Cdn Corps, Appendix 23; NAC, RG 24, vol. 13,796, WD "G" 5 CAD, 5 Cdn Armd Div RT [Radio Transmission] PROCEDURE (dated 8 June 1944), and Appendix 14, Exercise "FOLLOW-UP" (dated 17 July 1944); NAC, RG 24, vol. 14,056, WD 5 CAB, July 1944, Appendix 8, Signals Exercise (dated 6 July 1944).

29 The reports for 1 Canadian Corps, 1 CID, and 5 CAD are compiled in NAC, RG 24, vols. 13,690-13,691, WD GS 1 Cdn Corps.

30 NAC, RG 24, vol. 13,796, WD "G" 5 CAD, June 1944.

31 The leave period was 2-9 February 1944. Hoffmeister Collection (West Vancouver), Record of Promotions, Reductions, Transfers, Casualties: Bertram Meryl Hoffmeister.

32 NAC, RG 24, vol. 10,927, Summary of Ops 5 Cdn Armd Div (dated 6 July 1944).

33 Ibid.

34 The 5 CAD War Diary records that one colonel and one major visited 5 CAD headquarters and the two brigades 8-11 June. They met with Hoffmeister on the evening of 9 June and submitted a rough draft of their report on 11 June. NAC, RG 24, vol. 13,796, WD "G" 5 CAD, June 1944.

35 NAC, RG 24, vol. 13,796, WD "G" 5 CAD, 11 June 1944.

36 RMC, McAndrew Collection, Col. Clement Dick, former GSO I, 5 Cdn Armoured Division, interview with William J. McAndrew, 26 May 1980. Dick, who had served as Hoffmeister's brigade major in 2 CIB during the battle for Ortona, was also Snow's brigade major during the Liri Valley offensive. He served as GSO I 5 CAD from September 1944 to June 1945.

37 NAC, RG 24, vol. 13,796, WD "G" 5 CAD, June 1944, 5 CAD Report on Ops 23-31 May 1944. 11 Cdn Inf Bde Report on the Battle of the Liri Valley (n.d).

38 NAC, MG 30 E 157, CP, vol. 3, file GOC-in-C 5-0-3 vol. 1, 958C.009 (D178), Canadian Army Overseas Officer's Confidential Report on A/Brigadier T.E. Snow (dated 6 June 1944).

39 See NAC, MG 30 E 157, Crerar Papers, vol. 3, file GOC-in-C 5-0-3 vol. 1, 958C.009 (D178), Statement in Protest Against Adverse Report on A/Brigadier T.E. Snow (n.d); and Lt-Gen H.D.G. Crerar to CMHQ, 7 July 1944; and Major-General P.J. Montague to Lt.Col. T.E. Snow, 28 June 1944. See also ibid., vol. 7, file, 958C.009 (D183), Burns to Crerar, 7 June 1944.

40 NAC, RG 24, vol. 13,796, WD "G" 5 CAD, 6-7 June 1944.

41 NAC, RG 24, vol. 13,796, WD "G" 5 CAD, 16 July 1944; and Hoffmeister Collection, Service and Casualty Form, Maj. Gen Hoffmeister, B.M.

42 NAC, RG 24, vol. 13,796, WD "G" 5 CAD, 18 July 1944.

43 NAC, RG 24, vol. 13,687, WD GS 1 Cdn Corps, Appendix 26, Exercise "VITAL" – General Instruction (dated 20 July 1944).

44 NAC, RG 24, vol. 13,796, WD "G" 5 CAD, 8-9 August 1944.

45 NAC, RG 24, vol. 13,687, WD GS 1 Cdn Corps, Appendix 52, Traffic Control Units (dated 18 June 1944).

46 NAC, RG 24, vol. 13,797, WD "G" 5 CAD, June 1944, Appendix 23, 5 CAD Report on Ops 23-31 May 1944.
47 NAC, RG 24, vol. 13,796, WD "G" 5 CAD, July 1944, Appendix 4, Exercise "TIME OUT."
48 IWM, Leese Papers, box 4, Letters to MGen J.N. Kennedy, Leese to Kennedy, 8 June 1944.
49 See Nicholson, *Canadians in Italy,* 478-81.
50 NAC, MG 30 G6, Burns Papers, PWD, 2 July 1944.
51 NAC, RG 24, vol. 14,162, WD 12 Canadian Infantry Brigade (hereafter 12 CIB), July 1944, Appendices M6, 12 Cdn Inf Bde Memorandum No 6, 21 July 1944. See also appendices M1-M15.
52 Brigadier Spry left 12 CIB to take command of 3 Canadian Infantry Division (CID) in Northwest Europe.
53 RMC, William J. McAndrew Collection, General B.M. Hoffmeister, interview with B. Greenhous and W. McAndrew, 1980, 90.
54 The 5 CAD War Diary notes that Hoffmeister began searching for an appropriate area in which to hold a brigade exercise on 20 July. NAC, RG 24, vol. 13,796, WD "G" 5 CAD, 20 July 1944.
55 NAC, RG 24, vol. 13,796, WD "G" 5 CAD, 9 August 1944.

Chapter 9: Gothic Line to the End in Italy

 1 Royal Military College of Canada (hereafter RMC), William J. McAndrew Collection (hereafter McAndrew Collection), Brigadier I.S. Johnston, interview with William J. McAndrew, June 1980 (hereafter McAndrew-Johnston interview).
 2 On the planning for the Gothic Line offensive, see Douglas Orgill, *The Gothic Line: The Autumn Campaign in Italy, 1944* (London: Heinemann, 1967), 1-36; and Lieutenant-Colonel G.W.L. Nicholson, *The Canadians in Italy, 1943-1945* (Ottawa: Queen's Printer, 1966), 487-502.
 3 For Leese's memoir account, see Imperial War Museum (hereafter IWM), Papers of Lieutenant-General Sir Oliver Leese (hereafter Leese Papers), box 1, Autobiography Transcript, Chapter 14.
 4 National Archives of Canada (hereafter NAC), Record Group (hereafter RG) 24, vol. 10,431, file 210.B8008 (1), Extracts from W.D. [War Diary] – GS [General Staff] Eighth Army September 1944, Notes for Army Commanders Meeting 10th August.
 5 William J. McAndrew, "Eighth Army at the Gothic Line: The Dog Fight," *Journal of the Royal United Services Institute* (June 1986): 55.
 6 IWM, Leese Papers, box 4, Letters to Major-General J.N. Kennedy, Leese to Kennedy, 25 July 1944.
 7 NAC, RG 24, vol. 13,691, War Diary (hereafter WD) "G Staff" 1 Canadian Corps (hereafter GS 1 Cdn Corps), The Gothic Line Battle and the Advance to the F. Ronco – 1 Cdn Corps – 21 August to 28 October 1944 (hereafter 1st Canadian Corps Gothic Line Report), Appendix A, 1 Cdn Corps Operation Instruction no. 23 (21 August 1944). This operation instruction is incorrectly dated 23 August 1944.
 8 Ibid.
 9 Ibid.
10 NAC, MG 30 G6, Papers of Lieutenant-General E.L.M. Burns (hereafter Burns Papers), vol. 1, Personal War Diary (hereafter PWD), August 1944.
11 Burns conducted aerial reconnaissance on 16 and 19 August.
12 NAC, MG 30 G6, Burns Papers, PWD, 11 August 1944.
13 RMC, William J. McAndrew Collection (hereafter McAndrew Collection), General B.M. Hoffmeister, interview with B. Greenhous and W. McAndrew, 1980 (hereafter McAndrew/Greenhous-Hoffmeister interview), 93.
14 German 10th Army War Diary, cited in Nicholson, *Canadians in Italy,* 497.

15 NAC, MG 30 G6, Burns Papers, PWD, 11 August 1944.
16 NAC, RG 24, vol. 10,983, file 264C11.016 (D4), Appreciation by Brigadier I.S. Johnston on a possible attack by 11 Cdn Inf Bde Gp on MONTECCHIO posns on the GOTHIC LINE (n.d.).
17 Ibid.
18 Hoffmeister liked the idea of enveloping Point 120 from behind. On 20 August, he met with Burns and "proposed to bypass MONTECCIO [sic] and attack it from the rear." NAC, MG 30 G6, Burns Papers, PWD, 20 August 1944.
19 RMC, McAndrew Collection, McAndrew/Greenhous-Hoffmeister interview, 141.
20 NAC, RG 24, vol. 13,798, WD "G" 5 CAD, 5 Cdn Armd Div History of Operations – F. METAURO to F BEVANO (30 August 1944-27 October 1944) (hereafter 5 CAD METAURO to BEVANO), Appendix D, Report on Operations 12 Canadian Infantry Brigade Period 1 September 1944 to 5 September 1944 (hereafter 12 CIB Account 1-5 September 1944), 5-6.
21 RMC, McAndrew Collection, McAndrew/Greenhous-Hoffmeister interview, 141.
22 RMC, McAndrew Collection, C.H. Drury, interview with W. McAndrew and B. Greenhous, Montreal, June 1980 (hereafter McAndrew/Greenhous-Drury interview), 8.
23 To ensure that no staff coordination points were missed, Hoffmeister often brought his GSO II (an operations staff officer in the rank of major) to take notes on his visits forward. This was one of the lessons of the Liri Valley operations. See NAC, RG 24, vol. 13,796, WD "G" 5 CAD, 27, 29 August; NAC, RG 24, vol. 13,797, WD "G" 5 CAD, June 1944, Appendix 23, "5 Cdn Armd Div Report on Operations 23-31 May 1944 and Lessons Learned" (hereafter 5 CAD Report on Ops 23-31 May).
24 RMC, McAndrew Collection, Major General A.E. Wrinch, interview with William J. McAndrew, Toronto, June 1980, 7.
25 RMC, McAndrew Collection, Letter Hoffmeister to McAndrew, 30 July 1986. Emphasis in original.
26 Ibid.
27 Directorate of History and Heritage (hereafter DHH), J.L. Granatstein, *The Generals* interviews, "Notes on interview with Gen Bert Hoffmeister, Vancouver, 2 March 1992" (hereafter Granatstein-Hoffmeister interview).
28 On the differences between Crerar's and Simonds's planning methods and dealings with subordinates, see Stephen Ashley Hart, *Montgomery and "Colossal Cracks": The 21st Army Group in Northwest Europe, 1944-1945* (Westport, CT: Praeger, 2000), 160.
29 RMC, McAndrew Collection, McAndrew/Greenhous-Hoffmeister interview, 115-16.
30 Hoffmeister Collection, Personal Message from the Army Commander, May 1944.
31 Lt-Gen E.L.M. Burns, *General Mud: Memoirs of Two World Wars* (Toronto: Clarke Irwin, 1970), 178.
32 Nicholson, *Canadians in Italy,* 499.
33 DHH, Granatstein-Hoffmeister interview.
34 RMC, McAndrew Collection, Letter Hoffmeister to McAndrew, 19 August 1986; Hoffmeister to McAndrew, 30 July 1986. This was a widely held perception. Ian Johnston, although he thought Burns "very capable," believed that "he did not have a winning personality." RMC, McAndrew Collection, McAndrew-Johnston interview, 7.
35 RMC, McAndrew Collection, Letter Hoffmeister to McAndrew, 30 July 1986.
36 Hoffmeister Collection, Letter Vokes to Hoffmeister, 16 November 1944.
37 In fact, the written orders, from corps to brigade level were almost identical. Compare NAC, RG 24, vol. 13,691, WD GS 1 Cdn Corps, 1 Canadian Corps Gothic Line Report, Appendix A, 1 Cdn Corps Operation Instruction no. 23 (21 August 1944); ibid., vol. 13,796, WD 5 CAD, August 1944, Appendix 31, 5 Cdn Armd Div Op Instr no. 2 (21 August 1944); and ibid., vol. 14,056, WD 5 CAB, August 1944, Appendix 9, 5 Cdn Armd Bde Op Instr no. 1 (23 August 1944).

38 NAC, RG 24, vol. 14,159, WD 11 CIB, 25 August 1944.
39 On the breaking of the Gothic Line, see General Sir William Jackson, *The Mediterranean and the Middle East,* vol. 6, part 2 (London: Her Majesty's Stationary Office, 1987), 237-61. For the official Canadian perspective, see Nicholson, *Canadians in Italy,* 503-25.
40 The two divisions were 26 Panzer and 29 Panzer Grenadier. Nicholson, *Canadians in Italy,* 512-13.
41 1 CID Message Log, Serial 15124, 27 August 1944. Quoted in Nicholson, *Canadians in Italy,* 510.
42 NAC, MG 30 G6, Burns Papers, PWD, 27 August 1944.
43 Ibid., 29 August 1944.
44 NAC, RG 24, vol. 13,796, WD "G" 5 CAD, 26 August 1944.
45 Ibid., 27 August 1944.
46 NAC, RG 24, vol. 14,159, WD 11 CIB, 28 August 1944.
47 Ibid., 29 August 1944.
48 RMC, McAndrew Collection, McAndrew/Greenhous interview, 94.
49 NAC, RG 24, vol. 10,931, file 244 C5.015 (D3), 5 CAD Ops Log, Serials 592, 2105 29 August 1944.
50 Each echelon came from the parent organization behind it. Thus the numbers for strengths at each level are reduced accordingly. For example a company, normally consisting of 100 men was reduced to 80 to reflect the platoon that was in the vanguard.
51 IWM, Leese Papers, Autobiography, Chapter 14, 8.
52 NAC, MG 30 G6, Burns Papers, PWD, 30 August 1944.
53 NAC, RG 24, vol. 15,136, WD Perth Regiment 29-30 August; and NAC, RG 24, vol. 13,798, WD "G" 5 CAD, 5 CAD METAURO to BEVANO, Appendix C, History of Ops 11 CIB, Cape Breton Highlanders Report on Operations From 28 August Until 14 September 1944 (hereafter Cape Breton Report 28 August-14 September 1944).
54 NAC, RG 24, vol. 13,691, WD GS 1 Cdn Corps, 1 Cdn Corps GOTHIC Line Report, 4.
55 NAC, RG 24, vol. 13,690, WD GS 1 Cdn Corps, 1 Cdn Inf Div F. METAURO to F. MARECCHIA, 24 AUG-22 SEP 44, 8.
56 NAC, RG 24, vol. 10,983, 11 CIB Log, 30 August, 1045 hrs. At 1112 hrs, 11 CIB warned the Irish Regiment, "Do not let anyone get their feet wet today." Ibid. See also the Cape Breton Report 28 August-14 September 1944 in NAC, RG 24, vol. 13,798, 5 CAD METAURO to BEVANO.
57 The 11 CIB Log records that only "one patrol got out," but the Cape Breton after action reports record that two patrols mistakenly departed at 10:00 a.m. NAC, RG 24, vol. 10,983, 11 CIB Log, 30 August, 1220 hrs; and NAC, RG 24, vol. 13,798, 5 CAD METAURO to BEVANO, Cape Breton Report 28 August-14 September 1944.
58 NAC, RG 24, vol. 10,983, 5 CAD METAURO to BEVANO, Cape Breton Report 28 August-14 September 1944.
59 On the part played by the Cape Breton Highlanders in the breaking of the Gothic Line, see the regimental history: Alex Morrison and Ted Slaney, *The Breed of Manly Men: The History of the Cape Breton Highlanders* (Sydney, NS: Canadian Institute of Strategic Studies, 1994), 218-39.
60 NAC, RG 24, vol. 14,159, WD 11 CIB, 30 August 1944.
61 NAC, RG 24, vol. 10,931, 5 CAD Ops Log, 30 August, 1500 hrs.
62 RMC, McAndrew Collection, McAndrew/Greenhous-Hoffmeister interview, 96.
63 RMC, McAndrew Collection, McAndrew-Sparling interview, 11.
64 NAC, RG 24, vol. 10,931, 5 CAD Ops Log, 29-31 August 1944.
65 NAC, RG 24, vol. 14,158, WD 11 CIB, 30 August 1944.
66 NAC, RG 24, vol. 10,983, 11 CIB Log, 30 August 1944, 2335 hrs.

67   NAC, RG 24, vol. 13,798, 5 CAD METAURO to BEVANO, Cape Breton Report 28 August-14 September 1944, 2.

68   On the Perth Regiment at the Gothic Line, see Stafford Johnston, *The Fighting Perths* (Stratford, ON: Perth Regiment Veteran's Association, 1964), 85-93.

69   The Perth Regiment War Diary notes that the commanding officer, Lieutenant-Colonel Reid, actually went with the patrol commander at 0930 to confirm that the bridge was still in place and serviceable. NAC, RG 24, vol. 15,136, WD Perth Regiment, 30 August 1944.

70   Stanley Scislowski, *Not All of Us Were Brave* (Toronto: Dundurn, 1997), 254.

71   Ibid., 255-6.

72   NAC, RG 24, vol. 10,931, 5 CAD Ops Log, 30 August 1944, serial 659.

73   Ibid., serial 675.

74   From the Operations Log it is possible to determine that Hoffmeister returned to his Division Main Headquarters sometime between midnight and 0420. NAC, RG 24, vol. 10,931, 5 CAD Ops Log, 30-31 August 1944, Serials 664-686.

75   RMC, McAndrew Collection, McAndrew-Johnston interview, 4.

76   NAC, RG 24, vol. 10,931, 5 CAD Ops Log, 31 August 1944, 2320 hrs.

77   Ibid., 31 August 1944, 0435 hrs, serial 682.

78   Ibid., 31 August 1944, 1100, serial 725. See also NAC, RG 24, vol. 13,798, 5 CAD METAURO to BEVANO, Appendix B, 5 Cdn Armd Bde Account of Ops 30 AUG to 14 SEP 44, 1.

79   See, for example, the actions taken to clear traffic jams on the morning of 30 August, or the efforts taken to move 5 CAB units across the Foglia on the morning of 31 August. NAC, RG 24, vol. 10,931, 5 CAD Ops Log, 30-31 August 1944.

80   NAC, RG 24, vol. 10,983, 11 CIB Log, 31 August, 1127. On the brigade radio net, Hoffmeister was referred to as "Super Sunray."

81   Gordon Wood, *The Story of the Irish Regiment of Canada, 1939-1945* (Heerenveen, Netherlands: Hepkema, 1945), 41-44.

82   Nicholson, *Canadians in Italy,* 516.

83   NAC, RG 24, vol. 10,983, 11 CIB Log, 31 August 1944, 1403 hrs.

84   Ibid., 31 August 1944, serials 218, 219.

85   NAC, RG 24, vol. 13,798, 5 CAD METAURO to BEVANO, Appendix C, 11 Cdn Inf Bde – The Attack on the Gothic Line and the Capture of Coriano, 30 August-14 September 1944, 4.

86   For a good, low-level account of the BCD attack on Point 204, see R.H. Roy, *Sinews of Steel: The History of the British Columbia Dragoons* (Kelowna, BC: British Columbia Dragoons, 1965), 286-308.

87   Nicholson, *Canadians in Italy,* 517.

88   NAC, MG 30 G6, Burns Papers, PWD, 31 August 1944.

89   NAC, RG 24, vol. 13,798, 5 CAD METAURO to BEVANO, Appendix A, Intentions 5 Cdn Armd Div, 1.

90   Scislowski, *Not All of Us Were Brave,* 237-42.

91   Nicholson, *Canadians In Italy,* 521.

92   Hoffmeister Collection, Citation – Commander of the Most Excellent Order of the British Empire – Major-General B.M. Hoffmeister.

93   This point is well made in McAndrew, "Eighth Army at the Gothic Line," 57.

94   Ibid., 523.

95   "Put the enemy in the bag" is a colloquial wartime expression meaning to trap or capture the enemy.

96   NAC, RG 24, vol. 13,798, 5 CAD METAURO to BEVANO, Appendix B, 5 Cdn Armd Bde – Account of Ops From 30 AUG to 14 SEP 44, 3.

97   That was the time he gave orders to Lind. NAC, RG 24, vol. 13,798, 5 CAD METAURO to BEVANO, Appendix D, 12 CIB Account 1-4 September 1944, 7.

98 The division reconnaissance regiment had exactly the same type and scale of equipment as an armoured regiment in an armoured brigade.

99 At the outset of the operation, Leese talked about marching on Vienna. See G. Blaxland, *Alexander's Generals: The Italian Campaign, 1944-45* (London: William Kimber, 1979), 170.

100 On the plan for breaking the impasse at Coriano Ridge, see Nicholson, *Canadians in Italy,* 526-32.

101 NAC, RG 24, vol. 13,798, WD 5 CAD, 5 CAD METAURO to BEVANO, 7.

102 The 5 CAD plan mirrored the corps plan, which was to be conducted in eight phases. Compare 5 Cdn Armd Div Op Instr no. 2 (10 September 1944) in NAC, RG 24, vol. 10,931, WD 5 CAD, September 1944; and 1 Cdn Corps Op Instr no. 30 (10 September 1944) in NAC, RG 24, vol. 13,691, WD "G" 1 Canadian Corps, September 1944.

103 NAC, RG 24, vol. 13,798, WD 5 CAD, 5 CAD METAURO to BEVANO, 7.

104 Ibid., Appendix C, History of Ops 11 Cdn Inf Bde, 8.

105 RMC, McAndrew Collection, McAndrew/Greenhous-Hoffmeister, 100.

106 Nicholson, *Canadians in Italy,* 535.

107 RMC, McAndrew Collection, McAndrew/Greenhous-Hoffmeister interview, 99.

108 See Appendices A and B in Nicholson, *Canadians in Italy,* 685-86.

109 Ibid., 537.

110 For the official account of this action, see Nicholson, *Canadians in Italy,* 565-70, 572-74.

111 NAC, RG 24, vol. 13,798, WD "G" 5 CAD, Appendix D, Report on Operations, 12 Canadian Infantry Brigade, 22 September 1944 to 27 September 1944, 7.

112 Ibid., 10.

113 Daniel G. Dancocks, *The D-Day Dodgers: the Canadians in Italy, 1943-1945* (Toronto: McClelland and Stewart, 1991), 356.

114 The 1st Canadian Corps remained at the Fiumicino River from 28 September to 10 October, while the army main effort for the advance shifted inland to 5th Corps. Hoffmeister's division was then relieved by 2nd New Zealand Division on 10 October. A task force, based largely on 5 CAB and appropriately named "Cumberland Force" after its commander, advanced to the Savio 10-20 October. The entire division conducted a mostly unopposed advance from the Savio River to the Ronco River 24-28 October. The 1st Canadian Corps spent most of November in reserve.

115 NAC, RG 24, vol. 13,798, WD "G" 5 CAD, 13 December 1944.

116 McCreery, who had commanded 10th British Corps since landing at Salerno in September 1943, took over from Leese on 29 September 1944. Leese left the Italian theatre to become Commander-in-Chief, Allied Land Forces South-East Asia.

117 Clark succeeded Alexander as Commander-in-Chief, 15th Allied Army Group on 15 December. Alexander took up the post of Supreme Allied Commander Mediterranean when Sir Henry Maitland Wilson left to lead the British Joint Staff Mission in Washington.

118 See Nicholson, *Canadians in Italy,* 646-51. The most thorough study of this battle is Lieutenant-Colonel Mike Cessford, "'Crack Canadian Troops': Clearing the South Bank of the Valli Di Comacchio, 2-6 January 1945," *The Army Doctrine and Training Bulletin* 1, 1 (August 1998): 34-43.

119 RMC, McAndrew Collection, McAndrew/Greenhous-Hoffmeister interview, 106.

120 NAC, RG 24, vol. 10,928, file 2445C5.013(D4), History of Operations 5 Cdn Armd Div, Period 2 December-12 January [1945] (hereafter 5 CAD Ops 2 December-12 January), Part III. A short narrative of the Perth actions can be found in the regimental history. Johnston, *The Fighting Perths,* 109-11.

121 NAC, RG 24, vol. 14,160, WD 11 CIB, January 1945, Appendix 7.

122 RMC, McAndrew Collection, McAndrew/Greenhous-Hoffmeister interview, 106-7.

123 See Major J.E. Oldfield, *The Westminster's War Diary: An Unofficial History of the Westminster Regiment (motor) in World War II* (New Westminster, BC: Mitchell Press, 1964), 171-75.
124 NAC, RG 24, vol. 15,283, WD Westminster Regiment (Motor), 4 January 1945.
125 Some interesting firsthand accounts from Cape Breton soldiers and officers can be found in Morrison and Slaney, *Breed of Manly Men*, 293-300.
126 For an account of Sellars's gallant action, see Roy, *Sinews of Steel*, 360-1.
127 Ibid., 366.
128 NAC, RG 24, vol. 13,798, WD "G" 5 CAD, 6 January 1945.
129 Hoffmeister Collection, Lieut-General Sir Richard McCreery to Major-General B.M. Hoffmeister, 16 February 1945.

Chapter 10: Northwest Europe and After

1 Royal Military College of Canada (hereafter RMC), William J. McAndrew Collection (hereafter McAndrew Collection), General B.M. Hoffmeister, interview with W. McAndrew and B. Greenhous, 1980 (hereafter McAndrew/Greenhous-Hoffmeister interview), 111.
2 On the move of Canadian formations in Operation GOLDFLAKE, see Lieutenant-Colonel G.W.L. Nicholson, *The Canadians in Italy, 1943-1945* (Ottawa: Queen's Printer, 1966), 660-66.
3 RMC, McAndrew Collection, McAndrew/Greenhous-Hoffmeister interview, 112-13.
4 Ibid., 113.
5 RMC, McAndrew Collection, Major General A.E. Wrinch, interview with William J. McAndrew, Toronto, June 1980 (hereafter McAndrew-Wrinch interview), 9.
6 RMC, McAndrew Collection, McAndrew/Greenhous-Hoffmeister interview, 111.
7 The US First Army had seized a bridgehead at Remagan on 7 March 1945. Patton's 3rd Army bounced across the Rhine south of Mainz on 22 March.
8 National Archives of Canada (hereafter NAC), Record Group (hereafter RG) 24, vol. 10,941, file 245C5.013 (D3) Ops 5, 5 Cdn Armd Div History of Ops.
9 2nd Canadian Corps came back under command of First Canadian Army at midnight 1-2 April.
10 NAC, RG 24, vol. 13,798, War Diary "G" Staff 5 CAD (hereafter WD "G" 5 CAD), 13 April 1945.
11 Ibid., Appendix 22, 5 Cdn Armd Div Special Intelligence Summary, 14 April 1945.
12 Ibid., Appendix 21, OP CLEANSER (Notes on GOC "O" Gp Held at 141200B hrs), 14 April 1945. The 5 CAD War Diary entry for 15 April shows that Hoffmeister only briefed Brigadier Ian Johnston on the 11 CIB role in Op CLEANSER at 0730 on 15 April, one hour after the operation had started. However, the Ops Log shows that 11 CIB was informed at 8:30 p.m. on 14 April that it would be "in support" of 5 CAB for the operation. See NAC, RG 24, vol. 10,941, file 245C5.015 (D3), Ops Log, 5th Cdn Armd Div, 14 April 1945, Serial 654.
13 Before the GGHG and the 27th Lancers joined Cumberland Force, the 3rd Greek Mountain Brigade and "a group of New Zealand armour and artillery serving as infantry," made up the bulk of the force. On Cumberland Force, see Nicholson, *Canadians in Italy*, 583-84; Reginald Roy, *Sinews of Steel: The History of the British Columbia Dragoons* (Kelowna, BC: British Columbia Dragoons, 1965), 325-27.
14 See NAC, RG 24, vol. 14,195, WD 5 CAB, April 1945, Appendix 38, Present Sequence of Orders.
15 A flail is a device, mounted to the front of a tank, consisting of several heavy chains that spin rapidly on a rotor. When the rotor spins, the chains thrash the ground ahead of the tank, detonating anti-tank mines before the tank rolls over them.
16 NAC, RG 24, vol. 10,941, 5th Cdn Armd Div History of Ops in NWE, Part II, 1.
17 NAC, RG 24, vol. 10,941, file 245C5.013 (D3) 5th Cdn Armd Div History of Ops in NWE, Part II, 2. See also, ibid., Ops Log 5th Cdn Armd Div (hereafter 5 CAD Ops Log), 16 April 1945, Serial 729.

18 NAC, RG 24, vol. 15,283, WD The Westminster Regiment (Motor), 15 April 1945. Once "A" Company was relieved in its woods-clearing task by the Cape Breton Highlanders, it moved forward to provide security for 5 CAB headquarters, midway between Deelen and Lunteren.

19 NAC, RG 24, vol. 10,941, 5 CAD Ops Log, 16 April, Serial 738.

20 Ibid., Serial 720.

21 Despite the designation "tactical headquarters," this was not the same type of installation that Hoffmeister had attempted to use in the early stages of the Liri Valley Campaign; rather it represented the minimum the division commander needed to go forward and still remain linked into the principal control hub, the Division Main Headquarters. It consisted of two or three vehicles, a staff captain, and usually the artillery representative. See RMC, McAndrew Collection, Col. Clement Dick, former GSO 1, 5 Cdn Armoured Division, interview with William J. McAndrew, 26 May 1980 (hereafter McAndrew-Dick interview); and NAC, RG 24, vol. 13,798, WD 5 CAD, 15 April 1945.

22 NAC, RG 24, vol. 14,195, WD 5 CAB, Appendix 44, 2nd Canadian Armoured Regiment Lord Strathcona's Horse (Royal Canadians), Account of Operations, 12 April 1945-19 April 1945, 2-3. See also Lieutenant-Colonel J.M. McAvity, *Lord Strathcona's Horse (Royal Canadians): A Record of Achievement* (Toronto: Brigdens, 1947), 216-18.

23 NAC, RG 24, vol. 13,798, WD "G" 5 CAD, 16 April 1945; ibid., vol. 10,941, 5 CAD Ops Log, 16 April 1945, Serial 745.

24 Ibid., 16 April 1945, Serials, 757-58.

25 Ibid., Serial 781.

26 British Columbia Dragoons Archives (Kelowna, BC), author unknown, "The British Columbia Dragoons – History." Cited in Roy, *Sinews of Steel,* 389.

27 RG 24, vol. 14,230, WD BCD, Appendix 13, Report on operations of 9 Cdn Armd Regt (BCD) for period 14-19 April 1945, 3.

28 BCD Archives, Battle Accounts, April 1945, "Lieut. B.G. Hurst – Account of Voorthuizen Battle." Cited in Roy, *Sinews of Steel,* 391.

29 NAC, RG 24, vol. 10,941, 245C5.011 (D1), Ops 5th Canadian Armd Div, Otterloo, Account of the attack at Otterloo area night of 16-17 April 1945 ... by Lieut J Hobbson, the Divisional Interrogator, 23 April 1945.

30 RMC, McAndrew Collection, McAndrew/Greenhous-Hoffmeister interview, 119.

31 Gordon Bannerman, e-mail to author, 31 August 2003.

32 Gordon Wood, *The story of the Irish Regiment of Canada, 1939-1945* (Heerenveen, Netherlands: Hepkema, 1945), 64; NAC, RG 24, vol. 13,798, WD "G" 5 CAD, 17 April 1945.

33 NAC, RG 24, vol. 10,941, file 245C5.013 (D3) 5th Cdn Armd Div History of Ops in NWE, Part II, 3.

34 NAC, RG 24, vol. 13,798, WD "G" 5 CAD, 17 April 1945.

35 Gordon Bannerman, e-mail to author, 1 September 2003.

36 Ibid.

37 Douglas How, *The 8th Hussars: A History of the Regiment* (Sussex, NB: Maritime Publishing, 1964), 331-32; and NAC, RG 24, vol. 14,209, WD 8 NBH, 17 April 1945.

38 How, *8th Hussars,* 338.

39 NAC, RG 24, vol. 10,941, file 245C5.013 (D3) 5th Cdn Armd Div History of Ops in NWE, Part II, 5.

40 There was a total of seventy-six casualties in 5 CAB. C.P. Stacey, *The Victory Campaign: The Operations in North-West Europe, 1944-1945* (Ottawa: Queen's Printer, 1960), 580.

41 NAC, RG 24, vol. 10,941, file 245C5.015 (D3), Ops Log, 5th Cdn Armd Div, 18 April 1945, Serial 97.

42 Major-General B.M. Hoffmeister Scrapbooks, Citation – Companion of the Most Honourable Order of Bath, Major-General B.M. Hoffmeister.

43 NAC, RG 24, vol. 13,798, WD "G" 5 CAD, 20 April 1945.

44 NAC, RG 24, vol. 14,160, WD 11 CIB, Appendix 6, Report on Operations, 11 Cdn Inf Bde, The Battle for Delfzijl.

45 For accounts of the Battle of Delfzijl, see Stacey, *The Victory Campaign*, 591-94; and Daniel Byers, "Operation 'Canada': 5th Canadian Armoured Division's Attack on Delfzijl, 23 April to 2 May 1945," *Canadian Military History* 7, 3 (1998): 35-46.

46 For details on the Westminster's action, see Major J.E. Oldfield, *The Westminster's War Diary: An Unofficial History of the Westminster Regiment (Motor) in World War II* (New Westminster, BC: Mitchell Press, 1964), 196-206.

47 A brief account of the Irish Regiment actions in the fight for Delfzijl can be found in Wood, *Irish Regiment of Canada*, 65-66.

48 See Stafford Johnston, *The Fighting Perths* (Stratford, ON: Perth Regiment Veteran's Association, 1964), 117-19.

49 On the Cape Breton Highlanders' assault on Delfzijl, see Alex Morrison and Ted Slaney, *The Breed of Manly Men: The History of the Cape Breton Highlanders* (Sydney, NS: Canadian Institute of Strategic Studies, 1994), 311-32.

50 For a description of the BCD's dismounted operations near the Delfzijl pocket, see Roy, *Sinews of Steel*, 405-6.

51 Stacey, *Victory Campaign*, 594.

52 Diary of Reg Roy, Cited in Morrison and Slaney, *Breed of Manly Men*, 321.

53 NAC, RG 24, vol. 13,798, WD "G" 5 CAD, 2 May 1945.

54 Reg Roy recorded his impressions of the visit in his diary. Cited in Morrison and Slaney, *Breed of Manly Men*, 331 fn.

55 NAC, RG 24, vol. 13,798, WD "G" 5 CAD, May 1945, Appendix 44, 5 Cdn Armd Div Adm Order no. 1 – "FINALE."

56 RMC, McAndrew Collection, McAndrew/Greenhous-Hoffmeister interview, 126.

57 NAC, RG 24, vol. 13,798, WD "G" 5 CAD, 2 June 1945.

58 Ibid., 4 June 1945.

59 On the correspondence concerning Hoffmeister's early release from military service, see NAC, MG 30, E133, Papers of A.G.L. McNaughton (hereafter McNaughton Papers), vol. 262, file 963-28, Telegram Ian Mackenzie to A.G.L McNaughton 15 May 1945; ibid., Telegram Ian Mackenzie to A.G.L. McNaughton 21 May 1945.

60 NAC, MG 30, E133, McNaughton Papers, vol. 262, Army Message Murchie from Gibson, 22 May 1945; NAC, RG 24, vol. 10,624, file HQC 20-5-26-2, Record of Discussion between Gen. Murchie and Gen. Gibson, 28 May 1945.

61 RMC, McAndrew Collection, McAndrew/Greenhous-Hoffmeister interview, 131.

62 NAC, RG 24, vol. 13,798, WD "G" 5 CAD, 24 May 1945. See also Hoffmeister's recollection of the meeting in RMC, McAndrew Collection, McAndrew/Greenhous-Hoffmeister interview, 131-32.

63 NAC, RG 24, vol. 13,798, WD "G" 5 CAD, 25 May 1945.

64 RMC, McAndrew Collection, McAndrew/Greenhous-Hoffmeister interview, 132.

65 See Directorate of History and Heritage (hereafter DHH), file 112.1 (D64), Hoffmeister app[ointmen]ts for Can Pac Force, 27 July 1945.

66 Because the Pacific Force was to be raised with the same order of battle as a US division, the command and staff appointments have American designations.

67 Stone went on to distinguish himself as commanding officer of 2 PPCLI in Korea, where he won a second DSO for himself and a US Presidential Unit Citation for the battalion.

68 Donalda Hoffmeister, interview with the author, West Vancouver, 11 December 2000.

69 DHH, 112.1 (D64), Programme for the Reception of Major-General B.M. Hoffmeister.

70 Ibid., Minutes of Meeting held in the Council Chamber ... 1000 hours, 14 June 1945 to Acquaint Major-General Hoffmeister and members of his Staff with US Ts O & E and Progress To Date of Planning in Regard to CAPF.

71 Ibid.

72 Ibid., HQS 9131 FD 36, 16 June 1945.

73 The meeting with Marshall took place on 29 June 1945. See ibid., HQS 9131-2, Memorandum of CAPF Force Comd Visit to USA, 16 June 1945; and RMC, McAndrew Collection, McAndrew/Greenhous-Hoffmeister interview, 133-36.

74 Ibid., 134.

75 On the conscription crisis of 1944 and King's dilemma, see J.L. Granatstein, *Canada's War: The Politics of the Mackenzie King Government, 1939-1945* (Toronto: Oxford University Press, 1975), 333-81.

76 NAC, RG 24, vol. 10,941, file 245C5.015 (D1), Ops Log 5th Cdn Armd Div, 16 April 1945, Serial 800.

77 RMC, McAndrew Collection, McAndrew-Johnston interview, 4.

78 Ibid., McAndrew/Greenhous-Hoffmeister interview, 111.

79 These conferences took place on 20, 25, and 27 April. See NAC, RG 24, vol. 13,798, WD "G" 5 CAD, 20 April-2 May 1945.

80 Hoffmeister hosted Cumberland at 5 CAD main headquarters on 25 April. Between 25 April and 2 May, the period during which 11 CIB took the lead in the assault on Delfzijl, Hoffmeister met with Johnston daily – at Johnston's headquarters. See NAC, RG 24, vol. 13,798, WD "G" 5 CAD, 22 April-2 May 1945.

81 RMC, McAndrew Collection, Greenhous-Devlin interview, 22.

82 RMC, McAndrew Collection, Diary of Lt Col J.D. Christian (copy), 27 September 1944.

83 Lieutenant-Colonel Clement Dick was an exception. He had seen action as a platoon commander with the Royal Hamilton Light Infantry at Dieppe. DHH, Granatstein *Generals* interviews, "Notes on Col. Clement Dick interview, Toronto, 7 May 1991."

84 Clem Dick's recollection that he never produced a written order while he was Hoffmeister's GSO I was not entirely correct. McAndrew-Dick interview. Occasionally, Hoffmeister's staff would issue confirmatory notes following an important orders group. See, for example, the notes for Operation CLEANSER. NAC, RG 24, vol. 13,798, WD "G" 5 CAD, April 1945, Op Cleanser (Notes of GOC "O" Group Held 141200 B hrs), 14 April 1945.

85 RMC, McAndrew Collection, McAndrew/Greenhous-Hoffmeister interview, 3, 6.

Chapter 11: Hoffmeister and Command

1 Sergeant Ron Hurley, telephone interview with the author, 9 December 2000.

2 Archives of the Seaforth Highlanders of Canada, Personal Diaries, Memoirs, Interviews, Accounts of Battle, Diary of Capt W.H. Melhuish, Brig Hoffmeister lecture (n.d.).

Bibliography

Canadian Archives

BRITISH COLUMBIA ARCHIVES
J. Arthur Clark Papers (MS-0815)

CITY OF VANCOUVER ARCHIVES
Family History Files (Files on Hoffmeister, Bell-Irving, Forin, and Merritt)

DIRECTORATE OF HISTORY AND HERITAGE, NATIONAL DEFENCE HEADQUARTERS, OTTAWA
J.L. Granatstein's *The Generals* Interviews
Kardex Files (Pacific Force Files)

NATIONAL ARCHIVES OF CANADA
Department of National Defence Records. RG 24, War Diaries, Second World War (1939-1945)
General A.G.L. McNaughton Papers. MG 30 E 133
General H.D.G. Crerar Papers. MG 30 E 157
Lieutenant-General E.L.M. Burns Papers. MG 31 G6
Seaforth War Diaries (1939-1945). RG 24

ROYAL MILITARY COLLEGE OF CANADA
William J. McAndrew Collection

THE SEAFORTH HIGHLANDERS OF CANADA, VANCOUVER, BC
Personal Diaries, Memoirs, Accounts of Battle
Prof. R. Roy's Manuscript

UNIVERSITY OF BRITISH COLUMBIA SPECIAL COLLECTIONS
H.R. MacMillan Personal Papers
MacMillan Bloedel Limited Collection

United Kingdom Archives

IMPERIAL WAR MUSEUM, LONDON
Field-Marshal Viscount Montgomery Papers
General Sir Oliver Leese Papers
Lieutenant-Colonel Trumbull Warren Papers

LIDDELL HART CENTRE FOR MILITARY ARCHIVES, KING'S COLLEGE, LONDON
General Miles C. Dempsey Papers
Lieutenant-General Charles W. Allfrey Papers

Interviews, Massey Library, Royal Military College of Canada
Fairweather, David (Colonel). Interview with the author. Transcript. Vancouver, 7 December 2000.
Fairweather, David (Colonel). Telephone interview with the author. Transcript. 20 February 2001.
Gibson, Jock. Interview with the author. Transcript. Langley, BC, 9 December 2000.
Hoffmeister, Donalda. Interview with the author. Transcript. West Vancouver, 11 December 2000.
Hoffmeister, Rod. Interview with the author. Transcript. West Vancouver, 11 December 2000.
Hurley, Ron (Sergeant). Telephone interview with the author. Transcript. 9 December 2000.
Ketcham, Margot. Telephone interview with the author. Transcript. 8 December 2000.
Meade, Denis (Sergeant). Interview with the author. Transcript. Vancouver, 5 December 2000.
Moore, Dot. Interview with the author. Transcript. Vancouver, 8 December 2000.
Shaw, Ralph M. Interview with the author. Transcript. Vancouver, 10 December 2000.
Thomson, Sydney W. (Colonel). Telephone interview with the author. Transcript. 10 December 2000.
Worrington, Al. Interview with the author. Transcript. Vancouver, 8 December 2000.
Worton Billy. Interview with the author. Transcript. Vancouver, 8 December 2000.

Private Collections
Ken MacLeod Collection. In the possession of Ken MacLeod, Langley, BC.
Major-General B.M. Hoffmeister Collection. In the possession of Rod Hoffmeister, West Vancouver, BC.
Major-General B.M. Hoffmeister Scrapbooks. In the possession of Rod Hoffmeister, West Vancouver, BC.

Published Official Documents
21 Army Group. *The Armoured Division in Battle*. Holland: December 1944.
War Office (UK). *Field Service Pocket Book: Part I – Pamphlet no. 4. Appreciations, Orders, Messages, and Intercommunication*. United Kingdom: The War Office, 1943.
War Office (UK). *Field Service Regulations*. Vol. 2, *Operations – General*. Ottawa: King's Printer, 1939.
War Office (UK). *Infantry Training: Training and War, 1937*. Ottawa: King's Printer, 1941.
War Office (UK). *Infantry Training, 1937 Supplement: Tactical Notes for Platoon Commanders – 1941*. Ottawa: King's Printer, 1941.
War Office (UK). *Operations. Military Training Pamphlet no. 23. Part I – General Principles, Fighting Troops and their Characteristics – 1942*. Ottawa: King's Printer, 1942.
War Office (UK). *Operations. Military Training Pamphlet no. 23. Part III – Appreciations, Orders, Intercommunications and Movements – 1939*. Ottawa: King's Printer, 1941.
War Office (UK). *Operations. Military Training Pamphlet no. 23. Part VIII – River Crossings – 1940*. Ottawa: King's Printer, 1941.
War Office (UK). *The Training of an Infantry Battalion. Military Training Pamphlet no. 37 – 1940*. Ottawa: King's Printer, 1940.

Other Sources
Bercuson, David. *Maple Leaf against the Axis: Canada's Second World War*. Toronto: Stoddart, 1995.

Bidwell, S. (Brigadier), and D. Graham. *Firepower: British Army Weapons and Theories of War, 1904-1945*. London: Allen and Unwin, 1982.

–. *Tug of War: The Battle for Italy 1943-1945*. London: Hodder and Stoughton, 1986.

Bird, Will R. *Ghosts Have Warm Hands: A Memoir of the Great War, 1916-1919*. Nepean, ON: CEF Books, 1997.

Bishop, Arthur. *Courage on the Battlefield: Canada's Military Heritage*. Volume 2. Toronto: McGraw-Hill Ryerson, 1993.

Blaxland, Gregory. *Alexander's Generals: The Italian Campaign, 1944-45*. London: William Kinder, 1979.

Blumenson, Martin. *Mark Clark*. New York: Congdon and Weed, 1984.

–. *Salerno to Cassino: United States Army in World War II*. Mediterranean Operations, Part 3. Washington: Office of the Chief of Military History, 1969.

Blumenson, Martin, and James L. Stokesbury. *Masters of the Art of Command*. Boston: Houghton Mifflin, 1975.

Brown, Shawn R.G. "The Rock of Accomplishment: The Loyal Edmonton Regiment at Ortona." *Canadian Military History* 2, 2 (1993): 11-22.

Burns, E.L.M. (Lieutenant-General). *General Mud: Memoirs of Two World Wars*. Toronto: Clarke Irwin, 1970.

–. *Manpower in the Canadian Army*. Toronto: Clarke, Irwin, 1956.

Byers, Daniel. "Operation 'Canada': 5th Canadian Armoured Division's Attack on Delfzijl, 23 April to 2 May 1945." *Canadian Military History* 7, 3 (1998): 35-46.

Cessford, Mike (Lieutenant-Colonel). "'Crack Canadian Troops': Clearing the South Bank of the Valli Di Comacchio, 2-6 January 1945." *The Army Doctrine and Training Bulletin* 1, 1 (August 1998): 34-43.

–. "Hard in the Attack: The Canadian Army in Sicily and Italy, July 1943-June 1944." PhD diss., Carleton University, 1996.

–. "Warriors for the Working Day: The Fifth Canadian Armoured Division in Italy, 1943-1945." M.A. thesis, University of New Brunswick, 1989.

Chalfont, Arthur Gwynne Jones. *Montgomery of Alamein*. London: Weidenfeld and Nicholson, 1976.

Copp, Terry. *No Price Too High: Canadians and the Second World War*. Toronto: McGraw-Hill Ryerson, 1996.

Copp, Terry, and William J. McAndrew. *Battle Exhaustion: Soldiers and Psychiatrists in the Canadian Army, 1939-1945*. Montreal: McGill-Queen's, 1990.

Danchev, Alex, and Daniel Todman, eds. *War Diaries 1939-1945: Field Marshal Lord Alanbrooke*. London: Weidenfeld and Nicholson, 2001.

Dancocks, Daniel. *The D-Day Dodgers: Canadians in Italy, 1943-1945*. Toronto: McClelland and Stewart, 1991.

De Guingand, Sir Francis (Major-General). *Operation Victory*. London: Hodder and Stoughton, 1947.

Delaney, Douglas E. "Hoffmeister in His Proving Ground: Sicily, July-August 1943." *Canadian Military History* 12, 3 (2003): 19-34.

Dickson, Paul. "The Limits of Professionalism: General H.D.G. Crerar and the Canadian Army, 1914-1944." PhD diss., Guelph University, 1993.

Dinter, Elmar. *Hero or Coward? Pressures Facing the Soldier in Battle*. London: Frank Cass, 1985.

Doubler, M.D. *Closing with the Enemy: How GIs Fought the War in Europe, 1944-1945*. Lawrence, KS: 1994.

Douglas, W.A.B. "Filling Gaps in the Military Past: Recent Developments in Canadian Official History." *Journal of Canadian Studies* 3 (Autumn 1984): 112-24.

Douglas, W.A.B., and Brereton Greenhous, "Canada and the Second World War: The State of Clio's Art." *Military Affairs* 42 (February 1978): 24-28.

–. *Out of the Shadows: Canada in the Second World War.* Toronto: Oxford University Press, 1977.

Drushka, Ken. *HR: A Biography of H.R. MacMillan.* Madeira Park, BC: Harbour Publishing, 1995.

Eayrs, James. *In Defence of Canada.* 5 vols. Toronto: University of Toronto Press, 1964-1983.

English, John A. *On Infantry.* New York: Praeger, 1984.

–. *The Canadian Army and the Normandy Campaign: A Study of Failure in High Command.* New York: Praeger, 1991.

Este, Carlo d'. *Bitter Victory: The Battle for Sicily, 1943.* London: Collins, 1988.

–. *Patton: A Genius for War.* New York: Harper Collins, 1995.

Fraser, D. *And We Shall Shock Them: The British Army in the Second World War.* London: Hodder and Stoughton, 1983.

French, David. "Colonel Blimp and the British Army: British Divisional Commanders in the War against Germany, 1939-1945." *English Historical Review* 111 (1996): 1182-201.

–. "Discipline and the Death Penalty in the British Army in the Second World War." *Journal of Contemporary History* 33 (1998): 531-45.

–. *Raising Churchill's Army: The British Army and the War against Germany, 1919-1945.* Oxford: Oxford University Press, 2000.

Frost, C. Sydney. *Once a Patricia: Memoirs of a Junior Infantry Officer in World War II.* St. Catharines, ON: Vanwell, 1988.

Gagnon, Jean-Pierre. *The 22nd (French-Canadian) Battalion, 1914-1919: Socio-Military History.* Ottawa: Supply and Services, 1986.

Graham, Dominick. "Observations on the Dialectics of British Tactics, 1904-1945." In *Men, Machines and War*, edited by R. Haycock and K. Neilson. Waterloo, ON: Wilfrid Laurier University Press, 1984.

Graham, Dominick. *The Price of Command: A Biography of General Guy Simonds.* Toronto: Stoddart, 1993.

Graham, Howard (Lieutenant-General). *Citizen and Soldier.* Toronto: McClelland and Stewart, 1987.

Granatstein, J.L. *Canada's Army: Waging War and Keeping the Peace.* Toronto: University of Toronto Press, 2002.

–. *Canada's War: The Politics of the Mackenzie King Government, 1939-1945.* Toronto: Oxford University Press, 1975.

–. *The Generals: The Canadian Army's Senior Commanders in the Second World War.* Toronto: Stoddart, 1993.

Greenhous, Brereton. "Would It Not Have Been Better to Bypass Ortona Completely ...?" *Canadian Defence Quarterly* (April 1989): 51-55.

Griffith, Paddy. *Forward into Battle: Fighting Tactics from Waterloo to the Near Future.* Novato, CA: Presidio Press, 1990.

Groom, W.H.A. *Poor Bloody Infantry: A Memoir of the First World War.* London: William Kimber, 1976.

Hamilton, Nigel. *Monty: Master of the Battlefield 1942-1944.* London: Hamish Hamilton, 1983.

–. *Monty: The Field Marshal, 1944-1976.* London: Hamish Hamilton, 1986.

–. *Monty: The Making of a General, 1887-1942.* New York: McGraw-Hill, 1981.

Harris, Stephen J. *Canadian Brass: The Making of a Professional Army, 1860-1939.* Toronto: University of Toronto Press, 1988.

Hart, Stephen Ashley. *Montgomery and "Colossal Cracks": The 21st Army Group in North-west Europe, 1944-45*. Westport, CT: Praeger, 2000.

Hayes, Geoffrey W. "The Development of the Canadian Army Officer Corps, 1939-1945." PhD diss., University of Western Ontario, 1992.

Hendersen, Wm. Darryl. *Cohesion: The Human Element in Combat*. Washington: National Defence University Press, 1985.

Hickey, Des, and Gus Smith. *Operation Avalanche: The Salerno Landings, 1943*. New York: McGraw-Hill, 1984.

Horn, Bernd, and Stephen Harris, eds. *Generalship and the Art of the Admiral: Perspectives on Canadian Senior Military Leadership*. St. Catharines, ON: Vanwell, 2001.

–. *Warrior Chiefs: Perspectives on Senior Canadian Military Leaders*. Toronto: Dundurn, 2001.

How, Douglas. *The 8th Hussars: A History of the Regiment*. Sussex, NB: Maritime Publishing, 1964.

Howard, Michael. "Leadership in the British Army in the Second World War: Some Personal Observations." In *Leadership & Command: The Anglo-American Military Experience since 1861*, edited by G.D. Sheffield. London: Brassey's, 1997.

Hutchinson, W.E.J. "Test of a Corps Commander: Lieutenant General Guy Granville Simonds, Normandy – 1944." M.A. thesis, University of Victoria, 1982.

Jackson, W. (General). *The Mediterranean and the Middle East*. Vol. 6, parts 2 and 3. London: Her Majesty's Stationery Office, 1987, 1988.

Jackson, W.F. *Alexander of Tunis As Military Commander*. London: Batsford, 1971.

Johnson, Charles Monroe. *Action with the Seaforths*. New York: Vintage Press, 1954.

Johnston, Stafford. *The Fighting Perths*. Stratford, ON: Perth Regiment Veteran's Association, 1964.

Kitching, George. *Mud and Green Fields*. St. Catharines, ON: Vanwell, 1993.

Lamb, Richard. *Montgomery in Europe, 1943-1945: Success or Failure?* London: Buchan and Enright, 1983.

Lewin, Ronald. *Montgomery as Military Commander*. London: Batsford, 1971.

McAndrew, William J. *The Canadians and the Italian Campaign, 1943-1945*. Montreal: Art Global, 1996.

–. "Eighth Army at the Gothic Line: The Dog Fight." *Journal of the Royal United Services Institute*, June 1986, 55-62.

–. "Fifth Canadian Armoured Division: Introduction to Battle." *Canadian Military History* 2, 2 (1993): 43-55.

–. "Fire or Movement? Canadian Tactical Doctrine, Sicily – 1943." *Military Affairs*, July 1987, 140-45.

–. "Operational Art and the Canadian Army's Way of War." In *The Operational Art: Developments in the Theories of War*, ed. B.J.C. McKercher and Michael A. Hennessy. Westport, CT: Praeger, 1996.

McAvity, J.M. *Lord Strathcona's Horse (Royal Canadians): A Record of Achievement*. Toronto: Brigdens, 1947.

MacDonald, John A. "In Search of Veritable: Training the Canadian Army Staff Officer, 1899-1945." M.A. thesis, Royal Military College of Canada, 1992.

McDougall, Robert L. *A Narrative of War: From the Beaches of Sicily to the Hitler Line with the Seaforth Highlanders of Canada, 1943-1944*. Ottawa: Golden Dog Press, 1996.

Mackay, Donald. *Empire of Wood: The MacMillan Bloedel Story*. Vancouver: Douglas and McIntyre, 1982.

Malone, Richard S. *A Portrait of War*. Don Mills, ON: Totem Press, 1983.

Milner, Marc. "Reflections on the State of Canadian Army History in the Two World Wars." *Acadiensis* 2 (Spring 1989): 135-50.

Molony, C.J.C. (Brigadier). *The Mediterranean and the Middle East.* Vol. 5 and Vol. 6, part 1. London: Her Majesty's Stationery Office, 1973, 1986.

Montgomery of Alamein, Viscount (Field-Marshal). *The Path to Leadership.* London: Fontana Books, 1963.

–. *Memoirs.* London: Collins, 1958.

Morley, Alan. *Vancouver: From Milltown to Metropolis.* Vancouver: Mitchell Press, 1961.

Morrison, Alex, and Ted Slaney. *The Breed of Manly Men: The History of the Cape Breton Highlanders.* Sydney, NS: Canadian Institute of Strategic Studies, 1994.

Morton, Desmond. *When Your Number's Up: The Canadian Soldier and the First World War.* Toronto: Random House, 1993.

Mowat, Farley. *The Regiment.* Toronto: McClelland and Stewart, 1955.

Newman, Aubrey S. (Major-General). *What Are Generals Made Of?* Novato, CA: Presidio Press, 1987.

Nicholson, G.W.L. (Lieutenant-Colonel). *The Canadians in Italy, 1943-1945.* Ottawa: Queen's Printer, 1966.

Oldfield, J.E. (Major). *The Westminster's War Diary: An Unofficial History of the Westminster Regiment (Motor) in World War II.* New Westminster, BC: Mitchell Press, 1964.

Orgill, Douglas. *The Gothic Line: The Autumn Campaign in Italy, 1944.* London: Heinemann, 1967.

Perkins, Edward J. (Lieutenant). "Crossing the Melfa River," *Canadian Military History* 2, 2 (1993): 35-42.

Place, Timothy Harrison. *Military Training in the British Army, 1940-1944: From Dunkirk to D-Day.* London: Frank Cass, 2000.

Pope, Maurice A. (Lieutenant-General). *Soldiers and Politicians.* Toronto: University of Toronto Press, 1962.

Ritchie, Andrew L. *Watchdog: A History of the Canadian Provost Corps.* Burlington, ON: Canadian Provost Corps Association, 1995.

Roy, Patricia. *Vancouver: An Illustrated History.* Toronto: James Lorimer, 1980.

Roy, Reginald H. *1944: The Canadians in Normandy.* Toronto: Macmillan, 1984.

–. *Sinews of Steel: The History of the British Columbia Dragoons.* Kelowna, BC: British Columbia Dragoons, 1965.

–. *The Seaforth Highlanders of Canada, 1919-1965.* Vancouver: Evergreen Press, 1969.

Scislowski, Stanley. *Not All of Us Were Brave: Perth Regiment, 11th Infantry Brigade, 5th Canadian Armoured Division.* Toronto: Dundurn, 1997.

Shalit, Ben. *The Psychology of Conflict and Combat.* New York: Praeger, 1988.

Slim, Sir William (Field-Marshal). *Defeat into Victory.* London: Cassel, 1956.

Stacey, C.P. *Arms, Men and Governments: The War Policies of Canada, 1939-1945.* Ottawa: Queen's Printer, 1970.

–. "Canadian Leaders of the Second World War," *Canadian Historical Review* 66 (March 1985): 43-50.

–. *A Date with History.* Ottawa: Deneau, 1983.

–. "The Life and Hard Times of an Official Historian." *Canadian Historical Review* 51, 1 (March 1970): 21-47.

–. *Six Years of War: The Army in Canada, Britain and the Pacific.* Ottawa: Queen's Printer, 1966.

–. *The Victory Campaign: The Operations in North-West Europe, 1944-1945.* Ottawa: Queen's Printer, 1960.

Stevens, G.R. *A City Goes to War: A History of the Loyal Edmonton Regiment.* Brampton, ON: Charters, 1964.

–. *Princess Patricia's Canadian Light Infantry, 1919-1957.* Vol. 3. Montreal: Southam, 1960.

Swettenham, John. *McNaughton.* 3 vols. Toronto: Ryerson Press, 1969.

Thompson, Reginald William. *Montgomery, the Field Marshal: A Critical Study of the Generalship of Field Marshal the Viscount Montgomery of Alamein, K.G and the Campaign in North-West Europe, 1944/45.* London: Allen and Unwin, 1969.

Tooley, Robert. *Invicta: The Carleton and York Regiment in the Second World War.* Fredericton, NB: New Ireland Press, 1989.

Van Crevald, Martin. *Command in War.* Cambridge, MA: Harvard University Press, 1985.

Vokes, Chris (Major-General) with John P. Maclean. *My Story.* Ottawa: Gallery Books, 1985.

Whitaker, Denis, and Shelagh Whitaker. *Tug of War: The Canadian Victory that Opened Antwerp.* Toronto: Stoddart, 1984.

Wood, Gordon. *The Story of the Irish Regiment of Canada, 1939-1945.* Heerenveen, Netherlands: Hepkema, 1945.

Zuehlke, Mark. *Ortona: Canada's Epic World War II Battle.* Toronto: Stoddart, 1999.

–. *The Gothic Line: Canada's Month of Hell in World War II Italy.* Toronto: Douglas and McIntyre, 2003.

–. *The Liri Valley: Canada's World War II Breakthrough to Rome.* Toronto: Stoddart, 2001.

Index

Printed and bound in Canada by Friesens

Set in Minion and Helvetica Condensed by Artegraphica Design Co. Ltd.

Copyeditor: Andy Carroll

Proofreader: Gail Copeland

Cartographer: Eric Leinberger

Indexer: Noeline Bridge